"GRIPPING . . . THE PRIVATE EYEFUL OF GRACE KELLY!"

—The Philadelphia Inquirer

ONSCREEN she was the ravishing goddess reigning for eternity . . .

OFFSCREEN she was the bricklayer's beautiful daughter who married a prince and presided serenely over her fairytale kingdom of Monaco . . .

NOW JAMES SPADA REVEALS THE STUNNING TRUTH ABOUT . . .

* Her obsessive relationship with her father, the one man she could never please . . .
* The desperate need for love that drove her into the arms of her married leading men . . .
* Her complex relationship with Alfred Hitchcock, the director who saw—and revealed—the fire beneath the ice . . .
* Her struggle to cope with life as a princess and the disdain of her husband's family . . .
* Her frustrated attempts to resume her career . . .
* Her loneliness . . . her rebellious children . . . her drinking bouts . . .
* And much, much more!

How did one of the most sexually active women in Hollywood maintain her image of perfect chastity? The answer is here in an intimate biography that will engross you, move you, and surprise you.

"FASCINATING . . . A CAST OF CHARACTERS FAR RICHER THAN ANYTHING JACKIE COLLINS OR JUDITH KRANTZ COULD DREAM UP."

—London Today

"A COMPASSIONATE, WELL-BALANCED ACCOUNT . . . A FINE BIOGRAPHY OF A COMPLICATED WOMAN."

—Variety

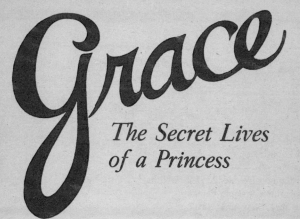

Grace

The Secret Lives
of a Princess

JAMES SPADA

A DELL BOOK

Published by
Dell Publishing
a division of
The Bantam Doubleday Dell Publishing Group, Inc.
1 Dag Hammarskjold Plaza
New York, New York 10017

For Christopher Nickens

Dell ® TM 681510, Dell Publishing, a division of the Bantam Doubleday
Dell Publishing Group, Inc.

ISBN: 0-440-20107-1

Reprinted by arrangement with Doubleday & Company, Inc.

Printed in the United States of America

May 1988

10 9 8 7 6 5 4 3 2 1

KRI

Contents

Acknowledgments

For sharing their memories of Grace with me, I'd like to express my gratitude to her sisters, Peggy Kelly Conlan and Lizanne Kelly LeVine, her niece Grace LeVine, her aunt Mildred G. Kelly, Cary Grant, James Stewart, Jean-Pierre Aumont, Don Richardson, Robert Dornhelm, Johnny Green, Mrs. Sandra Kelly, Stanley Kramer, Fred Zinnemann, Rupert Allan, Rita Gam, Judy Kanter Quine, Mark Miller, Mrs. Marie Magee, Gore Vidal, Arthur Jacobsen, Francisco (Chico) Day, Melvin Dellar, Mrs. Henry Hathaway, Lucille Ryman Carroll, Robert Slatzer, Mary Seaton Henderson, Mrs. George Seaton, Herbert Coleman, Teet Carle, John delValle, Mary Woolverton Naredo, Andy Hervey, Kathy McKenna, Bruce Vilanch, Craig Shepard, John Lupton, and Joseph Kenworthy.

Appreciation as well to those sources who preferred to remain anonymous.

Many people were generous with their time and assistance, and for that I am very grateful. In Philadelphia, Geraldine Duclow and Bill Harding of the Free Library and Tom Whitehead of Temple University were extremely helpful, as were Arthur Lewis and Frank Broderick.

In Hollywood, thanks to the staff of the Margaret Herrick Library at the Academy of Motion Picture Arts and Sciences, Jill Evans, Chris Nickens, Karen Swenson, Joe Goodwin, John Epstein, Allan France, Bob Thomas, Dick Deneut, Michael

Kamber, Michael Feinstein, Sylvia Bongiovanni, Miles Krueger, Craig Zadan, Milo Speriglio, John Strauss, and Dory Freeman.

In New York, I am grateful to the staff of the Lincoln Center Library of the Performing Arts, Margaret Holman of the American Academy of Dramatic Arts, Michel Parenteau, Donna Rosenthal, Nora Kelly Polinsky, Mel Shestack, Vito Russo, Robb Carr, George Zeno, Ben Carbonetto, Bruce Baughman, and Melanie Arwin.

In London, appreciation to the staffs of the British Film Institute Library and the *Sunday Mirror,* Don Short, Frank Howitt, and Paula James; Dave Kent of the Kobal Collection; and Peter Thompson, Gill Rowley, Dave O'Connor, and Robin Faircough.

In Paris, I'd like to thank Capt. Roger Bencze for allowing me to view the confidential police file on Grace's death, and for answering my questions. For their hospitality and assistance during my stay in their city, thanks to Pat Wilkins, Jose Mora, Jacques Snaiden, Mrs. Arthur Rubinstein, Maggie Nolan, Stuart Wilks, and Hans Lothar Bock.

In Nice and Monaco: Jenny Roca-Serra, Harriet Groote, Jean-Marc Almeras, and Valerie Borgna.

Thanks also to Margot Blue Borgo, Steven Englund, Fred Lawrence Guiles, David Hoag, Daniel Cooper, Joseph Laitin, Milli Janx, Mrs. Jonquil Trevor, and Kitty Kelley.

I'm grateful to Robert Slatzer for sharing with me information on Grace and Bing Crosby he was not at liberty to use in his 1981 book *Bing Crosby: The Hollow Man,* and to Don Richardson for permission to quote from Grace's letters to him and from an unpublished manuscript about his relationship with "Kelly."

Warm thanks to my editor, Paul Bresnick, and my agent, Kathy Robbins, for their consistent support and invaluable guidance. For their professional courtesies above and beyond the call of duty, appreciation to Loretta Fidel, Mary Hall Mayer, Alex Hoyt, Nancy Stouffer, Kathy Fowler, Charlotte

Brabants, Larry Alexander, Doug Bergstreser, and Karen Suben.

For their friendship and moral support, love to Dan Conlon, Dennis Lowman, Paul O'Driscoll, Joe Boutell, Karen Weismuller, George Schulman, George Pao, Ken deBie, John Cusimano, Steve Morris, Kevin Stalker, Alvin Kupperman, Michael Fishman, Michael Ruvo, Steve Lachs, Steve Macofsky, Colleen O'Rourke, Mark Meltzer, Bruce Wilson, Barbara Petty, Steve Mitchell, Rick Parker, Steve Early, Jerry Clar, Lance Benware, Lisa and John Vavoudis, Ken, Martie, and Jillian Weiss, Denyse LeBanc, and Mike Riepe.

Author's Note

Early in 1983 my publisher asked me to produce a lavish pictorial tribute to Princess Grace. I eagerly accepted the assignment; what better visual subject could one ask for than one of the world's most beautiful, elegant, and glamorous women? The book, however, was to include a forty-thousand word biographical sketch, and that concerned me. What could I possibly add to a life that had been chronicled for years and would soon be the subject of two full-fledged biographies? As I began to research Grace Kelly's life, it appeared that there was indeed little to reveal beneath the surface of her pristine, exemplary public image. The simultaneous publication of the two biographies in 1984 reinforced this belief.

I considered writing a series of impressionistic essays on Grace's life, not to add new facts to the story but to capture in word pictures the magic she had exuded since her days as a movie star. I also considered producing the book as "A Life in Pictures," a genre I was familiar with, and simply captioning each photograph with anecdotal information.

As I continued my research, however, I found a hint here, a fleeting reference there, to suggest that—although two major and well-produced biographies had not uncovered them—there were unrevealed elements of the Princess Grace story. I decided to write the book as an investigative piece, to interview everyone I could who was close to Grace, in the hope of turning up something new. It might not work, but I had to try.

My first dozen interviews revealed little I didn't already know. Then the tide turned. One of Grace's instructors at the American Academy of Dramatic Arts—who became her lover—gave me an extraordinarily frank interview that painted Grace in a completely different light than we have ever seen her before. After speaking with him for hours I wondered, Is he a reliable source? Did he have an ax to grind? Was he saying sensational things to assure that his name would be in print? My instincts told me he was being truthful —he was an instructor at UCLA, he had years of correspondence from Grace that he allowed me to see, he was careful to differentiate between what Grace had *told* him and what he had heard secondhand. And when I asked him again and again to reiterate stories he had told me, he related them exactly as he had originally, with no attempt at embellishment to make them more believable.

Of course, I still needed to verify what he had told me. With a new line of questioning, I interviewed and reinterviewed dozens of people who knew Grace—her sisters, her co-workers, her friends. I traveled to Philadelphia, New York, London, and Paris. With surprising speed an entirely new picture of Grace Kelly emerged—and almost all of what my source had told me was confirmed. I was stunned— and so was my publisher. When I submitted the first half of the manuscript to my editor, the decision was quickly made to abandon the "pictorial tribute" format—this was a different book than anyone had imagined it would be.

My intention has never been to do a "hatchet job" on Princess Grace; I hope that I have revealed the truth about her life with compassion. My motives are similar to my original source's. At one point during our interviews, I asked him, "Why are you telling me all this?" Without hesitation he said, "Because I think Grace Kelly was a far more fascinating and complex woman than anyone knows. Ever since she began in Hollywood, she's been painted as a nun. The truth of her life is far more interesting than the legend, and I think it should come out."

I agree.

James Spada

West Hollywood, California
November 1986

She has a blind confidence in the stars . . . the Scorpio woman, it is said, is born under the sign of sex and death, which gives her a passionate temperament—mysterious, extremely physical, eager to seize all the good things of life, all the joys of fortune and love—for life is brief, death is at hand. The princess once expressed her dread in this fashion: "I have had so much luck in my life that sometimes I am afraid . . ." She has a terrible fear of dying in an airplane or in a car. . . .

Madge Tivey-Faucon,
Princess Grace's former
lady-in-waiting, in 1964

✑ 1 ✑

Forging an Identity

We were always competing. Competing for everything—competing for love.
> *Grace Kelly on her early family life*

What's Grace sniveling about now?
> *Grace's father, Jack Kelly, to his wife*

Chapter One

On March 7, 1976, Monaco's Princess Grace, the former Grace Kelly of Philadelphia, stood on the stage of the auditorium in Philadelphia's Free Library. A tribute to her uncle, Pulitzer prize-winning playwright George Kelly, was in progress and, as 350 elegantly dressed invited guests applauded, the Princess presented the library's director, Keith Doms, with a large box. The Kelly family had made a gift of George Kelly's papers to the Free Library's Theater Collection. An important bequest, it was celebrated this evening with a gala reception attended by dozens of Kelly family members, their friends, and benefactors of the Free Library. The presentation of the Kelly papers was followed by a film-and-live-theater tribute to George Kelly's achievements.

No one except the library staff and the immediate Kelly family, however, knew that the box Princess Grace presented to director Doms was empty. The Free Library did not receive George Kelly's papers that evening—nor has it to this day.

Shortly before the festivities began, several peripheral members of the Kelly family, whose approval of the bequest was necessary, had withdrawn their permission, and no donation could be made until the intrafamily squabble was resolved. But the gala presentation had been planned, the invitations sent out. Everyone involved agreed to continue with the tribute—and an empty box was handed over to the library's director in front of hundreds of unsuspecting cultural patrons.

The situation itself is little more than amusing, but it takes on added significance because it symbolizes so succinctly an overriding tenet on which Grace Kelly was raised and by which she led most of her life: appearances are everything. It was a principle ingrained in her by her mother's example. To Margaret Kelly, it was extremely important that her family appear to all the world a happy, loving, stable, strongly religious, unfailingly moral one. When her husband dallied in extramarital affairs, Mrs. Kelly never considered divorce: the image must be upheld. When her son strayed from his marriage vows, she tried everything in her power to prevent his eventual divorce. But, he said, it wasn't because of her religious convictions: "She's not upset from the Catholic religious point of view. More because it makes her look like less than a perfect mother."

Grace Kelly learned her mother's lessons well; her entire life exemplified the triumph of appearance over reality. In Hollywood her public image was as a chaste, ladylike young woman who never dated except when chaperoned by her sister or a friend; her private affairs were quite the opposite. Her engagement to Prince Rainier of Monaco was presented to the world as a fairy-tale, whirlwind love at first sight; in reality it was only after a lengthy series of machinations, financial negotiations, interrogations, and a medical test that the marriage plans were finalized. Her marriage and family life were officially publicized as perfect; she tried at all costs to keep from public knowledge her tremendous struggle to be accepted by her husband's family and the people of his country, her emotional loneliness and creative frustrations, the rebellions of her daughters, her marital difficulties, and her drinking problem.

In the life of Grace Kelly, a dominant pattern establishes itself quickly: that of an extraordinary dichotomy. She was indeed successful in establishing a great chasm between appearance and truth, but there was also a large gap between what Grace wanted for herself and what she was forced to accept; between what she was and what she was expected to be. The sources of this dichotomy existed several generations before Grace's birth; they are present even in the land that spawned her forebears.

Today, much of the Irish countryside possesses a pastoral, pristine beauty that conjures up for most Americans romantic fantasies of simple pleasures, happiness through communion with nature, strength and healthy fortitude born of the invigorations of good hard work.

In the late 1860s, however, everyday life was quite different. For the family of nineteen-year-old John Henry Kelly, life in County Mayo was little more than numbing, backbreaking work that brought the family of seven an existence barely above the poverty level. Since the 1830s the potato famine and crop failures had reduced the Mayo population by nearly one third.

Religious persecution and discrimination against the Irish by their English governors turned a difficult life untenable. Thousands of Irish abandoned their native land for the infinite promise of America, joining the millions of other émigrés who swarmed through Ellis Island to face a future with as much uncertainty as potential. John Henry Kelly was one of these. Whether he was forced to leave because of his participation in an uprising against the British, or left simply to carve out a better life is unknown—and irrelevant. His journey set the stage for a remarkable family saga, surpassed in America only by that of the Kennedys—a clan the Kellys eventually paralleled, on a smaller scale, in attractiveness, vigor, ambition, success, wealth, idiosyncrasy, peccadilloes . . . and tragedy.

John Henry Kelly's first stop in America was Rutland, Vermont, where he met another Irish immigrant, Mary Costello, who was seventeen years old, five years his junior. They were married in 1869. Tall, handsome, and strong, John was a laborer and needed to relocate his family several times in search of work. A sojourn in Mineville, New York, ended when John lost his job, but a cousin of Mary's came to the rescue in 1873 with a job offer in the Falls of Schuylkill in Philadelphia.

His employment at Dobson's Textile Mill, while far from lucrative, proved lasting. While the bitter irony that he was now working for a wealthy English family was not lost on John Kelly, he could not afford the luxury of a moral indignation strong enough to keep him from reporting to work every morning—by 1890 ten Kelly children had been born.

There were six boys and four girls—Patrick, Walter, Ann, John (who died in childhood), Charles, Mary, Elizabeth, George, John Brendan (Jack, Princess Grace's father), and Grace, who died at twenty-two on the verge of a promising acting career. Mary Costello Kelly was a strong, highly intelligent woman who had educated herself and who possessed definite opinions. As such, she dominated her husband and her children; she never let him forget that he was not the world's greatest provider and never let the children lose sight of their mother's dream for a better future—if not for her, then for themselves. After several of her children had become famous enough to focus attention on their parents, Mary Kelly was interviewed for an *American Magazine* article entitled, "Oh, For a Million Mothers Like Mary Kelly!" In it "the dowager" left little doubt about who ran the family: "I've been a lawyer, for I laid down the code of justice in the family; and I was the policeman that kept order, and the jury that decided the cases, and the judge that handed out the punishment . . . [I've been] the accountant that kept the books—in my head . . . I had to know groceries and dry goods, fuel and light, plastering and papering and carpentering. That is what it means to be the wife of a poor man and the mother of ten children."

All the Kelly boys worked at Dobson's mill (Jack started there at age nine, working after school), and their earnings were turned over to their mother—but the family never rose much above the subsistence level. It is a measure of Kelly family strength, though, that no fewer than five of the siblings became highly accomplished, famous, or rich—or all three. There was a streak of ambition in the Kellys, instilled in them principally by their mother, who wanted her children to rise above the poverty she had known as a girl in Ireland and the daily struggles of the family in Philadelphia. Their mother gave the Kelly brood a sense that nothing was beyond their reach, particularly if they pulled together and put their considerable intelligence to work.

A good example of this occurred around 1900, when twenty-eight-year-old Patrick, who, although a skilled bricklayer, had been for most of his life a low-paid employee, decided to go into the construction business for himself. The only thing he lacked was money. Taking note of a local newspaper's contest in which readers were asked to vote for the most popular town employee, who would be awarded a five-thousand-dollar house, Patrick conferred with his family and a plan was hatched: Brother Jack would follow the neighborhood paperboy on his morning rounds and make note of the newspaper's subscribers. Then another of the Kelly brood would pay a friendly call on these neighbors and urge them to vote for Patrick.

In any small election, of course, such a personal touch is all-important, and Patrick Kelly won the vote—and the house—in a landslide. A quick sale of the property gave Patrick the capital he needed, and the P. H. Kelly Building Co. was born. Eventually the new enterprise supplied most of the Kellys with employment.

The strength of character of Mary Kelly and her indomitable sense of what one "should" do with one's life had some negative effects on her family. Mary Kelly's domination of and disappointment in her husband made him a somewhat shadowy figure for the children and drove him into extramarital affairs. Years later, after Grace Kelly had become world-famous, her cousin Charles Kelly, Jr., would say, "There never has been a good Kelly marriage"—and the union of Mary Costello and John Henry Kelly does not appear to have been the exception.

The pressures of living up to Kelly expectations were tremendous, and they led three of Mary Kelly's children into fantasy. Grace was on her way to an acting career before her death at twenty-two; Walter went into vaudeville and became famous for a "Virginia Judge" routine; and George became a playwright, winning the Pulitzer prize for *Craig's Wife.*

In one of many patterns that would repeat themselves in the offspring of Princess Grace's father, John Brendan Kelly, John Henry Kelly's children each reacted quite differently to the powerful forces that molded them. The competitive spirit was evident in all of them, but it took discrete forms. Athletics were extremely important in the Kelly family, but George Kelly detested sports and only Jack truly excelled at them; practicality and a good business sense were hallmarks of the Kellys, yet Walter, George, and Grace preferred the arts; most of the Kelly men were quite fond of women—and with their strapping good looks their attentions were returned— but George Kelly was a homosexual whose plays, it was charged, were often misogynist.

Jack Kelly's athletic prowess took the form of sculling, a sport in which a rower propels an almost paper-thin shell through the water using only two oars and his own strength —a test not so much of finesse or technique as sheer physical power.

Jack's almost fanatical single-mindedness in practicing his passion disturbed even his mother, who had worked hard to instill determination in her children. She told him she was concerned that he was neglecting other facets of his life for his practice. "Rowing is something special to me, Ma," he answered. "It's a real he-man sport, and it takes guts and willpower. It sort of proves to a man what he's made of."

Jack proved to the world what he was "made of" after an incident that devastated him. The winner of several national titles, Jack set his sights on the Diamond Sculls at Henley, England, in 1919—the most prestigious rowing event short of the Olympics. Jack bought a new scull and trained himself into peak condition, only to be notified three days before the event that his application had been denied. No official reason was ever given. Jack was convinced he knew why, however: because he was "not a gentleman"; he had worked with his hands, and as a manual laborer would have a strength advantage over the more genteel English entrants. There was more to it than that—a feud between the Henley stewards and Jack's sponsor—but the greatest hurt came from the fact that, as he saw it, this was just one more body blow delivered by the English to Irish pride and achievement.

"Did you ever know an Irishman who would take a thing like that lying down?" his daughter Grace asked proudly many years later. "So John Kelly, grandson of an Irish pig farmer, two months later won the Olympic singles gold medal. And whom did he beat? The English champ! So, he sent his victorious green rowing cap to the King of England with his compliments!"

Later the same day at the 1920 Olympics Jack and his cousin Paul Costello won the doubles gold medal. But Kelly's victories couldn't erase the lingering hurt and bitterness of the Henley snub, and it wasn't until thirty years later that Jack Kelly would get his ultimate revenge—but not without his son paying a high emotional price.

All the Kellys were strikingly attractive—the girls pretty and robustly healthy, the boys strong, tall, and handsome. But perhaps the most impressive of the lot was Jack, whose innately powerful physique had been made awesome by years of rowing, and whose strong, chiseled face surrounded bright, compelling eyes. His personality was a strong one too—Jack Kelly had a reputation for going after what he wanted and getting it. His mother, worried about the welfare of her sons George and Jack in Europe during World War I, wrote to Walter that she was far more concerned about George because "I don't worry about John being cold as I know if there is one blanket in France, he will have it."

By 1921 thirty-two-year-old Jack Kelly was not only an Adonis and an Olympic champion, but the proprietor of a very promising business as well. He had worked for his brother Patrick at the P. H. Kelly Building Co. for years as a mechanic and an apprentice bricklayer—but, like Patrick, he was hardly content to be an employee. He had practically no money at all, much less the capital to start a business: "Coming back from World War One," he said, "I rolled too many double sixes in a crap game on a transport and was cleaned." This time, however, there was no necessity of winning a newspaper vote as most popular employee in order to raise capital—two of Jack's brothers were now in a position to help him out. Walter handed him a check for five thousand dollars that he had just received from RCA Victor Records for a "Virginia Judge" recording, and George, a successful actor about to turn to writing, gave him another two thousand. "Neither of them would take any stock or any interest," Jack said in retrospect, "but years later I persuaded them to take their money back."

This time, however, the pulling together of the family resulted in bad blood. Patrick wasn't happy about Jack's going into business for himself—Jack's company, Kelly for Brickwork, would be in direct competition with his firm—and when Charles left Patrick's employ to join Jack's company a serious split developed within the family. It was Charles, apparently, who developed Kelly for Brickwork into a thriving enterprise, pinching pennies and watching over every facet of the business while Jack concentrated primarily on sports, women, and having fun. By the time he'd settled down and begun to take a serious interest in his own company, brother Charles had made sure he was a millionaire.

Even before he had amassed such enormous wealth, Jack Kelly was, by any standard, a "catch," and there was no dearth of pretty young women vying for his attentions. These were often hard to win; what time he didn't spend practicing sculling he devoted to building his business. But there *was* a girl Jack liked and dated off and on. Like Jack's mother, she was a strong-willed young woman used to getting what she wanted—and waiting for it as long as necessary.

Not that she spent much time pining for the love of Jack Kelly. Rather, Margaret Majer, a pretty, vivacious, popular girl with a talent for swimming, treated him with ambivalence during the ten years between their first meeting in 1914 and their marriage; she had pursuits of her own. By the time she wed Jack Kelly, Margaret Majer had earned a two-year certificate in physical education from Temple University, modeled for national magazines as "the girl next door," and become the first woman to teach physical education at the University of Pennsylvania.

Jack Kelly had met his match in Margaret, and although he could have had a number of other girls much more easily, his sense of challenge was enjoyably stirred by this singular young woman who traced her German ancestry back to sixteenth-century nobility. After ten years of on-again, off-again courtship, Margaret succumbed to Jack Kelly's charms and became Mrs. John B. Kelly on January 30, 1924.

Chapter Two

Like her mother-in-law, Margaret Majer Kelly was a strong-willed woman, but unlike his father, Jack Kelly was not easily dominated. The influence of the Kelly side of the family can be gauged by the fact that Margaret, raised a Lutheran, converted to Catholicism in order to marry Jack. Despite this concession to Ma Kelly, Jack's mother never did warm to her daughter-in-law. There was, perhaps, *too* much similarity between the two women, and Mary feared that Margaret's strength might undermine her own influence over her son. Two years after the marriage, however, Mary Kelly died—and the wheels were set in motion for a striking re-creation of the John Henry Kelly family in that of Jack Kelly.

Within nine years of their marriage, Jack and Margaret had four children—Margaret (Peggy), born in 1925; John Jr. (Kell), born in 1927; Grace, born November 12, 1929; and Elizabeth Anne (Lizanne), born in 1933. By the time of Kell's birth, the Kellys had moved from an apartment into a grand, seventeen-room house on Henry Avenue in fashionable Germantown—which Jack Kelly built, of course, with Kelly bricks. The John B. Kellys, never considered for membership in Philadelphia's renowned Main Line society, had nonetheless become one of the city's wealthiest families. It was one of the few ways in which Jack Kelly's family differed from his father's. But there were many more similarities.

Like her mother-in-law, Margaret Kelly was a woman who dominated her children and ran her household with an iron hand. When they were old enough to verbalize a certain wry bitterness about their upbringing, her children often referred to Margaret as "our Prussian general mother." Mrs. Kelly wouldn't take umbrage at the description: "I wasn't the sort of mother who waited to discipline the children until their father came home."

Jack Kelly wasn't home all that much. He tended to his business six days a week and played golf religiously every Sunday. Later he dabbled in politics and, after his youngest daughter was born, had several extramarital affairs. So Margaret Kelly had little choice but to run her household herself, especially since all the parental energy, ambition, and drive that Jack Kelly possessed was spent on just one of his children: Kell. Jack's only son, and a typically sturdy Kelly progeny, Kell represented to his father an opportunity to avenge the humiliation and disappointment he had suffered at the hands of the Henley stewards in 1919. With a singleness of purpose that some might describe as fanatical, Jack Kelly began, when his son was just seven, to mold him into as exceptional a sculler as he himself had been. Throughout his high school years Kell spent every minute of his spare time practicing and training. He forswore a social life, did not date, and had little of what most young people consider "fun"—not because he was as internally driven as Jack Kelly had been as a boy, but because this was what his father "expected" of him. Kelly family biographer Arthur H. Lewis has said that Kelly "messed up his only son's life by forging him into an instrument of personal revenge."

Kathy McKenna, who served for ten years as Kell's administrative assistant when he was a Philadelphia city councilman, says, "Kell wanted to play football. He didn't want to row on the river, but it didn't matter. You have to understand the nature of John B. Kelly, Sr. He was the boss. And Ma Kelly was the boss. I don't think any of those kids had a shot. They were raised in a family where children were seen and not heard. You speak when you're spoken to. You do what you're told. 'My way or the highway.' Kell spent his entire life, even after his father died, trying to measure up."

So great was Kell's sense of duty that when he lost his first

Henley race he was so devastated his hands had to be pried from the oars. Kell ultimately fulfilled his father's destiny by winning the Henley championship twice, as well as a bronze medal in the 1956 Olympics. But he remained forever in the shadow of his father, whom most sculling enthusiasts consider the greatest sculler in history. In middle age Kell broke free of the emotional constraints that had been inculcated into him, left his wife and six children, and had a relationship with a transsexual which resulted in a near-scandal and helped ruin his chances to become mayor of Philadelphia. Those close to the Kelly family blame Jack Kelly that his son missed out on his adolescence and attempted to have one after forty. Jack Kelly's influence on his daughter Grace would be as great—and, in many ways, as damaging—but for a totally different reason. Within her family, little Grace was an outcast, a pariah.

Of all his children, Jack Kelly appreciated and understood Grace the least. He was a sportsman, and his son and two of his daughters inherited athletic talent from him. The child Grace was a meek, sickly girl, uninterested in sports, and timid and shy amid a rambunctious, energetic family. Jack Kelly disdained intellectuals and the arts; Grace demonstrated an early aptitude for reading, theater, and reverie. Her father never came to understand her or relate to her—preferring boys, he was delighted by his tomboy daughters and puzzled by the feminine Grace. "I don't get that girl," Jack Kelly once told a friend. "We're an athletic family, very good athletes, and she can barely walk."

Jack Kelly made no secret of the fact that he favored his firstborn, Peggy, over all his other children. Even Kell would feel the sting of Jack's sometimes crudely insensitive outspokenness about his preference for Peggy. When Kell's first child, a girl, was born, he expressed mild disappointment to his father that the child had not been a boy. "Don't worry," Jack Kelly told the son who had put the name John B. Kelly on a Henley trophy, "My greatest joy in life has been Peggy."

Grace's early years were spent battling a series of illnesses

—frequent colds and inner ear problems. "We'd all have head colds," Peggy says, "but Grace's would settle in her ear and linger." Grace was the only Kelly child not robustly healthy; Kell recalled that she was made to drink the blood juice of the family roast "to build her up." Her sickly state affected her personality, made her even shyer and more withdrawn than she already was. Jack Kelly, for one, couldn't understand this un-Kelly-like behavior, and he offered little "Gracie" scant sympathy. He was frequently heard to ask his wife, "What's Grace sniveling about now?"

Most of Grace's later drives in life would be motivated by a deep-seated need for her father's love and approbation, but it seemed that there was nothing she could do to impress him. Even after Grace won an Oscar, Jack Kelly told the press, "I always thought it would be Peggy. Anything Grace could do, Peggy could do better. How do you figure these things?"

Grace turned to her mother for the love and attention she wasn't getting from her father. "Grace was always a mommy's girl," Lizanne says. "We have pictures of Peggy, Kell, and Grace when Grace was about two, and she's on Mother's lap, but Mother is lying down so as not to be in the picture— Grace wouldn't sit for the picture unless my mother held her."

Despite this, Grace did not receive an overabundance of love from her mother either. Mrs. Kelly instilled in her children a strong sense of religious righteousness and social propriety, competitiveness, ambition, and determination, but she did not shower them with affection—least of all Grace. She once described the difficulty of her position in the family: "My older sister was my father's favorite, and there was the boy, the only son. Then I came, and then I had a baby sister and I was terribly jealous of her. I loved the idea of a baby but I was never allowed to *hold* it. So I was always on my mother's knee, the clinging type. But I was pushed away, and I resented my sister for years."

A series of governesses cared for the children, the first a German woman who frightened Grace: "She told such terrifying stories," Grace recalled, "that I'd be afraid to go to sleep. I kept asking Peggy, 'Can I sleep in your bed?' "

This strange woman was replaced, after Lizanne's birth, with a spinster friend of Mrs. Kelly's, Florence Merckle. A warm, affectionate woman who took as much interest in Peggy, Grace, and Lizanne as she would have had they been her own, "Aunt Flossie" became a surrogate mother for Grace. "Flossie was wonderful," she said. "I remember how I'd feel when she came to school to watch me in a play. Just having her in the audience mattered a lot to me. Although I think it did make me wish my mother could have come more often too."

Children deprived of parental love and attention often forge a strong bond with their siblings, but this was not so with Grace. Her brother paid scant attention to her; her sisters didn't understand her much more than their father did, and they alternately mistreated and took advantage of her. Peggy exploited her younger sister's worship of her: "I was always telling her what to do," Peggy recalled, "and she always did it." Grace may have balked once or twice, but to no good end—neighbors remember Peggy once dragging Grace along the ground by her hair. With the compassion of adult hindsight, Peggy later said, "I wonder if I imposed on her."

A younger sibling dominated by an older one is fairly common in a family; often the harassed child turns around and bullies the next in line. Not Grace. Sister Lizanne, as boisterous as Peggy, quickly began to terrorize her frail older sister. As Lizanne later admitted, "I gave Grace the most trouble. For three years she was the baby of the family. Then I came along and elbowed her out of the way. I used to beat her up —yes, I really did! And let her say she wanted something, and I'd grab it first. When she grew older, I was the brat sister who made her life miserable . . . I was awful!

"Grace used to be very nice to Peggy and she used to say to me, 'Why aren't you nice to me like I was nice to Peggy?' She was Peggy's lackey—Peggy used to make her do things for her and get things for her and she would try the same thing on me and I wouldn't do it. I guess I was a little more stubborn than Grace."

Grace, so much a misfit in the Kelly clan, developed a protective shell, and a considerable ability to amuse herself. She read a great deal, lost herself in reverie, and made up little plays for her dolls to act out, providing each of them with a distinct voice and personality. Lizanne says, "Grace never went to Mother and said, 'What can I do now, Mommy?' She always entertained herself." Lizanne remembers a vivid example of Grace's almost preternatural calm and resourcefulness: "I don't remember how old Grace was. Probably nine or ten, maybe eleven. We had a fight—we fought constantly—and I locked her in the closet in our room. I don't even know why I did it, but I refused to let her out all day. Mother kept asking me where Gracie was, and I kept telling her I had no idea . . . I gave Grace a pillow and her dolls. That was all she needed. She stayed in the closet until I let her out at suppertime, and she was perfectly happy there. She didn't seem angry. She didn't even tell Mother."

Reminded of the incident years later, Grace admitted she was indeed angry—but even at that early age she had developed a philosophical serenity: "What's the use of getting angry? You can't improve the situation . . . I can't quarrel. I'd rather give up. I don't like fighting, all the loud voices and the angry words . . . when it's finished I feel as though a steamroller had gone over me. And I remember it for a long time."

As Grace grew older, her health improved, and her innate Kelly athleticism finally showed itself. She began to take dance lessons, developed an interest in tennis, then—in an attempt to be more like the rest of the Kellys—she became involved in sports. In time, she grew proficient. Lizanne recalls, "Grace was a very good athlete. She was captain of her hockey team, she was a good swimmer, and a good diver. She wasn't *consumed* with sports, but she was always first team on every sport she went out for. It wasn't like it was with me and Kell, but to say she wasn't an athlete is entirely wrong. At camp she won all sorts of medals and honors." But as her mother recalled, "While the rest of us went in heartily for sports of all kinds and were eager competitors, Grace participated only because she liked the people she played with, not because she was anxious to win."

If Grace, in some small way, hoped to win the acceptance of her family by participating in sports, she wasn't successful. Still "mild and timid," as her mother described her, Grace continually faded into the background of this boisterous group—which put her at a distinct disadvantage in a family in which, she later said, "we were always competing. Competing for everything—competing for love." She often got lost in the noisy family shuffle; friends recall Grace's mother introducing her daughters to people and forgetting about Grace. Once, Grace's birthday cake carried an incorrect number of candles.

In this kind of atmosphere, young "Gracie" was a very lonely little girl, and her possessions—particularly her dolls—became extremely important to her. "Grace always liked to save her dolls," Lizanne recalls. "We would always get the same dolls. When someone came to the house, they would bring two dolls, one for Grace and one for me. My dolls got to be an absolute disgrace because we'd both play with mine. Grace kept hers safely away. Years later, when I visited the palace, I looked into her closet and saw all her old dolls. I said 'My God, Grace, you still have those dolls!' And she said, 'Don't you still have your dolls?' I said, 'No, we destroyed mine playing with them.'"

Lizanne's perception of Grace's "timidity" was that it did not reflect her sister's true personality. "She was very strong-willed and determined, but very mild about it. She had a way of making people think she needed help. You always thought, 'Oh, I better go over and help her.' But she did not need help at all." Lizanne isn't sure why the disparity existed, but she has an idea. "It might have been a conscious thing—maybe she was more conniving than I thought she was."

Grace's interest in acting began when she was nine or ten. By the time she was twelve, she and Peggy were performing regularly with the East Falls Old Academy Players. For Peggy it was a lark, but Grace took her roles seriously and developed an ability that brought her increasingly important roles as she entered her teens.

Acting, for Grace, was the best way she knew to shine the way a Kelly was expected to. Unable to compete with her siblings in personality and athletic skill, she was able to take her inner fantasies and act them out on stage, where people *had* to listen to her. And there can be little doubt that Grace saw theatrics as her way to the fame and accomplishment that her father and two of his brothers had enjoyed, and that he was grooming Kell to achieve. If she couldn't—or didn't want to—follow in her father's athletic footsteps, she could at least emulate his famous theatrical brothers.

It was no coincidence that Grace felt closest to her uncle George during her formative years. Both were pariahs within their families. Like Grace, George had no love for physical pursuits. He was a quiet, book-loving pretender to sophistication amid a rough-and-tumble Kelly tradition. A homosexual in a family of womanizing men, George Kelly knew what it was like to be different, and Grace strongly sensed his empathy with her plight within her own family. Like Grace, George was enraptured of fantasy, but he took his several steps further than Grace: throughout his life he invented a background for himself considerably more impressive than the one he had lived. To many, George Kelly was an insufferable snob—he refused to consider tea brewed from a tea bag —but to Grace he was the epitome of sophistication, style, and taste. Indeed, many of Grace's own refinements were developed through careful observation of her uncle George.

It was George Kelly, above all others, who fostered Grace's continued interest in the theater—both by his exalted example and by his active encouragement. George had tried to discourage his sister Grace from becoming an actress, telling her the life was "too hard." But after his own great success, George felt more confident in prodding his niece along a path he sensed she was headed anyway.

Grace did something about her interest when she joined

the Old Academy Players. Mature and dedicated beyond her years, Grace was a godsend to the company's director, Ruth Emmert. She was never late for rehearsals, always knew her lines, and was able to raid her house for impressive props and wardrobe. Tall, and with a poise and sophistication uncommon for her age, Grace was given ingenue roles when her peers were still playing juveniles. Ruth Emmert, in fact, thought Grace was fourteen or fifteen. When she found out otherwise, Grace begged her not to tell anyone else, so that she could continue to have a wide range of roles.

One of Grace's Academy Players performances elicited a rare word of praise from her father. As he told it, "The woman who played Grace's mother forgot her part. Grace dropped her handbag. As she came up with it, she fed the older actress her lines. Turning to Margaret, I said, 'We've got a trouper on our hands.' "

Grace's first newspaper notice came with her performance in her uncle George's play *The Torch Bearers,* and the critic agreed with Jack Kelly's observation: "For a young lady whose previous experience was slim," he wrote, "Miss Kelly came through this footlight baptism of fire splendidly. From where I sat it appeared as if Grace Kelly should become the theatrical torch bearer of her family."

Even at Ravenhill, the Convent of the Assumption, where Grace spent her grammar school years, the nuns sensed in her a talent for the stage when she played the Virgin Mary in the school's annual Nativity play. One of her teachers, Sister Elizabeth, recalled being impressed by her performance: "She understood the drama of the thing—she was reverent and serious . . . she came in majestically and sweetly, laid down baby Jesus, and made a deep genuflection."

By the time she was graduated from Stevens, a public high school, Grace's theatrical ambitions were so well known that her yearbook photograph bore the caption, "She is very likely to become a stage or screen star."

High school years are either among one's happiest or a period that one cannot wait to be over. For Grace, it appears to have been largely the latter. "The teens are rather awful to live through, aren't they?" she said. "I was rather shy—certainly never much of an extrovert. They were wonderful years and terrible years. Anxious years. Not very happy."

Between the ages of fourteen and sixteen, according to her mother, Grace went through an awkward period: "She was nothing but a giggly somebody with a high, nasal voice. She always has had trouble with her nose, and in her childhood winters she had been the victim of one long sustained cold in the head. That gave her the peculiar voice. Her enjoyment of food gave her a little extra weight. And she had been nearsighted for several years, which made it necessary for her to wear glasses. All in all, she was nobody's Princess Charming in those days . . ."

Joseph Kenworthy, then a seventeen-year-old high school junior, dated the fourteen-year-old Grace and disagrees with Mrs. Kelly's unflattering assessment of her daughter at this time. "There was nothing awkward about her looks, in any way, shape, or form. Ever. She was beautiful, intelligent, fun —you name it, she had it. She had a great personality, and she was all kinds of fun. Everyone who took her out fell in love with her, believe me."

Despite Grace's recollections of unhappiness in high school, she seems to have been the kind of lovely, popular young lady every adolescent girl envies; by most accounts Kenworthy's assessment appears to be accurate. One friend described her as "the best giggler I ever knew," and her high school yearbook contained this description of her, obviously written by a friend: "One of the beauties of our class. Full of fun and always ready for a good laugh, she has no trouble making friends." A classmate said after she became famous, "Grace was a wild teenager, but everybody hides it. She gets loyalty from everybody, but those of us who knew her remember her."

If Grace ever did go through an awkward period, by the time she was sixteen she possessed the loveliness that would make her world famous. Even in her yearbook photograph—

those pictures usually being notoriously bad depictions of even the most attractive young people—she looks more like a movie ingenue than a typical high school student.

With her beautiful complexion, blond hair and blue eyes, a carriage and sophistication rare for her age, and her "great personality," Grace was inordinately sought after by young men, usually several years older than she. "Men began proposing to my daughter Grace when she was barely fifteen," Mrs. Kelly has said, contradicting her statement that Grace was "nobody's Princess Charming in those days." "She probably won't like my saying this at all—but I'm sure that if she had added a charm to a bracelet for each proposal, she would scarcely be able to lift that bracelet today."

A clue to the reason such a disparity existed between Mrs. Kelly's perception of her daughter at this time and everyone else's is supplied by Candy Barr, who went on a double date with sixteen-year-old Grace. "When we picked Grace up at her house, she came out with glasses on, no makeup, her hair in a ponytail, a sensible sweater over her skirt and blouse. She looked perfectly prim and proper. We went to a dance place on the pier in Atlantic City, and Grace excused herself to go to the ladies' room. When she came out, her hair was down around her shoulders, she'd put makeup on, and she took off her glasses and sweater. It was as though an entirely different person came out of that washroom."

Just as she had been with her family, Grace was pliable, deferential, and accommodating with the young men she dated. One remembered, "Grace had a pleasing way about her. She didn't talk too much, just listened. Instead of showing off and chattering all about herself, like most teenagers, she was attentive to her dates. She made each escort think he was king bee, and you know, some girls never learn that."

Another concurred: "I think she was popular because she made a man feel comfortable. If you wanted to sit, she'd sit; if you wanted to dance, she'd dance. And if you took her to a party, she wouldn't float off with another fellow. She was your date, and she remained your date."

Grace's accommodation of her dates did not, at this time, extend to providing sexual favors, but neither was she prudish or off-putting with her boyfriends. Joseph Kenworthy recalls, "It may not have been as free and easy as it is today, but there was plenty of what we used to call necking and that kind of thing. Certainly there wasn't as much sleeping around as there is today—unfortunately. But there was nothing cold about Grace. She was a normal girl on a date. There was no way that you got the feeling that she was trying to freeze you out—but she wasn't free and easy either."

Grace fell in love in high school, with a young man named Harper Davis. He was a friend of her brother's at the William Penn Charter School, and he used this "in" with the family to convince Mrs. Kelly to allow him to escort Grace to a Penn dance—although she was only fourteen (Harper was sixteen). "Because she was so young, I was concerned," Mrs. Kelly said later. "I waited until they got home; I couldn't force myself to go to sleep as long as she was out of the house. When she did get back she said, 'Oh, Mother, I had a wonderful time!'" Mrs. Kelly liked Harper Davis: "He was a nice clean-cut boy with brown hair and eyes," Mrs. Kelly recalled. "He and Gracie made a handsome young couple. And he took her out many times, to dances, sports events, and sometimes to the movies."

That Harper and Grace were a school "couple" can be gauged from a mock "gossip column" item which appeared in the Penn Charter Class Diary in March 1944: "Rumors of a rift between a Buick salesman's son and a brickmaker's daughter. The buzzards gather . . ."

Immediately after Harper was graduated from Penn Charter, he enlisted in the Navy. He and Grace wrote to each other faithfully and dated while he was on leave. The next year Harper contracted multiple sclerosis. "I suppose we never knew how much he meant to her," Mrs. Kelly said. "The first intimation of Grace's deep feeling for Harper came only after he was stricken . . ."

At first Harper was confined to his house, and Grace spent

hours with him, trying to keep his spirits up. Not long afterward, his condition worsened, and he was transferred to a hospital. "It became terribly apparent that he would never recover," recalled Mrs. Kelly. "Toward the end it was more saddening than ever for her to visit him. The people who today regard Grace as cold and emotionless should have seen her after she came home from an hour by the bedside of a boy who could neither move nor speak."

Harper remained ill for seven years and eventually died. Grace flew in from Hollywood for his funeral, and a year later, she admitted to a reporter, "I was in love with my first boyfriend. His name was Harper Davis, and he died."

As Grace prepared to graduate from Stevens in 1947, family attention was focused away from her even more than usual —Kell was about to make his father's dream come true. Later that summer he won the Diamond Sculls at Henley on his second try. "At last," wrote his father years later, "after twenty-seven years of waiting and hoping, the name of John B. Kelly was on the Diamond Sculls."

Grace had been her brother's most enthusiastic booster in the family—once deeply embarrassing him by becoming inconsolable over one of his losses—but his success only made her more eager to carve out achievements of her own. By this time, she knew she wanted a career in the theater, but she hadn't expressed this ambition to her family. Although most of her contemporaries aspired to little more than marriage and children—Peggy was already a mother by the time Grace was graduated from high school—Grace found her mother sympathetic to her hope of furthering her education.

The school Grace wanted to attend was the American Academy of Dramatic Arts, but she was too meek to make the suggestion to her mother, who was more enthusiastic about her daughter attending a good East Coast college to get a "proper" academic education. In the hope that she could have it both ways, Grace suggested Bennington, the women's college in Vermont. "At the time I wanted to be a dancer," she explained, "and Bennington has a wonderful four-year course in all forms of the dance."

Grace applied to Bennington, but a series of roadblocks confronted her. "That was the year all the boys who had been in the war came back to school, creating such a jam that hundreds of girls who would have gone to coeducational schools had to go to women's colleges. Bennington just had to raise its entrance requirements to keep from getting too over-crowded, so instead of asking that each girl have one year of math, it asked that she have two. Me, studying to be a dancer, I had only one year, and that was that."

When she found out she had been denied admission to Bennington, it was too late for Grace to apply anywhere else. Along with her uncle George's encouragement, this rejection emboldened her to broach to her parents the subject of where she *really* wanted to go. Neither, unsurprisingly, was enthusiastic. Her father warned her against entering the the-atrical life. "My husband knew, from hearing his brothers talk of the stage," Mrs. Kelly said, "what a difficult and often dismal life it could be. I was not too fond of the idea of my little girl all alone in New York."

"My parents were afraid that she wouldn't make it and she'd be disappointed," Lizanne recalls. "I don't think they were unhappy about the profession; they were afraid she wasn't determined enough. But she was."

For one of the few times in her life, Grace was insistent. "She had never wanted anything so badly before," Mrs. Kelly said, "so we couldn't hold out." Jack Kelly relented, allowing her to audition—probably because he thought she'd be turned down and finally get this nonsense out of her head; his comment, according to a family friend, was, "Let her go. She'll be back in a week."

Her father, as he would through most of her life, underes-timated Grace's mettle—and her shrewdness. "Deep down," Lizanne would later say, "Grace had to prove to Daddy that she could do it." Later, Grace would usually avoid use of her family name to create an advantage for herself, but she was not above doing exactly that at key times—and this was one of them. Asked to explain her theatrical goals on her application to the Academy, Grace wrote—with marvelous disingenuousness—"I hope to be so accomplished a dramatic actress that some day my uncle George will write a play for me and direct it."

Her relationship to the revered George Kelly played a larger part in her admission to the Academy than Grace could have imagined it would. When she applied, enrollment had already been closed, and she was told that there simply was no additional room in the class for anyone, not even the next Eleonora Duse. But when Grace's "aunt" Marie Magee took her to see Emil Diestel, the secretary of the school's board of trustees, she told him that he simply had to hear this girl: she was the niece of *George Kelly*. Marie recalls, "Mr. Diestel said, 'Oh, in that case, have her come tomorrow and read for me.' And he gave her twenty sides of dialogue to learn." The dialogue—by wild coincidence—was from George Kelly's *The Torch Bearers*.

The door may have been opened because of her family ties, but Grace was on her own once the audition began. Although her evaluation sheet contained the notation "niece of George Kelly," it was Diestel's favorable impressions of the girl herself that guaranteed Grace admission to the Academy: she had, Diestel noted, a "good" personality, "very good" stage presence; "good" intelligence; "expressive" dramatic instincts; and "positive" imagination. The only negative remarks were reserved for Grace's speaking voice, described as "nasal" and "improperly placed." But Diestel very much liked what he saw. "Lovely child," he concluded. "Should develop well."

And thus Grace Kelly embarked on her first major step toward independence from her family—and, she hoped, success in a field she herself had chosen. Her boldness in tearing herself away from the Kelly nucleus won her the admiration of her brother. Asked years later why Grace had been able to succeed to such an astonishing degree, Kell replied, "She got away from home early . . . none of the rest of us managed to do that."

Shortly before Grace left for New York to cross a major threshold in her life, she crossed another quite different one in Philadelphia. At the age of eighteen, Grace Kelly lost her virginity. In a pattern that would repeat itself again and again over the next eight years, her partner was a man several years older than she—and married. Describing her first sexual experience to a later lover, she said, "It all happened so quickly. I dropped in unexpectedly at a girlfriend's house—I remember it was raining very hard—and her husband told me she would be gone for the rest of the afternoon. I stayed, talking to him, and before I knew it we were in bed together."

Grace was aching to have her sexual and artistic vistas broadened, and her life in New York would do just that—to a degree she never imagined in 1947. Outwardly Grace was everything her mother had wanted her to be—demure, sensible, and refined. But she possessed a strong rebelliousness, a thirst for experience, a burgeoning sexual drive and curiosity, and resentment against the strictures of her upbringing. Most important, Grace's drives and motivations were inspired by her almost pathological need for her father's approbation. Lizanne's assessment that Grace "needed to prove to Daddy that she could do it" is an accurate but mild one. Most of Grace's actions in the next eight years were motivated by this need—and the result was extraordinary success. But her "father complex" also left her with an obsessive attraction to older, accomplished, authoritative paternal figures. She allowed this attraction to take her into imprudent liaisons that caused her great public embarrassment and no small amount of private guilt, and ironically, infuriated the very man whose love and approval she most sought.

But for Grace in 1947, her first thrust of independence and her acceptance into the august Academy of Dramatic Arts—alma mater of such celebrated performers as Spencer Tracy, Lauren Bacall, and Kirk Douglas—represented her first step toward the freedom and emotional fulfillment she had never before been able to attain. "Now," she said to her mother as she prepared to leave, "I'm really going to do what I've always wanted to do."

Chapter Three

Unlike most aspiring actors and actresses who descend upon New York each year, Grace did not have to suffer the indignity of living in a cockroach-infested, five-floor walk-up while at school. One of the conditions of her parents' approval of her move to New York was that she stay at one of the city's most irreproachable institutions, the Barbizon Hotel for women—something a young girl could not do unless underwritten by her family. For the first year of her stay in New York, all of Grace's living expenses, and her Academy tuition, were paid by her father.

The Barbizon was the kind of place designed to placate all the fears that mothers suffer when their daughters leave home; so Victorian was it that electrical appliances were banned. The "good character" of the girls who lived there was ensured by the requirement of three references; and their continued acceptable behavior was guaranteed, their parents were assured, by an early curfew and a strict "no men" regulation, which was enforced by burly matrons who guarded the elevators to the girls' private quarters. Every morning at seven, rooms would be checked to ascertain that the girls had spent the night sleeping alone.

With Grace's sexual drive aroused by her encounter in Philadelphia, she wasn't about to let the rules of the Barbizon rein her in too tightly. Of course, the Barbizon wasn't a prison and the girls were free to come and go as they pleased. Any activity frowned upon by the management of the Barbizon could always be conducted away from its hallowed halls —and frequently was by Grace over the course of the next two years. But her newly developed rebellious streak led her to a very risky breach of the regulations, one for which she could have been thrown out of the hotel.

Grace had met Herb Miller during her first day at the Academy. Miller, who later changed his name to Mark Miller and costarred in the television sitcom *Please Don't Eat the Daisies,* recalls, "We were turned on to each other from the first day we met. We were two young, vital, horny kids, and our relationship was very physical. It was a hot and heavy thing. There was a recreation room on the thirteenth floor of the Barbizon, and Grace used to bring me up there and we'd smooch. We were very much in love, and we had an awful lot of fun. Sometimes you can have a physical relationship with someone, but not *like* them. But Grace and I really liked each other."

Grace's indiscretion within the walls of the Barbizon was never discovered—possibly because, as was true for most of her life, her image was so pristine that no one would have suspected her of such a flagrant flaunting of the rules. The genteel façade of the Barbizon suited Grace perfectly; she had by then well assimilated the Kelly credo of appearance as everything.

Grace had taken her mother's concept of how a respectable young woman looks and acts and adopted it whole as her personal style. "She was terribly sedate," a friend recalled. "Always wore tweed suits and a hat-with-a-veil kind of thing. She had any number of sensible shoes, even some with those awful flaps on front."

She also wore white gloves, a badge of genteel femininity harking back to the 1930s. Her Barbizon roommates recall Grace sitting alone through dinner, quietly reading a book. Within public view she was always flawlessly polite, a model of decorum. Grace would have been the last of the girls the Barbizon guardians would have suspected of bringing men into the establishment.

But the inner tug-of-war between what she wanted to project publicly and what she wanted to experience privately not only led Grace to break the rules, it also caused her to flirt with the exposure of her indiscretions. She could have gone to Herb Miller's apartment to be intimate with him there,* but there was something about the danger of discovery that excited her. Another, milder example of this is her roommate's recollection that despite a ban on loud music and dancing Grace would frequently perform wild dances in the hallways, dressed only in panties, and skitter back to her room whenever the elevator approached.

This wild side of Grace, usually so well hidden beneath layers of propriety, sometimes surfaced even in public—when Grace had been drinking. Those who thought her chilly and decorous were stunned one night at a New York party when Grace suddenly jumped on top of a table, flipped off her shoes, and began to writhe sensuously to the guitar music being strummed by one of the other guests. Moving sinuously, she became more and more sexually provocative, undoing her topknot until her hair fell about her face and shoulders. One of the male guests watching this display with fascination muttered, "I've said all along there's fire under all that ice."

But if Grace flaunted authority, she also took her studies at the Academy very seriously, even when her assignments seemed silly in the extreme. "We would be assigned to go to the Bowery and watch a drunk," Grace explained, "and come back and act out a drunk. Or we would have to study a workman on an excavation for several days and play him. We also had to go to the zoo and study a llama." And, one presumes, come back and play him.

Grace's greatest diligence in school was in the effort to improve her speaking voice, the one area in which she was criticized at her audition. The Academy's policy was to smooth out regional accents, giving everyone an "American"

---

* On other occasions, she did just that. Classmate John Lupton recalled, "I went to a party at Mark's once, and he and Grace spent the entire evening making out in a corner."

way of speaking that could not be localized. Mark Miller recalls working very hard with Grace on both their voices. "I
had this Texas drawl and she had the worst, most nasal Philadelphia accent you could ever imagine. We were both very
conscientious about trying to lose our accents—we'd stay up
until one in the morning doing speech exercises. It was very
funny really, us doing all these umlauts and *oow-ooh* sounds. I
finally lost my drawl, but Grace corrected her accent a little
too much—she started sounding British." Grace liked her
new manner of speech; it was refined and mellifluous and
went very well with her prim image.

Casting directors would later find Grace's new voice quite
fetching, but when her sisters first heard it they teased her
unmercifully. Finally Grace told them, with a touch of hauteur, "I must talk this way—for my work." Mrs. Kelly recalled, "They saw that she was serious and stopped joking."

The only thing Grace was as serious about as her acting
was her determination to become financially independent of
her parents. Theatrical jobs were out of the question until
she graduated, and Grace was at a loss to figure out a way to
make her own money. On a weekend trip with Mark Miller,
an unexpected opportunity presented itself. "I was doing
some modeling at the time," Miller relates, "and had become
friends with a photographer who had begun doing covers for
Redbook magazine. He invited me out to his house for the
weekend, and I brought Grace with me. When he saw her he
flipped. He said to her, 'You've got great bone structure. Do
you mind if I take some pictures of you?' Grace said he could,
and a few weeks later he called me for her phone number—
Redbook wanted to use her on its cover."

Grace had thought about modeling, but she wasn't at all
convinced she could make any real money at it. The *Redbook*
cover encouraged her to put together a portfolio and, with
the moral support of her friend Carolyn Scott, she approached several modeling agencies. Her wholesome pretti-
ness was perfect for the kind of all-American image advertis-
ers sought to project, and a top agency quickly signed her.

She began working at the excellent 1948 wage of $7.50 an hour, doing both print jobs (newspaper and magazine ads) and commercials; the first featured her spraying a can of insecticide around a room. She was most often used for household ads, prettily promoting the latest cleanser or appliance, and she more than once bemoaned the fact that although she aspired to be a career woman it still seemed as though she'd be stuck in the kitchen.

Although Grace made the covers of other important national magazines like *Cosmopolitan* and *Ladies' Home Journal,* she never could project the kind of high-fashion modeling image that would have put her in the pages of *Vogue.* A photographer for Macy's department store, which used Grace frequently for its newspaper ads, explains why: "She was very beautiful and certainly tall enough, but she was not as painfully thin as most of the fashion models, so by the accepted standards she was just not *chic.* As a result of this criteria we couldn't use her for 'high fashion' clothes. We used Grace Kelly only for lingerie."

Ruzzie Green, another photographer who shot Grace for a toothpaste ad, described her as "what we call good clean stuff in our business. She's not a top model and never will be. She's the girl next door. No glamour, no oomph, no cheesecake. She has lovely shoulders but no chest. Grace is like [Ingrid] Bergman in the 'clean' way."

She may not have become a "top" model, but by any standards she was a success. Within a year she was earning a steady four hundred dollars a week, often much more. Still, she wasn't happy modeling. She resented some of the things she was called on to do (like wearing lingerie and being flirtatious with men at conventions while handing out cigarettes), and the grueling work was especially difficult for someone who was doing it only to make ends meet. (After a year of work, she had stopped accepting money from her parents and moved into her own apartment in Manhattan.) Her lack of real enthusiasm for modeling affected her performances: "I was terrible," she said about a cigarette commercial she'd done for television. "Anyone watching me make a pitch for Old Golds would have switched to Camels."

Grace's success as a model created some problems with her fellow Academy students. John Lupton recalls that Grace was "a candidate for Miss Rheingold, and that was like being Miss America if you lived in New York. There were big billboards all over the place. You looked up at the top of a five-story building and there was a picture of Grace Kelly's face. It just made her seem that much bigger than life."

The reaction that this, and Grace's personality, engendered in many of her Academy classmates was, in many ways, similar to the kind of response she would get years later in Hollywood: a combination of awe, jealousy, and resentment. "I had several classes with Grace," Mary Woolverton, now Mrs. Daniel Naredo, recalls, "and like everybody else in that class I'll never forget her when she got dressed for exercise class. We had to get into our leotards and Grace was absolutely exquisite. She was *so* beautiful. But I always thought she was kind of cold. I didn't think she had much talent. I remember thinking, though, that she would become a success just on her looks—and that thought kind of amazed me."

Grace, Mary remembers, "wasn't particularly popular. She was a loner. She looked like a model who came in, did her thing, and left. There were students who were in awe of her because of her beauty and that distant quality she had. No one believed she had any particular talent. I remember once we were all sitting around and talking about where we'd be after we graduated, who'd be doing what. Grace said there was no doubt in her mind that she would be a success. It was taken by the others as her being presumptuous and snobby, and they resented it."

Classmate Craig Shepard confirms that there was a good deal of resentment toward Grace at the Academy. "People would see her on the street and say to each other, 'Did you see Grace Kelly? Get her! Who does she think *she* is?' Of course, she was working and most of us weren't, so there was a lot of jealousy, I'm afraid."

Shepard had his own problems with Grace, though. "Grace, I found, was very cold. We graduated together, and later I worked with her on a *Philco/Goodyear Playhouse*. She played Mrs. Lincoln, which was the lead, and I was just an extra. Never once did she say, 'Hiya, Craig.' I mean, we had been *classmates*! I'm not bitter about Grace, but I don't think she was a saint. She was always a lady, always well groomed, but she was not always charming."

One of Grace's most serious problems with the other students at the Academy was their sense that she had an unfair advantage over them. As Shepard puts it, "I never thought Grace could act. She wasn't an imaginative actress, a creative actress. All she had was technique. She knew her craft, but as for the actor's temperament, innate talent, forget it. But she had other things going for her that were obviously more important. She had good connections. Her uncle was George Kelly, and she came from a wealthy family. And she had perseverance, drive. I'm sorry I can't say better things about Grace. She was beautiful and—I was going to say she was kind, but I'm not sure she was kind."

Occasionally her classmates expressed their resentments toward Grace with childish tauntings. Once, in a crowded elevator, a student continually pushed a puppy he was holding into Grace's face until she began to cry. The young man ridiculed her tears until an instructor who had entered the elevator put a stop to it.

The instructor was twenty-seven-year-old Don Richardson, a married man separated from his wife, who has since directed hundreds of theater and television shows and now teaches acting at the University of California at Los Angeles. He had never met Grace before, and he found himself drawn to the teenage girl. "I was amazed to realize that without knowing her at all I felt immediately protective . . . I found myself treating her as tenderly as a child."

Richardson offered to walk Grace back to the Barbizon, but when they got there, she was reluctant to say good-night. Richardson asked her if she would like to come over to his apartment. "She said yes," Richardson recalls, "and we went over to my place. I started a fire, and within forty minutes we were in bed together. It was an amazing sight, seeing a girl as beautiful as Grace lying naked in my bed, bathed in the light from the fireplace. I thought to myself, 'Boy, you sure got lucky.'"

Grace and Richardson began an affair, the first of many she would have with older men. In the months that followed, he often took her to parties at the homes of theater and television professionals he knew. One of these was Irving Pincus, producer of *Ellery Queen,* a TV show Richardson was directing at the time. "There were a few important agents present, with their wives," Richardson says. "At this gathering, like all the previous ones, Kelly—that's what I called her —sat wringing her white gloves, listening and listening, but deeply enclosed. When one of the women would direct a question or comment at her, she would answer in a high young voice with a slight Philadelphia ring to it, articulately and poised, but then, having made a reply, she asked no question or made any comment in turn. The next day Pincus called me on the phone and said, 'Jeez, you've brought some dull broads to my house, but last night was the dullest.'"

Richardson didn't think Grace was dull. "Her public persona was so completely different than her private self that it was phenomenal. She was so proper, people thought of her as a nun. But when we were alone together, she used to dance naked for me to Hawaiian music. And if you don't think that was an incredible sight, you're crazy. She was a *very* sexy girl."

Before long, Richardson found himself falling in love with her. Grace too was infatuated. Richardson was exactly right for her—nine years older, separated from his wife, worldly and accomplished, an authority figure, and a man in a position to help her who believed strongly in her potential for success. "Even then," Richardson says, "I was convinced that she was going to be a major movie star. She wasn't a great actress, and her voice was minimal, which was a problem for the stage—I don't think she would have become a great stage star—but I knew that the special qualities she possessed would come across beautifully on the screen."

Several of Grace's fellow students were aware of her relationship with Richardson. "Grace and Don Richardson were very much in love," Mary Naredo volunteers. "He was the first great love of her life." John Lupton recalls that this affair between an instructor and a student became a prime topic of classroom conversation. "It wasn't a very common thing," Lupton says. "I think the general reaction was 'Wow!' "

One classmate who wasn't aware of Grace's new romance was Mark Miller, even though he continued to see her for much of the time she was involved with Richardson. Ironically, Miller recalls a fight they had over his discovery that Grace was dating someone else. "I found out she was seeing this stud from Philadelphia, a real big handsome guy. I thought, Where did this guy come from? and I got real pissed off. Very jealous. I had *no* idea about Richardson. We resolved the problem of this guy from Philadelphia, but we broke up over something else, but I can't remember what it was. It was shortly before graduation. It was very tragic for me. I'd dated a lot of girls, and I was 'pinned' in college and all that, but I never adored anyone like I did Grace. But I'm happy that we were able to segue into a friendship—we remained friends all her life."

For his part, Don Richardson wasn't in the habit of falling for his students, but Grace fulfilled several important emotional needs in him. "I fell in love with Grace," he says, "for reasons that were very different from why I thought she was going to be a great movie star. When I met Grace, she seemed very pathetic, very helpless, very fragile. She was terrified of people, and very uncomfortable with herself. I felt protective toward her; she needed somebody to look after her. She was friendless, she had no warmth at home of any kind. And so my heart went out to her almost as though she were a waif."

Part of Grace's appeal for Richardson, of course, did stem

from the qualities she possessed that he felt would make her a star. "I also fell in love with Grace because to me she was the ultimate shiksa. To a Jewish boy that kind of blond, blue-eyed beauty was the forbidden thing. Apart from that, I was madly in love with her sculpturally, pictorially. I'm also a sculptor and I paint. I used to sit and admire her wrists or her ankles or her hands. I found her a terrific art object, aside from being a human being."

Grace returned Don's affections, he says, "not just because I was a very handsome man, but because, as a Jew, I was forbidden to *her*. We were like yin and yang—we were total opposites. And I guess I was La Bohème to her. When you're raised with money, bohemia can have its attractions."

Richardson was surely living the part. After separating from his wife, he had moved into a small apartment on west Forty-fourth street. To furnish it, he turned to his father, who owned a boardinghouse in Coney Island and sent him some old furniture that had been stored in the basement: a bridge table, eight wooden restaurant chairs, and an army cot. "That was my pad. That was where Grace and I spent week-end after weekend. You can only explain it as La Bohème, because, compared to her wealth, this looked like Raskolnikov's lair in *Crime and Punishment*."

As the relationship became more and more serious, Grace began to talk of marriage. "I wasn't terribly interested in getting married," Richardson says, "because I'd just been through a separation. But Grace kept talking about it. I told her that her church would never allow it, because I'd be a divorced man. But she told me that because I'd never been baptized, everything that went before could be wiped out. I'd have a clean slate in heaven, or something like that."

After several months of increasing involvement with Richardson, Grace made a weekend trip home to Philadelphia. Almost immediately Mrs. Kelly sensed a dreamy distraction in her daughter, and that could mean only one thing. "Gracie," she asked her, "there's a man, isn't there?" Grace told her mother about Richardson and added that he had asked her to marry him. Richardson, Mrs. Kelly recalled, had convinced Grace that "he could make her into a wonderful actress within a very short time . . . She was flattered. She was intrigued by the idea of becoming a big star—and even more beguiled by the fact that someone thought she could be a star. When she spoke about him, she was carried away. There were all these big things they were going to do . . ."

Mrs. Kelly advised Grace to wait, telling her, "You can make it on your own. You don't need anyone." Later she recalled that "I went on in that vein at length, and I believe I convinced her . . ."

"Convinced" is not exactly what Grace was; "bullied" is a more accurate term. Mrs. Kelly did not want Grace involved with a "theater person"—or with an older man, a New York sophisticate, or a Jew: Kellys were expected to marry within their religion. Even before she met Richardson, Mrs. Kelly decided he wasn't right for Grace. And she sensed, correctly, that her importunings for her daughter to "wait" (meaning "forget it") would not be heeded. When Grace told her mother that she wanted to bring Richardson home to meet the family, Mrs. Kelly felt she needed to take swift rearguard action. What ensued was Grace's first jarring realization that when it came to matters of the heart, her life was not her own.

On the Friday evening that Grace and Richardson were due to arrive on Henry Avenue to spend a weekend, Mrs. Kelly asked Kell to bring over two of his more obnoxiously macho athlete buddies while Richardson was in the house—and Kell knew exactly what he and his friends were meant to do. "I gave them the word," he admitted years later, "this fellow was a bit of a creep."

"I didn't want to go," Richardson says, "because I'd been through that before with my first wife, and I could have done without it. But Grace insisted. I knew nothing about her family—she wasn't famous at this time, remember." When Richardson entered the Kelly home, the family was gathered in the den. Mr. Kelly told him to sit down and asked if he would like a drink. Richardson replied that he would. "He went to the bar and unlocked it—everything in that house was locked, including the refrigerator. He poured me a drink and then locked the bar again. I found myself sitting there with this bourbon and water, feeling like I was a drunkard or something—I was the only person in the house with a drink."

Feeling awkward and self-conscious, Richardson looked around the room. "There was a painting of Papa sitting in a chair with a rifle in his lap and a hound dog, you know, the typical bullshit painting." Nothing was said for several minutes, then Kell and his friends began to needle Richardson.

"They gave me a real hard time, making Jewish jokes and doing Jewish imitations . . . It was real uncomfortable for me. But I'll tell you," Richardson continues, "I felt worse about the way they treated Grace. She was as removed from the family orbit as I was. She sat in the corner with her kid sister, totally isolated from the rest of the family. They seemed to take no interest in her at all. During the course of that evening, we went to his country club for dinner. On the way, we stopped at Peggy's house, and Papa went around making a whole show of himself, touching things and saying, 'This is holding up pretty good. They told me it would when I bought it.' He kept saying 'I bought this, I bought that, I bought this.' Then we continued on, stopping three times to look at churches, where he announced that he had donated this wall, and we stood there looking at bricks. And during this, nobody paid any attention to Grace whatsoever. When we sat down to dinner, all his conversation was with his son and those two bully boys he'd brought along to humiliate me, and they talked about athletic scores, that kind of thing.

"I was seated at the far end of the table with Mama and Grace and the kid sister. Grace mostly sat with her head down and looked totally separate from all of them. At one point Mama asked me, 'How is Grace doing at the Academy?' And I said, 'Oh, your daughter's going to be a very important movie star.' She looked at me as though I'd wounded her mortally. 'It's only a childish whim,' she said. Mr. Kelly called from the other end of the table, 'What's going on down there?' And Mama said, 'This young man says that Grace is gonna be a great movie star.' And he said, 'She'll get over that nonsense and settle down.' "

Richardson spent the night; the following morning, things got worse. Mary Naredo supplies an interesting piece of information of which she became aware. "That next morning, after Don left his bedroom, Mrs. Kelly actually went through his briefcase—and she found a letter from Don's wife's lawyer about their divorce. Well, Grace had never told her mother that Don was married, and that's when things really hit the fan."

Told of Mary Naredo's comment, Richardson says, "You know, I'd completely forgotten about that. But it's true. When Mama found that letter from my wife's lawyer, she asked me to leave the house. They threw me out. I'm sure things were made much worse by the fact that also in my briefcase were condoms. Grace was very naïve at that time; she didn't even use a diaphragm. So it was up to me to make sure she didn't get pregnant. I can only imagine Mama's reaction when she realized that Grace and I were having an affair."

The Kellys forbade Grace ever to see Don Richardson again. When he returned to Manhattan, he did so alone, and after Grace was graduated from the Academy a few days later, she was moved out of the Barbizon and sent to the Kellys' summer beach house in Ocean City, New Jersey. She was not allowed to return to New York and pursue the theatrical roles her two years of training had prepared her for. Several weeks elapsed before she telephoned Richardson. "When the call came at last," he says, "she said she had walked a mile up the beach to a public phone in order to call me."

At the end of the summer Grace made a furtive trip into Manhattan to see Richardson. All she could do was sit talking with him in Penn Station for half an hour. "During which," Richardson says, "she sat on a bench and cried."

"Grace said she was in love with Richardson," Lizanne recalls, "and she was very upset about that horrid weekend. But my parents didn't understand him at all. They didn't understand his way of life. He was so different from the boys Grace had dated in school, the boys from Penn Charter. They were friends of my brother's, athletes, Joe College types, and all of a sudden here was Grace with a sophisticated man from New York. They didn't like that. Their age difference was a problem too. But you know, my father was nine years older than my mother, and we always used to throw that in her face when she'd say, 'I think that man's too old for you.' It came up a lot with Grace, because she definitely had a thing for older men."

The Kellys allowed Grace to return to the Barbizon that fall, after extracting a promise that she would not see Richardson again. "It was a promise neither of us could keep," he says, and they resumed their affair, spending weekends at his apartment. Before long, Richardson found an unexpected visitor at his door.

"Papa came to see me. There was Mr. Kelly in all his grandeur, in a gray homburg and dark overcoat and suede gloves, and he looked at my place and he just couldn't believe it. I asked if I could take his coat, and he said no and just stood there in the middle of the room. He said, 'Let me put it to you straight—how would you like a Jag?' Well, in New York City in those days, no one had a car, and I didn't understand him. I thought he meant to go on a jag, you know, go out drinking together. I thought he was trying to make amends for that horrible weekend. And then he said, 'Any color,' and I realized it was an object meant to bribe me into leaving Grace alone. I then made a great speech about how dare you, I love your daughter, and I don't want anything from you, how dare you insult me. He left in a great huff."

Then, Richardson says, Mr. Kelly changed his approach. "The following week I got a phone call; a young male voice advised me that if I didn't stay away from Grace, I would have every bone in my body broken. I replied, 'Her father's offer was better.' "

The phone calls continued, "threatening all kinds of mayhem," Richardson says, but he never told Grace about them, or about her father's visit. "I found myself unable to talk to Grace about her family. Her family was off limits. Her devotion to them was actually kind of pathological when you consider how much rejection they gave her."

Grace would never have criticized her parents to anyone, but she was left angry, frustrated, and hurt by their combination of distance and self-serving possessiveness. Her reaction took the form of renewed resolve to achieve her own success, but she also rebelled against the heavy-handed moral strictures forced upon her and became sexually promiscuous. It was this, ironically, that drove the wedge between her and Don Richardson that the Kellys could not.

"We continued to see each other for three or four years," Richardson says. "But I began to see the other side of her nature, which was that she was cold as steel. She was like a Patton tank on her way somewhere. The thing that ended our romance was that she started to get interested in people who I found unworthy of her. She started to go around with the maître d' of the Waldorf, because he was connected with a lot of big society people, and he knew a lot of celebrities. She became his mistress.

"Then, one night she had a date with Aly Khan, and a few months later, after she had started to be in the movies and she was still living on the East Side, she called me up and invited me to come and have dinner. She made dinner, and later in the evening she said to me, 'Would you like to see some beautiful things?' and she started modeling clothes for me. I thought they were pretty clothes, but I couldn't understand her great pride in them. She'd always had wealth, so what was so important about these clothes? And then she brought out a bracelet. It was a gold bracelet with several emeralds in it. Unfortunately, I recognized the bracelet. I had known several other girls who had the same bracelet. When

Aly Khan had a date with a girl, he used to give her a cigarette case with one emerald in it. When he fucked her, he
gave her the bracelet.*

"I took the bracelet and dropped it into her fishbowl and
left in a huff. That was the end of our romance. I thought her
values had gone gaflooey, you know. I knew our relationship
couldn't go anywhere because I was never interested in social
climbing, celebrities, that sort of thing. I loved the work.
When I asked Anne Bancroft, who was also one of my students, what she aspired to, she said, 'To be a great actress.'
Grace's reply was 'I want to be a big movie star.' There was
the difference, you see."

Grace and Richardson remained friends and corresponded
until the end of her life. But he found it difficult to accept
what he saw as a tragic spiral into which Grace had fallen.
"From the time of the bracelet incident, she screwed everybody who she came into contact with who was able to do
anything good for her at all. I lost all respect for her. She
screwed agents, producers, directors. And there was really no
need for it. She was already on her way.

"Ironically, her Catholicism, which she believed in, didn't
prevent her from being promiscuous. She would jump out of
bed on Sunday morning, wearing nothing but the crucifix, go
to church, come back in an hour, and jump into bed. Catholicism is a very flexible religion.

"It wasn't that she was a nymphomaniac, in any way at all.
I saw no signs of that. She was a normal girl. But she just had
a terrible need to have someone put his arms around her.
What she needed, constantly, was reassurance that she existed. She was starved for affection because of the family. She
was afflicted with a great sense of emptiness, terrible loneliness, and this was her way of alleviating it."

---

* Mark Miller reports as well that Grace told him that Aly Khan proposed
marriage to her; she turned him down, because at that point her career was
the most important thing in her life.

Chapter Four

The myth of Grace Kelly as a paragon of virtue is matched by the legend that her professional Midas touch began in high school and never failed her, that success came to her quickly and easily. Such is rarely the case, and it certainly wasn't with Grace. Any actor or actress with enough individuality to achieve superstardom is usually too unique to impress any but the most discerning casting directors; if a performer doesn't fit into a "type," too often no one knows what to make of him.

This was true of Grace. Armed with her degree from the Academy, she optimistically set out to make the "rounds" of theatrical auditions in New York. It was a discouraging and debilitating experience. Her first shock came when she discovered the catch-22 that has vexed neophytes in many fields: "Whenever they asked me what I'd done," Grace later said, "I had to explain that I had just graduated from the American Academy of Dramatic Arts, and, you know, that name was so long that sometimes I didn't think I'd be able to get it out. Then the receptionist would be terribly condescending and tell me to come back when I had a little experience. All the kids would get together in the drugstore, and I'd be right there with them, moaning about how impossible it was to get experience if everybody kept telling you to get it first before they'd consider you for a job."

Even worse for Grace was that she always seemed to be "too" something for the role she was seeking. She was "too tall" for most parts, "too intelligent-looking" to play an ingenue, "too chinny," "too leggy." It didn't help her inferiority complex. Her height, it seemed, was the biggest "problem": "Everybody said I was too tall. I've read parts in my stocking feet in the offices of every play producer in New York. I couldn't get to first base because I was five feet six and a half."

One of Grace's auditions turned into a nightmare. She had heard that Al Capp, the creator of the cartoon "Li'l Abner," had written a Broadway musical based on his Dogpatch characters and was auditioning girls for the part of Daisy Mae. Despite Don Richardson's opinion that Grace "wasn't exactly the Daisy Mae type," Grace insisted on auditioning.

"I took her to Capp's office," Richardson recalls, "and waited for her in a little coffee shop nearby. About a half hour later, she came back with her hair messed up, her lipstick smudged, and her dress ripped. Capp had tried to rape her. He physically attacked her. She was in tears and told me how she had had to flee his office to get away from him. Well, I was ready to kill him, but she pleaded with me not to do anything about it. 'I'm okay,' she said, 'the poor man has only one leg—leave him alone.'

"Of course, Capp was arrested for that same sort of thing years later, but no one ever knew that Grace had been one of his victims."*

Despite her experience with Capp, Grace needed to continue to audition for strangers. Finally, she got a job with the Bucks County Playhouse near New Hope, Pennsylvania. It was a prestigious assignment; Bucks had featured performances by some of the finest actors of the American stage. Grace, in fact, probably deserved the nod less than some of her Academy classmates, but the Playhouse owner was a friend of the Kelly family, and once again Grace's family ties helped her cause. (Her program biography said more about

---

* Capp was arrested in April 1971 and charged with adultery, sodomy, and indecent exposure after inviting a married college student back to his room for further discussion after he had given a lecture. In February 1972, he struck a bargain that dropped two of the three charges, pleaded guilty to attempted adultery, and was fined five hundred dollars plus court costs.

her father, uncle, and brother than about her.) Regardless of the reason she was there, Grace was determined to make the most of her opportunity.

Again not likely by coincidence, Grace's first professional performance at the Bucks County Playhouse was in her uncle George's *The Torch Bearers.* In a bit of typecasting, she played an amateur actress, and she did reasonably well. What impressed her co-workers about her was her aura of experience. The play's leading lady, Haila Stoddard, said with admiration: "Even at this early time in her acting career, she had an almost innate sense of what *not* to do. She effortlessly avoided the common affectations or mannerisms of young actors."

Afterward, back in New York, Grace began anew the arduous process of asking for work, something she found "humiliating." Her height continued to be a problem, but in the fall of 1949, she got lucky. As she cried joyously to her mother over the phone, "I've got a part in a Broadway play—and I'm not too tall for it because it's with Raymond Massey!"

The play, August Strindberg's tragedy *The Father,* about a Swedish cavalry captain driven to madness by his evil wife's insinuation that their daughter is not his child, featured a prominent ingenue role in the person of the daughter. Grace was convinced she had been cast in the part because both Massey and leading lady Mady Christians were tall and towered over all the other aspirants except her. Massey—who, as director as well as star, made the decision to hire Grace—has denied this. "She got the part because she showed the most promise. All through the rehearsal period we were impressed with her earnestness, her professionalism, and her good manners. She was organized and dedicated. Between rehearsals she would ask Mady if she could sit in her dressing room and talk about the theater. She was a delight to have in the company. A rare kind of young person who had a hunger to learn and to improve herself." (Grace later told a reporter that she had learned more talking with Mady Christians in her dressing room than she had in two years of study at the Academy.)

The Father began its out-of-town tryouts in Boston, and Grace, eager for her family to see her in a Broadway-bound show, invited them to see it. After the performance Mrs. Kelly held a cast party in their hotel suite. "When Raymond Massey arrived," Mrs. Kelly said, "he was delighted to see Jack—Massey used to row for Toronto and all old oarsmen know each other. But he didn't understand why Jack was there. It took him several minutes to realize that he was Grace's father, for Grace hadn't said a word."

The Father opened on Broadway on November 16, 1949. Carolyn Scott, who had urged Grace to try modeling partly because she doubted her potential as an actress, remembers sitting in the audience on opening night. "Though I knew how thrilled Grace was, I didn't expect to get goose bumps myself. But when she walked out on the stage, looking so fresh and pretty and breathtaking, I burst into tears. I think it was then that I realized she was going places."

Most of the critics agreed with Scott. Ironically, considering that Grace was in such august company, at least one critic thought she was the best thing in the show. George Jean Nathan commented, "Only the novice Grace Kelly, convincing as the daughter, relieves the stage from the air of a minor hinterland stock company on one of its off days."

With notices like that, *The Father*'s days were numbered, and it closed after just sixty-nine performances. Grace returned to the search for work and once again was told she was "too" something or other. Still, this was a good period for Grace, one she would remember with great happiness. She loved being surrounded by the other young actors who had become her friends, and with them she could be herself, allowing them to see her warm, funny, silly side. Her new apartment on fashionable East Sixty-sixth Street was unpretentious and often cluttered; Mrs. Kelly recalled constantly picking up after Grace whenever she visited and telling her to become successful so she could afford a maid. Grace's only pet was a parakeet named Henry, but she was seldom lonely: friends dropped in almost constantly to talk about acting and the theater, to commiserate about parts not won and the arbitrary nature of auditions.

They were a lively bunch, full of energy and fun. One of their favorite games was "giggle belly," in which they all lay on the floor, their heads on one another's stomachs. Then they'd tell funny stories, which would get them to laughing, and their heads would bounce up and down with their bellies. That would produce more laughter, until the room was full of hysterical, violently jerking people. "We did a lot of silly things," Grace recalled, "and we all laughed a lot."

Grace didn't win another part on Broadway for almost two years, but she wasn't without work. The early 1950s were the golden age of television, when live drama of the first order was presented nearly every night. It was a rich new opportunity for young actors, and a grueling testing ground. The good impression Grace had made in *The Father* helped her win important roles in shows like *Studio One, Robert Montgomery Presents, Lights Out, Kraft Playhouse, Lux Video Theatre, The Somerset Maugham Theatre, Hallmark Hall of Fame, Philco/Goodyear Playhouse,* and *Playhouse 90.* She even did a singing-dancing stint on *The Ed Sullivan Show.* It has been said that Grace's initial entrée into television, on CBS, was facilitated by the fact that CBS executive Isaac Levy was a partner with the Kellys in an Atlantic City racetrack. But as usual, Grace took her advantage and made the most of it. In all, she appeared in over sixty television shows in two years, a prodigious output, and she constantly improved her craft. Grace Kelly, in fact, was one of television's pioneer actresses, a fact forgotten in the later glitter of her Hollywood and world fame.

Live television work was fraught with hazards, as Grace quickly learned. "How did we ever get through it?" she wondered years later. "It was like working on the edge of a precipice! I'll never forget one time I was playing a scene in bed with all my clothes on under the covers so I'd be ready to run into the next scene dressed. But the camera didn't stop in time, and they didn't cut away—so there I was, on the screen getting out of bed with all my clothes on!"

Another time Grace and "a wonderful English character man" were supposed to arrive at an orphanage with a hot Christmas pie. "We were to wave through the window," Grace recalled, "and the pie was too hot. So I set it down and the old actor stepped in it. He came limping into the place with half the pie spread over his shoe. 'Look what we've brought you—this nice, hot pie—Merry Christmas!' "

Television helped Grace perfect her craft, and she was noticed. *Life* featured her in an article on "TV's Leading Ladies," looking quite sexy in fishnet stockings for a *Lights Out* role as a music hall singer. Most of her roles typecast her as an elegant sophisticate, usually the daughter of a wealthy man. One of her directors, Fred Coe, explained what made Grace special: "She wasn't just another beautiful girl, she was the essence of freshness—the kind of girl every man dreams of marrying."

Well, perhaps not *every* man. Grace was still encountering opposition from people who found her cold and remote. "She has no stove in her belly," director Sidney Lumet was heard to complain. And a 20th Century-Fox talent executive, choosing not to screen-test her, explained his decision succinctly: "She's got no sex!"

The road was not completely clear of obstacles, but Grace was making progress. Both Don Richardson and Mark Miller referred her to Edie Van Cleve, an agent with the powerful MCA agency whose clients included newcomer Marlon Brando. "Edie just flipped when she saw Grace," Miller recalls. "She signed her up almost immediately." Although Grace's first love was the theater, Van Cleve was working behind the scenes to get her assignments in Hollywood, where the big money was. She succeeded in getting Grace a small part in director Henry Hathaway's drama for 20th Century-Fox, *Fourteen Hours,* based on a real-life incident in which a young man jumped to his death from a New York hotel. Hathaway cast Grace as Mrs. Fuller, a nattily dressed young woman discussing a divorce with her lawyer when the life-and-death drama begins. This close encounter with the tenuousness of life changes the woman's mind about the divorce.

Grace's Hollywood debut was inauspicious (*Fourteen Hours* was financially disappointing), but it did bring her some industry attention, a mink coat she bought with her earnings, and her first devoted fan—a young girl in Oregon who began a "Grace Kelly Fan Club" and wrote to Grace weekly with the names of new members she'd signed up. Grace thought it very funny and cried out in triumph after receiving an update, "We've got a new girl in Washington! I think she's ours, sewed up!" Silly as it may have seemed, it was a strong early indication of Grace Kelly's potent screen appeal that a tiny role in a minor film would inspire someone to start a fan club for her.

While she was filming *Fourteen Hours,* Grace met Hollywood great Gary Cooper, who was impressed by her. "I thought she looked pretty and different, and that maybe she'd be somebody," he said later. "She looked educated, and as if she came from a nice family. She was certainly a refreshing change from all these sexballs we'd been seeing so much of." The paths of Grace Kelly and Gary Cooper would cross again.

An opportunity to play a major movie role came to Grace with a frantic phone call from 20th Century-Fox: director Gregory Ratoff wanted her to audition for a part in his new film, *Taxi,* and she was told to rush over to Fox's New York offices. The urgency of it all rang false to Grace, who put so little stock in the whole thing that she simply stopped by on her way to an acting class wearing her usual "bumming around" outfit—tweed skirt, well-worn shirt, flat shoes, no makeup, and with her hair tied behind her head.

When she arrived, an MCA representative was there to greet her, and he was mortified at her appearance amid a roomful of sensational-looking girls dressed, coiffed, and made-up as though for a *Vogue* magazine cover sitting. But, as sometimes happens in situations like this, Grace's appearance delighted Ratoff. He was casting for a plain Irish immigrant girl, and when he saw Grace, he proclaimed, "She's perfect! I like the fact that she's not pretty." The MCA representative protested that she *was so* pretty, but Ratoff wasn't dissuaded. Grace, when plain and dowdy, in fact did not have the beauty that makeup, lighting, and good photography could bring out in her. Ratoff asked Grace if she could speak in an Irish brogue, and she replied, "Of course," explaining that she was Irish. Luckily, Ratoff took her word for it, because she spent the next two days preparing for the screen test by practicing the accent. By then, Grace badly wanted the part—it was a good one, it did not rely on her beauty so much as her talent, and it could be hers without having to sign a long-term contract with Fox, something she did not want to do.

Grace made the test and Ratoff was delighted. He wanted to hire her, but his bosses nixed her in favor of Constance Smith, an English actress already under contract to the studio. Grace was disappointed, but she soon realized that the whole episode had in fact been a lucky break: *Taxi* wasn't a hit and did nothing for Constance Smith's career, but Grace's screen test for the part was to be instrumental in winning her two other roles which began her ascension to Hollywood stardom.

At this point Grace had received contract offers from several major studios, including MGM, and she could easily have become a part of the MGM stable of contract players, an opportunity most aspiring actors would have leaped at. But she turned the offer down, as much because of an East Coast disdain for Hollywood as because, to her, it smacked of indentured servitude. Grace sensed, too, that she would be lost amid hundreds of young players, that she didn't have the experience to win roles larger than the one she had played in *Fourteen Hours.* She would rather play large parts on the stage, refine her acting abilities, and be better prepared for Hollywood stardom if the chance again presented itself.

The opportunity for Grace to gain theatrical experience and to star in her first Hollywood movie came simultaneously. She received an offer from producer Stanley Kramer and director Fred Zinnemann to star opposite Gary Cooper in a Western, *High Noon.* The names alone were enough to brighten any young actor's eyes. Cooper, of course, was a Hollywood legend and Kramer and Zinnemann had already begun to establish their impressive Hollywood reputations. The men involved in the production, especially Cooper, intimidated the twenty-one-year-old Grace, Mark Miller recalls. "She said to me, 'I don't know if I'm ready. I'm scared.' Now, Grace wasn't the kind of girl to be scared of anything, but she *was* just starting out. I told her, 'You have a good director. Just do what he tells you to do. You know you photograph beautifully. You'll do fine.'"

An offer from the prestigious Elitch Gardens stock company in Denver, Colorado, took Grace off the hook temporarily. She wanted to do more stage work, she told Edie Van Cleve, and the agent agreed that it would be advantageous, but Van Cleve didn't want to give up on having her client costar with Gary Cooper in her second movie. Fully aware that most starting dates for motion picture filming are put off several times, Edie advised Grace to go to Colorado, gambling that her client could have her theater experience and her movie too. She stalled the producers, telling them that Grace was doing theater work and that she would consider their offer when a definite start date for the film was set. The gamble paid off.

Grace's 1951 summer at Elitch was a marvelous one for her. The work was hard—ten plays in eleven weeks—but she felt herself coming into her own as an actress. She won acclaim in such plays as *The Man Who Came to Dinner, The Cocktail Party,* and *Ring Around the Moon,* and she told a fellow actor that she would be happy to "stay here forever." Her joy wasn't just a result of creative fulfillment. Grace had once again fallen in love.

Gene Lyons was a fellow actor, a ruddy Irishman with

intelligence, good looks, and a brooding charisma that led some observers to compare him to Brando. Most of his associates fully expected him to be a major star. Ten years older than Grace, he was, like Don Richardson, a talented theater professional and a potential mentor.

Their relationship developed to the point where Grace felt the need, once again, to inform her family of it. Mrs. Kelly recalled asking Grace how she knew she was in love with Gene. "She explained that since she had gone out on her own, she found that her Philadelphia friends who were not in the theater no longer interested her as much as they once had. Some of them told her frankly they thought she was foolish to want to be an actress. [This] young man was exactly the opposite. He not only knew how she felt, but he felt the same way. He kept telling her that they could be stars in the theater together, that they would stimulate each other to success and fame."

Lyons had been romantically involved with actress Lee Grant, who described him as a man with "an inner fragility and loveliness that were very special and very endearing." When Lyons met Grace, he was in the process of annulling his marriage. Like Grace, he was essentially shy and reserved —but their affection was obvious enough for a fellow company member to describe them as "besotted with each other."

In retrospect the description appears an unfortunate choice of words, because Gene's "fragile psyche" resulted in a drinking problem that eventually doomed his relationship with Grace. Mrs. Kelly, once again, tried to steer Grace away from thoughts of marriage. "I felt that he was not the stable sort of young man I'd hoped Gracie would marry . . . and I had real reservations toward her marrying someone in her profession."

Grace continued to see Gene, dining frequently and romantically at the Russian Tea Room in New York after the stint at Elitch Gardens. The couple did a television drama together, *The Rich Boy,* in which a young woman leaves her lover because of his drinking. It was a case of art imitating life; the more she saw Lyons, the more Grace realized that his psychological problems were so deep-seated that she would not be able to "reform" him. There would be no need for Lyons to go through the trial-by-fire Richardson had and meet Grace's family because, although she continued to see Lyons for another year, she had dropped all thoughts of marriage.

(All this time, Don Richardson was under the impression that he was Grace's only paramour. "I didn't find out about Gene Lyons until years later," he says. "Apparently Grace had several other lives she kept completely secret from me. The girl got around, I tell you.")

After Grace broke off the relationship with Lyons (and as her star ascended while Gene's career failed to ignite as everyone predicted), his alcoholism grew worse and worse. He hit his nadir in the mid-1950s but pulled his life together enough to appear recurringly in the TV series *Ironside* in the early 1970s. Once again down on his luck after that series ended, Lyons died in 1975.

While Grace was still working at Elitch Gardens, Edie Van Cleve's hunch proved correct—filming on *High Noon* had been postponed, and now that things were ready to go the producers still wanted Grace. On August 10 she received a telegram: CAN YOU REPORT AUG. 28, LEAD OPPOSITE GARY COOPER, TENTATIVE TITLE "HIGH NOON." It was an opportunity no one in his right mind would turn down, and Grace timidly asked if she could leave Elitch before the season ended. She was told that actors did it all the time, and it would be no problem. And so Grace Kelly, after five years of study and apprenticeship, was making her second movie as the "lead opposite Gary Cooper." It was only the first in what was to be an astonishing string of professional "good breaks" for Grace.

2

Sexual Elegance in Hollywood

Behind that frigid exterior is a smoldering fire . . . In the Hollywood of the chippies and the tramps, a lady is a rarity. That makes Grace Kelly the most dangerous dame in the movies today.

Confidential magazine

Chapter Five

*H*igh Noon was the first of a series of film offers that gave Grace the opportunity to work with the finest
actors, directors, and screenwriters of her time. It is difficult
to call to mind another Hollywood newcomer so consistently
surrounded by top-echelon talent without a prior reputation
in another medium. Grace, who had begun a lifelong fascination with astrology, did indeed seem to have a fateful run of
professional luck in Hollywood.

Producer Stanley Kramer had scored successes with *Home
of the Brave, The Men* (Marlon Brando's screen debut), and
Cyrano de Bergerac and would go on to produce and direct
such classics as *Judgment at Nuremberg, Ship of Fools,* and
Guess Who's Coming to Dinner. Director Fred Zinnemann
had scored as well with *The Men,* and his nine previous films,
although not classics, had evidenced the talent that would
result in *From Here to Eternity, Oklahoma!, A Man for All
Seasons,* and *Julia.*

Screenwriter Carl Foreman *(Home of the Brave* and *The
Men)* had fashioned a spare Western, based on John Cun-
ningham's story "The Tin Star," around the saga of Will
Kane, an aging sheriff who has rid a frontier town of lawless-
ness, taken a young Quaker bride, and is preparing to hang
up his guns. Word gets to him, however, that an outlaw he
put behind bars five years earlier is free again and is gunning
after him. Kane returns to face the killer, despite the pleas of
his violence-abhorring bride. In a climactic showdown in the
town's main street, Amy Kane's love for her husband over-

comes her pacifist upbringing and she shoots one of his ad-
versaries, saving Kane's life.

High Noon was to be a relatively low-budget "art" picture,
and one of the considerations in casting Grace was that, as a
neophyte, she would be available at a considerably lower fee
than a more established star. More than that, however, Grace
seemed perfectly suited to play Amy Kane; the Quaker bride
was written as a young, beautiful, innocent, refined, even
repressed woman.

"[MCA agent] Jay Kantor brought Grace to my attention,"
Stanley Kramer recalls. "I saw her in a show off Broadway.
She was very pretty and very refined, and I took it upon
myself to hire her. I suppose that required a certain arro-
gance, but I was convinced that she was right for the part."
Director Zinnemann was shown Grace's photograph, and he
too was impressed by her beauty and her "look": "She was a
new face," Zinnemann explained, "and had the kind of quality from the photograph that I thought was important . . .
with a kind of inhibition about it, very straitlaced and very
virginal."

Grace was called in to meet Zinnemann and she didn't
disappoint him. She wore the white gloves that before long
would become a Kelly trademark. "It wasn't so much the
gloves," Zinnemann said later, explaining the impression
Grace made on him, "as that she had the personality and
manner to go with them. Most actresses are more . . . *uninhibited.*" It was a quality Zinnemann particularly liked in
Grace, for Amy Kane was nothing if not inhibited.

Grace was so shy, in fact, that she responded to Zinnemann's questions with little more than yes or no answers.
It got so bad that Zinnemann told her: "You ought to learn
how to speak to people and what to say to them when you
meet them." It was odd advice from Zinnemann, who himself
was often at a loss for words, and the interview did not
breeze along. But Grace's reserve worked for the part she was
seeking, and all concerned agreed with Kramer that Grace
should play Amy.

Then came an unforeseen complication: Gary Cooper, a Hollywood legend, was available to play Sheriff Kane. Kramer had wanted to hire him but wasn't sure he could meet Cooper's price with the film's five-hundred-thousand-dollar budget—Cooper was a *big* star. But he was also fifty-one and hadn't had a hit in years. He knew a good part when he saw one, and he wasn't going to lose it with "star" demands that Kramer couldn't meet. "I paid him a good salary," Kramer recalls—but it was not what Cooper had been used to getting.

The producers were also uncertain about the casting of Grace Kelly to play Gary Cooper's bride; there was an age difference of twenty-eight years. Kramer particularly thought Grace was now miscast, and he remembers that Cooper himself was concerned about how audiences would react to the age difference: "Coop muttered a few times under his breath, 'What's an old goat like me doing playing opposite such a young girl?' "

There was nothing to be done, however; a commitment had been made to Grace's agents and there wasn't time to look for another actress. And, no small matter, everyone concerned *wanted* Grace to play the role: "She was just too special, her face too attractive and photographically interesting," Zinnemann said. "So we stuck with her." The age issue soon faded; Hollywood, after all, had a long tradition (continued to this day, usually by older men in charge of casting) of hiring young actresses as the love interests of older men (almost never is the opposite true). In fact, Grace may be the Hollywood champion in that respect: the average age of her eleven leading men was forty-six; the only Kelly costar less than eleven years older than she was Louis Jourdan. With her penchant for older men, Grace very likely didn't complain about the situation.

Indeed, Gary Cooper soon became the first in a series of these much older leading men with whom Grace conducted affairs of varying seriousness during her Hollywood career. Impressionable, star-struck, drawn to men of maturity and achievement, Grace found herself romantically helpless among the sophisticated, attractive, celebrated, and accomplished men with whom she was surrounded in Hollywood. "I prefer older men," she said. "They're more interesting. I like people who know more than I do. I always have preferred older people." Lizanne adds, "Grace fell in love very easily; too easily, really. Every time I turned around, it seemed she was talking about some other man, saying, 'Isn't he divine?'"

Gary Cooper, handsome, rugged, as much a man's man as he was a ladies' man, the celebrated star of classics like *Mr. Deeds Goes to Town, The General Died at Dawn,* and *Beau Geste,* and an Oscar winner for *Sergeant York,* was exactly the kind of man to make Grace Kelly smitten. And she was. "Grace was infatuated with Gary Cooper." Lizanne says. "She was in awe of him, very star-struck."

The sentiment was returned; as Stanley Kramer discreetly puts it, "Coop felt warmly toward Grace." Separated from his wife* and winding up a tempestuous affair with the beautiful young actress Patricia Neal, Cooper was vulnerable to the charms of this warmly attentive, gorgeous young newcomer. Robert Slatzer, who worked on the Paramount lot as a publicity and rewrite man in the early 1950s and has since written biographies of Marilyn Monroe, Bing Crosby, and John Wayne, befriended Gary Cooper, among many other Hollywood celebrities, and frequently went hunting and fishing with him. "Coop was the kind of guy who could sit down and talk to you about anything and was never evasive. He was quite a ladies' man, and he told me that he and Grace were having an affair. I was on the set a couple of times, and, when Grace would come up to him, just the way she looked at him you could tell she was melting. She'd embarrass him, sometimes, by coming over and putting her arms around him and being obvious in front of other people."

Before long, Grace and Cooper were linked in gossip col-

---

* Cooper had married Veronica "Rocky" Balfe, an actress known professionally as Sandra Shaw, in 1933. In 1938 they had a daughter, Maria. Through frequent separations, and Cooper's romantic dalliances, they remained married until his death in 1961.

umns, and whispers began of a romance between the two. Word got back to Philadelphia, and Grace's parents were concerned; Cooper was clearly too old for Grace, even if she didn't think so. First Lizanne, then Mrs. Kelly flew out to California to "chaperone" Grace and Cooper on several dates near the location in California's Sonoma Mountains. It was a scenario that would occur again and again during Grace's career as word of her dalliances got back to Philadelphia, because her parents were very concerned about her interest in men they found too old, too worldly, and, in several cases, too married for Grace. In Cooper's case, the affair was short-lived.

Publicly, Cooper simply expressed admiration for Grace's artistic potential: "She was very serious about her work. . . . She was trying to learn, you could see that. You can tell if a person really wants to be an actress. She was one of those people you could get that feeling about."

Cooper, Grace has said, worked with her to improve her performance. "He's the one who taught me to relax during a scene and let the camera do some of the work. On the stage you have to emote not only for the front rows, but for the balcony too, and I'm afraid I overdid it. He taught me that the camera is always in the front row, and how to take it easy."

From all reports, director Zinnemann had a curiously ambivalent attitude toward Grace during filming. He found her visually delightful—asked years later why he had cast her, his response was "She was a *very* pretty girl"—and he consequently gave her an inordinate amount of camera attention. His loving close-ups, in fact, disturbed not only Grace's female costar, the fiery Katy Jurado, who accused Zinnemann of being "half in love" with Grace, but producer Kramer as well. Part of Zinnemann's reason for so emphasizing Grace was to keep her screen impact on an even keel with Cooper's and Jurado's. Grace expressed appreciation of him: "I'll never be able to thank Fred Zinnemann for what he did for me. He and Mr. Kramer were the ones who proved to me that movie-making is as great a creative art as the stage, and that those on the stage who talk down the movies just haven't seen or been in the right pictures."

On the other hand, Zinnemann's major preoccupation as director was with Cooper's performance, and Grace, as a screen neophyte, suffered from the lack of strong guidance from her director. Her performance inspired such critical adjectives as "bloodless and flat," "mousy," and "wooden," and when Grace saw the rushes she was mortified. "Everything is so clear working with Gary Cooper," she explained later. "When I look into his face, I can see everything he is thinking. But when I look into my own face, I see absolutely nothing. *I* know what I'm thinking, but it just doesn't *show*. For the first time I suddenly thought, 'Perhaps I'm not going to be a great star; perhaps I'm not any good after all.' "

What Grace didn't know was that, to Zinnemann at least, her performance was exactly right. Her awkwardness and acting reticence was, he thought, perfectly suited to the Quaker bride. "She was very, very wooden . . . which fitted perfectly, and her lack of experience and sort of gauche behavior was to me very touching," he commented. "To see this prim Easterner in the wilds of the Burbank Columbia back lot —it worked very well."

Zinnemann left Grace to her own limited devices because he felt that to direct her would be to risk eliciting an "actorish" performance from her, and that was the last thing he wanted—"I wanted the whole thing to look like a newsreel." One of Grace's biographers, Steven Englund, noted, "An experienced, older professional actress would have had to possess very considerable acting talent indeed to do what Grace did (and somewhat rued) naturally."

High Noon was an artistic and commercial success. "It cost five hundred thousand dollars and grossed eighteen million. That's *very* good," Kramer says. Reviews, including most of Grace's notices, were excellent, although few spent more than a line or two discussing her performance. The film was a triumph for Gary Cooper, winning him an Academy Award and reviving his career. The film is, in fact, one of Grace's best movies. "It was a wonderful picture," Grace commented. "I loved every minute of it, except when the wife was on the screen. I just wasn't in the same class with the rest. Oh, they were nice to me, and they told me I had done a fine job, but I knew better. I left Hollywood as fast as I could, and I told myself I wouldn't go back until I could carry my own weight in a picture."

Grace's fear that she was "not going to be a great star" was reinforced when she returned to New York. She resumed her acting lessons and attempted to get back into television. This brought her a rude surprise: "I discovered that in television they forget quickly. I'd been doing leads before I left, and although I was in California just five months, when I got back I could hardly get bit parts. That was when I had to face up to the possibility that I might not be a great actress. And I knew I had to come to a decision in my own mind. Would I be happy if all I could ever be was a character actress, playing subordinate roles? I thought about it a lot, and my final answer was yes, I *could* be happy if that was how it had to be."

No sooner had Grace made this important decision than it became quite moot. After just a few months in New York she received an offer that would change her life: legendary director John Ford wanted her to costar with Clark Gable and Ava Gardner in *Mogambo,* a remake of the 1932 Clark Gable-Jean Harlow vehicle, *Red Dust.* Grace would play Linda Nordley, a proper young Englishwoman, the wife of an engineer, who becomes involved in a romantic triangle with a white hunter (Gable) and a sexy show girl (Gardner). It was another astonishing opportunity, particularly in light of the deflating reaction she'd gotten from television executives. So much so that Metro-Goldwyn-Mayer managed to wrangle Grace's signature onto a seven-year contract, something she had steadfastly avoided for three years.

John Ford had been unmoved by Grace's performance in *High Noon.* "All she did," he said, "was shoot a guy in the back. Cooper should have given her a boot in the pants and sent her back East." When he saw her *Taxi* test, though, he was more intrigued and told Metro executive Dore Schary, "Darryl [Zanuck, head of 20th Century-Fox] miscast her in that test—but this dame has breeding, quality, class. I want to make a test of her—in color. I'll bet she'll knock us on our asses."

Schary recalled, "He made the test. It and Grace Kelly were stunning. We signed her to a long-term contract. John Ford enabled me to even the score with Darryl Zanuck. He got Monroe, we got Grace Kelly."

Ironically, Schary has said that signing Grace at the time he did was somewhat unique, because long-term contracts were becoming passé. But Grace was given an ultimatum: sign a six-month contract with options every six months extending to seven years, or you don't do *Mogambo*. Grace wasn't prepared to lose such an important role; after some soul-searching, she agreed to the contract—but only when MGM acquiesced to some of *her* terms. She would make just three pictures a year (in those days, even major stars might make four or five); she wanted one year off every three, and she wanted to be able to make her home in New York rather than having to live in Hollywood (as some actors had been constrained to do so that the studio might "keep an eye on" them).

Lucille Ryman Carroll, wife of actor John Carroll, was head of talent at MGM in the fall of 1952 when Grace Kelly was signed, and she remembers Grace sitting in her office to discuss the contract. Contrary to what has been reported, Mrs. Carroll says, MGM had few problems with Grace's demands. "We certainly didn't object to her wanting to take time off for stage work, because our belief was that doing a Broadway show could only enhance the popularity and reputation of our actors, making them more valuable commodities for us."

MGM wouldn't budge on one of Grace's demands, however. "She told me that it was very important for her to choose her own roles," Mrs. Carroll recalls. "I told her that we never allowed that, that we always chose roles for our contract players, and that these roles were designed to make them top-notch stars. She said to me, 'But I'm afraid that you might put me into something that doesn't suit me.' I told her, 'Don't worry about that, my dear, we can be trusted to put you in roles that will enhance your career.'"

Mrs. Carroll recalls being impressed by the "self-confidence" Grace showed during the interview, but she didn't feel that MGM had latched on to a sure thing. "I was puzzled, for one thing, over the fact that she'd been sent to see me rather than Mr. Mayer [Louis B. Mayer, head of MGM], which was the usual procedure. And I had heard that she wasn't exactly setting the world on fire. No one else seemed to want her, really, and the word on her performance in *High Noon*—some of our people had seen a rough cut—wasn't ecstatic. So I felt that I could get her for a good price, and I offered her seven hundred and fifty dollars a week to start— fifteen hundred was more common in those days. She accepted."

Grace might have held out for more money—she could make more a week modeling full-time—but she sensed, as Dore Schary later said, that "nobody in the picture business was that impressed with her," and she did, after all, want to go to Africa and make *Mogambo*. As she said later, speaking of the contract, "If *Mogambo* had been made in Arizona, I wouldn't have done it."

Its contract with Grace allowed MGM to pick up (or drop) her option every six months; at the end of seven years, she would be making between four and five thousand dollars a week. It also guaranteed her twenty-three thousand dollars a year in bonus money and allowed for all of her requirements except one: MGM, not Grace, would choose her roles. It was a point that would create much contention between Grace and her studio over the next three years, Mrs. Carroll's assurances notwithstanding.

By signing the MGM contract, Grace paved the way for a momentous career move. That, however, wasn't uppermost in her mind. What was important to her can be surmised by the telephone call she made to her mother: "Guess what I'm going to do next?" she gushed into the phone. "I'm going to Africa . . . *with Clark Gable!*"

Gable, of course, had been known as the King of Hollywood—and the quintessential cinema heartthrob—ever since *Gone With the Wind* fourteen years earlier. Although he was now fifty-one, age had stolen little of the dashing sex appeal that had made him a star, and he had been idealized as a sophisticated older man who knew how to keep a woman satisfied. His 1939 marriage to blond comedienne Carole Lombard—a match that set millions of movie fans' hearts a-flutter—was no less romantic for the fact that Lombard, seven years younger than Gable, called her husband "Pa."

Gable's reputation as a gentleman of warmth and sensitivity was matched by his fame as a hard-living, hard-drinking womanizer. Devastated by Lombard's death in a 1942 plane crash, Gable took to bouts of drink, during which his personality could turn ugly and unpredictable. He had just come out of a much-publicized, brief marriage to a woman close to his own age, the wealthy English aristocrat Lady Sylvia Ashley,* and Mrs. Kelly was worried about her daughter going so far away in the company of such a volatile man. After the Cooper affair, she worried too that Grace might be vulnerable to Gable's charms. "Clark Gable?" Mrs. Kelly responded to her daughter's announcement. "All the way to Africa with him? . . . How can I allow you to go over there all by yourself? What will people say? Do you think it's proper?"

"Oh, Mother," Grace replied, "you've got such old-fashioned ideas."

Mrs. Kelly allowed Grace to go to Africa, but her fears

---

* Gable's first marriage, in 1924, was to Broadway actress and teacher Josephine Dillon, seventeen years his senior. It ended in divorce in 1930. His second wife was Houston socialite Ria Langham, also seventeen years older than he. They were wed in 1930 and divorced in 1939. His fifth marriage, to eighteen-years-younger Kay Williams Spreckels in 1955, lasted until his death in 1960. On March 20, 1961, Kay gave birth to Clark Gable's only child, John Clark Gable.

turned out to be well-founded: Grace did indeed fall hard for Gable. "Grace was mad for Clark," Lizanne confirms. Gable himself, returned from filming, told Louella Parsons, "She should never have been allowed to go all that distance without a chaperone." From the outset of filming Grace was constantly at Gable's side; she became known among the company as "the girl with Gable." She went so far as to accompany him on early-morning safaris with famed white hunter Bunny Allen. This puzzled even Gable. "What is there about this that you like?" he once asked her. She replied, "It's the strangeness and the excitement of it all. I want to be able to tell my grandchildren about it some day." What she didn't add was that it also afforded her the opportunity to be with Gable as often as possible.

That Grace Kelly and Clark Gable were taken with each other cannot be denied. But exactly what *form* their affection took may never be known. There are those who claim there was a physical affair, among them Don Richardson and an anonymous Gable friend who said, ungallantly, "Grace was just a one-night stand for Clark." Others insist it was merely a platonic, although quite special, father/daughter closeness. According to Gore Vidal, who was writing screenplays at MGM at the time, Grace had a strong sexual interest in Gable which he did not return. "Grace almost always laid the leading man," Vidal says. "She was famous for that in this town. One of the few she failed to was Clark Gable. *Mogambo*'s producer, Sam Zimbalist, with whom I've made several pictures, was wildly funny about how they got on during the location shooting in Africa. Gable liked older women, preferably society ladies, and by that time was more into the bottle than into sex anyway. But Grace set her eye on Gable, who complained to Sam, saying, 'What am I going to do about this girl? She keeps staring at me and she wants moonlit dinners in my tent,' and so on. And Sam said, 'Well, that's your problem.' So Gable invited her to a candlelit dinner alone in his tent and got her dead drunk, which didn't take much with Grace, and she threw up. So that was the end of that romance, Gable's body was saved yet again, and she never went back."

Despite Gable's apparent lack of interest in Grace's romantic overtures, a tender friendship nonetheless developed between them. She admired Gable's fearlessness, and he was surprised and impressed by hers. Once, told that Grace was reading down by the ocean, Gable became concerned, principally because the Mau Mau uprisings in that part of Africa presented a threat to everyone. He went to look for her and found her with a book in her lap, crying. He asked her why. "It's the most beautiful thing," she explained softly. "I'm reading *The Snows of Kilimanjaro,* about the leopard in the snow, and I looked up and I saw a lion walking along the seashore."

He was astonished: "She saw a lion walking along the shore and she wasn't frightened!" Gable liked nothing better than a girl with spunk, and he and Grace grew closer and closer. Bunny Allen recalled that Grace at first seemed terribly prim and proper, but after a while she'd "pass the bottle around with the rest of us." That, too, was a quality Gable liked in Grace. And she was impressed by macho man Gable's sensitive side: more than once he was seen reading poetry to her while they sat on the banks of the wild Kagera river.

Inevitably word leaked out about the special closeness of Kelly and Gable, and rumors began to circulate of a romance. Before long, a London newspaper columnist sent Gable a telegram: RUMORS SWEEPING ENGLAND ABOUT YOUR ROMANCE WITH GRACE KELLY. PLEASE CABLE CONFIRMATION OR DENIAL. According to Grace, Gable laughed when he read it and said, "That's the greatest compliment I've ever had. I'm old enough to be your father."

Gable was likely unaware that it was that very fact that made him so attractive to Grace. She called him "Ba," the Swahili word for father, and it often sounded to Gable like Carole Lombard's "Pa," summoning up complicated emotions within him. But with all that, Lombard was just seven years younger than Gable, not, as with Grace, nearly thirty. He held back, not unattracted but unwilling to become involved with so emotional a young girl. (Gable's unwillingness to become physically intimate with Grace led her into fits of uncontrollable sobbing.) Once filming ended and Grace was saying goodbye to Gable at the London airport, she broke down again. The crying jag, witnessed by reporters, was cited as proof that Grace and Gable had had an affair and now it was over—against Grace's wishes. Rather, it was Grace's realization that her desire for Gable, with shooting at an end and everyone saying goodbye, then had no possibility of developing into a real relationship.

Asked about her tears, Grace replied in the flip, coy manner of someone skirting the truth: "If I cried, and I don't remember doing so, it was probably over the fact that I had to leave all that beautiful Georgian silver behind in customs." But later, in a more serious vein, she revealed as much as she ever would: "I was very fond of Clark Gable . . . Perhaps, if there wasn't so much of an age discrepancy, it might have been different."

It might well have, because by the end of filming Gable had become very fond of Grace. A friend of his revealed that when Clark returned from Africa he talked incessantly about her: "It was almost as if he were talking about Carole . . ." Despite his special feelings for Grace, however, Gable chose to stick with his decision not to pursue a relationship with her.

With the exception of the disappointing outcome of her relationship with Gable, Grace's experiences in Africa were all she'd hoped they would be. She read dozens of books about the continent and its natives, and she remarked, "I've always been fascinated by Africa, and believe me, I wasn't disappointed." The film crew traveled over ten thousand miles of the continent, reaching into primitive areas never before photographed. Grace was mesmerized by it all—the strange plant life, the seemingly docile elephants and rhinoceroses that might attack at any moment, the Watusi natives—even the danger. An enraged rhinoceros rammed a

Jeep carrying Clark, Grace, and Ava, almost turning it over before the beast was shot. A tribe of warlike Samburus, after completing an ancient courage ceremony for the cameras, frightened everyone when they, as if in a trance, began a weird war dance, jumped in the air and waved their spears threateningly at the film crew. Another time three crew members were killed when their Jeeps overturned in the thick jungle overgrowth. Dozens more were injured in various ways, and the crew suffered generally from the intense heat, the maddening mosquitoes, and persistent tropical infections.

Grace took it all in stride. She wrote home about how beautiful Africa was, recounting the time she looked out of her mosquito-netted tent to see a moon so enormous she felt she could reach out and touch it. Reading about the country and accompanying Gable on safari weren't the only ways Grace tried to get the most she could out of Africa. She also endeavored to learn Swahili, and she was the only member of the crew to do so. If nothing else it resulted in an amusing anecdote, told by Donald Sinden, the English actor who portrayed Grace's husband. The first night in Nairobi, Sinden, Clark, and Grace dined together at the New Stanley Hotel. "Our waiter was a Kikuyu," Sinden related, "and Grace proceeded to astonish Clark and me by ordering the entire meal for the three of us in Swahili . . . Having served the coffee, the waiter was just moving away when Grace called after him, *'Lete, ndizi, tafadhali.'* By then we had learned that *lete* meant 'bring' and *tafadhali* meant 'please,' but Clark, with some incredulousness, asked her, 'What's an *ndizi?'*

"Before she could reply, the waiter had turned and in a bored American accent answered, 'It's a banana,' and wearily made his way."

As the company prepared to move to a new location in Uganda, Clark decided that he would take Grace, Ava, Ava's husband Frank Sinatra, and a few others on a sightseeing trip along the Indian Ocean. The only transportation available for such a trip was a decrepit old plane that the pilot insisted was safe, but that Clark thought must have been "held together with chicken wire." Everyone piled in, and their marvel at the breathtaking sights was matched only by their nervousness in the rickety aircraft. MGM executives, considering the value of the cargo, would have had a collective heart attack had they known of Gable's adventure.

Grace and Ava Gardner became friends during the filming, and both she and Frank Sinatra remained close to Grace throughout her life. Ava seemed an odd choice by Grace for a friend; their public images could not have been less alike. But Gardner's personality appealed to the earthy, sexy, private Grace; she enjoyed Ava's ribald sense of humor, admired her open sexuality and frank, often profane, outspokenness— something Grace's sense of propriety did not allow her. Even so, Ava's lasciviousness did sometimes shock Grace, and Gore Vidal offers an illustrative anecdote, told to him by Sam Zimbalist: "The location was full of these tall Watusis, beautiful warriors who had been hired as extras, wearing their breechclouts. The girls were walking along, and Ava said to Grace, 'I wonder if their cocks are as big as people say? Have you ever seen a black cock?' Grace turned purple, of course, and said, 'Stop that, don't talk like that!' Ava said, 'That's funny . . . neither have I'—and with that she reached over and pulled up the breechclout of one of the Watusis, who gave a big grin as this huge cock flopped out. By then Grace had turned absolutely blue. Ava let go of the breechclout, turned to Grace, and said, 'Frank's bigger than that.' "

Robert Surtees, cinematographer of *Mogambo*, tells another Ava Gardner anecdote, one also revealing of Grace: Ava, during a trip to Rome with Surtees and Grace after filming was completed, told him "as a joke that she wanted to see every whorehouse in the city in one night. I had worked there on *Quo Vadis* for over a year so I knew where all the brothels were. She knew I'd know. Grace Kelly was staying, like Ava, at the Hotel Excelsior. I went over and picked the two of them up, as that cool, dignified Grace also wanted to go on the tour. Well, at one dive we got to a guy who became attracted to Grace and got in the backseat to neck with her as we drove along. Ava laughed till I thought she'd burst."

The least enjoyable aspect of the *Mogambo* filming for Grace was working with John Ford. A "man's director," renowned for his Westerns, Ford had little affinity for directing women under the best of circumstances. With the exigencies of filming on an African location and his deteriorating health, Ford had little time to help a newcomer like Grace, and he left her to her own devices. At least once this resulted in a Ford blowup—when Grace took a position indicated in the script. "Kelly, what the hell are you doing?" Ford bellowed. "Well," Grace stammered, "in my script it says she walks over here . . ."

Ford turned livid. "We are shooting a movie, not the script!"

Despite such unreasonable anger and Ford's lack of sensitivity to her, Grace turned in a much better performance in *Mogambo* than she had in *High Noon.* Typecast as a prim, frigid wife, Grace brought the proper mixture of refinement and repressed passion to Linda Nordley. Her finest moments on-screen delineate her growing love for Gable. Grace's role was a difficult one, but reviewers thought she handled it admirably; *Newsweek*'s critic provided one of the first perceptive analyses of Grace's screen appeal: "Grace Kelly makes one of the loveliest patricians to appear on the screen in a long time. Her particular quality is the suggestion that she is well born without being arrogant, cultivated without being stuffy, and highly-charged without being blatant."

By the time *Mogambo* was released in October 1953, Grace Kelly was fast becoming a media celebrity, and it was this hoopla, as well as her performance, that won her *Look* magazine's designation as the Best Actress of 1953 and an Academy Award nomination as Best Supporting Actress. She lost the Oscar to Donna Reed in *From Here to Eternity,* but it hardly mattered: by the end of 1954, Grace Patricia Kelly, the bricklayer's daughter from Philadelphia, had become a Hollywood phenomenon—and, with several indiscretions which soon became embarrassingly public, something of a scandal as well.

Chapter Six

In the fall of 1953, Alfred Hitchcock sat in a studio screening room and viewed the test Grace had done for Gregory Ratoff's *Taxi*. The world-famous "suspense" director, who had produced a string of hits over the previous twenty years and substantially advanced the art of cinema in the process, had seen Grace in *High Noon* and a rough cut of *Mogambo* and was not impressed. But as he sat watching her test for Ratoff, something about her moved him profoundly. He himself may not have understood the full import of his feelings at the time, but as his career intertwined with Grace's over the next four years he would find himself making a considerable emotional investment in the young girl then before him on the screen.

Grace's dichotomy fascinated Hitchcock. She was in manner and bearing every inch a lady. She was also a vibrant, sensual, sexually arousing young woman. Her sex appeal, wrapped as it was in decorum, became all the more potent. For many men, Grace solved the whore/madonna dilemma: she possessed elements of both. And for Hitchcock, this combination promised a great deal of vibrancy on celluloid. "An actress like Grace, who's also a lady," he said, "gives a director certain advantages. He can afford to be more *colorful* with a love scene played by a lady than with one played by a hussy. With a hussy such a scene can be vulgar, but if you put a lady in the same circumstances, she's exciting and glamorous." Hitchcock dubbed this quality of Grace's "sexual elegance."

Hitchcock was the first director to utilize these warring elements of Grace's personality, and although he wouldn't fully exploit them until his next film with her, *Rear Window,* the role he wanted Grace to play in *Dial M for Murder* was a departure for her: an unfaithful wife whose husband tries to murder her.

The plot was a typically stylish Hitchcock suspense yarn. Tony Wendice (Ray Milland) discovers that his wealthy young wife, Margot, has taken a lover (Robert Cummings). Fearful that she will divorce him and he will be left without money, Tony hires a former school chum to murder her.

They act out an elaborate scenario: Tony calls Margot while he is out with friends (to establish an alibi) and distracts her while the killer sneaks up from behind and strangles her. Tony listens impassively to the struggle, then is shocked when Margot returns to the phone and sobs that she has stabbed her attacker with a pair of scissors.

Tony rushes home and eventually calls the police, but not until he has manipulated the evidence to make it look like Margot murdered the man because he was blackmailing her. Margot is arrested, and Tony's scheme seems to have worked until a suspicious police inspector turns up an incriminating duplicate key to the apartment. He then exposes the truth.

The first meeting between Grace and Alfred Hitchcock was an awkward one. She was tongue-tied with nervousness ("In a horrible way it was funny to have my brain turn to stone," she said later), and Hitchcock's only comment after the interview was that he would "have to do something about her voice," which was still too high and thin. Nonetheless, he wanted her to play Margot.

Warner Brothers approached MGM about "lending" it Grace to do Hitchcock's picture, and the studio's executives readily agreed. They had nothing else lined up for her, and by charging Warner twenty thousand dollars, MGM would clear fourteen thousand after paying Grace one thousand a week for the six weeks of shooting.

When filming began in the fall of 1953, Hitchcock worked hard to make Grace comfortable and at home on the set. Assistant director Melvin Dellar remembers that "Hitch made her very much at ease, and she in turn made everyone comfortable."

The most important reason for Grace's ease and openness on the *Dial M* set was the fact that Hitchcock worked with her more closely than any movie director had before him. Grace was used to being virtually ignored by Zinnemann and Ford, and the very personal attention showered upon her by a man of Hitchcock's brilliance and stature came as a gratifying surprise. Ironically, the director who once said that "all actors are cattle" was teaching Grace what twenty years as a film-maker had taught him. "Working with Hitchcock was a tremendous experience and a very enriching one," Grace later said. "As an actor, I learned a tremendous amount about motion picture making. He gave me a great deal of confidence in myself."

She offered a specific example shortly after the filming. "Every good dramatic coach and every good director would like you to think of the story as a whole, and not just your part in it. But Hitchcock was the first one to show me *why,* and then teach me *how.* In the telephone scene I used all the tricks to show horror that I had ever learned in school or in television, and thought I had done particularly well with my eyes. But all he used in that scene were my hands on the telephone. I was hurt, but he flattered me by telling me my hands were good actors, too. What he meant was that acting was more than a trick of waving your eyelashes, and that to be a success, you had to learn to act with your whole body. I worked so hard after that."

Grace, Hitchcock, and his wife, Alma, soon became close friends; she frequently dined at their house. "I have such affection for him and his wife," Grace said, "that he can do no wrong." There were many light moments between them on the set; Hitch's love of word games and puns tickled Grace, and she held her own in coming up with new examples of his latest game. Ever since meeting Lizabeth Scott, Hitch had amused himself by imagining other famous names minus their initial letter: Rank Sinatra, Ickey Rooney, Reer

Garson, Scar Hammerstein, Orgie Raft, Lark Gable, Ugh Marlowe—the list was endless, and every time Hitch or Grace would come up with a new one, they'd giggle like schoolchildren.

Hitchcock's humor had its wry side as well, and sometimes that was aimed at Grace. He loved to tell off-color stories in her presence, all the time checking to see whether she looked shocked. At one point, disappointed by Grace's apparent indifference, Hitchcock turned and asked her, "Aren't you shocked, Miss Kelly?" She gave a reply that absolutely delighted him: "No. I went to a girls' convent school, Mr. Hitchcock. I heard all those things when I was thirteen."

Although Hitchcock was a director who knew exactly what he wanted—he once said that filming was anticlimactic for him because he'd already worked the entire movie out in his mind—he listened to Grace's suggestions, and in at least one instance deferred to her. Every visual aspect of a scene was important to Hitchcock, and for the key moment when Margot Wendice gets up out of bed to answer the phone call from her husband, Hitch wanted Grace to put on a richly red velvet robe to contrast with her blond hair and create a visual tension on the night-dark screen.

Grace, working from her understanding of her character, told Hitchcock that a woman alone, roused from sleep, would not bother to put on her robe: "I'd just get up and go to the phone in my nightgown." Hitchcock agreed to try it, and he quickly saw that Grace was right; he was also happily surprised to discover that the nightgown added a sexiness to the murder attempt that was perfectly in keeping with his skewed sensibilities.

So taken was Hitchcock, in fact, with the dance of death he had choreographed between Margot and her would-be killer that he spent nearly a week filming it. Although it lasts just a few moments on-screen, it is one of the director's most heart-stopping scenes.

As filming progressed, Hitchcock became increasingly enamored of Grace's charms. Mel Dellar recalls that "Hitchcock was fascinated by the way she looked, the way she walked, the way she moved." Donald Spoto, in his Hitchcock biography, *The Dark Side of Genius,* presents a convincing case that Alfred Hitchcock was in love with Grace and tortured by her lack of reciprocation. If he couldn't have her personally, though, he'd have her professionally. Said John Michael Hayes, who wrote the screenplay for Grace's next Hitchcock film, *Rear Window,* "[He] would have used Grace in the next ten pictures he made. I would say that all the actresses he cast subsequently were attempts to retrieve the image and feeling that Hitch carried around so reverentially about Grace."

Hitchcock never made any overt attempts to woo Grace, and by the time *Rear Window* filming began she may have been aware only of a "sweet" affection for her on Hitchcock's part. By the early 1960s, however, Hitchcock's interest in Tippi Hedren, the lovely blonde he cast in *Marnie* when Grace turned down a return to the screen, would result in clumsy sexual propositions which greatly disturbed Hedren.

Grace soon found herself enmeshed in a sexual imbroglio, but it had nothing to do with Hitchcock. Her forty-nine-year-old costar Ray Milland was another highly attractive leading man, an Oscar winner in 1945 for *The Lost Weekend,* and powerful and well liked in Hollywood. The fact that he was married did little to dampen twenty-three-year-old Grace's ardent interest.

Milland had married the former Murial Weber in 1932, and they had a son, Daniel, born 1940, and a daughter, Victoria, adopted in 1949. Like Gary Cooper, however, Milland appreciated women other than his wife, and he often succumbed to temptation. He was particularly susceptible to Grace's considerable charms, and he fell hard. So did Grace. "It was very serious between Ray and Grace," Lizanne recalls. They began to see each other, making little effort to conceal their romance. "I was aware of it," Mel Dellar says. "My wife and I saw them out having dinner a couple of times, and late in the evening, after we finished filming, they'd go to some little place and have a few drinks."

Milland surprised Lizanne one day by confiding the depth of his feelings for Grace to her. "I flew back from Hollywood on the same plane with him," she recalls, "and we had a long talk. He told me he really was very much in love with her."

Gossip in Hollywood spreads faster than Southern California fires whipped by hot Santa Ana winds, and Milland's wife, known to her friends as Mal, soon heard talk about her husband and this beautiful newcomer. She feared it was true, but there was no proof. Several weeks after her suspicions were first aroused, her fears were confirmed. A close friend of the Millands, who requested anonymity, recalls: "Jack—his friends call Milland 'Jack'—was going on a trip, and he had just left the house. Mal's sister Harriet was there, and Mal poured her heart out to her about her suspicions. Harriet got in her car, followed Jack to the airport, and sure enough, there was Jack with Grace, going off on a tryst somewhere."

The Millands separated; Grace and Ray discussed marriage. He took an apartment in Hollywood and Grace spent a great deal of time there. Teet Carle, a publicist at Paramount at the time, says, "I don't know if they were living together, but the story got back to me that someone from the studio went over to Ray's apartment and Grace answered the door."

Grace's indiscretion soon became common knowledge in Hollywood, and she was unprepared for the animosity directed toward her. Mal Milland was extremely well liked in this company town; she and Ray had a family, and none of their many friends wanted to see the marriage destroyed. A tearful late-night telephone call from Mrs. Milland to Louella Parsons about "this young girl who's trying to steal my husband" did little to help Grace's cause.

It wasn't the publicity, which the veteran Milland was more used to and less affected by than Grace was, but rather his realization of the impracticality of his divorcing Mal that caused Milland to reconsider. Studio publicist Andy Hervey recalls that Mrs. Milland had an ace up her sleeve: "Mal told

Ray, 'You go ahead and get a divorce and marry Grace Kelly. That's okay with me, because all the property is in my name.' Needless to say, it wasn't long before the marriage plans were off."

The previously quoted friend of the Millands adds, "Jack finally came to his senses and realized that he had a wonderful woman in Mal—and of course, they're still together to this day.* Mal still refers to the Grace Kelly period as 'those agonizing days.' "

Not only was Milland being pressured to break off the romance, so was Grace by her family. After the Cooper and Gable "situations," Jack Kelly had asked publicist Scoop Conlan, a family friend, to "keep an eye on Grace," and Conlan reported back to him about his daughter's latest potentially embarrassing liaison. The Kellys were very displeased. "My father was concerned about Ray Milland," Kell said later. "He didn't like what he had heard about him." Jack Kelly himself huffed to a reporter a short time later, "I don't like that sort of thing much. I'd like to see Grace married. These people in Hollywood think marriage is like a game of musical chairs."

Lizanne recalls, "In our family at that point divorce was not the thing to do, and going out with a married man or a divorced man was a no-no. If Milland had been single, things might have been different." Once again, Mrs. Kelly flew to Hollywood to make sure her daughter kept her head. Jack Kelly later said, "She and Scoop sat down and talked things over with Grace. They found her willing to listen."

"My mother and father were very strong-willed people," Lizanne says, and they convinced Grace that she simply had to drop Ray Milland. "Grace came to realize that Ray hadn't quite gotten over his wife, and that it was wrong for her to be the cause of his divorce. That was the main reason Ray and Grace never pursued it."

The gossip in Hollywood about Grace and Milland was so fierce—and the reaction so virulent—that both Grace's own

---

* This interview was conducted before Milland's death in 1986.

studio and Warner Brothers feared a tidal wave of bad publicity that could harm her very promising career. Robert Slatzer recalls, "In those days the studios would routinely pay off reporters to keep unsavory things out of the newspapers. In Grace's case, it got to be very expensive because the studios were always buying off journalists in order to keep her image pure."

A few gossip column items did appear, but it was always possible to dismiss these as exaggerations of a few innocent dates. One publication that couldn't be bought off, however, was *Confidential,* the *Enquirer* of its day, and before long the magazine blew the whistle on the Kelly/Milland liaison in a salacious account that caused Grace deep consternation and public humiliation. In its colorful style, the magazine detailed Ray's infatuation with Grace and the domestic discord it caused: "After one look at Gracie he went into a tailspin that reverberated from Perino's to Ciro's. The whole town soon hee-hawed over the news that suave Milland, who had a wife and family at home, was ga-ga over Grace. Ray pursued her ardently and Hollywood cackled. Then mama Milland found out. She lowered the boom on Ramblin' Ray and there followed one of the loudest, most tearful fights their Beverly Hills neighbors can remember."

Grace was shaken. She had never experienced the glare of the spotlight in quite this way before. Perhaps *Confidential* could be dismissed as a rag, but disapproving tidbits soon began turning up in respectable newspapers as well. "I felt like a streetwalker," she told an interviewer later.

A good deal of the resentment against Grace in Hollywood stemmed from what many saw as the hypocrisy of her Goody Two-shoes image in light of her healthy sexual appetite. Mrs. Henry Hathaway, the widow of Grace's first motion picture director, feels bitter toward Grace to this day. "I have nothing good to say about Grace," she says. "She had an affair with my best friend's husband, Ray Milland. And all the time wearing those white gloves!" Asked whom else in Hollywood Grace may have had affairs with, Mrs. Hathaway replies,

"You name it. *Everybody.* She wore those white gloves, but she was no saint."

Many in Hollywood shared Mrs. Hathaway's feelings. They mocked Grace as "Little Miss Prim and Proper." Columnist Kendis Rochlen cackled in the Los Angeles *Mirror-News,* "She's supposed to be so terribly proper, but then look at all those whispers about her and Ray Milland."

Hollywood's reaction to Grace's behavior upset her deeply. She never looked upon her frequent sexual dalliances as promiscuous—and they were not, in the true sense of the word. They were neither indiscriminate nor casual. When Grace gave herself to a man, it was, as Don Richardson has said, because of a deep-seated desire for affection and acceptance from father substitutes, much more than the physical delights of sex. And, more often than not, she felt herself truly in love before she would have sex with a man. She wanted to marry Ray Milland, and the fact that her conviction that he would leave his wife and marry her was rooted more in naïveté than reality does not make it any less genuine.

Still, before long Grace developed an underground reputation in Hollywood, as Don Richardson put it, as "an easy lay."* Some observers cluck-clucked while others saw opportunity. "Word got around Hollywood that you could lay Grace Kelly," Richardson says, "and so everybody in town started asking her out on dates."

Robert Slatzer was introduced to Grace by Gary Cooper and took her out several times. "She was a very 'touchy' kind of girl," Slatzer says. "She thought nothing of touching you, putting her hand on your thigh, that sort of thing. She had a very strong aura of availability, and she was very sexy."

Why then did Grace Kelly win—and maintain, despite future indiscretions—a public reputation as, in Don Richardson's words, "a nun"? The answer lies with those people who

---

* Joe Regan, a former rowing partner of Kell's and employee of Kelly for Brickwork, used exactly that term to describe Grace to Kelly family biographer Arthur Lewis.

knew and loved her. Everyone close to her was extremely fond of her. Arthur Jacobsen, who later co-produced two of Grace's films, recalls, "You couldn't work with Grace without falling in love with her. I certainly did. She was a marvelous, marvelous girl and everyone adored her." It is a sentiment echoed by many other of her friends, and they banded together to protect her against those people who were out to "get" her in Hollywood.

Grace's intimates knew of her peccadilloes, but they were also aware that she was a sweet, sensitive young woman. The fact that she was acting upon her sexual needs did not make her a hypocrite; and her friends knew as well that Grace's dalliances were never the result purely of lust. As her roommate Rita Gam said, "Grace was used by some of these men. For them, it was not serious. For her, it was. They could not have suffered as desperately, or as silently, as she did."

Her protective allies helped create the first great Grace Kelly myth: that she was a young woman who, simply by being, aroused uncontrollable, intemperate desire in otherwise sophisticated men and made them act like smitten schoolboys. Despite their foolhardy pursuits, the story went, Grace kept them all at bay. Occasionally she might agree to accompany them to dinner, but purely out of affection or professional regard.

Grace made sure this public reputation took hold by having a chaperone along whenever she went out after the Milland affair. Scoop Conlan explained to a reporter at the time, "She's very cagey about doing anything the gossip columns can hop on. Put yourself in her shoes. If, to use an old-fashioned expression, you felt you had been put upon by the tiger cat gossip columnists and rumormongers, you'd watch your conduct in public extra carefully too, wouldn't you?"

Grace faced the inevitable breakup with Milland with great sorrow. Her realization that now, even apart from her family, her life was truly not her own left her shaken. The success she had longed for was close at hand, and yet it had already extracted a toll. If she were not a rising Hollywood star, and subject to public scrutiny, could she and Milland have been successful at a relationship? She couldn't help but wonder.

Grace's "desperate and silent" suffering soon turned to anger against Hollywood. "Sometimes I think I actually hate Hollywood," she said shortly after the Milland affair. She fled to New York. "For some personal reasons," she explained later, "I really wanted to stay in New York." In the cloak of anonymity that city offered she could try to put Milland out of her mind and escape the harsh and judgmental spotlight that had begun to follow her.

Her sojourn in New York, however, was a mercilessly short one. Soon after she arrived at her apartment, Hitchcock phoned to offer her a costarring role opposite James Stewart in *Rear Window,* the story of a photographer, wheelchair-bound after breaking a leg, who spies on his neighbors through his telephoto lens and comes to believe that one of them has murdered his wife. Grace would play Lisa, his sophisticated, wealthy girlfriend, a woman of wit and sexual playfulness. The role appealed to her, and she wanted to work with Hitchcock again—so, despite the fact that she wanted a respite on the East Coast, she accepted the assignment. MGM once again agreed to lend her services to a competing studio, this time Paramount—for a fee of twenty-five thousand dollars. MGM's profit on this latest Kelly deal would be fifteen thousand.

Again there was potential for attraction between Grace and her leading man, but Stewart had just recently married and he did not succumb to Grace's charms. There wasn't a breath of scandal surrounding Grace and Stewart, but in the great tradition of "I'm married but I'm not dead," Stewart admitted that he *appreciated* Grace's attributes. Scoffing at suggestions that she was aloof, he said, "Grace, *cold?* Why Grace is anything but cold. She has those big warm eyes—and, well, if you ever have played a love scene with her, you'd know she's not cold . . . besides, Grace has that twinkle and a touch of larceny in her eye."

Stewart says today that from the beginning he was pleased

about the prospect of working with Grace. "This was her fifth picture, and I'd seen the other pictures, and I was very impressed with her and I was looking forward to working with her. She really made an impression on everybody out here in the short time it took her to go to the top.

"A lot of things impressed me about her. She seemed to have a complete understanding of the way motion picture acting is carried out. And she was so pleasant on the set; she was completely cooperative. She was really in a class by herself as far as cooperation and friendliness are concerned."

By now Alfred Hitchcock was determined to create as strong a Grace Kelly on-screen image as possible. *Rear Window* scenarist John Michael Hayes recalled that Hitchcock asked him to spend a few days with Grace to "see what you can do with her dramatically." The director didn't want Grace to play Lisa as written, rather he wanted Lisa written to accentuate Grace's more compelling characteristics. Hayes recalled that he himself was fascinated by Grace: "I was entranced by her . . . I couldn't get over the difference between her personal animation and, if I may say so, her sexuality. . . . There was an alive, vital girl underneath that demure, quiet façade; she had an inner life aching to be expressed. . . ."

Hayes's script drew on the polarity of Grace's personality; Lisa was elegant and controlled, but quick to tease her crippled (and therefore sexually limited) fiancé: wearing a flimsy negligee, she notices his appreciation and says coyly, "Preview of coming attractions." The promise of sexual delights from a seemingly elegant and unattainable object of desire titillated audiences and brought into sharp focus all the elements of Grace's appeal—exactly the result Hitchcock wanted.

Grace was willing to put herself entirely in Hitchcock's hands. Stewart recalls, "She was completely cooperative. There was no selfishness connected with her. She was there to do a job, and she depended on her director as much as she depended on her own ability, which she didn't force on her director or on the other players. I think she was, in that respect, an ideal actress."

The highly personal concern for Grace's performance and appearance Hitchcock had shown while filming *Dial M for Murder* bordered on the obsessive during *Rear Window*. Costume designer Edith Head recalled Hitchcock's intense interest in Grace's clothes: "There was a reason for every color, every style, and he was absolutely certain about everything he settled on. For one scene he saw her in pale green, for another in white chiffon, for another in gold. He was really putting a dream together in the studio . . . Hitch wanted her to appear like a piece of Dresden china, something slightly untouchable."

That Hitchcock also wanted Grace to look as sexually inviting as possible is clear from another story, told by Grace. When she first appeared wearing her negligee, Hitchcock looked her over and, with a frown on his face, called Edith Head to his side. "The bosom isn't right," he said tactfully, then made clearer what he meant. "We're going to have to put something in there." Head went with Grace back to her dressing room and suggested falsies. Grace protested that they'd be obvious—and besides, she didn't want to wear them. Instead, Grace recalled, "We quickly took it up here and made some adjustments there and I just did what I could and stood as straight as possible—without falsies. When I walked out onto the set Hitchcock looked at me and at Edith and said, 'See what a difference they make?' "

Despite Hitchcock's consuming interest in Grace, James Stewart doesn't subscribe to Donald Spoto's theory that he was tortured by unrequited love. "I think it's all ridiculous," he says. "Why anybody would think that, I have no idea. I don't think there was a dark side to Alfred Hitchcock. He *was* a genius, certainly, in the brightest light that could possibly be."

Grace's working habits quickly gained her a reputation as one of Hollywood's most conscientious, considerate actresses. Jimmy Stewart praised her concentration. "She's easy to play to," he said. "You can see her thinking the way she's supposed to think in the role. You know she's listening, and not just for cues. Some actresses don't think and don't listen. You can tell they're just counting the words."

Grace was well liked too by the film's crew. (This was true on all her films.) Herbert Coleman, Hitchcock's assistant director, recalled that Grace "wasn't the slightest bit temperamental. She came to work, knew her dialogue, knew what she was going to do. You'd call her on the set and she'd be right there, ready to work, all the time. I'd place her right alongside Barbara Stanwyck in that respect."

Stewart agrees. "She came out here, completely out of the blue, and after five pictures she was in demand all over town. And she took this in such a pleasant, ladylike way, without going out and blowing her own horn and being starlike about it. She didn't do that at all. And aside from being a very admirable thing, I think that helped to make her a hit not only with the audiences but with her fellow workers out here in Hollywood."

Herbert Coleman was surprised to discover another aspect of Grace's personality. "Grace was kind of a tomboy," he said. "I've never heard anyone write about that particular facet of her life. She loved to joke and have fun. She had a tendency to kid around and play like a girl much younger than she actually was."

Coleman continued, "I never saw her have problems with anyone. People just loved her. You couldn't help but be fond of Grace. She was not cold or distant at all. She was very warm and very, very friendly to the people she liked and worked with. In my opinion that 'aloof' stuff was built up by publicity people. That was part of the image they wanted to present to the public. And of course Hitch presented that kind of image of her. He did that with all the blond women he worked with. He tried to present them as cold and distant and aloof. And none of them were like that at all."

James Stewart became a lifelong friend of Grace's, and he recalls with great affection that "her humor was very quiet, it wasn't a joke-type humor, but she looked at the bright and the amusing side of life. It was a very delicate type of humor. It's so important, especially in the acting profession. That kind of humor is a wonderful, gemlike thing to have. She was a genuine, kind, humorous, caring, wonderful person."

The very special regard for her that Stewart and Hitchcock both had made the filming of *Rear Window,* completed early in 1954, an extremely pleasant experience for Grace. Moreover, there hadn't been a hint of scandal. The release of the film in August 1954 created a Grace Kelly sensation, and by the end of the year she was the biggest star in Hollywood. By that time as well, a new scandal would take place, and its ramifications would send Grace into a tailspin so severe she sought psychiatric help.

Chapter Seven

The day after MGM received Hitchcock's request to lend him Grace for *Rear Window,* it was asked to consider another from the production team of William Perlberg and George Seaton *(Miracle on 34th Street),* who owned the screen rights to James Michener's bestselling Korean War novel, *The Bridges at Toko-Ri.* Perlberg and Seaton wanted Grace for the relatively minor role of jet pilot William Holden's worried wife.

MGM executives were puzzled by all this outside interest in Grace. *Mogambo* had yet to be released, and while they thought Grace was an interesting new addition to their roster, they didn't see the kind of potential for stardom in her that Hitchcock, for instance, did. They were happy to oblige, especially since once again they were clearing fifteen thousand dollars on Grace's loan-out fee. At this rate, MGM could make a hundred thousand a year on Grace without ever putting her in a movie of its own.

Her role in *The Bridges at Toko-Ri* didn't intrigue Grace much; the script revolved around the male characters, four of whom had more screen time than Grace did, and the film was little more than a war picture. She accepted the role primarily because of the prestigious nature of the property and the reputations of Perlberg and Seaton.

As so often before, Grace was required to "audition" in a meeting with the producers, and once again she set herself apart from the other young actresses present. "The part of the wife," Perlberg recalled, "wasn't big enough to attract an important star. But there were a few spots in it that had to be right, and we needed more than just an ordinary actress who could get by with it. Our problem was to find an unknown with real talent."

Seaton and Perlberg sensed that they'd found her when Grace arrived "dressed as if she were walking down the street window-shopping. She wore glasses and flat-heeled walking shoes." Grace had read the book and wore to the interview precisely what a budget-minded Navy pilot's wife would have worn. It was a canny ploy; not only did it set her apart from the other girls (who all looked, as Perlberg recalled, like Sadie Thompson), it allowed the producers to better visualize her in the part—and it told them as well that this was an intelligent actress who'd done her homework. They were suitably impressed; Grace reminded Seaton of "the girls at the Actors' Workshop in New York—they're so intensely dedicated."

Most of *The Bridges at Toko-Ri* was filmed in Japan, but Grace's scenes were shot in Hollywood, after the company returned to the United States. As Holden's wife, she spends one last week with him in Tokyo before he is to fly on a war mission. They try to have fun and do as much as possible (including a day of swimming, which gave us Grace in a bathing suit for the first time on-screen) and there is a poignant bedroom scene between the soon-to-be-parted couple.

Grace's brief scenes with William Holden—her work encompassed just three weeks' time—were enough to create a strong attraction between the two. Once again, Grace's leading man was a handsome, masculine superstar (soon to be an Oscar winner for *Stalag 17)* and at thirty-six twelve years her senior. Once again, that leading man was susceptible to her charms. Although married,* Holden was a dedicated woman-

---

* Holden married actress Brenda Marshall, née Ardis Ankerson Gaines, in 1941, when she was a bigger star than he. She had a daughter from her first marriage to Richard Gaines, and within five years she and Holden had two sons, Peter and Scott. They remained married through numerous Holden dalliances (he told fellow actor Warren Oates in the early 1950s that one of his goals was to sleep with at least one girl in every foreign country he visited), and Ardis was extraordinarily understanding of her husband's roving

izer with a soft spot for young ladies of refinement and class. (He fell hard for the lovely Audrey Hepburn when they worked together six months earlier on *Sabrina*.) Holden biographer Bob Thomas describes a "brief but satisfactory romance" between the two during the *Toko-Ri* filming; but their feelings for each other apparently did not flourish until they worked together again on *The Country Girl* a short while later.

Grace's involvement in *The Bridges at Toko-Ri* was of little importance to her career. The film was a moderate success, but her role was so minor that most reviewers paid scant attention to her; *Time,* alluding to the pool scene, noted that the film "does little more for Grace than establish that she has a better figure than normally meets the eye."

Alfred Hitchcock said of Grace, after she completed *Rear Window,* "so far she has only played leading women. She has yet to play the character about whom a film is built. That will be her big test." Her association with Perlberg and Seaton brought Grace that "big test," the great dramatic opportunity that had so far eluded her in Hollywood. The producers owned screen rights to the Clifford Odets play *The Country Girl,* which had won a Broadway Tony for the impressive actress Uta Hagen. The story concerned Georgie Elgin, a young woman whose promise in life is destroyed by her devotion to her alcoholic, self-destructive actor husband. Beaten down by ten years of neglect, abuse, and worry, she lives a life of fatigue and monotony. But her husband needs her, and her love for him is such that she will never leave his side.

Perlberg and Seaton (who had written the screenplay and would direct it) had signed Jennifer Jones to costar with Bing Crosby as the actor and William Holden as a director who offers him a chance to make a comeback and falls in love with

---

eye. In fact, Holden made it a point to introduce all of his leading ladies, including those he was romantically involved with, to her. Grace was no exception. In 1970 the Holdens were divorced.

Georgie. But just before filming was set to begin, Jones became pregnant. Her husband, RKO czar David Selznick, told the producers that they could complete the picture before Jennifer's condition began to show. But to them, a potential disaster had turned into an unexpected opportunity: "George and I don't tear our hair out at the news," Perlberg remembered. "We just look at each other. We're both thinking the same thing at the same time: *Grace Kelly.*"

Unexpectedly, the producers faced an obstacle in getting Grace for *The Country Girl.* MGM executives had seen the rough *Rear Window* cut, and although they had been myopic in the past where Grace was concerned, they weren't blind. Grace's impact on Hitchcock's film was undeniable; and even months before its release there was intense interest in Grace from both the press and Hollywood's most influential filmmakers. With so many requests coming in from other studios for Grace's services, MGM figured if she were going to develop into a strong box office draw, it had better put her into a few films of its own.

Thus, when the producers routinely asked MGM for a second loan-out of Grace, they were turned down. "We have big plans for Grace," Dore Schary told them. But Perlberg and Seaton knew that Grace was unhappy with the projects MGM had offered her, and they also knew that she was one of the studio's most independent—and headstrong—contractees. Rebuffed by MGM, they decided to try an approach from the opposite side; but it had to be done discreetly. "*Somehow* we let Grace know we were negotiating for her," Perlberg recalled. "And *somehow* she got a copy of *The Country Girl* script. No court on earth can make us tell how she got it. Just say that I suspect Seaton and he suspects me."

Grace read the script and realized that Georgie Elgin was the role of a lifetime for her, exactly what she needed to prove her dramatic mettle in Hollywood. "I just *had* to be in *The Country Girl,*" she said. "There was a real acting part in it for me." She had never had to act before, she said, "Not like this. Sometimes I had to act, but I had beautiful clothes, or beautiful lingerie, or glamorous settings to help me. And lots of times, too, I was just the feminine background for the male stars who carried the action and the story on their shoulders." Yes, she told Perlberg after reading the script, she very much wanted to do *The Country Girl*.

"Metro won't let us have you," he told her.

"Why not?" Grace asked.

"They're making a thing called *Green Fire*," Perlberg replied, "and they want you for it. It's rumored that Eleanor Parker walked out on it, and Robert Taylor won't have anything to do with it, but they want you for it anyhow."

Grace was furious. It was bad enough that in eighteen months MGM hadn't offered her a single script except *Mogambo* she would consider acting, but now it was trying to prevent her from doing one of the most desirable and coveted roles in Hollywood. Legend has it that Grace stormed into Dore Schary's office and shouted, "If I can't do this picture, I'll get on a train and never come back. I'll never make another film!"

Years later Grace said, "I'm always being given credit for being bolder than I am. I never said any such thing to anybody. I couldn't, even if I wanted to. My agent handled the whole matter. It's true that Bill Perlberg kept telling me to say something like that. But people are always telling me what to say."

Knowing his client as he did, Lew Wasserman, Grace's Los Angeles agent, told MGM that unless it allowed Grace to do *The Country Girl* she might indeed walk out on Hollywood. The studio wasn't in a position to feel secure about what Grace might or might not do. It knew, of course, that Grace's winning *The Country Girl* sweepstakes could only enhance her box office pull for its later Kelly projects. It was thus inclined to let her do the movie, but it wasn't going to let Perlberg and Seaton have her cheap. Its terms, MGM informed Paramount, were a fifty-thousand-dollar fee (it would clear forty thousand) and five thousand dollars for each day the film went over schedule. This last item was to ensure that

Grace could begin filming *Green Fire*—which she was required to do as a condition of the loan-out—as soon as possible.

Everyone agreed to the terms, and Grace was set to play
Georgie Elgin. Arthur Jacobsen, assistant producer of *The
Country Girl*, remembers that Seaton called him into a
screening room to watch the rough cut of *Rear Window*. "I
saw this *gorgeous* girl on the screen—God, she was beautiful.
George turned to me and said, 'What do you think?' I said,
'She's very good and she's gorgeous.' He said, 'Yeah, but *what
do you think?*' I had no idea what he was talking about. He
said, 'What do you think of her for Georgie?'

"I looked at him and said, 'George, she's too beautiful!' *The
Country Girl* had to be a drab woman who'd been married to
a drunk for ten years. And George said, 'Well, use your imagination. You know what we can do.' So I thought and thought
and said, 'Okay, let's find out. Let's try. We'll bring her in,
dress her as Georgie, and see what happens.'

"Well, between Edith Head, George, me, and Grace herself, Grace Kelly was transformed. She walked into the office
a few days later with her drab dress on and I said, 'You win,
George, you win.'"

Jacobsen says that there was more method to Seaton's apparent madness than simply being aware that Grace's vibrant
beauty could be camouflaged with drab clothes and plain
makeup. "Georgie Elgin, when she first met her husband, was
a classy, beautiful woman. She sacrificed the wonderful life
she had before she met him in order to help him. The only
way to project that is to find a woman who had all this innate
vibrancy, class, and beauty and strip her of it, just as Frank
Elgin had Georgie. Otherwise, she would have had nothing to
lose and it wouldn't have been as effective.

"George Seaton was an expert at spotting people for incon-
gruous roles, and he was at his best in choosing Grace as the
Country Girl."

Another person who had difficulty envisioning Grace as
Georgie was Bing Crosby. His contracts assured him leading-

lady approval, so his opinion of Grace was important. To Perlberg and Seaton's chagrin, Crosby expressed strong doubts to them about Grace's ability to look the role, and he wondered whether she was experienced enough to perform the part adequately.

Crosby's doubts about Grace were purely professional, because the two had been intimately involved a year and a half earlier. In mid-1952 Crosby's wife, Dixie,* lay dying of cancer. The Crosbys were close friends of Alan Ladd and his wife, the former Sue Carol. Bing frequently dropped in to use their pool, but on many an evening he visited with a different recreation in mind. Sue complained to friends that while Dixie fought for her life Bing would knock on the Ladds' door at nine-thirty or ten o'clock at night with a girl at his side. Most frequently the girl was Grace Kelly. The Ladds would graciously entertain their unexpected guests; Alan talking with Bing by the bar, Sue and Grace conversing in the kitchen or out by the pool.

Always the scenario was the same: the evenings would drag on until, past midnight, Ladd would announce that he and Sue were going to bed; he had to be at the studio first thing in the morning. Crosby would make no move to depart, and Ladd would tell him, "Bing, we're going to bed. You're welcome to stay, just lock the door when you leave."

On several occasions, Sue came down in the middle of the night to find Bing and Grace enmeshed in each other's arms on the couch. Robert Slatzer recalls talking with Sue Ladd about it. "Sue said it really hurt her to be talking to Dixie every day on the phone as she lay dying, and there was Bing, coming over, never mentioning Dixie, and flaunting these girls in front of her. Alan was very upset with Bing, and he'd say to Sue, 'Jesus, doesn't he know any place else where he can go at night? There must be hotels or motels . . .' "

---

* Bing and former actress Dixie Lee (née Wilma Winifred Wyatt) had been married since 1930 and had four sons, Gary, Dennis, Philip, and Lindsay. Dixie died late in 1952, and Bing married actress Kathryn Grant in 1957.

Grace and Bing soon drifted apart and did not see each other again until they were brought together to make *The Country Girl.* Attracted by Grace's youth, beauty, and vibrancy when he first met her, Crosby found it difficult to imagine her as the slatternly, exhausted Georgie. Perlberg and Seaton assured him that in their professional judgment Grace could do the job; Crosby's response was, "Well, if you guys are convinced, I'll trust you to know what you're doing" —hardly a ringing vote of confidence for Grace.

Crosby's doubts remained throughout the first week of filming. Assistant director Francisco (Chico) Day recalls that Bing "thought the part was a little too heavy for Grace. I realized that even when we were doing the picture, in the beginning. But after we got into it, I'm telling you, Bing felt just fine."

Bing's comment to Perlberg and Seaton after that first week was widely quoted: "I'll never open my big mouth to you two about a casting problem again. I'm sorry I had any reservations about this girl. She's great."

Everyone else in *The Country Girl* company agreed; Grace was well liked among the crew members, Chico Day recalls. "She was very sweet, very amiable, very pleasant. Always had a wonderful smile. She had a wonderful expression she used whenever anyone would call her to come to the set; even if she was busy with an interview or other business, she'd always say, 'All rightie!' That was one of the things I admired about her. With some of the stars I've worked with, whenever they were having an interview or a business deal or something, it was an imposition for someone to call them to work—and their reply certainly wouldn't be as nice as it was with Grace."

The proximity of Grace and the fifty-year-old Crosby during filming renewed their attraction to each other, and they once again became romantically involved. William Holden, who also found his feelings for Grace flaring anew, discovered that he had a rival for her affections one night when he went to Bing's dressing room at nine-thirty in the evening.

When Holden knocked on the door, Bing answered, a drink in his hand. Holden could see Grace sitting inside as Crosby told him, "Hey, ol' buddy, why don't we talk tomorrow? I'm sort of tied up for the night."

Holden was aware of Crosby's earlier intimacy with Grace, but Bing didn't know that Holden too numbered among Grace's paramours. When Grace told him about her relationship with Holden, Crosby feared that bad blood would develop between himself and a friend. He asked Bill to come to his dressing room and said, "I don't mind telling you, Bill, I'm smitten with Grace. Daffy about her. And I was wondering if—"

"I felt the same way," Holden replied. "What man wouldn't be overwhelmed by her? But look, Bing, I won't interfere."

Grace and Bing began to date, appearing in Hollywood restaurants and nightclubs. As a widower, Crosby was not likely to stir up the kind of bad publicity Grace had endured with Milland, but she was nonetheless careful. On all her public dates with Bing she was accompanied by either Peggy or Lizanne—and the latter recalled that "Bing was mad for her, really mad for her, taking her out all the time." Accounts of the dates made the newspapers, along with photographs of the couple on the town with chaperones carefully cropped out. Soon, newspapers dubbed Crosby and Kelly "Hollywood's Newest Romance."

Before long Bing fell deeply in love with Grace. So much so, Lizanne reveals, that "Grace called me up one night and said, 'Bing has asked me to marry him.' But she wasn't in love with him. She loved him, but she was not *in love* with him."

Sorrowfully, for she didn't want to hurt someone of whom she was so fond, Grace turned Bing's proposal down. And, to avoid hurting him further, she refused to see him again.

Crosby was crushed by Grace's rejection. A friend of Bing's recalled, "I remember when Grace and Bing had it bad they used to go to a restaurant called Scandia on the Sunset Strip and sit for hours, always at the same table. Then she ended it

—and it took Bing a long time to get over the fact that she was the one who walked away from the romance, she was the one who brushed him. He used to keep going to Scandia alone, sitting at the same table, brooding over a drink, almost as if he hoped she'd walk through the door any minute."

Bing, in fact, carried a torch for Grace all his life. In February 1978 Crosby's widow, Kathryn, asked Princess Grace to appear in a television documentary tribute to Bing. She signed the letter, "Yours with love and jealousy." When Grace sent her regrets, Kathryn persisted, asked again by telegram and explained her letter's cryptic closing: "I have been jealous of you because Bing always loved you." (Grace agreed to read poetry on the program.)

Shortly after the breakup, Crosby implied to a reporter that there had never been any strong interest on his part: "If I were fifteen or sixteen years younger, I'd fall willingly into the long line of limp males who are currently competing madly for her favors." It was a disingenuous remark in light of Grace's penchant for older men and Crosby's marriage, three years later, to Kathryn Grant, a contemporary of Grace's. But it served to save face for Bing.

Once Holden realized that Crosby was no longer in the picture, he resumed his own romantic pursuit of Grace Kelly. Gun-shy because of the Milland publicity, Grace was hesitant to resume an affair with a married man; she and Holden had been able to conduct their initial liaison without arousing public curiosity. Why tempt fate a second time? But Holden was a persuasive charmer. Grace let herself be swept up by his ardor—so much so that Holden became concerned. "She fell head over heels in love with him," Robert Slatzer recalls. "In fact, he told me that it sort of scared him in a way, because she was really serious. He was sort of making the rounds, you know; he liked to have affairs. But her romances were always very serious. He told me, 'She really throws her heart into a love affair.'"

Mel Dellar was a good friend of Holden's; they had served together in the Army, where Dellar directed him in several training films. The impression Mel got from Holden was that his feelings matched Grace's. "Bill was absolutely crazy about her and they had quite a fling," he says. "I was hoping they would get married, because that's what Bill wanted, and he was a wonderful guy."

Grace and Holden did discuss marriage. There was, of course, the not inconsequential problem of his existing wife, but at that point his relationship with Ardis was particularly acrimonious, and thoughts of divorce were not far from Holden's mind. Removing that obstacle, however, would create another: Holden would then be persona non grata in the eyes of the Roman Catholic Church. As she had with Richardson, though, Grace felt that there were ways around the roadblocks. She spoke to her family priest, Father John Cartin, who reconfirmed to her the church doctrine she had spoken of to Richardson: if a non-Catholic divorced man embraced the Catholic Church, his previous marriage would be considered invalid. Expectantly, Grace told all this to Holden, but he didn't share her enthusiasm. "I couldn't do that," Bill told his close friend, actor Broderick Crawford. "I loved Grace and wanted to marry her. But I'd be damned if I'd let any church dictate what I could do with my life."

Lizanne confirms that Grace and Holden wanted to get married and adds, "Bill liked Grace an *awful* lot. I'll tell you, whatever quality she had, she should have bottled it—she would have made a fortune! I mean, there was something about her that men just went ape over. It was amazing to see these big Hollywood stars falling all over themselves."

Robert Slatzer recalls, "Bill Holden told me that it was impossible *not* to fall in love with Grace. He said that she fell in love easily, and he thought she was in love with him and Bing Crosby simultaneously." The real possibility of marriage for Grace and Holden may never have existed, however. To Holden, the primary pleasure was in the pursuit, and he never had any intention of divorcing his wife. He told several intimates, "If I were to lose Ardis, I would lose everything."

At first Grace and Holden were successful in keeping their

affair private. Chico Day says, "You'd never know from their actions on the set that there was anything going on. I never saw Bill or Grace together in a dressing room, either hers or his. Whatever was going on was a thing that belonged to them, not to anybody else. I think that was a tribute to their acting ability, because when you love somebody, you're in love. When you're having an affair with somebody, there's no way to hide it—and they were absolutely sensational in keeping it to themselves."

For a while. Grace's latest indiscretion would soon be revealed—ironically, because of a totally innocent incident. The seemingly omniscient *Confidential* magazine blew the lid once again, gleefully describing Kelly/Holden trysts at Grace's apartment. Their "evidence" was the sighting of Holden's car outside Grace's apartment early one morning.

With two roommates, Grace would hardly use her apartment for a tryst with Bill Holden. Arthur Jacobsen explains why Holden's car was there: "It was all so innocent, it's comical. Grace called me late one evening to say that her car broke down, and could I send a car for her in the morning. I said I would, and then I remembered that Bill had to pass by Grace's apartment on his way to work, and I called and asked him if he would pick Grace up the following morning. That's all there was to it."

Although the magazine got most of the details wrong, there *was* a relationship between Grace and Holden, and thus Grace's private life was once again revealed salaciously in a national magazine. She was devastated. Holden demanded a retraction and got it. But the follow-up story was little comfort to Grace. After informing its readers that Miss Kelly "wasn't grabbing for a guy who already had a ball and chain" and "explaining" Holden's presence at Grace's apartment in that light ("far from enjoying an ardent interlude, Holden was being given firm notice by Miss Kelly that he belonged at home"), the magazine went on to note that as long as a man was single, Miss Kelly was very much available. The article cited an unnamed Hollywood bachelor's opinion that "a lot of glamour girls like Monroe and Russell aren't as eager as you think. Their sex appeal goes into their looks. They use low-cut dresses and a wriggly walk for what they really don't have. Now that Gracie . . ."

Confidential concluded that with Grace Kelly, "behind that frigid exterior is a smoldering fire . . ." Grace possessed, they opined, "what the older fellows go for—she looks like a lady and has the manners of one. In the Hollywood of the chippies and the tramps, a lady is a rarity. That makes Grace Kelly the most dangerous dame in the movies today."

Confidential's reportage did nothing to help Grace's reputation, and before long she experienced in person the kind of sniggering that was going on behind her back. Leaving a restaurant with a date, she was mortified when confronted by a young man who said to her, "I see you're going out with single men now. How about a date?"

Back in Philadelphia, the Kellys were again distressed over the public airing of their daughter's sexual dirty linen. Grace, it seemed to them, had become uncontrollable, chaperoning sisters or not. Frustrated at his inability to keep his daughter in line, Jack Kelly took his fury out on *Confidential*—on the theory, one supposes, of killing the messenger. Arthur Jacobsen recalled, "Jack Kelly and his son stormed into the *Confidential* offices and roughed up the magazine's editors."

Grace went into a depression, and her personality changed markedly on the set. Chico Day recalls, "She would just keep within the confines of her dressing room. Very seldom would she sit out on the set between shots. She didn't even go to the commissary—she'd eat her lunch in her dressing room."

Grace's Academy classmate Mary Woolverton Naredo says that Grace was deeply troubled not only by this latest public humiliation, but by a guilty conscience as well. "It doesn't take any stretch of the imagination to realize how very emotional this would be for a young girl, getting all this attention from older, more mature men for the first time. I don't care who the woman is, there's too much guilt associated with promiscuity. Especially when a girl's been raised as Grace was."

Finally, Grace sought professional counseling to deal with all the pressures and conflicting emotions she was being subjected to in Hollywood. "I know she got psychiatric help out there," Mary Naredo reveals. "She was very emotionally overwrought."

In a surprisingly frank 1979 interview, Grace spoke of her embarrassment and the bitterness she felt toward Hollywood, and she defended herself against charges that she was a "home wrecker": "As an unmarried woman, I was thought to be a danger. Other women looked on me as a rival and it pained me a great deal. The worst was when the Hollywood gossip columnist Hedda Hopper started to persecute me with her hatred. She warned all producers, directors and actors against me. Bing Crosby told me that Hedda had described me as a nymphomaniac!

"The persecution didn't last long. I had a circle of good friends. But even so, I hated Hollywood. It's a town without pity. Only success counts. Anyone who doesn't have the key that opens the doors is treated like a leper. I know of no other place in the world where so many people suffer from nervous breakdowns, where there are so many alcoholics, neurotics and so much unhappiness."

Whether because of the psychological help, or simply as a result of her own inner strength, Grace was not defeated by Hollywood. She simply fought back, did not allow herself to be left vulnerable. She was never again publicly linked to any of her leading men, and press attention soon turned to her first "legitimate" romance.

For all of Grace's personal upheaval, her unfolding performance as *The Country Girl* was impressing her associates more and more. Her concentration was unshakable; as Holden commented during filming, "With some actresses you have to keep snapping them to attention like a puppy. Grace is always concentrating. In fact, she sometimes keeps me on track." Crosby, too, expressed admiration for Grace's work.

"She worked her head off to get the performance the director wanted from her. And what's more, she got it and she got it good."

Seaton's directorial style was perfect for Grace at this emotionally charged point in her life. "George was so willing to help Grace," Chico Day recalls. "I thought he was the person who contributed most to her performance. He was so patient in rehearsals. The way he operated was so beautiful—I never heard one word louder than the other. He was always quiet and sweet in explaining his opinion."

During the filming the 1953 Academy Awards were presented, and Grace failed to win as Best Supporting Actress for *Mogambo*. The crew gave her a consolation plaque inscribed, "This will hold you until you win *next* year's Academy Award." Grace's performance so impressed most of the crew, many of whom had felt at first the way Bing Crosby did about Grace's inexperience, that the sentiments expressed on the plaque were more than just ego-massage; Grace's associates were certain she would be in the running the following year for Best Actress in *The Country Girl*.

Chapter Eight

While Grace was treated with respect and admiration by her directors and costars, her own studio continually assaulted her sensibilities with offers of silly, secondary roles she would have disdained years earlier, much less now, after her work with some of Hollywood's greatest talents. Despite Lucille Ryman Carroll's assurances that she could "trust" MGM to choose roles "right" for her, Grace found herself forced to balk at a series of assignments her studio had already announced as her next project. One of these was *Quentin Durward,* of which Grace said, "All the men can duel and fight, but all I'd do would be to wear thirty-five different costumes, look pretty and frightened. There are eight people chasing me—the old man, robbers, the head gypsy, and Durward. The stage directions on every page of the script say, 'She clutches her jewel box and flees.' I just thought I'd be so bored . . ."

Her faith in MGM's judgment hadn't been furthered by her experience with *Green Fire,* which she flew to South America to begin filming immediately after completing *The Country Girl* in the late spring of 1954. A melodramatic romantic adventure set among the Colombian emerald mines, it required, like *Quentin Durward,* little more of Grace than to look lovely and wear a great variety of outfits. The film wasn't one she would have chosen except that her appearance in the film was the quid pro quo required in order for MGM to release her for *The Country Girl.* Making the picture, Grace said, "was a wretched experience. Everyone knew it was an awful picture, and it dragged on in all the heat and dust because nobody had any idea how to save it."

Grace's unhappiness was obvious to her costars. Stewart Granger, playing her love interest, recalled that Grace "was watching us all, she wasn't happy on the film because she knew she was in a potboiler. At the beginning she was rather looking down her nose at us. I felt sorry she was seeing us in this lousy movie."

Happily married, Granger didn't enter into an affair with Grace, but he was nonetheless quite taken with her "delicious behind" and "tempted" by her flirtatiousness: "She would look at me in a contemplative sort of way . . . she was very nice to kiss." According to Granger, his only indiscretion with Grace was one she did not give prior consent to: "Our last scene was played in a torrential downpour and when the final kiss came we were both soaking wet, which accentuated that fabulous behind. To save her embarrassment I covered it with both hands. She was so delighted at finishing the film that she didn't even object, but if you look closely at that kiss you'll see Grace give a start as those two eager hands take hold."

Granger was impressed as well by Grace's courage. "I remember one time we had to go out in a little motorboat during a storm. I was shaking like a leaf, I was so scared. But Grace stepped into the boat and said calmly, 'Well, if we have to, let's go.' I got in too, but I remember thinking at the time, 'Most women would be screaming like mad if they had to do this.'

"She has a mental attitude that says, well, if there's nothing she can do about a bad situation, she's perfectly calm. If there's something she *can* do about it, then she's not calm. It's a wonderful philosophy of life."

Many young actresses would have assumed that there was nothing they could do about contractual obligations and calmly accepted the roles offered by their studio. Certainly hundreds did, and many promising careers were thus sabotaged with bad scripts and typecasting. Grace would not let that happen. MGM announcements of Grace Kelly's next movie appeared regularly in Hollywood's trade papers, only to be retracted when the star, whom the studio had not consulted beforehand, refused to make the picture.

To save further public embarrassment, the studio began submitting scripts to Grace—which she regularly turned down. She was appalled that even after her success in *Rear Window* and the favorable advance word about her performance in *The Country Girl,* MGM continued to see her as merely decoration for overblown, male-dominated melodramas. She refused, she said, to become "a beautiful but dumb clotheshorse": "I don't want to dress up a picture with just my face. If anybody starts using me as scenery, I'll return to New York."

MGM's lack of insight into Grace's appeal was Alfred Hitchcock's gain, for it was he, before all others, who saw in Grace the qualities that would make her a superstar in a remarkably short period of time. Dore Schary and others of the MGM brass, however, were astonishingly thickheaded when it came to Grace. Even as late as 1955, when the "Grace Kelly Phenomenon" was in full flower, they continued to offer her insulting properties that she had no choice but to reject.

Grace's problems with MGM, according to Lucille Ryman Carroll, resulted from Dore Schary's takeover of the studio from Louis B. Mayer in the early 1950s. "Dore Schary should have been a rabbi," she says, "because he didn't know what sex was like. That's the reason we didn't have Marilyn Monroe—because he felt that Marilyn was just a little trollop he could pick up anytime for one day's work at $350 a day. He didn't understand Marilyn, and he didn't get Grace either. He didn't know how to run a studio. Everything had to be just his way—makeup, wardrobe. Mr. Mayer used to let his people do the job they were trained to do. He couldn't worry about that kind of thing. But Schary had to have his hand in everything. And just because he personally didn't find Grace appealing—didn't think she was sexy—he had no idea what to do with her."

If Dore Schary and MGM were myopic about Grace, the press and the public were not. As early as the spring of 1954, with only *Mogambo* in release, *Life* magazine featured Grace on its cover, announcing that 1954 would be "a year of Grace." The rather daring prediction was based on rough footage the editors had seen of *Dial M for Murder* and *Rear Window,* as well as their knowledge of Grace's upcoming challenge as *The Country Girl.*

That *Life's* editors were aware of Grace's potential for sex appeal is indicated clearly by the cover photo, taken by Philippe Halsman (who had created a sensation with a come-hither portrait of Marilyn Monroe, used by *Life* as her first major magazine cover in 1952). In three-quarter profile, her hair over one eye, Grace looks mischievously into the camera lens in a shot remarkable for its lack of regard for her "de-mure" reputation.

The magazine's prognostication wasn't fulfilled by the release of *Dial M for Murder;* Grace's reviews were good and the film was a success, but her part was a relatively minor one and not designed to show her off to maximum advantage. That was left to *Rear Window,* and when the film was released in August 1954, *Life's* prophecy had come true four months early. The "sexual elegance" that Alfred Hitchcock had elicited from Grace caught the public's imagination, and suddenly Grace Kelly was a box office draw. Theater owners began putting Grace's name in letters the same size as Hitchcock's and Stewart's; a few marquees declared, "Grace Kelly in Rear Window."

It was at this time that Grace became the subject of intense journalistic interest, most of it puzzled. One article after another described Grace as an enigmatic figure, a paradox even to those who knew her. Titles such as "Who Is Grace Kelly?" "What Makes Grace Kelly Different?" and "The Seven Graces" abounded, and the astute and incisive *Saturday Evening Post* reporter Pete Martin found himself no closer to understanding Grace after researching his profile of her than he was before. "The tough thing about the Kelly story," he wrote, "is this: You run yourself black in the face tracking down everyone—including Grace herself—who can give you an angle on her. You talk to those who've worked with her, those who are related to her and those who are her friends. And when you have finished all this, she is still such an elusive subject that writing about her is like trying to wrap up 115 pounds of smoke."

The biggest problem for the press and public in "getting a handle" on Grace, of course, was that she possessed any number of quite discrete personalities. She was clearly a lady, well brought up, possessing a refinement rare in a Hollywood abrim, as Van Johnson put it, with "a broadside of broads." But she was also, as most of Hollywood knew, a young woman with a healthily expressed sexual appetite. The "cool, distant, and aloof" image was the easiest one for the press to stress, especially since that was the way she acted toward them. But those who knew her could think of nothing less descriptive of the real Grace. "The publicity people didn't know what to write about her," James Stewart said. "So they had to hang this tag 'aloof' on her, for lack of anything else."

Cary Grant, who starred with Grace in her next picture and who became a lifelong friend, agreed that Grace was not aloof, but he provided a strong clue as to *why* many people thought of her that way: "If you made a gaffe with Grace, she didn't respond to it in any way. She'd just change the subject if she felt she had to say anything at all. Or she'd just enclose herself in what my wife at the time used to call her 'plastic egg'—that she could see out of, but you couldn't get in. She didn't respond at all. She was very nice about it, not impolite, not ungracious. But she had her own set of rules by which she conducted herself. If you wanted to make an ass of yourself, that was up to you. She wasn't going to go along with it."

A large group of people who frequently made "asses" of themselves in Grace's mind was the press. Much of her reputation for aloofness was the result of her fear and distrust of the Fourth Estate, and her aversion to revealing the details of her private life. "Until I know people," she said at the time, "I can't give much of myself. A year ago when people asked me, 'What about you?' I froze. I'm better now, but I'm still not cured."

Grace was shocked at first by the prying questions that were asked of her; when one reporter early in her career asked her if she wore falsies, she became so upset she left the room in tears. Later, more self-possessed, Grace replied coolly to a query, "I don't think it's anybody's business what I wear to bed."

"I have been accused of being cold, snobbish, aloof," Grace said. "I don't think I am any of those things. I just don't think it's asking too much to have a private life of my own. I am aware that people are interested in a person who's a star, but a line has to be drawn somewhere. There was a reporter, for instance, who asked me, 'How big are you?' I started to tell him how tall I am. 'Not that,' he said impatiently, 'I mean your bust. Not very big, I imagine.' "

Occasionally Grace's discomfort with interviewers exploded into anger. Edith Head recalled an evening when Grace dropped by to see her on the Paramount lot for a night fitting: "It's nine-thirty, and in addition to working on *Green Fire* with Stewart Granger all day, which can bush anybody, she's been on 'The Bob Hope Show' and she's tired. She's thinking about this idiot who asked her, 'What makes you so hard to talk to?' and by the time she gets here, she's exploding. People tell you she's cool and collected. This isn't true. Annoy her, and she boils. 'If I don't feel like talking, that's my business,' she tells me. 'I'm not employed to give monologues. I'm hired to be an actress!' "

The chary relationship between Grace and the press wasn't helped by the fact that the studio publicity people, whose job is to smooth relations between journalists and movie stars, were just as mystified and resentful of Grace as many writers were. At the height of the studio system, stars were expected to cooperate fully with the press. The studio, in return, would do everything in its considerable power to make sure that the resulting reportage was favorable. Joan Crawford, for example, would do practically anything to accommodate the press and ensure positive coverage of her life and career.

Grace was one of the first stars to reject this symbiotic relationship; and her independent attitude, coming as it did as the studio system was crumbling, threatened and angered the men and women whose jobs depended on goodwill between players and press. Edith Head offered a succinct summation of the problem studio "flacks" were faced with when she was asked to provide a "Grace Kelly anecdote." She replied, "I don't think Grace Kelly would allow an anecdote to happen to her." So frustrated were they that several PR men uncharacteristically allowed their ill feelings toward Grace to show. One, assigned by MGM to help Pete Martin piece together his profile of Grace, told him, "I'm hoping you'll tell me what the excitement about this girl is all about." Martin was astonished: "I kept thinking, *He's* asking *me* the questions. I'm supposed to do that!"

Hollywood's more cynical insiders might not have appreciated Grace, but the public certainly did. By the end of 1954, a year in which *Dial M for Murder, Rear Window, The Country Girl, The Bridges at Toko-Ri,* and *Green Fire* were all released, Grace was the number one female box office attraction in America. She received more fan mail than any other MGM player, and she was surrounded by more excitement and publicity than anyone had been since Marilyn Monroe's rise to prominence in 1952 and 1953.

What was it that made Grace Kelly such a big star so fast? Her beauty would have guaranteed a successful film career, but her meteoric rise can be traced primarily to the fact that Grace Kelly was the right person at the right time. Her compelling combination of refinement and sexual charisma was perfect for the 1950s, when America's more conservative attitudes were being pushed aside ever more boldly by sexual frankness, especially in cinema. Americans were intrigued by sexuality, but many found Marilyn Monroe's sometimes fla-grant brand of it offensive. In some ways, Grace Kelly was "the pious man's Marilyn."

William Holden's analysis of Grace's appeal was particu-larly perceptive: "Popularity goes in eras and depends on the mood of the world. In the late twenties and early thirties the grand movie stars like Norma Shearer and Joan Crawford provided the elegance and glamour that people wanted. Then came war, chaos, economic turmoil, religious insecurity—all those things. All this created a mood in which the emphasis was on bodily pleasures and excitements. For a long time our actresses were popular in proportion to the size of their breastworks. Phoniness didn't matter. But now I think the world wants something else. I hate to impose this on Grace . . . but I think she had become a symbol of dignity and all the good things that are in us all. I do think she has an honesty and a dignity, and I think the world *wants* to get back to honesty and dignity. Women like Grace Kelly and Audrey Hepburn help us to believe in the innate dignity of man—and today that is what we desperately need to believe in."

Don Richardson agrees that Grace was right for her time. "The boys came back from the war, and they'd seen dark-haired Japanese girls and dark-haired Italian girls. Grace was a tall blonde, the all-American girl back home they'd been longing for."

But timing wasn't everything for Grace, Richardson be-lieves. "Grace was like a blank piece of paper. Her personality was such that everybody saw in her what they wanted to see in her. The poet Yeats said, 'I clothe you in the colors of my longing.' Grace was a perfect canvas for everyone to paint a dream on."

Jimmy Stewart's assessment of Grace's appeal was less re-flective but still telling: "She has great beauty and a quality that hits you like a cyclone. The public is like an old setter dog in smelling out anything good and Grace is good. She has class. Not just the class of being a lady—I don't think that has anything to do with it—but she'll always have the class you find in a really great racehorse."

Mary Seaton Henderson, the daughter of George Seaton and a teenager in the mid-1950s, saw Grace as a role model. They formed a friendship as Mary visited her father's sets, and Grace spent time at the Seaton home. Mary's reaction to Grace, born of her personal knowledge of her, was one shared by millions of young women who had seen her only on the screen: "She was my ideal. She was always the perfect lady. She walked well, she spoke well, she always knew how to carry herself. She always said the right thing at the right time. I looked at her as the epitome of what I wanted to be like when I became a full-grown lady. I found her one of the most gracious, most hospitable, most endearing women I will ever know in my life."

Young actresses who quickly become popular phenomena in Hollywood have traditionally been the most at risk for engendering critical ridicule; many cinema purists regard wide audience popularity as the antithesis of artistic integrity. Too, the chances that a studio will stereotype a young performer increase proportionately with his or her rise in popularity and the studio's desire to continue to "cash in" as quickly as possible on public acceptance, a phenomenon which in many cases is short-lived.

This might have happened to Grace, except for her own well-defined sense of self and her unwillingness to turn herself over, body and soul, to the MGM "star machine." Grace's reviews for *The Country Girl* were those usually reserved for our most revered actors, and certainly they were of a kind rarely accorded a pop phenomenon: "Crosby and Miss Kelly," wrote *Look*'s critic, "play this human tragedy with a compassion and psychological insight reaching the best traditions of dramatic skill." *Cue* agreed: "The Crosby-Kelly-Holden team comes just about as close to theatrical perfection as we are likely to see on-screen in our time."

Despite such praise for Grace's acting ability, MGM once again failed to offer her a role to which she felt herself suited.

It sent her two scripts it considered top-notch properties, *Something of Value* and *Jeremy Rodock,* a Western to costar Spencer Tracy. Grace informed MGM that although she agreed the projects were first-rate, they were not "right for me personally," and she declined to do them.

MGM executives were furious. To them, Grace's latest refusal smacked of simple insubordination, and when press reports began appearing asking whether Grace wasn't in fact attempting to break her MGM contract, the studio's hand was forced: it ordered Grace to report for *Jeremy Rodock.* When she didn't, MGM suspended her.

For many contract players the cessation of a weekly paycheck can be devastating, an effective bargaining tool for the studio. It wasn't with Grace. Hollywood observers, noting the Kelly family wealth, suggested that Grace could merely call on her family if the financial crunch got too severe. She wouldn't have done that, but neither did she need to: her father had already given her a substantial sum. "Dad gave each of us money when we reached twenty-one," Lizanne says. "It had been kept in trust for us." Grace, when asked by a reporter what hardships a lack of studio income would create for her, replied with an insouciance that galled the MGM bigwigs: "I'm afraid I'll have to stop decorating my new apartment for the present." Hardly a hardship compelling enough to force Grace into acquiescing to her studio's demands.

Moreover, even with Grace's endowment from her father and the fact that she had been making between $750 and $1,500 a week for more than two years, she led her life with the frugality of a struggling young extra. She lived in a small apartment in a lesser section of Hollywood—with two roommates. In no way had Grace become caught up in the Hollywood nouveau riche life-style chase of mortgaged-to-the-sky Bel-Air mansions and loaded Rolls-Royces. The rent on her New York apartment was well within her budget as well. With such frugality, she had added to her already substantial nest egg during her years in Hollywood, and she was prepared to delve into it for as long as necessary. "I guess there's nothing I can do," she told a reporter, "but sit here and wait till they want me back."

Aware of Grace's financial independence, the MGM brass wavered among themselves about keeping her in suspension. What's more, Grace had been nominated as Best Actress of 1954 for her role in *The Country Girl,* and as the presentation night approached, word in Hollywood was that Grace and Judy Garland (for *A Star Is Born)* were neck and neck in the race. MGM didn't relish the embarrassment of having that year's Oscar winner on suspension from the studio, so on March 21 it informed Grace that she was once again on salary and that it would like her to report as the star of the film version of Elizabeth Barrett Browning's autobiographical novel, *The Barretts of Wimpole Street.* Grace replied through her agent that she didn't think it was right for her, but that she would consider it. True to its style, MGM announced that Grace's suspension had been lifted and that she would soon report to begin work on *The Barretts of Wimpole Street.* Dore Schary told the press, "We respect Grace, and we want to do everything possible for her during this important time in her life when she is up for an Academy Award."

And so Grace Kelly attended the 1955 Oscar ceremonies as an employed actress. A victory was anything but assured her, however; Judy Garland, as a child of Hollywood, was thought by many to be the sentimental favorite, and Grace, accompanied to the awards by Edith Head, did not expect to win.

A backlash against Judy because of her celebrated temperament had developed, however—to Grace's benefit. She won the Best Actress Oscar and, after shedding a few tears, gave a gracious acceptance speech in which she spoke of her inability to express all the love and gratitude she felt in her heart. Backstage, a reporter asked her to kiss co-winner Marlon Brando. Ever demure, Grace replied, "I think he should kiss me." Brando complied.

The Academy Awards had been televised nationally for several years, and the fact that her family was watching her receive Hollywood's ultimate accolade added to the emotion which overcame Grace when she won. Her father's derogatory comments about her ambitions came to mind as she accepted her trophy; when a reporter later asked her what she was thinking when she began to cry that night, she replied, "I was just happy, because it meant that now I, too, belonged to the family."

But even this supreme achievement could not bring Jack Kelly to give his daughter her due. For months Grace's father had been making less than gallant comments about his daughter's success. At one point he had said, "Peggy's the family extrovert. Just between us, I've always thought her the daughter with the most on the ball." He expressed "bewilderment" at Grace's stardom, saying, "I thought it would be Peggy. Anything that Grace could do Peggy could always do better."

Grace had been deeply hurt by her father's insensitivity; it was bad enough to make comments like that privately, but to make them to reporters seemed to Grace in her more resentful moments cruelly calculated attempts to keep her in her place. No amount of success, it seemed, could shake her father's low opinion of her. Winning the Academy Award—equivalent in her profession to an Olympic gold medal—would finally, she had hoped, bring her the paternal approval she so craved. But it was not to be. To a reporter, in a comment wired to every newspaper across the country, Kelly expressed amazement at Grace's accomplishment: "I can't believe it. I simply can't believe Grace won. Of the four children, she's the last one I'd expected to support me in my old age."

During Grace's next visit home, all the Kellys, except for her father, who'd been detained on business, gathered in the den, enjoying cocktails. Grace, because of her new stature and her rare trips to Philadelphia, became the center of attention, answering breathless questions from her sisters and jocularly revealing inside information about the "real" Hollywood. Laughing gaily as she drank champagne, Grace became more and more uninhibited, and soon broke into one of her rare and wicked imitations of Bette Davis.

In the middle of Grace's "Petah, Petah, Petah," with everyone dissolved into helpless laughter, Mr. Kelly walked into the room. He watched impassively for a few moments as Grace continued her impersonation. Then he spoke up. "Grace," he said, "that will be enough. You're among the family now. You don't have to put on an act."

Grace stopped, walked over to her father and gave him a kiss, and didn't say another word for the next hour.

Chapter Nine

After the public humiliation and the private torment of her abortive affairs with Milland and Holden, Grace vowed never again to become involved with a married man. Her next lover was indeed single, and there were no recriminations, no sniggering in the press when the relationship became public. But he was also divorced, a Continental playboy, and a Greek orthodox. This time, Grace faced another, even more formidable obstacle: her family.

Oleg Cassini, of Russian and Italian descent, raised in Florence, had by 1953 become a well-regarded fashion designer and a card-carrying member of the international jet set. Forty years old, married and divorced twice (to heiress Merry Fahrney and actress Gene Tierney), Cassini was renowned as a womanizer who charmed ladies young and old with his Continental manner and mustachioed good looks.

Cassini could have almost any woman he desired, but the only one he wanted was Grace. "I fell in love with her after I saw her in *Mogambo*," he said later. "She was all that I wanted—beautiful, clean-looking, ethereal enough, sexy enough . . ." Cassini told a friend who was with him in the movie house that Grace Kelly would be his new girlfriend. The friend laughed at Cassini's chutzpah, but within minutes Oleg got his chance: as he walked into one of his favorite French restaurants in Manhattan, he spotted Grace, dining with the French actor Jean-Pierre Aumont, whom she had been seeing for several months. Cassini and Aumont were acquaintances, which gave Cassini a perfect opening. After an effusive greeting, Oleg left Jean-Pierre little choice but to introduce him to Grace and ask him to join their table. Aumont watched with growing irritation as Cassini showered Grace with compliments and charm. It was just the beginning of what Cassini later called "the greatest, most exhilarating campaign of my life, using every bit of fantasy and energy I had. The goal, to get this incredibly beautiful, superficially cool woman interested in me."

Grace found herself inundated with flowers over the next few days, sent anonymously. Finally Oleg called, identified himself as "your friendly local florist," and asked for a date. Skeptical, Grace assented to lunch—with sister Peggy along —only after Oleg assured her that she had already met him. They had a pleasant meal, but Grace did not encourage his attentions, because—as she told him then—she was leaving for the West Coast shortly and—as she told him over the telephone weeks later—she was very much in love with Ray Milland.

Cassini continued his courting via long distance, with flowers, telephone calls, and letters. Over the next few months Grace kept things with Oleg casual, seeing him only occasionally, inviting him to Hollywood and the set of *The Country Girl*—even as she was involved with Crosby, and then Holden. Cassini, like Don Richardson and Gene Lyons before him, was not aware of Grace's relationships with her two costars. He told *People* magazine nearly thirty years later, "When she broke up with Milland she sent me a postcard asking me to come to the South of France while she filmed *To Catch a Thief.* 'Those who love me follow me,' she wrote."

While Grace was seeing Crosby and Holden, Oleg was an amusement, an ego booster, a charming companion; their relationship remained platonic. Not until those affairs ended and Grace had endured the public embarrassment and family pressure they created did she begin to see Cassini in a new light. He was charming, yes, and a more ardent paramour a young woman could not hope to enjoy. Better still, he was unmarried, and thus unlikely to cause scandal. Grace barely considered her family's reaction to a serious affair with Cassini, but whenever she did she convinced herself it would be favorable, despite Cassini's marital failures and his religion, because he was, at least, single.

Cassini did follow Grace to France in the summer of 1954, and their relationship flourished in the romantic atmosphere of the Riviera. Cassini was in his element, and his sophistication and savoir faire captivated Grace—she was still, despite her lofty experiences over the past year and a half, a young woman who had led a very sheltered life. As roommate Rita Gam later put it, "Considering that the world saw us as glamorous movie stars, we were terribly naïve . . ."

Grace gradually fell in love with Cassini while she made *To Catch a Thief.* "We were very isolated there," he said, "and when she finished working, we spent the evenings together." The platonic nature of their relationship changed, Cassini says, and Grace "asked me what my intentions were. I told her I wanted to marry her . . . I don't think Grace could have had an affair with me unless she thought honestly that she was going to marry me."

Cassini and Grace became, in his words, "secretly engaged." Secrecy was necessary, she admitted to him (and, finally, to herself), because she anticipated some opposition from her family. "We had an understanding," Cassini says. "We decided that when we got back to the States, Grace would win over her mother, who would then win over her father. She saw no difficulty."

It was a foolhardy faith on Grace's part; Cassini would soon be subjected to the same Kelly family treatment Don Richardson had been. But that was several months in the future. In the meantime there was a movie to be made.

Mid-1953: Paramount Pictures suggests to Alfred Hitchcock that he film David Dodge's novel *To Catch a Thief,* a property the studio owned. The story appeals to Hitchcock: John Robie, a highly successful cat burglar, retires to the French Riviera, only to discover that a series of burglaries patterned after his own are taking place around him. He meets Frances Stevens, the beautiful, sophisticated, and sexually flirtatious daughter of an American socialite, and amid a great deal of sexual cat and mousing they discover the identity of the burglar and take suspicion off Robie.

The enticing fact that the movie would have to be made on location on the Côte d'Azur attracted Hitchcock's interest as much as the story did. He knew immediately the actors he wanted to play John Robie and Frances Stevens: Cary Grant and Grace Kelly. Hitchcock had worked with Grant twice, in *Suspicion* and *Notorious,* and knew that his suave urbanity was perfect for Robie. And who better than Grace Kelly to play a cool, elegant, yet passionate blond beauty?

Hitchcock's first feeler went out to Cary Grant. As Grant recalled, "I had left the business, or thought I had, and I was in Hong Kong when Hitch sent me a cable to call him. I did, and he told me about an idea for a script he had to be set in the South of France. Well, both of those things were very attractive—that Hitch had glommed onto a script that he enjoyed, and that we would travel to the South of France. I asked him, 'Who do you see as the leading lady?' and he said, 'I have a girl I think is absolutely marvelous by the name of Grace Kelly.'"

Grant had seen Grace in both *Fourteen Hours* and *High Noon,* and he liked what he saw. "I recognized her even then as a brilliant actress. She had control, and she was obviously listening to the person she was doing the scene with. That isn't always the case. So I said to Hitch, 'I agree with you— I've had my eye on her too.'"

Grant agreed to come out of retirement to make *To Catch a Thief,* but it wasn't until the summer of 1954 that filming began—after Grace had made four other films. When Hitchcock asked MGM for yet another loan-out of Grace's services, the studio once again balked. It wanted Grace to begin making movies for MGM, not every other studio in town. Word leaked to the press about Hitchcock's interest and MGM's reluctance, and both Hedda Hopper and Louella Parsons wrote unequivocally that Grace's bosses would not budge this time.

Grace was sure they would. She told Edith Head, "No matter what anyone says, dear, keep right on making my clothes. I'm doing the picture." Grace had refused all the scripts MGM had offered to her, and the studio was still afraid that if it denied her something she wanted badly enough, she might well make good on her *Country Girl* threat and renounce Hollywood forever. Paramount helped Grace's cause as well by telling MGM that it would be happy to honor Metro's request for a loan-out of William Holden—who, as the 1953 Best Actor Oscar winner, was a hot property—if MGM would be good enough to return the favor by releasing Grace. That enticement, and a lot of money, led MGM to acquiesce yet again, and Grace was free to make another Alfred Hitchcock film opposite another of Hollywood's most popular matinee idols.

Grace was excited about the prospect; Stewart Granger recalled that during *Green Fire* filming, "Three quarters of her mind was in France . . . I really think she was planning her Riviera wardrobe most of the time." When she arrived in France, however, she had done four motion pictures in the space of little more than six months, and she was, in the words of Steven Englund, "In a state bordering on clinical exhaustion." She asked Hitchcock to allow her "to sleep" for a few days before filming began, but location shooting is very expensive, and he couldn't afford the delay—Grace had to report. Her enthusiasm for the project and the instant rapport that developed among herself, Grant, and Hitchcock helped to rapidly restore her strength and vitality. Grant, in fact, did not recall that Grace was anything but rested and ready to work. "If she was exhausted," he said, "it wasn't apparent to me. I think I would have noticed it. But it may well have been, because making a film is not an easy matter. The layperson doesn't understand it at all. But whether she was tired when we began, I couldn't say."

The *To Catch a Thief* company was a happy one, particularly so for Grace. Hitchcock's regard for her was something she had come to expect and look forward to. That Cary Grant shared Hitchcock's esteem came as a happy extra. Grant and Grace became lifelong friends, an affection first engendered, he said, by his respect for her as an actress: "Most young actors are inclined to worry about how they look to the camera, and therefore their concentration isn't totally on the conversation. You can tell they're not really listening to what you're saying. I've often tested actors by switching the dialogue, which leaves them completely up in the air because they expected a certain line, and if I change it to a line which alters the words but not the sense, you can see their hesitancy, because it doesn't exactly fit. Grace didn't do that.

"Grace acted the way Johnny Weissmuller swam, or Fred Astaire danced. She made it look so easy. Some people said Grace was just being herself. Well, that's the toughest thing to do if you're an actor, because if you're yourself, the audience feels as though that person is living and breathing, just being natural, not 'acting'—and that's the hardest thing in the world to do."

Grant enjoyed Grace's outspokenness. Shortly after working with her he said, "She will probably go through life being completely misunderstood, since she usually says completely what she means." Asked in 1985 about the quote, Grant said, "I'm afraid that the connotation was that she was therefore brutally frank. That wasn't so. But if she was going to speak, she said exactly what her thoughts were."

Grace's "equanimity," Grant said, surprised him. "But then again, it didn't really surprise me, because I had seen her act." Still, he didn't expect her calmness in the face of often painful professional requirements: "Grace never complained about anything," Grant said in 1956. "We had a scene where I had to grab her arms hard while she was fighting me and push her against a wall. We went through that scene eight or nine times, but Hitchcock still wanted it again. Grace went back alone behind the door where the scene started, and just by chance I happened to catch a glimpse of her massaging her wrists and grimacing in pain. But a moment later she came out and did the scene again—she never complained to me or to Hitch about how much her arms were hurting.

"She isn't one of those girls who waste time by being angry . . . if a dress didn't fit, well it just didn't fit, and that was that, with no hysterics. So of course they got the dress fixed for her faster than they would have for a girl who was screaming about it. No wonder she was popular with the wardrobe people, even if she didn't go around slapping them on the back."

Alfred Hitchcock's vision of Grace Kelly as a beautiful iceberg covering a molten core of sensuality was never more fully realized than in *To Catch a Thief*. From the beginning of the picture the motif was unmistakable. As Hitchcock explained, "I deliberately photographed Grace Kelly ice-cold and I kept cutting to her profile, looking classical, beautiful, and very distant. And then, when Cary Grant accompanies her to the door of her hotel room, what does she do? She thrusts her lips right up to his mouth . . . I think the most interesting women, sexually, are the English women. I feel that the English women, the Swedes, the northern Germans, and Scandinavians are a great deal more exciting than the Latin, Italian, and the French women. Sex should not be advertised. An English girl, looking like a schoolteacher, is apt to get into a cab with you and, to your surprise, she'll probably pull a man's pants open."

That Hitchcock's intuition about the sexual chemistry between his stars was correct is never more evident than in the film's several double entendre sequences. So potent was the charge between the two stars that once again rumors of a romance between Grace and her leading man surfaced. Grant dismissed such speculation. "Grace and I were never romantically inclined in any possible way," he said. "We shared a professional regard and admiration for each other, and that was all."

For Hitchcock and *To Catch a Thief* that was enough. Grant's and Kelly's reading of the script's more provocative lines bordered at times on the lascivious, as in the following exchanges:

> GRANT: What do you expect to get out of being so nice to me?
> KELLY: Probably a lot more than you're willing to offer.
> GRANT: Jewelry—you never wear any.
> KELLY: I don't like cold things touching my skin.
> GRANT: Why don't you invent some *hot* diamonds?
> KELLY: I'd rather spend my money on more tangible excitement.
> GRANT: Tell me, what do you get a thrill out of most?
> KELLY: I'm still looking for that one.
> GRANT: What you need is something I have neither the time nor the inclination to give you—two weeks with a good man at Niagara Falls.
>
> *Later, during a picnic lunch, Kelly offers Grant a piece of chicken:*
>
> KELLY: Do you want a leg or a breast?
> GRANT: You make the choice.
> KELLY: Tell me, how long has it been?
> GRANT: Since what?
> KELLY: Since you were in America last?

A classic cinematic example of both visual and verbal double entendre takes place a few scenes later, when Frances invites Robie to her hotel room to watch a fireworks display:

> KELLY: If you really want to see fireworks, it's better with the lights off. I have a feeling that tonight you're going to see one of the Riviera's most fascinating sights. *(She walks toward him, her gown strapless and low-cut.)* I'm talking about the fireworks, of course.
> GRANT: I never doubted it.
> KELLY: The way you looked at my necklace, I didn't know.
> GRANT: . . . I have about the same interest in jewelry that

I have in politics, horse racing, modern poetry, and women who need weird excitement. None.

KELLY *(As she reclines seductively on a divan):* Give up—admit who you are. Even in this light I can tell where your eyes are looking. *(Close up of her necklace, revealing as well her inviting décolletage)* Look—hold them—diamonds! The only thing in the world you can't resist. Then tell me you don't know what I'm talking about. *(The fireworks begin in the background. She kisses his fingers, then places his hand beneath the necklace. We cut to a close-up of the fireworks.)* Ever had a better offer in your whole life? One with everything!

GRANT: I've never had a crazier one. *(Cut again to fireworks)*

KELLY: Just as long as you're satisfied. *(More fireworks)*

GRANT: You know just as well as I do this necklace is imitation.

KELLY: Well, *I'm* not! *(They kiss, and we cut to fireworks again. Back to a long, passionate kiss, then a final, climactic frenzy of fireworks to end the scene.)*

The filming of *To Catch a Thief* was one of the happiest moviemaking periods of Grace's life. She loved the Riviera, just as she thought she would, and she went sightseeing with cast and crew members whenever fatigue didn't completely overtake her. She and Oleg Cassini, Hitchcock and his wife, Alma, and Cary Grant and his wife, Betsy Drake, dined together most nights in the small, atmospheric restaurants that dot the hillsides of southern France. But, Grant remembered, "There wasn't that much time to see the French Riviera; it's a tiring day when you're filming." Grace did manage to visit nearby Monaco and one of its casinos in Monte Carlo; she was giddy when she won a few hundred francs at a gaming table.

One romantic scene between Grant and Kelly on the Moyenne Cornich above the Mediterranean featured, in the background, the palace of Prince Rainier Grimaldi, the absolute monarch of the tiny principality of Monaco. When Grace and several of the crew members later drove around the country, she was entranced by descriptions of a spectacular garden on a high plateau which was impossible for them to reach.

"Whose gardens are those?" she asked screenwriter John Michael Hayes.

"Prince Grimaldi's," Hayes replied. "I hear he's a stuffy fellow."

"Oh," Grace said wistfully. "I'd like to see his flowers."

While at work or play, there was a rare camaraderie among Grant, Grace, and Hitchcock. Even when the director was dissatisfied, the mood was jocular. "With Hitch," Grant recalled, "one sort of set up the scene for his inspection. We knew what the scene was going to be about; he'd let us work it out between ourselves initially, because he knew that we weren't complete idiots. Then he would watch us do it in rehearsal, and sometimes we knew as we were doing it, on our feet, that it wasn't right. And very often he would ask, 'Is that the way it's gonna go, fellas?' And we'd say, 'All right, we'll start again,' and he'd give us a few thoughts and ideas, and go back to his bungalow, and we'd start to rehearse again. Hitch always made us feel that we were collaborators. Working with Hitchcock was very *comfortable*."

It could also be very funny. Hitchcock was famous for his wit and his love of puns, and that was one of the reasons he admired Grace so much. "She had a marvelous sense of humor," Grant said. "Otherwise I don't think Hitch would have been attracted to her, because he too had a wonderful sense of humor." Grant recalled a word game that the three of them played continuously during filming, in which everyone in the company was renamed according to his or her job: "The cameraman was Otto Focus, the script girl was Mimi O'Graph. The guy in charge of costumes was Ward Robe. Then there was Alec Trition, and you'll never guess what the art director's name was—Art Director! It got so that if anyone came on to the set while we were waiting for a shot to be set up, we'd ask them for some contributions, and if they came up with a good one, they could stay. But if not, they were out—*out!* There was May Kupp and Mike Shadow and Dolly Shot. We had a long, long list. The set builder was Bill Tit. Sometimes they got impossibly obscure; people would stand around trying to think of a new one all the time."

The only unpleasantness for Grant during filming was during a scene in which Grace drives him through the small, winding roads in the hills above the Mediterranean. At a 1982 tribute to her in Philadelphia, Grace joked that her driving "caused Cary Grant to turn dead white under his tan." Grant acknowledged that "I *was* rather anxious about it. Grace had started the scene without her glasses, and it was a continuation, so that when she offered to drive me wherever I was going, she got into the car without her glasses. Her driving was erratic, and there was other traffic around, and I must say that I was uneasy. I asked her where the hell she thought she was going, and she said, 'Don't be silly, I haven't got my glasses on.' I thought, *No wonder,* and I took hold of the wheel below camera range."

As the finale of *To Catch a Thief,* Hitchcock designed an elaborate costume ball, the sole purpose of which, according to Donald Spoto, "was to show off his leading lady in a shimmering ball gown." Its filming required over a week, and Hitchcock worked closely with Grace to present her in the most stunning way possible. But Cary Grant, like Jimmy Stewart, dismissed Spoto's theory of Hitchcock's unrequited passion for Grace: "We *all* were in love with Grace for goodness' sake—we had a lovely combine. We were all in love with each other. We enjoyed each other's talents. In fact, if Grace hadn't married the Prince and left acting, she, Hitch, and I were going to form our own production company together and do a series of pictures, *Thin Man, Mr. and Mrs. Smith* kinds of things. It would have been delightful. Hitch may have been sexually attracted to Grace, but so were a lot of other people. So what's the big deal?"

To Catch a Thief opened in August of 1955 and disappointed many Hitchcock purists with its uncharacteristic slackness and lack of strong suspense. Still, it was a beautiful, stylish, witty film, and it presented the ultimate Hitchcockian vision of Grace Kelly as the queen of "fire and ice." Reviews were mixed, but audience reaction was similar to the London *Daily Telegraph* critic's: "The mood throughout is one of cynical humor, with witty dialogue and amorous overtones. The young American beauty pursues the former jewel-thief with a Shavian frankness and zest, and their love scenes will entertain many people not ordinarily over-fond of thrillers. Mr. Grant and Miss Kelly dominate the film with easy charm . . ." *To Catch a Thief* was a commercial success, won an Academy Award for its cinematography, and further cemented Grace's position at the top echelon of movie stardom.

Grace had spent three months on the French Riviera, romanced on-screen by one of Hollywood's most glamorous leading men, and wooed off-screen by a suave, sophisticated jet-setter. Back home in Philadelphia, however, she was still "our little Gracie" and under the unrelenting control of her parents. The romantic idyll shared by Grace and Oleg Cassini on the Côte d'Azur came to an abrupt end when, because she was seriously contemplating marriage, Grace felt compelled to introduce Cassini to her family.

The Kellys, of course, were aware of Grace's relationship with Oleg, which had made the papers long before their sojourn in France and was now much discussed in gossip columns from coast to coast; Cassini was Grace Kelly's first publicly acknowledged paramour. If Jack Kelly's opposition to Don Richardson was intense, it tripled in ferocity against Cassini. Kell echoed his father's feelings in *Time* magazine's cover story on Grace: "I don't approve of these oddballs she goes out with. I wish she would go out with more athletic types." The all-American Kelly men had no time for European smoothies oozing charm. Told Cassini would be coming to meet him, Jack Kelly sneered, "Should I shake his hand or kiss it?"

Because Mrs. Kelly had expressed some admiration for Oleg, Grace felt that she could enlist her mother's help in softening her father's opposition to Cassini. Margaret called one of her closest friends, Dorothea Sitley, who, as director of publicity for Gimbel's department stores, had worked with Oleg. "I just received a letter from Grace," Mrs. Kelly told her friend, "and she said she wants to bring Oleg Cassini down to Ocean City to stay there at the place. Jack says he'll kill him if he walks through the door. You know Oleg. I don't dare let Jack know I even called you. But I can tell him if what you say about Oleg is all right. Then Jack will let him come."

Mrs. Sitley's response was not encouraging. "Now wait a minute," she replied. "Oleg is *not* for Grace. Definitely he is not for her. He's charming, but he's careless, just like a child wandering around." She then told a story of Cassini forgetting his wallet when they went out for drinks, and allowing Mrs. Sitley to pay for them. This was considered a serious breach of gentlemanly etiquette.

Mrs. Kelly decided to forestall any Cassini visit and, to that end, she met with Grace and Oleg in New York. Over lunch she tried to dissuade Cassini from his marital intentions. "Oleg," she told him, "you're terribly charming and Continental, and I can certainly understand Grace's wanting to date you, but as a marriage risk you're very poor."

Expecting Cassini to wilt, Mrs. Kelly was taken aback when he vigorously defended himself, anticipating all objections against him. Yes, he began, he'd been divorced, but he remained friendly with Gene Tierney and close to his children. His own substantial wealth should put to rest any suspicion of fortune hunting. And he was not a womanizer, he concluded, despite his reputation: "Once I am involved with a woman, as I now am, I do *not* date others."

Cassini then turned the tables, suggesting that Mrs. Kelly's religious principles, which condemned his divorces and romantic dalliances, were flexible when it came to a homosexual friend of her family's and her husband's well-known philanderings. Margaret Kelly was shocked, but she also admired Cassini's spunk—a Kelly might have reacted to a prospective mother-in-law's opposition in much the same way. She told Cassini that the family would not stand in the way of Grace's seeing him, as long as they did not publicly announce any marriage plans for at least six months. Then, perhaps believing that the rest of the Kellys would admire Cassini's strength of character as much as she had, Mrs. Kelly invited him to a weekend in Ocean City.

Like Richardson, Cassini dreaded the trip, but he agreed to go for Grace's sake. As before, it was a fiasco. Oleg had a room of his own in the family's beachfront house, but he had to walk through Mr. and Mrs. Kelly's bedroom to get to it. "The weekend I spent in Ocean City was the worst of my life," Cassini has said. "I ate razor blades for breakfast there . . . Nobody would talk to me except Grace's sisters. It was awful, and I suffered, was humiliated night and day. Grace's father positively refused to talk to me. He mumbled something to the effect that there was no communication possible between us, ever."

Also present that weekend was Lizanne's beau, Donald Le-Vine, who was Jewish and also facing Kelly antagonism. Cassini took him aside at one point and muttered, "Don, you're slipping in because all the attention is on me." Cassini may have been right, because Lizanne and Don LeVine were wed shortly thereafter.

Her family's treatment of Cassini appalled and deflated Grace. Their interference in her life was bad enough when she was an acting student having an affair with one of her instructors. Now she was almost twenty-five, an internationally famous movie star, an Oscar nominee, a woman whose portrait would in a few months appear on the cover of *Time* magazine—and her family was treating her like a high school girl bringing home the leader of the neighborhood motorcycle gang.

If it had not been clear to Grace before, it was now. Her life, as it differed from Kelly family strictures, was simply not her own, no matter how many leading men kissed her or how many important magazines ran profiles of her. It was a depressing realization. Her choice of a marriage partner, she feared, could not be made based upon her own needs and desires, but rather on what was best for the Kelly family, what advanced their position in the eyes of their neighbors and the world. As Cassini put it, "Her family regarded her as a prize possession, a property, like a racehorse that must be handled, above all invested, wisely—not wasted."

Just as unsettling to Grace, her desire for the respectability of marriage had again been thwarted. She felt great guilt over the promiscuity of her days in Hollywood, and she was prepared to be faithful to one man for the rest of her life once she married. Cassini said, "I know for sure that she went to confession regularly—I sometimes accompanied her to the church—and I believe she was often troubled in her conscience." Her lifelong friend Judy Kanter Quine, then married to Grace's agent Jay Kanter, added, "If one has carefully defined values, as Grace did from the time she was very young, then breaking the rules brings very little pleasure and much remorse and guilt."

Grace was furious with her parents, who on the one hand condemned her sexual dalliances, and on the other prevented her from "legitimizing" her affair with Cassini by marrying him. Had she been a different young woman, she might have defied her parents; she did, in fact, seriously consider that option, so great was her anger. "She kept seeing me despite her family's opposition," Cassini says, "even suggesting we get married right away. She told me to find a priest who would marry us." But Grace was much more a dutiful daughter than a rebellious one, and Cassini soon discovered that "she had changed her mind. Her parents had talked her out of it."

So much of Grace's psychology revolved around winning her father's approbation that she would never have risked his fury by defying his wishes in so serious a matter as marriage. "The most amazing thing about Grace," says Don Richardson, "is that in all the years I knew her, and with all the terrible things her father did to her, she never once said a negative word to me about him. She constantly defended his actions."

Grace continued to see Cassini for several months after the visit to Ocean City, but the affair was doomed. After Grace returned to California, she telephoned Cassini in New York and told him that Frank Sinatra had asked her out. He and Ava Gardner had been divorced, and the passionate singer wanted to renew the friendship he and Grace had developed during *Mogambo* filming. Grace asked Cassini if he would mind her seeing Sinatra. "Yes, I *would* mind!" Oleg exploded. He was, he reminded Grace, planning to be in Los Angeles the following week, which was when Sinatra wanted to see her. "How in hell do you think I'll look in the papers if you're photographed on Sinatra's arm going into Chasen's while I'm sitting in my room at the Beverly Hills Hotel? That's all Hedda will need to write tomorrow morning—'Cassini is out of the picture.' So no, you do *not* have my permission."

Grace went out with Sinatra anyway, and although she and Cassini continued to date, the relationship ended early in 1955. Overlooking the Sinatra incident, Cassini recalled that he reacted to the parting with magnanimity. "It was very difficult for me to go through our breakup," he said. "Everybody had Grace Kelly on their lips. She was the number one creature of the world at that moment. And there I was, suddenly eliminated. But I think I showed the better part of me then. I was reasonable, understanding, and supportive, rather than narrow-minded, jealous, and argumentative . . . it's not that easy to be the big man. Love has a possessive quality about it. I thought she was mine. But I really supported her and never said a word about how I felt. At that moment I grew up, and I think it was my finest hour."

Her family's rude and heavy-handed opposition to yet another of her suitors left Grace more depressed and angry than ever. She was physically exhausted after making six major films in a year and a half, and psychologically battered by her seemingly futile efforts to impress her father. Rather than enjoy her success, she fixated on small injustices and allowed them to send her into tailspins of despondency. Academy classmate John Lupton recalls a lunch he had with Grace in Hollywood around this time. "There had been a lot of magazine coverage of Grace, which I thought would please her—she was a star, which is what she always wanted to be. But one of the pieces had called her 'the girl with the stainless steel interior,' and that really upset her. She said to me, 'I don't know why they think of me that way.' I was astonished at how upset she was—it was like someone had kicked her in the stomach. She had put a wall of protection up around herself, and now she felt that she was defenseless. She was saddened by the outlook for her in Hollywood. It really struck me that the lady we had all put up on a pedestal at school was *so* hurt by what was being written about her."

Grace needed to get away from Hollywood, and she took advantage of the contract clause that allowed her to spend a year working in New York. She returned to her apartment there as soon as she had completed the final *To Catch a Thief* interiors on Paramount's lot in Hollywood.

Her sojourn in New York during the fall of 1954 and the spring of 1955 was a recuperative one. She didn't set foot in front of a movie camera for over six months, and she enjoyed the respite immensely. Living again in her beloved Manhattan helped revive her spirits and dispel her depression. For the first time she began to put down roots somewhere other than in Philadelphia—she moved into a two-bedroom apartment on Fifth Avenue, across the street from the Metropolitan Museum of Art, and hired the decorator George Stacey to help her furnish and decorate it exactly as she wanted.

This was a major step for Grace; it symbolized her growing independence from her family. Her apartment on East Sixty-sixth Street, in a building constructed of Kelly bricks, had been decorated, Don Richardson says, by Mr. and Mrs. Kelly: "You wouldn't believe what this place looked like. It was all Grand Rapids furniture, right out of Zody's."

Grace's own taste ran to eighteenth-century French, and she and Stacey scoured New York's antique stores for just the right desk, chair, and chaise longue. (A year earlier, Grace had rented Lucille Ryman Carroll's house in Hollywood. "She came to see it with Oleg Cassini," Mrs. Carroll recalls, "and when she came upon a French desk in the bedroom, she cried out, 'Oh, Oleg, look, it's just like the one you have I love so much.' That desk convinced her to rent the house. It was odd though—once she rented it she almost never stayed there.")

In New York, Grace renewed the friendships that had lapsed in her absence. In Hollywood, she had said, she had "many acquaintances but few friends." Here, she felt at home among people who shared her love of theater and acting for art's sake. Friends were important to Grace; like her romantic liaisons, they provided her with some of the affection and moral support she craved from her family. To have a friend, in Grace's mind, meant to be a friend—and her friends continually marveled that, no matter how busy she was, no matter how much the center of glamorous attention, Grace never slighted them. Judy Quine recalled this singular quality: "In the middle of the most dazzling event, which was centered and focused only on her, [she had this capacity] to do what she should do within that context and at the same time to be as sensitive to each of her friends who was there or involved in a way as though nothing was happening . . ."

Although she was still gun-shy about romantic dalliances with Hollywood leading men, Grace around this time had a brief and very discreet affair with David Niven, one which never reached the point of press speculation. Grace and Niven became close and lifelong friends, and he and his wife frequently visited the palace at Monaco once Grace became a princess. On one occasion Prince Rainier asked Niven whom among his reputedly large number of Hollywood conquests had been the most satisfying. Unhesitatingly Niven replied, "Grace." Seeing the Prince's shocked expression, Niven added the highly unlikely clarifier, "Er, Gracie . . . Gracie Fields."

Chapter Ten

Once Grace had settled anew into a New York lifestyle and created for the first time a world entirely her own (even if only within four walls), her movie career was considerably lower on her list of priorities than it had been a year earlier. So it was with little enthusiasm that she greeted a March phone call from Rupert Allan (*Look* magazine's West Coast editor and a friend since writing three cover stories on Grace) to tell her that the French government wanted her to attend the Cannes Film Festival in early May. Grace told Allan she didn't want to go; when he persisted, she told him she would think about it.

The next day Allan called again, and he put considerable pressure on her. The French, he said, were eager to have her there; she was becoming very popular in Europe. *The Country Girl* would be shown at the festival, and it was a film of which Grace was justifiably proud. And, he reminded her, she had loved the South of France while making *To Catch a Thief* there. Allan's weren't the only such exhortations to Grace; the head of the Motion Picture Association of America, again at the behest of the French, urged her to attend "as a representative of America." With her participation put in those terms—and after assurances from Allan that he would accompany her and run the gauntlet of press and fans—Grace agreed.

As she prepared to fly to France, Grace was unaware of a conference taking place in the offices of *Paris Match* magazine—a meeting that set in motion a series of events that would ultimately change her life forever. It began with the magazine editor's desire for a photo feature that would pique his readers' interest in the Cannes Film Festival, one of France's most publicized, glamorous, and lucrative events.

Pierre Galante, *Paris Match*'s movie editor, read aloud a list of celebrities scheduled to attend, and all agreed that Grace Kelly, who had just won the Oscar, would be the festival's center of attention. They wondered, however, how to cover her in a provocative enough way that their story in itself would be newsworthy. Managing editor Gaston Bonheur, musing aloud, asked Galante, "Do you think you could arrange a meeting between Grace Kelly and Prince Rainier of Monaco?"

Galante later recalled, "The words were barely spoken and already the room's temperature had climbed. 'Prince Charming Meets Movie Queen!' someone said. 'I can see the headlines now!' someone else added."

The publicity value of the story was obvious to everyone. Few Frenchmen were unaware of Prince Rainier, the thirty-two-year-old absolute monarch of the tiny, shimmering principality bordering France which boasted the world's best-known gambling casino at Monte Carlo, or his long love affair with popular French actress Gisele Pascal. Expected to marry Gisele, the Prince had abruptly broken off the relationship when his doctors told him that she would be unable to conceive children. That the Prince's wife be fertile was an overriding matter of state in Monaco; by the terms of a 1918 treaty, should Rainier die without an heir the country would revert to French control.* To the native Monegasques, many of whose families date back eight centuries, such a turn of events was unthinkable—as was the inevitable taxation and military service that would follow: neither responsibility is required of Monaco's citizens.

Thus, the marital prospects of Rainier, already Europe's

---

* The Prince could have adopted a child, but this was not considered a viable option; the Monegasques wanted a birthright heir to their throne.

most eligible bachelor, were watched with an unusually high degree of interest. A meeting between a beautiful, popular, *single* American actress and the young, handsome, eminently marriageable Prince Rainier couldn't help but excite celebrity watchers in all corners of the Continent. Charged with arranging everything, Galante set out with trepidation. "Was it possible to bring off? Princes are busy men, and movie stars have just as many demands on their time. I knew. I had just married Olivia De Havilland . . . but I had my assignment and, despite my doubts, I would do my best to get it."

Grace arrived in Paris on May 4, accompanied by Gladys de Segonzac, with whom she had struck up a friendship when Gladys served as wardrobe mistress on *To Catch a Thief*. As they prepared to board the overnight train to Cannes, they ran into Pierre Galante and Olivia De Havilland, also on their way to the festival. Gladys was an old friend of Pierre's, and she made introductions all around.

Galante was relieved by the unexpectedly personal way in which he met Grace. Her ten days in Cannes would be busy ones, and since protocol required that the Prince be given forty-eight hours' notice before he would issue an invitation to the palace, time was of the essence. There was room for embarrassment all around if Grace demurred at meeting the Prince, because Galante had already sent out feelers to the palace. "It would not do," Galante recalled thinking, "to have the Prince issue an invitation and then have the actress turn it down. So you see, there was a lot that could go wrong. I was happy that I packed plenty of aspirin."

With a mutual friend breaking the ice between Grace and Galante, he was more confident of his ability to convince her, and he had his chance the following morning. As the train approached Cannes, Grace asked Olivia, "Tell me about the festival. What is it like? What is one supposed to do in Cannes?"

Galante had his opening. He told Grace that her round of official receptions would be exhausting unless she got away from the festival itself a few times. "Why don't you visit Monaco?" he asked her. She recalled how intrigued she'd been by the beautiful country on the hillside when she was last on the Riviera, and she asked Galante, "What is Monaco like?"

He explained that it was less than half the size of Central Park, had twenty thousand residents and the world's smallest army—ninety men and four officers who essentially guarded the palace: "Their red and blue uniforms and matching feathered helmets are straight out of an operetta." Grace smiled when Galante added that Monaco's prince, scion of the oldest ruling family in Europe, was "a handsome young bachelor."

"Well, why not?" Grace replied. "If I can get away from the festival for a few hours, it sounds like an interesting place to visit." Galante's luck held out. A few hours later, word came from Monaco that Prince Rainier would be happy to meet Miss Kelly at 4 P.M. the following day. Pierre then asked Elias Lapinere, MGM's representative at Cannes, to convince Grace that it would be a good idea to allow *Paris Match* to photograph the meeting for a layout in the magazine. Grace, who had considered the whole thing a remote option, was puzzled. "I still don't see why it's so important that I meet the Prince," she said. "But if you all think it's such a good idea, I'll do it."

Before long, Grace regretted the decision. She was "overwhelmed by the hordes of press and fans who crowded her wherever she went" her first day in Cannes, Galante recalled, and she was frazzled. The next day she would be acting as hostess of an official American reception for festival VIPs at five-thirty. It would be impossible for her to meet the Prince at four in Monaco—more than an hour's drive from Cannes —and be back in time. In the lobby of the Carlton Hotel, shouting over the heads of a swarm of reporters and photographers around her, Grace yelled to Galante, "Cancel the Prince!"

Panicky, Galante phoned the palace and, as gingerly as possible, explained the situation and asked the Prince's secretary if the appointment could, possibly, be pushed up to three. The secretary fell silent, but when Rainier was asked, he agreed. Galante was told, "His Serene Highness kindly agrees to move up the hour to three. He is entertaining friends at his villa in Beaulieu, but he will do his best to be back by three."

Once again Grace agreed to meet the Prince—and once again the following morning, she rued the decision. With her clothes just unpacked and wrinkled, and her hair just washed and wringing wet, she discovered that the electricity had gone out—a strike, she was told. With nothing to wear, and no way in which to style her hair, Grace was frantic. She called Rupert Allan. "It's unbelievable—and now I'm committed," she told him.

"Well, don't do it," Allan said. "I told you to clear things through me. I'll tell *Paris Match* to drop dead."

"No, no," Grace responded, "you can't get someone like the Prince of Monaco waiting there and not do it."

Grace put in a frantic call to Gladys de Segonzac, who came to her room to assess the situation. There was one dress unwrinkled enough to wear—but it had a loud, splashy design of large red-and-green cabbage roses on a black satin background, snug around the hips, then flared to midcalf. A fashion risk on any occasion, but entirely inappropriate for meeting a prince in his palace. Still, it would have to do. And Grace's hair would just have to be combed dry and pulled back into a bun.

Convinced that she and Gladys had saved a disastrous situation, Grace faced another problem when she met Galante in the lobby of the Carlton. Pierre looked at her and exclaimed, "You cannot be introduced to the Prince without a hat!"

"But I don't have a hat," Grace replied. "I didn't even bring one. Can't we go out and buy one?"

It was one-thirty, the middle of southern France's "sacred" two-hour lunch break, and all shops were closed. Gladys again came to the rescue, recalling that Grace had a headband of artificial flowers in her suitcase. She rearranged the flowers, stretched the material, and fashioned a combination hat and tiara for Grace to wear over her hair. "It looked wonderful when she finished," Galante recalled. And so Grace Kelly—pushed, pulled, smoothed, and improvised into presentability—set out to meet the Prince of Monaco.

An observer given to superstition might be forgiven for suspecting that some outside force was doing everything possible to prevent Grace Kelly's meeting Prince Rainier on May 6, 1955. Any of the myriad obstacles Grace had faced over the last two days might have changed her mind about the advisability of making the trip to Monaco; once she was on her way, they didn't stop. As the car carrying Grace, Gladys, Galante, and Elias Lapinere sped along the winding roads leading to the palace, Elias jammed down on the brakes to avoid a crash—and his car was struck from behind by the car carrying the *Paris Match* photographers.

No one was hurt, damage was minimal, and the party arrived at the palace with minutes to spare. But Prince Rainier had not yet arrived from Beaulieu. An aide-de-camp suggested that everyone take a tour of the palace. As Grace walked through the grand apartments, private apartments, and museums, the photographers shot away, at one point capturing her gazing at the royal bed.

As the tour continued, Galante remembers, Grace's behavior began to betray nervousness. She fidgeted, then asked, "What do I call him? How old is he? Does he speak English?" Then, aware that it was three forty-five, she became annoyed. "I think he's very rude to keep us waiting like this," she snapped. "Let's get out of here."

As Galante's stomach sank, a guard announced that the Prince had arrived, and in he walked. Grace saw before her a man younger than she had imagined him, and better-looking. As he extended his hand to her, she curtsied slightly. "How do you do?" the Prince said. "I am pleased to meet you. I am sorry I am so late." Nervous, charmed by the Prince's unexpectedly apologetic attitude, and surprised by how attractive she found him, Grace said nothing; she merely smiled back at him.

"Would you like to visit the palace?" the Prince asked her.

"We just have."

"Then let's go and look at the gardens." With Grace at his side, the Prince led everyone outside, stopping first at his private zoo, which housed two lions, several monkeys, and an Asian tiger. As camera shutters clicked, Rainier put his hand through the bars of the tiger's cage and nonchalantly petted the beast. Grace was impressed with his courage and his affinity for animals. "She looked at him with a new expression on her face," Galante later wrote. As they continued walking, the Prince showed Grace the magnificent flower gardens and the breathtaking view of the Mediterranean Sea. They seemed completely absorbed in each other, oblivious of the others present. "We felt like indiscreet onlookers," Galante recalled. And, he said, "Grace's complexion seemed to acquire a new glow."

Rainier was surprised as well by this American movie star. Grace Kelly was unlike any other actress he'd ever met: refined, quiet, even shy. Her beauty could not be overlooked, but neither could her unusual dignity and quiet elegance. The Prince found his emotions enjoyably stirred. Lapinere signaled forcefully that Grace must be leaving if she were to make the reception in time. The Prince, feeling a puzzling shyness, told Grace that he was tentatively planning a trip to the United States sometime in the near future, and he hoped that he might see her again. Grace replied that that would be a pleasure. She then said her goodbyes.

On the way back Grace seemed lost in thought. Galante interrupted her reverie to ask what she had thought of the Prince. "He is charming," she replied. "So very charming."

Grace's visit to Cannes resulted in a furor of press speculation about her love life. Ironically, this had nothing to do with Prince Rainier. Before she left for France, she wrote to Jean-Pierre Aumont and asked to see him while she was at

Cannes. He was happy to oblige; from his point of view, their romance in 1953 had ended much too soon.

They had met while playing Mr. and Mrs. John Audubon in the television drama *The Way of an Eagle*. Aumont was a handsome French star just beginning to make his mark in America. Widowed when his wife, actress Maria Montez, died after an accident in her bathroom, Aumont had been seen in the company of some of France's most beautiful actresses. Twenty years older than Grace, he had just the kind of charm and sophistication guaranteed to appeal to her. Initially, however, she resisted his advances. The first day Grace arrived for rehearsals, Aumont says, "I was immediately stunned by her beauty—and by her behavior, which was rather cold and aloof. She just put her glasses on and started to read the part. After a while there was a break and I asked her if she would like to have lunch with me. She said, 'No thank you, Mr. Aumont.' I found that very odd, because usually during rehearsals, especially in New York, people become very friendly and they immediately call each other by their first names. But Grace kept calling me 'Mr. Aumont.' "

Strongly attracted to Grace and "furious" when she continued to decline his invitations, Aumont became more and more frustrated. "Then, several days into filming, we were in a dance hall where young people hang out on Saturday nights. There was graffiti on the walls. I saw something written that I thought Grace should see. I grabbed her arm and said, 'Grace, look at this.' The graffiti said, 'Ladies, be kind to your men—after all, they're human beings too.'

"Grace laughed—and the ice was broken. And after that we were the best of friends." They began a romance that lasted several months: "She showed me around New York and gave me tours of her favorite places, like Greenwich Village. For three months we never left each other . . . then life separated us." Aumont had to return to France, and although Grace kept up a regular correspondence with him, her relationship with Oleg Cassini precluded any reunion while she was making *To Catch a Thief*.

Now, traveling to France again, this time alone, Grace let Jean-Pierre know she wanted to see him. He wasted no time in telephoning her; they spoke on her first day at the festival. "She told me she was scheduled to meet Prince Rainier of Monaco, but that she had to see her hairdresser and was going to cancel. I said to her, 'Grace—you can't do that!' She asked, 'Why?' I said, 'Because he's a reigning prince and seeing him is more important than seeing your hairdresser. And it could be embarrassing for America if you canceled the appointment.' Then she changed her mind and said she would go."

When Grace returned from Monaco, Aumont asked her how things had gone. "She replied, 'Oh fine. The Prince is charming.' And that was all. Maybe she'd had a stronger reaction than that, but she certainly wasn't going to let me know about it."

After two days in Cannes, Grace had not yet had time to see Jean-Pierre, and she suggested they meet at a party the following evening to be given by professional hostess Elsa Maxwell.

At the party Grace and Aumont became immediately reenchanted with each other. They conversed intimately, danced gazing into each other's eyes, and ignored everyone else present. So their endearments wouldn't be heard, they sent billets-doux back and forth and smiled at each other as they read them. Aware that Grace enjoyed waltzes, Aumont sent a note to the band, asking that they play every waltz they knew. He and Grace danced into the early morning hours. "The secret of Jean-Pierre's charm," a friend of the actor's said, "is that he spoils women. A woman yearns to feel wanted; she craves attention and thirsts for tenderness. Jean-Pierre understands this. He worships a beautiful woman, not from afar, but with words and gestures and constant devotion."

No one, least of all the assembled journalists, could fail to notice that Grace, the darling of the festival so far, seemed to have lost her heart to one of her host country's most romantic leading men. The reporters were gleeful—and a photograph of the couple dancing turned up in the normally staid *Time* magazine. "Grace Kelly, commonly billed as an icy goddess," the caption read, "melted perceptibly in the company of French actor Jean-Pierre Aumont . . . had Aumont, who came and thawed, actually conquered Grace?"

"The press," Aumont says, "didn't know that we knew each other from before. So they thought it was love at first sight. They thought the minute she saw me in the middle of that dinner party she threw herself into my arms."

New romance or a rekindling, the obviously enamored Grace and Pierre, as she called him, kept the press breathless. They were inseparable at festival functions and stole away whenever possible. They spent a day in St. Paul-de-Vence, an artists' village, wandering through the narrow twisted streets and visiting pottery shops.

The next day they met for lunch at a small, out-of-the-way restaurant. During the meal, they held hands and kissed; Grace took Aumont's hand in hers and nibbled on it. These private moments did not remain so for long; a photographer had followed them and, with a telephoto lens, secretly recorded their billing and cooing in a voyeuristic series of photographs published, as the Cannes festival was ending, in *Paris Match* and *Life*.

Once again, Grace was confronted with one of the unpleasant realities of celebrity. She blushed deeply when she saw the photographs and muttered, "How embarrassing!" Worried about her family's reaction, she rushed a telegram off to Philadelphia: I HAVE LOST NEITHER MY HEART NOR MY HEAD.

Reports began to circulate that Aumont, hopeful of publicity, had told the photographer about his rendezvous with Grace. After denying this for years, Aumont now admits he did reveal where he would be having lunch that day—but in a casual, unthinking way. "My brother-in-law," he explains, "was one of the great reporters for *Paris Match*. He and his family lived with me and my little girl, and he would always have his friends from *Paris Match* around. That day one of them asked me nonchalantly, 'Where are you having lunch today?' and I told him. I didn't think anything of it until the pictures were published. Grace was very upset—and so was I."

Despite her embarrassment over the publication of the pictures and her guilt-prompted reassurances to her parents, Grace did not behave any more circumspectly with Jean-Pierre after the festival ended. "She looked upon this time as a kind of 'Roman Holiday,'" Aumont says. "She was away from the strictures of her parents and the studio, and she was determined to make the most of it." Mr. and Mrs. Kelly certainly would not have been the least bit pleased by Grace's behavior in Paris, where she and Aumont went after the festival. They took adjoining rooms in the Raphael Hotel and began a blatant and whirlwind series of rendezvous which kept the press in a state of extreme agitation for a week. They attended a popular play, taking turns nibbling on a single ice-cream bar at intermission. They walked hand in hand along the Champs-Élysées. They remained oblivious of stares and comments at the popular club La Regence as they ate chicken and gazed into each other's eyes.

Rumors began circulating that Grace and Aumont would soon be married. The English papers, in fact, reported that Aumont had "announced" his engagement to Grace. Asked shortly afterward if he wanted to marry Grace, Aumont replied, "Who wouldn't? I adore her. She's wonderful. She's charming, adorable, intelligent, and, in spite of her beauty, modest."

Confronted with the same question, Grace replied, "A girl has to be asked first." Told that Aumont had informed several people that he *had* asked her, she blushed. "We live in a terrible world. You can't have secrets from anyone. A man kisses your hand, and it's screamed out from all the headlines. He can't even tell you he loves you without the whole world knowing about it."

After a week in Paris, the couple traveled to Aumont's country house at Rueil-Malmaison. There Grace met

Aumont's nine-year-old daughter, Marie-Christine, his brother and sister-in-law, and Maria Montez's sister and her husband. Grace brought her knitting and spent a comfortable, relaxed weekend among this close-knit extended family. A photographer friend snapped Grace sitting with her glasses on, her needlework in her lap, and Jean-Pierre at her feet. The domesticity of the scene fanned the marriage rumors, and despite an official MGM denial, Grace seemed to waver as Aumont saw her off at the Paris airport. "I do not know," she responded to the incessantly repeated question. "I cannot at this time tell you."

When Grace returned to the United States at the end of May, she found herself the center of a frenzy of publicity about her relationship with Aumont, fueled by *Life*'s publication of the photos of their cozy luncheon. Again bombarded by questions, Grace at first said that she and Aumont were "just good friends," but when a reporter suggested that Aumont was "too old" for her, and a foreigner to boot, she replied, "Differences in age or nationality present no obstacles in marriage between two persons if they love each other." Then she added, "I love France and the way Frenchmen's minds work."

According to Aumont, it *was* their different homelands that presented the biggest obstacle to their relationship. "I knew that our lives were too different. She was living in America, and I in France. She had a great many film commitments in her country. I don't think it would have worked, really."

When Elsa Maxwell asked Aumont about his relationship with Grace, he replied that he was "desperately" in love with her, but he added, "I don't think she feels that way about me at all." In France, Grace was caught up in the heady romanticism of Paris in the spring, but back in America, she had time to reflect on the daunting realities of their situations. Mrs. Kelly, to test her daughter's feelings for Aumont, asked her, "Gracie, shall I ask Mr. Aumont to visit us in Philadelphia?"

Grace, recalling the experiences of Richardson and Cassini, replied coolly, "Mother, that's entirely up to you."

Mrs. Kelly later wrote, "I knew then that she was not planning to marry him. She was still waiting for her prince."

When she returned from Cannes, Grace could no longer avoid her contractual obligations to MGM. She had turned down so many scripts that she knew she would have to accept *something* from the studio quite soon. Luckily she was sent a script that, if it wasn't *The Country Girl,* at least appealed to her: a movie version of Ferenc Molnár's play *The Swan,* a work her uncle George admired. The showpiece lead role, which Grace had played on television, was a lovely princess who must choose between love and duty to her country. The project might well have been tailored to appeal to Grace in its theatrical roots and its theme of noblesse oblige, a concept by which she had frequently conducted her affairs, particularly in regard to her family. Her affection for the project was influenced too by her meeting with Prince Rainier. To the relief of MGM, she accepted the role and filming began in the late summer of 1955.

MGM spared no expense to make *The Swan* as lavish as possible; designer Helen Rose remembered that "I used beautiful fabrics on all the costumes, the best I could find." For a white chiffon ball gown, Rose's artisans spent weeks embroidering hundreds of camellias, placing each petal upon the gown by hand. "I had never seen a star so thrilled as Grace was the day we fitted [the gown]. She stood before the mirror, gently touching the embroidered camellias on the background of the gown, saying, 'How simply marvelous—what talented people you have here at MGM.'"

Even more overwhelming to Grace was the fabulous Biltmore, a loving replication of a French Renaissance château built by George Vanderbilt in Asheville, North Carolina, and used as a location for *The Swan.* "It's like a palace," Grace told Jay Kantor. "I love it." Grace found herself caught up in the regal trappings surrounding her, and her demeanor in *The Swan* is almost preternaturally graceful, elegant, and serene.

Still, the Irish Kelly in her was never far from the surface. MGM, in a typically overbearing attempt to keep Grace happy, treated her as though she were, in fact, a princess, which embarrassed her. When the stewardess on the MGM-hired airplane carrying Grace to North Carolina forgot the silverware, forcing Grace and Alec Guinness to eat their steaks with penknives and plastic spoons, fawningly apologetic airline executives promised to fire the hapless girl. Grace circulated a petition among the others on the plane, asking that the stewardess not be fired.

Despite the regal trappings of her role, Grace retained her sense of humor—and mischief. She played word games with Guinness and reacted to his English wit with abandon: "The other day," Guinness said, "I told her a joke and Grace actually fell off the couch laughing." She and another costar, Jessie Royce Landis, teased Guinness unmercifully about a fan letter he'd received from a woman named Alice, and for days had Guinness paged by "Alice," driving the actor to distraction until he caught on.

One small bit of playfulness on Guinness's part resulted in a twenty-five-year battle of wits between the two. During filming, Jessie Royce Landis picked up a large, unwieldy tomahawk from a local Indian reservation and gave it to Guinness. Not wanting to lug the thing back with him after filming ended, Guinness asked a hotel porter to place it "in Miss Kelly's bed." Grace never mentioned finding it, and Guinness forgot about it until, years later, he discovered it in his bed at his English country cottage. How it got there his best efforts could not determine.

More years elapsed, and Grace was in America for a poetry reading tour with the Shakespearean actor Richard Pasco. In Minneapolis she found the tomahawk in her hotel bed and suspected Pasco—who, she reasoned, must know fellow actor Guinness. He didn't, and said so. "That really baffled her," Guinness chuckled when asked about it later. Pasco was in fact the culprit, but he hadn't lied about not knowing Guinness; a mutual friend made the arrangements between Pasco and Guinness, whom Pasco had never met.

Grace's next opportunity came when Guinness was awarded a Lifetime Achievement Oscar in 1980. She made elaborate arrangements with the Beverly Wilshire Hotel staff to put the tomahawk in Guinness's bed while he was attending the ceremonies. Overlooked when invitations to the Governor's Ball went out, Special Oscar recipient Guinness simply went back to his room when the awards show was over. But the discovery—when he least expected it—put a wonderful cap on a nostalgic evening.

The final exchange, twenty-five years after the first, occurred in Chichester, England, while Grace was there for a poetry reading. She discovered the hatchet in her attaché case.

Grace enjoyed filming *The Swan,* but her total concentration was not on her work. His costar's distraction became obvious to Guinness, who recalled, "Sometimes I saw her waiting on the set, just looking into space, and I asked her, 'Grace, are you feeling all right?' Then she came to, but always with a little start of surprise, as if she had been far away."

She *was* far away—in a reverie about what life would be like for her as the Princess of Monaco. For, shortly after she returned home from Cannes, and all during the filming of *The Swan,* Grace was being courted—by mail, telephone, and envoy—by Prince Rainier. During the evening of the day he met Grace, Rainier conferred with Fr. Francis Tucker, his spiritual adviser and a man intimately concerned about the Prince's marital status. Originally from Wilmington, near Philadelphia, Father Tucker knew Jack Kelly and had more than once considered Grace Kelly, "a lovely young woman from a good Catholic family," as a suitable mate for his "Lord Prince." Told that Miss Kelly had that day visited the palace, Father Tucker hopefully inquired as to Rainier's reaction. "I've met her," the Prince told his priest. "I've met the one." Rainier revealed to *Paris Match* in 1976 that "I made up my mind, one evening during the spring of 1955, to go to the States and ask Grace's father for permission to marry her."

Rainier's wooing of Grace began with a discreet letter to her from Father Tucker. Tucker wrote, "I want to thank you for showing the Prince what an American Catholic girl can be and for the very deep impression this has left on him." Grace was enormously buoyed up by the letter, because she had been much more taken with Rainier than she let on to anyone after the meeting. "I almost knew I was in love with the Prince before we met for the second time," Grace said later. "I don't know how I knew . . . and yet, something . . ." Grace responded to Father Tucker in an equally discreet but encouraging way, and a correspondence began between Grace and Rainier. When the Prince became aware that Grace shared his interest, Father Tucker reported, he was "all aglow," and full of "little exuberances."

The correspondence and telephone communication between Grace and Rainier became more and more intimate, and eventually the Prince broached the possibility that their attraction might lead to marriage. Grace was dumbstruck. Here she was, playing a princess, surrounded and deeply impressed by the trappings of royalty, and a reigning prince was subtly suggesting he might like to make her his bride. It was all too much to believe, and she often put it out of her mind. Still, she just as often found herself lost in daydreams of what it would be like to be a real-life princess.

Grace kept the Prince's interest from everyone, including her family and friends, because she feared that the press might somehow get hold of the story and she did not want to cause the Prince any embarrassment. Thus, when Kelly family friends Edie and Russell Austin visited Monte Carlo, they knew nothing except that Grace and Rainier had met. Still, when they found there were no tickets to a gala at Monte Carlo's Sports Club they wished to attend, Edie suggested to her husband that he telephone the palace, mention that they were friends of Grace Kelly's, and request that the Prince help them get a table. Russell did so, leaving a message with Rainier's secretary.

Several hours later, Father Tucker called the Austins back. The Prince would be happy to reserve a table at the gala for the couple, Tucker told them—and, if it was convenient, he would very much like to have them to tea at the palace the next day. Rainier was eager for news of Grace, a fact Father Tucker discreetly conveyed to them.

The next afternoon's tea was a polite one, at which the Prince listened with rapt attention to news of the Kellys in Philadelphia and turned the conversation to Grace whenever possible. As they said their goodbyes, the Austins—undoubtedly prompted by Father Tucker and encouraged by the Prince's obvious interest in Grace—suggested that he visit them in Margate, New Jersey, if he "happened to be in the United States" in the near future. The Prince thanked them, and said that yes, he did hope to make a trip there soon. As soon as the Austins returned to the United States, Edie excitedly called Mrs. Kelly with the news that Prince Rainier of Monaco was very interested in renewing his acquaintanceship with Grace. "He's a bachelor, you know," Edie told Mrs. Kelly rather unnecessarily, "and he's looking for a bride."

A few weeks later, the Prince told Grace that he would be coming to the United States late in November, and if she didn't know it outright, she sensed that if their reunion were as successful as their first meeting, it could well lead to a proposal. Again Grace fought down her flights of fantasy with doses of hard reality; the chances of such a situation leading to marriage were very remote indeed. Still, she would of course allow the Prince to visit her. She thought to herself, *Que será, será.*

The possibility that the Prince would propose to her seemed less remote to Grace when she read, just before his arrival in the United States, an interview with him published in *Collier's* magazine. Entitled "Where Will the Prince Find His Princess?" the piece by David Schoenbrun detailed Rainier's need to marry and produce an heir in order to keep his country independent of France. It also told of his planned visit to the United States and speculated that he might just be coming to America to find a princess. Rainier denied it, saying, "I am not shopping for a bride." This was indeed true. Rainier already knew who it was he wanted to marry.

The clues were present for all the world in Rainier's description of his "ideal woman": she should be "pretty," "natural and charitable," not "flashy or spoiled." She should be "an intelligent girl, but not an intellectual." It would be beneficial, Rainier went on, if the girl he was to marry were "five to ten years younger" than he: "I would not want some teenager who likes to stay up all night dancing, any more than I would want a stay-at-home who could not keep up with me."

His wife should be able to handle servants (family wealth would thus be a plus) but she should as well be able to cook and manage a household herself: "Servants do not respect you if you are not a competent housekeeper. How can she order dinner, or tell the cook what to make unless she herself knows how to cook?"

That the description might have been tailor-made to fit Grace wasn't lost on her. A further musing of the Prince's touched her, but she could in no way imagine how uncannily his words presaged what the next six weeks of her life would be like: "A bachelor's life is lonely, empty, and particularly so for a prince. I cannot behave like any ordinary bachelor. I have no private life. I cannot go out without being followed, watched and gossiped about. Every time I am seen with a girl someone starts a rumor about a love affair. Why, only recently I met your lovely American actress, Miss Grace Kelly, a charming girl, and the next day I read in the press that I was going to marry her. That sort of thing embarrasses both me and the girl. It is very difficult to be natural and at ease with a girl when both of you are secretly wondering whether something will come of it, and when the whole world is openly speculating about marriage.

"You see, this is perhaps my greatest difficulty, knowing a girl long enough and intimately enough to find out if we are really soul mates as well as lovers . . . if *you* met a pretty girl at a party and you were attracted to her and she to you, well, you could say: 'What are you doing next Saturday evening?' You could ask her to go to a movie, or a dance, or perhaps a dinner at some little restaurant . . . I cannot do that. I have neither the free time nor the privacy."

In America, Rainier would have considerably more of both than in his day-to-day life in Monaco, and, he hoped, he could conduct his courtship of Miss Kelly in privacy. Grace had given him every encouragement short of a "yes," and Rainier arrived in America with the expectation of leaving as a betrothed man. He was accompanied by Father Tucker, the man most intimately involved in the Prince's quest for a wife, and his personal physician, Dr. Robert Donat, whose job it would be to make sure that the Prince's future bride could bear him children. He intended to woo and win Grace Kelly's hand within a few weeks, then return to governing Monaco. It was an extraordinary way to go about things, to be sure, but as Rainier had said, "I cannot behave like any ordinary bachelor."

To an extent even Rainier could not have imagined, Grace's personal, professional, and family situations were, in many ways, just as extraordinary as his. Moreover, they had all come together, in this December of 1955, to make her as eager and ready for marriage as he was.

3

Princess Grace

Of course I consider marriage. But I've considered my career longer. If I were to quit now to get married—and I'd have to quit because marriage is a full-time job to my way of thinking—then I'm afraid that all the rest of my life I'd be fretting about what a great actress I might have been.

Grace Kelly, March 1955

Chapter Eleven

Prince Rainier had hoped to see Grace immediately upon his arrival in the United States with a visit to the set of *The Swan* (with *Look* magazine photographers dutifully in tow). When this proved impossible, plans were made for the Prince and Grace to be reunited at the Kelly home on Christmas day; the film was running behind schedule and would not be completed until a few days before Christmas.

By this time Grace was aware of the seriousness of Rainier's intentions; barring total disaster in Philadelphia, the Prince was going to ask for her hand in marriage. She wasn't certain what her response would be, but she knew that she could very well say yes. She found the prospect thrilling—and frightening. The latter so much so that she almost declined to meet the Prince again. Until the last moment she wasn't sure she'd have the courage to go through with it. "At one point," she admitted years later, "I almost didn't go home for Christmas, even though the Prince was to visit us. I made up my mind I wouldn't go. And then—I can't remember how it happened—I just went and bought a plane ticket anyway."

The Prince was scheduled to arrive at Henry Avenue on Christmas day night, and up to the last minute Grace was racked by misgivings. "Christmas morning," she said, "I was sorry I'd gone home. I wished I'd remained in California." As the Prince's appearance drew near, Grace was rattled with anxiety. She phoned her sister Peggy and implored her to "be over here with me."

According to Peggy, the rest of Grace's family were not at all nervous about meeting the Prince. "We knew almost nothing about him. It wasn't like he was well known in the United States; we weren't reading about him in the papers every other day. So it wasn't like Prince Charles coming to your house for dinner."

When the Prince, Father Tucker, and Dr. Donat arrived at the Kellys' at 7 P.M., introductions were made all around, and Peggy later said she noticed "sparks flying" between her sister and Rainier. The evening was convivial; Mrs. Kelly found the Prince more charming than she'd imagined him, and Father Tucker's wit kept all in high spirits. Soon, as they had done in the palace gardens, Grace and Rainier became enthralled with each other and conversed together to the exclusion of the others. Peggy, sensing that the couple would be more comfortable away from her parents, suggested that "the young people" go back to her house and continue with the party. They did, and Jack Kelly drove Father Tucker to a local rectory, where he spent the night.

Grace, Rainier, and Dr. Donat played cards with Peggy and her husband until 3 A.M. "Grace and Rainier seemed very relaxed and comfortable with each other," Peggy recalls. Afterward they returned to the Kelly house, and Mrs. Kelly offered the Prince and Dr. Donat the guest rooms. They happily accepted and donned Kell's too-large pajamas for the night. As Grace prepared for bed, she went to her mother's room. A "radiance" Mrs. Kelly had noticed in her daughter earlier was even more evident now, and—bursting with curiosity—she asked Grace what she thought of the Prince. "She hesitated," Mrs. Kelly later wrote, "as if she didn't want to reveal the full extent of what was going on inside her. 'Well, I think he's most attractive in every way.' Then she added, 'Yes, I think he's very nice.' "

Fantasies aside, Grace found herself startlingly attracted to Rainier. He was a good-looking, sturdily built man, with the kind of Continental charm Grace had found so alluring in Oleg Cassini and Jean-Pierre Aumont. Although he was one of Grace's youngest suitors, he was—as the ruler of a country —the ultimate father figure. The strong chemistry between them at their half-hour meeting in Monaco, which had led Grace to sense that she fell in love with him that day, was cemented that first night in Philadelphia, and they both knew immediately that everything was going to work out between them. The day after Christmas, Lizanne recalls, they visited the LeVines' apartment for dinner: "Rainier was helping with the dishes and we were having a good time. Toward the end of the evening, Rainier was talking to Don, and Grace said to me, 'How do you like him?' I had just met him, because I wasn't there Christmas day; I was in Pittsburgh with Don's family. Grace said to me, 'I'm going to get married—we're getting engaged.' Well, I just about fell off the couch. I said, 'Oh my God, Grace—you don't even *know* this guy!' "

But Grace was certain. "Everything was perfect," she explained later. "When I was with him, I was happy wherever we were, and I was happy with whatever we were doing. It was a kind of happiness . . . well, it wouldn't have mattered where we were or what we were doing, but I'd have been happy being there and doing it . . . I just can't explain it."

In Philadelphia, Grace and the Prince spent every possible moment together: they dined, strolled, visited Grace's friends, talked about themselves, opened up their hearts and souls to each other. On the 27th, Rainier and Dr. Donat accompanied Grace to Manhattan, where she was taking singing lessons to prepare for her next film, *High Society,* a musical version of *The Philadelphia Story.* In New York, Grace and the Prince did the town, and mention of their dates was made in the newspapers, but the significance of those dates could not have occurred to the reporters. On the 29th, Grace telephoned her mother to tell her what she had already told Lizanne—that she and the Prince were very much in love and wanted to get married. Mrs. Kelly was ecstatic. "Imagine," she told a reporter later, "here I am a bricklayer's wife, and my daughter's marrying a prince!"

Years later Peggy was quoted to the effect that her sister's marriage to Prince Rainier was an "arranged" one. To most people—especially in America—this suggests a marriage of convenience, one based upon considerations other than passionate love. Certainly the second meeting of Grace and Rainier had been "arranged," but it couldn't have come about any other way. And while the extraordinary behind-the-scenes events that followed Grace's "Yes" to Rainier might understandably be construed as part of an arrangement, they were dictated by the Prince's position and should not suggest a lack of romance. There can be no doubt that Grace Kelly and Prince Rainier were dizzily infatuated with each other within hours of their reunion.

Still, Lizanne says, "I don't think Grace was in love. She didn't have time to *really* be in love. She had been more in love with other people than she was with Rainier when she first met him. But there was a great attraction between them. Other than that, I don't know why she decided to marry him so quickly."

A family friend, Bill Hegner, once said, "I think they bought each other out of a catalogue." Although it's highly cynical, Hegner's notion isn't that farfetched in one respect: it was necessary for Rainier to marry not only someone he loved but someone *suitable.* Had Grace become known to him through a dating service, she would have won the highest "match rating" possible. She was young, she was beautiful, she had been brought up with wealth, she was Catholic, she had a reputation, outside Hollywood at least, for refinement and chastity. And, equally important, she was a world-renowned celebrity, a glamorous film star whose presence as the Princess of Monaco would undoubtedly help increase its tourist trade, the major contributor to the country's treasury.

Had the marriage of Grace and Rainier been purely a convenience of state, it would have been ideal. That the two were also mad about each other made things well-nigh perfect. The Prince found himself happily surprised, in fact, by how comfortable he felt with Grace. "As the Prince of Monaco," he said not long after the wedding, "I quickly learned that many of those around me were trying to use me for their own purposes. I trusted nobody. I knew from the start that I could trust the Princess. It was one of the reasons that I felt so surely that she was the person for me. With her, I felt complete. I could relax and be myself."

Before the engagement of Grace and Rainier could be announced, however, there were several important hurdles to be cleared. Rainier's taking a wife was a matter of state, and as such it carried with it certain unavoidable necessities. The first of these was medical assurance that Grace Kelly was physically able to bear an heir to the Monegasque throne. "I must get married and raise a family," Rainier had told *Collier's*. "I told my people recently that I am keenly sensitive to the political implications of my bachelorhood." Even had Rainier been more cavalier about this very singular example of noblesse oblige, his advisers could not be. The survival of Monegasque life as they knew it hung in the balance; the fertility of a future princess would have to be all but guaranteed—or Rainier would not be allowed to marry her.

This had been made painfully apparent to Rainier in 1953. He had been in love with Gisele Pascal; she had, for several years, lived in his Beaulieu villa where he spent most of his time with her. So entrenched was she in Rainier's life that the citizens of Monaco thought of Gisele as their "uncrowned princess." After six years of romance, Rainier wanted to marry Gisele, and the thought of becoming the Princess of Monaco thrilled her. She refused even to discuss the romance, lest she say something wrong: "I am living in a dream and nothing must spoil it."

Unfortunately for Gisele, something did. When Rainier told his advisers that he planned to marry her, they reminded him that it would be necessary for her to take a fertility test. Instead, Gisele presented a letter from her Paris doctors certifying that she could conceive. This was not sufficient for the Monegasque officials, who insisted that the Prince's own doctor perform the test. When the first test came back negative, the physician took another, then a third. All indicated that

Gisele was infertile. Rainier was told that he would not be allowed to marry her.

Although he seriously considered it, abdication for the woman he loved was not a solution for Rainier, since there was no one to assume the throne; such an action would have the same effect as a childless marriage: Monaco's seven-century Grimaldi rule would end and the country would become a French protectorate. Bitterly Rainier broke off his relationship with Gisele. The Prince told Francis Tucker, "Father, if you ever hear that my subjects think I do not love them, tell them what I have done today." (Gisele later married and had a child, and one can only imagine the Prince's reaction to the news.)

Now Rainier was faced with the same dilemma, and it was as distasteful to him as it had been several years before. He knew it must be done, and by his own doctor. (Hence Dr. Donat's otherwise inexplicable presence in America; the first reason proffered was that the Prince had come to have a checkup at Johns Hopkins University Hospital and wanted his own doctor along; later it was said that Rainier had brought Donat here to enroll in the school. Neither explanation makes any sense; Rainier didn't have to travel three thousand miles for a medical checkup, and neither would the Prince of Monaco's private physician have any compelling reason to attend an American university. But it was necessary to explain Donat's presence thus, in order to avoid speculation about the *real* reason. Rainier sensed, correctly, that Americans would neither understand nor sympathize with the need for a fertility test of Grace Kelly before she could marry him.)

Rainier was loath to broach the subject to Grace. "Her family is very religious, very conservative," the Prince told one of his advisers. "I don't dare even suggest it to her!"

But it simply had to be done. Father Tucker, who had already spent hours questioning Grace about her religious beliefs, informed her of the need for the test. Faced with the fact that without a test there was no possibility of marriage, Grace agreed.

The test—kept secret from Grace's family—was performed at a private sanitarium on the outskirts of Philadelphia, because its director was a man Grace knew and trusted. She was terribly anxious about undergoing the examination—not only because so much depended on it, but because Prince Rainier was under the impression that she was a virgin.

During this emotionally charged period, Grace fell back on her intimacy with Don Richardson, and she telephoned him every day, confiding her innermost thoughts. He vividly recalls her telling him about the fertility test. "They had her in stirrups, taking all kinds of tests to make sure that she could produce an heir for Monaco. She was frantic about the fact that the test would reveal she wasn't a virgin, because the Prince thought she was. She told me she explained to the doctors that her hymen had been broken when she was playing hockey in high school."

Could Prince Rainier, a sophisticated man, have actually believed that Grace, a well-traveled movie actress of twenty-six, was a virgin? "You have to remember that this was 1955," Richardson says, "when twenty-six-year-old virgins were a lot more common than they are today. And that was Grace's image. People believed she was a nun. Everything about her spoke of virginity and pureness; the Prince knew she came from a 'good Catholic family.' When you looked into the face of Grace Kelly, you couldn't believe she was anything but unblemished, untarnished, and virginal. It's entirely possible that the Prince, worldly as he was, believed she was a virgin."

Grace passed the test; she and Rainier, the doctors told him, could have as many children as they wanted. That obstacle cleared, there was next the question of a dowry, and it presented a serious problem, one that almost prevented the marriage—because her father balked. "Grace told me," Richardson says, "that her father kept storming out of meetings with the Prince's lawyers in a rage. She'd say, 'Daddy's being impossible!' These heavy negotiations went on for days, but he finally came through and paid the dowry. The last figure Grace mentioned to me was two million dollars."

Americans would have understood the necessity of the dowry even less than that of the fertility test, and first Mrs. Kelly, then Grace, denied that there had been one. Jack Kelly's initial refusal was rooted in his deep-seated American aversion to such an alien tradition—and his fear that Rainier was marrying Grace because he needed money. Again it was Father Tucker whose gentle, patient explanation of the need for a dowry brought Jack Kelly around. In long conferences with the priest, Kelly bellowed, "I don't want any damn broken-down prince who's head of a country over there that nobody ever knew anything about to marry my daughter!"

Father Tucker explained that the presentation of a dowry was a time-honored European tradition, especially among royalty. (Rainier's great-grandfather, Prince Albert, in fact, had received six million dollars in 1889 from his second wife, American Alice Heine, the widow of the Duke of Richelieu.) If Rainier were just after money, Tucker went on, he could have married any number of women much wealthier than Grace. The Prince loved his daughter, Tucker told Jack Kelly, so he needn't worry on that score. And the Prince was in fact a man of considerable wealth.

Then why, Jack Kelly demanded to know, did he need a dowry? Father Tucker explained that a downturn in tourism and gambling in the Monte Carlo casinos had left Rainier and his country cash-poor. But there was fabulous wealth in the real estate and the property that made up Monaco, not least of which was the Prince's 220-room palace. When Rainier's "real" wealth—in the millions—was proven to Jack Kelly, the astute businessman realized that the Prince's financial troubles at the moment were no more than a cash-flow problem. Unlike any other property holder, however, the sovereign of a country could not very well mortgage his holdings to raise money.

Still, why would Jack Kelly agree to pay a virtual stranger such a large sum of money to marry his daughter? The reasons are complex, having more to do with Kelly's own personality than with Father Tucker's assurances that this was *what was done* in Rainier's social strata. To be sure, Kelly was under a great deal of pressure from his family not to throw any monkey wrenches into the exhilarating events that were unfolding on Henry Avenue. But he was also, despite his innate suspicion of the situation, deeply pleased by the prospect of his daughter becoming a princess. Mrs. Kelly's exclamation about the daughter of a bricklayer marrying a prince sums up not only her own attitude but her husband's as well. The Kellys' most compelling drive was to be accepted in Philadelphia society, but Main Liners had for years continually snubbed them, considering the Kellys and their wealth hopelessly *nouveau*.

How better could Jack Kelly show Philadelphia society than to be the father-in-law of a prince who was a member of Europe's oldest ruling family? As Don Richardson puts it, "The Kellys were social climbers. Their plan originally was to get Grace married into Philadelphia society. Papa was very angry that he never made it into the social register, even though he'd made a lot of money."

Oleg Cassini agrees with this assessment. "For Grace to have married a matinee idol or a clothes designer," he says, "would have done no good at all" in advancing the family's social position. "Rainier brought the highest prestige that was religious as well as social and financial."

Jack Kelly, convinced of the Prince's bona fide position as a European monarch and a man of impressive lineage and old wealth, saw his daughter's marriage as his family's ultimate chance for the kind of status he had devoted his life to achieving. That money needed to be paid for the privilege was merely a business matter, a small detail in what was a priceless opportunity for a man obsessed with his family's place in the eyes of the world.

One needs to consider too Jack Kelly's well-developed ego. The position he himself would occupy after his daughter's marriage to Prince Rainier was not lost on him. While having a princess as a daughter didn't exactly make him a king, it would make him the closest thing to one America would ever have.* Kelly agreed to pay the dowry.

The announcement of the betrothal of Grace Patricia Kelly of Philadelphia and His Serene Highness Prince Rainier III of Monaco was made simultaneously on both sides of the Atlantic. In Philadelphia, Rainier got his first taste of the American brand of journalism at a press conference in the Kelly manse. Hard-bitten reporters from New York and Philadelphia weren't about to treat a foreigner from a country most of them had never heard of with any more respect than they would treat anyone else. Standing on the piano, pushing furniture aside, and jostling for position so violently that the pregnant Lizanne had to flee upstairs for safety, they fired questions and impudent orders in a dizzying staccato: "Hey, Prince, give her a kiss!" "Was it love at first sight, Prince?" "Hold it, Rainier . . . smile! . . . That's fine, Prince."

Rainier became angry; at one point he growled to Father Tucker, "After all, *I* don't belong to MGM." Mrs. Kelly attempted to smooth things over by exhorting the newsmen, "Now, not too familiar with the Prince . . ." The journalists then turned their attention to Grace. "Show us your engagement ring, Gracie!" "Will you give up your career?" "Was this an arranged marriage?" "How many children will you have?"

Grace blushed and squirmed, and Mrs. Kelly once again helped out by answering the last question for her daughter. "I hope they'll have many children," she burbled. "I like a big family."

When the conference ended, the furor really began. The media, both in America and Europe, knew instinctively that this very well could be the wedding of the century. The story had it all: Hollywood glamour and royal mystique, fairy-tale

---

* Columnist Earl Wilson referred to Grace's parents as "King John" and "Queen Margaret" in his wedding dispatches from Monaco.

romance, the drama of surprise, the conflict of differing cultures, a beautiful bride, and a dashing, handsome groom.

Grace and Rainier occupied the front pages of the world's newspapers for weeks as reporters scrambled for angles, controversies, and scoops. A few days were devoted to speculation about where the nuptials would be held. The New York *Daily News* began its dispatch on the issue as if it were a major matter of state: "An international fog of conflicting reports yesterday surrounded the question of when and where Grace Kelly will marry Prince Rainier of Monaco . . . In Philadelphia, Miss Kelly's mother said the announcement her daughter would wed the charming prince in Monaco 'must be a misunderstanding.' And the prince's personal chaplain said Rainier wants a quiet wedding in Philadelphia."

Rainier at first agreed to hold the wedding in Philadelphia "in deference to his bride, her family, and the American people." But once again, matters of state intervened when the Monegasques let out a collective shriek of disapproval; their prince's wedding must be held there. And—no small matter—Monaco's waning tourist trade and dwindling income would be helped tremendously by the presence of thousands of guests, reporters, and curiosity seekers at the wedding. Further, the focus of world attention on the beautiful little country during the nuptials would entice thousands of people to visit Monaco for years to come.

If most of the world was surprised by the unexpected announcement from Philadelphia, Grace's acquaintances, indeed the entire Hollywood community, were shocked. Most of her friends knew only that she had met the Prince in Monaco the previous year as a publicity stunt, and she had told none but her closest intimates that he was even coming to visit her. (Her desire to avoid publicity and possible embarrassment caused her to keep the Prince's visit secret from as close an associate as Rupert Allan; this led to the erroneous perception that Grace was unaware of the Prince's impending visit until after she arrived home for Christmas.)

Hedda Hopper wrote in her syndicated column, "Her

friends are completely baffled; half of them don't believe she and the Prince will ever reach the altar." The Hollywood community couldn't understand why Grace, at the pinnacle of her career, would give everything up to marry a man she barely knew and "live in a glorified gambling casino." Some suspected an elaborate publicity ploy arranged with the help of MGM. But the studio, informed by Grace of her intentions before the official announcement, was as dumbstruck as everyone else. James Stewart recalls, "Grace told Dore Schary, 'Mr. Schary, I'm going to get married.' And Schary said, 'I think that's wonderful, Grace—we'll have a big reception for you upstairs here at the studio.' And Grace said, 'You don't quite understand, Mr. Schary . . .'"

MGM's executives reacted to the news with mixed emotions. Although Grace was noncommittal on the subject, they sensed that after she completed *High Society* she would not make any more films. To lose a star of Grace's stature was not pleasant, but at the same time the publicity value of her wedding was incalculable, and the studio did have two films of hers yet to release—in one of which she played a princess. No wonder many in Hollywood suspected that in some shadowy way MGM was behind all this. On the contrary, Grace had once again maddened her studio bosses by doing exactly what she wanted to do without any regard for her legal obligations to MGM.

The suddenness of Grace and Rainier's decision to marry is much easier to fathom from the Prince's standpoint than from Grace's. For him it was necessary that a decision be made quickly. Rainier couldn't spend months in the United States courting Grace; he had a country to attend to. She couldn't move into the palace to make sure she was compatible with Rainier; she had a movie to make. "She would never have done anything like live with Rainier before they got married—under any circumstances," says Judy Kanter Quine. "Things like that weren't done in those days, and certainly wouldn't have been by Grace."

But why did Grace agree to marry a man she barely knew? That she wanted to be married and have children is clear; the facets of her personality that pushed her to forge a life as a career woman were embattled over another tenet that had been bred into her since girlhood: a woman's greatest achievement is being a wife and mother. Every new artistic triumph was balanced by the knowledge that in this very simple way she was a failure, and this tormented her. Donald Sinden recalled Grace's meeting his two-and-a-half-year-old son Jeremy: "She looked at him with absolute *envy.*"

When Grace met Prince Rainier, she was ready and eager to make a drastic change in her life. She was deeply disappointed in Hollywood, wounded by the salacious publicity her romantic liaisons had engendered, and afraid that she had achieved all she could professionally, that her career could do nothing but wane. While she was making *High Society,* Gore Vidal asked Grace at a luncheon at composer Jule Styne's house, "Why on earth would you want to leave Hollywood now that you've finally made it to the top?" Her reply is as revealing as it was droll. "She answered," Vidal recalls, "by asking me if I knew what makeup call is. I said, 'Of course.' And she said, 'Well, I'll tell you one of the reasons. When I first came to Hollywood five years ago, my makeup call was at eight in the morning. On this movie it's been put back to seven-thirty. Every day I see Joan Crawford, who's been in makeup since five, and Loretta Young, who's been there since four in the morning. I'll be goddamned if I'm going to stay in a business where I have to get up earlier and earlier and it takes longer and longer for me to get in front of a camera.'"

Vidal says, "I think she saw that her career would just be more of the same and would begin to slide. There are always new girls coming up. Women's careers are very short in this town, and always have been, unless you want to graduate to doing Bette Davis horror roles. She got out at the top."

Don Richardson, too, thinks that Grace's doubts about her career influenced her decision to marry the Prince. "Grace had terrors about where she would go from the point she was at. She knew that her abilities were minimal. I don't think she had great confidence about being able to go the next step. What was she going to become? A character actress? She definitely wasn't going to become a great theater star. I think inside she knew that her career was mostly a lot of razzmatazz and hype, and it had nowhere to go."

On a deeper level, however, Grace in late 1955 was a restless, dissatisfied, and unhappy woman. Her Catholic upbringing left her guilty about her sexual dalliances and angry at her family for continually objecting to her attempts to legitimize herself in their eyes through marriage. In 1957 she said, "If I'd met the Prince two or three years earlier, perhaps I wouldn't have married him—at least, not so soon. But we came together at the right time . . . It couldn't have been any different. It had to be that way. It seemed right, and it felt right, and that was the way I wanted it. I knew that I was going to do it, even if there was a chance that I was making a mistake. I would find out later. Right then and there, nothing mattered to me except our staying together."

Oleg Cassini discussed her upcoming marriage with Grace: "She talked to me about Prince Rainier, and about how marrying him was the solution to her life. By marrying him she was satisfying a large group of people who had power over her—her family, church authorities . . . Grace sacrificed a lot for the establishment."

A friend added another element: "The fact is, she had no turf. Her turf wasn't Philadelphia, it wasn't New York, and Hollywood was just borrowed turf. Monaco would be *her* turf . . . In Philadelphia she was a nobody. In Hollywood she became somebody. In Monaco, she would *really* be somebody."

Don Richardson was upset when Grace told him she was going to marry Prince Rainier. "I raised hell with her—I said, 'Don't do that. Jesus, don't do that.' I told her it was just awful—because I knew why she was doing it. Her whole life revolved around pleasing that father of hers. The thing she wanted most in the world was to win his approval, to make him think highly of her. And, despite everything she had accomplished, she still hadn't been able to achieve that. He was much more impressed with athletics—his son's rowing medals were far more important to him than Grace's acting awards.

"When I went to the Kelly house that famous weekend, Grace took me upstairs and showed me a walk-in closet in which were kept all the rowing medals of the father and brother, pictures of the mother as a model, certificates that Papa had gotten for making donations, that kind of thing. There was absolutely nothing relating to Grace in that closet —not even a snapshot of her—and she had been on the covers of magazines by then."

All of this left Richardson with a definite conclusion about Grace's motivations. "As far as I'm concerned, the real reason that she married the Prince was to make a bigger splash than a pair of oars."

Chapter Twelve

Grace learned most of the history of Monaco, and of the man she was about to marry, in the same way her fellow Americans did—through newspaper accounts published after the sunburst of publicity that surrounded the announcement of her engagement. Few Americans knew much about Monaco; Mrs. Kelly thought at first that Rainier was the Prince of Morocco. Peggy recalls correcting her. "It's *Monaco,* Mother—you know, where Monte Carlo is." Mrs. Kelly remained confused. "I've been to Monte Carlo," she mused, "but never to Monaco."

The Morocco misconception was widespread. On the set of *High Society,* a co-worker said to her, "Really, Grace, I can't picture you living with all those camels." Common too was Mrs. Kelly's perception of Monte Carlo as somehow its own entity, not a part of anything else—except possibly France, a notion guaranteed to give a Monegasque apoplexy. For Monaco, although the smallest country in the world, was one rich with history, tradition—and national pride bordering on chauvinism.

Located on the Mediterranean coast of France, Monaco is situated approximately 700 kilometers (435 miles) south-southeast of Paris, ten miles east of Nice and a few miles west of the Italian border. Less than one mile square, the country's 28,000 residents make it the most densely populated nation in the world. It consists of four districts: the capital, Monaco-Ville, or old Monaco, which sits atop Le Rocher (the Rock), a towering promontory jutting out into the sea on top of which sits Rainier's enormous pink palace;

La Condamine, the port area; Fontvieille, a light industrial and residential area; and Monte Carlo, part of a smaller promontory opposite Le Rocher, the hub of the country and home of the gambling casino, some of Europe's most glamorous hotels, the Opera House, and the Sporting Club. It is here that the world's wealthiest people had come to play for almost a century by 1956.

What is now Monaco was originally inhabited by the Phoenicians, came under Roman control for a time, then was Christianized around A.D. 100. It was ruled for centuries by a succession of French and Italian princes, who lived in a fortress atop Le Rocher. In 1297 the country came under Grimaldi family control when Genoese Francesco Grimaldi, disguised along with several of his men as a Franciscan monk, penetrated the fortress, overwhelmed the guards, and took control. The Italian Grimaldis, through centuries of intermarriage, became predominantly French, as did Monaco: its language, its political and cultural ties, its *esprit* today owe far more to France than to Italy.

The power and wealth of the Grimaldi princes grew with their talent for political intrigue, judicious marriage and, when necessary, skulduggery and murder. By the eighteenth century, Monaco's land holdings included a coastal area comprising Menton and Roquebrune. The princely family lived in a lavish palace atop the Rock, owned several elaborate estates in France, and held dozens of aristocratic titles, most won through marriage. The French Revolution of 1789, however, stripped the Grimaldi family of all its financial holdings; they were left only a plundered palace and a decimated country.

Prince Charles III, Rainier's great-great-grandfather, who reigned until 1889, both oversaw Monaco's greatest defeat and initiated its development into one of the world's richest countries. Charles, faced in 1861 with the threat of an Italian takeover, acceded to France's demand for the return of Menton and Roquebrune in exchange for French protection of Monaco's sovereignty. Charles now reigned over a secure country, but one even tinier than before, and very nearly bankrupt. Europeans spoke derisively of the minuscule "nation" and its prince's "delusions of grandeur." But it was just those delusions that would soon make Monaco excessively more important than its geographic area would ever suggest.

Charles, now nearly blind, envisioned the course he needed to steer to bring prosperity to Monaco: wealthy Europeans must be lured into spending their money within its borders. There were plenty of fashionable vacation spots along the Mediterranean; that would not be enough. What Monaco needed to provide, Charles realized, was a gaming center—a place where the titled, the wealthy, and the bored could gamble. Casino gaming was illegal in both France and Italy; where it was permitted, in Belgium and Germany, the weather was cold and the environs unfashionable. Monaco's sunny, scenic location would lure the world's "beautiful people" as nowhere else could.

Charles created a casino corporation charged with establishing Monaco as the gaming capital of Europe. In this era of Queen Victoria's reign, however, the appearance of a more suitable enterprise was necessary, and thus the corporation was christened the *Société des Bains de Mer* (Society of Sea Bathing [SBM]). Now, the Prince of Wales, the Emperor of Austria, various grand dukes, and other worthies could come to Monaco under the guise of physical rejuvenation. In fact, sea bathing was one of the few things one *couldn't* do in Monaco—its beaches, covered with pebbles rather than sand, were inhospitable to ocean frolicking.

His casino corporation in place, Charles looked forward to instantaneous new wealth for Monaco, but it didn't come. For eight years, under a succession of entrepreneurs, the corporation foundered, unable to change the disdain in which the aristocracy held Monaco. In 1863 Charles brought in François Blanc, who had had great success with casinos in Homburg and Baden. By the turn of the century, under Blanc's and then his son's direction, Monte Carlo had become the glittery play spot Charles had envisioned. The casino's enormous yearly income was put back into Monte Carlo to make it one of Europe's most spectacular showplaces. The casino building itself was a breathtaking example of *belle époque* architecture, ornate and palatial. Within its walls was built a glorious opera house, designed by Garnier, the architect of the Paris Opera, and it opened with a gala featuring Sarah Bernhardt.

Monte Carlo's two hotels, both within feet of the casino, became the talk of Europe with their grandiose splendor. The casino's standards were high enough to please the haughtiest aristocrat; Britain's foreign secretary was denied admittance because of improper dress. It was all designed, of course, to make Monte Carlo *the* place for Europe's wealthiest to holiday, and it worked. By the early 1900s the casino was making fifty million francs a year, employed a sixth of Monaco's citizenry, and became the principality's banker—and its mainstay, turning over 73 percent of its receipts to the government. So wealthy was Monaco by the 1880s, in fact, that Charles excused his subjects from paying income taxes—a privilege still enjoyed by the Monegasques.

Prince Charles was succeeded in 1889 by his son, Prince Albert I. Albert ruled for thirty years and distinguished himself and his country in ways quite unlike his father had. Looked upon as a playground and perceived as little more than Monte Carlo, Monaco was brought a degree of distinction both by Albert's remarkable war record in the French Navy and by his establishment of the Institute of Human Paleontology in Paris and the Oceanographic Institute in Monaco. The Oceanographic Institute was unparalleled in its facilities for marine research and became world-renowned for scientific excellence. The International Hydrographic Bureau later chose Monaco as the site for its headquarters "in recognition of the luster of the great oceanographic works of this prince."

World War I ravaged many of the great families of Europe, but it had little economic effect on Monaco. The principality remained neutral, but Monegasques assisted the Allies by fighting in the French Army and working in hospitals and convalescent centers. Prince Albert, now a pacifist, spent most of the war in the harbor aboard his yacht. To him, the war's only benefit was that it brought closer political ties between France and Monaco. A 1918 treaty between the two countries, superseding that of 1861, guaranteed France's protection of Monaco's sovereignty in return for Monaco's deportment "in perfect conformity with the political, military, naval and economic interests of France."

The treaty guaranteed Monaco military assistance and allowed France, with the Prince's approval, to draft Monegasques into its own army in times of emergency. Another provision called for the absorption of Monaco into France (and thus the end of Monaco's status as a sovereign nation) if a Monegasque prince should have no heir—a clause prompted by France's fear that the German branch of the Grimaldi family (created by the marriage of Charles III's sister Florestine to the Duke of Urach-Württemburg) would win control of Monaco and create a potential strategic advantage for Germany on the coast of France during any future conflict between the two countries. With Albert's son Louis II the crown prince, the provision was of little immediate import; but it greatly affects public and private decisions in Monaco to this day.

Louis II took over the helm of state in Monaco at his father's death in 1922. In 1897 Louis had married Juliette Louvet, the daughter of a washerwoman, and she bore him a daughter, Charlotte. Prince Albert considered Juliette unsuitable as the consort of Monaco's crown prince and refused for nearly twenty-five years to recognize the marriage—or Charlotte—as legitimate. As he neared death, however, he realized that Charlotte, his only grandchild, must be declared Prince Louis's heir, lest the Grimaldi succession be interrupted.* A year after her father's ascension to the throne, Charlotte, married to a French nobleman, Comte Pierre de Polignac,

---

* Contrary to general belief, a Monegasque prince's heir need not be male.

gave birth to a son, Rainier III, and further assured continued Grimaldi control of Monaco.

Prince Louis's reign was as undistinguished as his father's had been remarkable. Neither a visionary nor a statesman, he was content with the status quo, which served him well in the first two decades of his reign. But unlike World War I, World War II had a devastating impact on Monaco's economy. So far-reaching and debilitating were the war's effects that at its conclusion in 1945, few people remained who could indulge themselves in Monaco's effulgence. By the late 1940s the casino was operating at a loss, there was little money for Monaco's people or its prince, and the country was physically and spiritually run-down. The palace, long neglected by Prince Louis, who lived in Paris much of the time, was in serious disrepair. A symbol of Monaco, its dilapidated condition was a sorry symbol of the principality's declining fortunes.

Neither Prince Louis nor most Monegasques looked favorably upon the succession of Princess Charlotte to the throne; a male monarch was preferred to a female. Beyond that, Charlotte was not well thought of among her people. She had waged boisterous public battles for several years with Pierre and divorced him in 1929. This, in a Catholic country, was anathema. She had expressed pro-Mussolini sentiments during the war, an ill-advised action in Monaco. Pressured from several quarters to renounce her claim to the throne, she reluctantly did so in 1944. On June 2 of that year, Louis named his grandson Rainier as Monaco's crown prince.

Rainier's childhood was not a particularly happy or nurturing one. After his parents' divorce in 1929 (when he was six), the child became a pawn in a bitter battle between Pierre and Charlotte. Pierre was awarded custody by a court and sent Rainier to an English preparatory school, Summerfield's, at St. Leonard's-on-Sea. Later he attended a public school, Stowe, in Buckinghamshire. Fearful at one point that Charlotte would take the boy out of the school, Pierre spirited him away and was charged with kidnapping. Prince Louis then obtained a court order to keep Pierre from removing Rainier from school.

Life in the English public school deeply upset the boy. Used to royal perquisites, he was not prepared for what happened to him at Stowe. The time-honored, cruel practice of "caning," he said, "shocked" him, as did the need to "fag" for (do the bidding of) the older boys. Worse, the young Prince was the only foreigner among 560 boys, and a Catholic. As such he faced derision and ostracism. Classmates called him "fat little Monaco." He became a loner—so unfavored that even his one fellow Catholic avoided him—and developed a deep-seated shyness and reserve. He learned to internalize his emotions, to put a "brave face" on everything, and to never express fear, insecurity, or vulnerability. Friendships were very difficult for Rainier to develop; intimacy was beyond his capability. He became adept at a solo sport, swimming, and released his aggressions through boxing. And, as do many people unable to express themselves well, be became interested in dramatics. He appeared in amateur theatricals, delighting in all the attendant artifice and (as one of his biographers put it) "gussying himself up."

At fourteen, Rainier transferred to a school in Geneva, where he felt more at home and which he found "wonderful." He was a good student. At seventeen he entered college and in 1944 was graduated from the prestigious academy, École Libre des Sciences Politiques. He returned to Monaco where, just named crown prince, he prepared to apprentice at his grandfather's side. Things did not go well. Independent, and with strong opinions of his own, Rainier was appalled at Louis's refusal to fire an old friend, Monaco's minister of state, Émile Roblot, despite Roblot's support of the German occupational government in France. As an Allied victory over the Germans drew near, and Roblot forbade anti-Nazi demonstrations in Monaco, Rainier pleaded with Louis to disavow Roblot, arguing that his actions could harm Monaco's future after the Allies liberated France. Louis, irresolute, did nothing.

Frustrated and angry, Rainier joined the French Free Forces, informed them of Roblot's activities, and so distinguished himself fighting the Nazis at Alsace that he was awarded the Croix de Guerre and the Bronze Star. Later, he attained the rank of chevalier in the Legion of Honor.

After the war, Rainier went to Berlin to work in the Economic Section of the French military mission, where he rose to colonel. Returned to Monaco in 1947, he found his beloved country in a disastrous state and his grandfather indifferent to its plight. Aware that within a few years the burden of governing—and reviving—Monaco would fall upon him, Rainier adopted a devil-may-care lifestyle. He risked his life with reckless auto racing and snow skiing, stalked a killer boar, and nearly drowned in a stubborn effort to retrieve an arrow from the bottom of the sea.

When Rainier became Monaco's ruler in 1949 at the age of twenty-six, however, he was prepared for the formidable task ahead of him. His country's fortunes had never been at a lower ebb. Worried about the future of the principality, Rainier did everything within his power to revitalize the SBM; he even allowed Greek shipping tycoon Aristotle Onassis to buy up controlling interest in the corporation, a situation that would ultimately vex him. But nothing worked to restore Monte Carlo as a tourist attraction *par excellence.* Nothing, that is, until Rainier decided to get married. A politically savvy man, the Prince was fully aware that a glamorous, popular American movie star as its princess would do much to restore Monaco as a tourist attraction. What he didn't foresee was the extent of the obsessive fascination people the world over would have for what was heralded as "the wedding of the century."

On January 10, an official engagement celebration was held for Grace and Rainier at a "Night in Monte Carlo" gala at New York's Waldorf-Astoria. Grace, looking more beautiful than ever, danced with her prince, posed with him, and nuzzled with him when she thought photographers weren't watching. At one point, as the press gleefully reported, a slight schism developed between the soon-to-be royal couple. The New York *Daily News* contained the following account of the incident: "If Prince Rainier thinks this girl is going to be the type who will sit idly by and let him have his own way, he may have another think coming. He may have had an inkling of things to come the other night when he and Grace attended a party at the Waldorf-Astoria.

"An unidentified woman came up to the Prince, gushing congratulations, and then impulsively planted a kiss on the Prince's right cheek. Moments later, Grace's cool gaze found the red smear of lipstick. 'Wipe that lipstick off your cheek,' she said. It wasn't a request. It was an order. The girl's Jack Kelly's daughter, all right!"

A few minutes later, Grace demanded, "Who was that woman?" Rainier replied that he didn't know. The following day, the woman, Ecuadorian socialite Graciela Levi-Castillo, told the press, "He knows who I am." She explained that she was an old flame of the Prince's and wanted to remind him of that. "This engagement business burns me up," Graciela said. "In six months it'll all be over. It won't last."

"I was upset," said Grace. "And I don't think Rainier liked it either."

By January 17, Grace had returned to Hollywood to film *High Society,* and Rainier began a brief tour of the United States. Grace was excited about her new film; it was a remake of MGM's highly successful 1940 film of Philip Barry's play *The Philadelphia Story,* which had starred Katharine Hepburn (for whom it was written and who starred in it on the New York stage), Cary Grant, and James Stewart. Grace had been fond of the play since she performed its lead role her senior year at the Academy. This version was a musical and contained several new elements, including a different setting and a cheerier story line. The plot, however, remained essentially the same: headstrong socialite Tracy Lord (Grace), divorced from C. K. Dexter-Haven (Bing Crosby), plans to wed hopelessly square George Kittridge (John Lund). Two reporters from *Spy* magazine (Frank Sinatra and Celeste Holm) are sent to cover the society nuptials, and Tracy, unhappy about their presence, sets about trying to confound them. After a flirtation with the male reporter, Tracy comes to realize that she and Dexter-Haven are still in love. Her marriage is to Dexter-Haven instead of to Kittridge.

No sooner did Grace arrive on the West Coast to begin production than she received a shock: her mother had given a series of revealing interviews to a reporter from Hearst's King Syndicate, published in newspapers all over the country—including the Los Angeles *Herald and Examiner.* "My Daughter Grace Kelly—Her Life and Romances by Mrs. John B. Kelly as told to Richard Gehman" described Grace as a "frail, ethereal child" who—although she had a few awkward years —was being proposed to by dozens of young men by the time she was fifteen. Mrs. Kelly detailed with varying intimacy Grace's relationships with Harper Davis, an unnamed Don Richardson and Gene Lyons, Clark Gable, Bing Crosby, Ray Milland, Oleg Cassini, and Jean-Pierre Aumont. Three segments of the ten-day series were devoted to Prince Rainier's courtship of Grace. It was a remarkable journalistic coup; most of America, and especially Hollywood, read each installment voraciously.

Grace, who learned about the series from a newspaper promo, was angry, hurt, and deeply embarrassed. As Rainier put it, the series "struck Grace a terrible blow. She just didn't understand how her own mother could do something like that." To a woman who had tried so hard to retain a degree of privacy for herself, and who had felt so violated by accounts of her personal life like those in *Confidential,* her mother's action was a bitter betrayal. The fact that, as the articles pointed out each day, Mrs. Kelly's royalties from the series would be donated to her favorite charity did little to soothe Grace's feelings; to her that indicated that her mother was willing to expose her daughter's life to public inspection for the sake of something dear to *her.* In tears Grace told a friend, "I've worked so hard and now my mother's going to destroy everything overnight."

MGM was just as surprised as Grace when the series appeared, and very unhappy that it had had no control over the contents. (Later, when the articles appeared in Europe, the studio convinced editors to remove some of the more "objectionable" material.) Angrily, Grace confronted her mother, who told her that she had spoken to the reporter much less intimately than the articles suggested, and that he filled in material he did not get from her in a way as to suggest that he had. Mrs. Kelly's explanation did little to placate Grace, who during her first two weeks on the set of *High Society* felt great discomfort with the knowledge that everyone from her co-stars to the grips was reading some very private things about her over morning coffee.

Grace's new, exalted position as a princess-to-be may have inspired a little awe among her co-workers, but that was dissipated on the second day of filming when her engagement ring became the object of good-natured ribbing from the crew. Grace asked director Chuck Walters if she could wear her own ring as Tracy Lord. Walters, tongue in cheek, told her he'd have to see it to make sure it was good enough. Next day, Grace brought in an enormous, spectacularly beautiful ring: intertwined diamonds and rubies (to represent Monaco's official colors) set with Grimaldi family heirloom jewels. It was, Celeste Holm recalled, "as big as a skating rink." When, reacting to the oohs and ahs of all who saw it, Grace said, "It is sweet, isn't it?" there were shrieks of laughter from everyone at her absurd understatement. Till the end of filming, Holm said, "Grace was teased about her 'sweet' diamond ring."

High Society called upon Grace to make her singing debut in a duet with Bing Crosby of "True Love," one of the Cole Porter songs in the sound track. The film's co-musical director and conductor, Johnny Green, recalls that "I vehemently opposed Grace singing her own track. I had spent a lot of time in my own projection room listening to any number of samples of Grace's dialogue, the timbre, the quality of her voice and diction, and I listened to her sing informally in my office, and I decided that she was not capable of singing her own track. I was well on my way to picking a voice double for her when I ran head-on into what became a Sherman tank called Grace Kelly. She insisted on singing her own track, and she came on like Refrigerator Perry. This disagreement between Grace and me went all the way to the head of the studio, Dore Schary, and I lost."

Grace had taken singing lessons for months, and she was determined to sing with Bing Crosby; she gave a charming rendition, offering a sweet counterpart to him. "At the end of the song, they sang in *harmony* yet. I made the arrangement, God help me," Green says. "She made a real monkey out of me, because the record not only went Gold, it went Platinum." Grace proudly displayed her Gold Record Award in the palace for years afterward. (Frank Sinatra was never thereafter reminded of Grace's Gold Record without good-naturedly grumbling that she had earned the accolade before he had.)

Early in September, Prince Rainier flew to Los Angeles and rented a posh villa in Bel-Air. For six weeks he and Grace spent evenings together, with Grace frequently barbecuing their dinner. For a time Rainier's father, Prince Pierre, visited as well, to meet Grace for the first time. He was, he professed, "completely charmed" by her.

Rainier and his father visited the movie set one day, and a luncheon was held for them by Dore Schary. "I could tell Grace was panicky," Celeste Holm recalled, because Dore Schary was not famous for his tact and director Charles Walters, as Holm put it, "never finished a sentence without a four-letter word in it." The meal progressed smoothly until Schary asked the Prince how big Monaco was. Rainier replied that it was five square miles, and Schary said, "Jesus, that's not even as big as our back lot."

"The silence that followed was deafening," Holm recalled. "I figured anything was kosher if it drew attention away from that reply, so I immediately stuck my fork into my steak and splattered juice and gravy all over the tablecloth, and exclaimed loudly, 'Dear me, you can't take me any place.'" Holm remembers thinking that after Schary's comment Grace "would never make another picture."

Indeed, the question of whether or not Grace's marriage would end her career arose immediately after the announcement of her engagement. Whenever the question was put to her, Grace referred to her MGM contract, implying that she would have to honor it, like it or not. Even into *High Society* filming, she responded to the oft-repeated query by saying, "My contract has four years to run. I've always been faithful to any agreement I have made."

Grace maintained that stance to placate the studio and buy time in what she feared would turn into a legal battle with MGM, because she was well aware of the Prince's feelings on the subject. Rainier, less compelled to be coy, went public with his decision just a few days after Grace's comment about being "faithful" to her MGM agreement. "I don't want my wife to work," he said somewhat churlishly. Then he added, perhaps to soften things, "She thinks I am right that she should end her film career."

Grace's public statements contradicting her future husband's prompted press reports of "premarital discord." Grace had in fact tried to convince the Prince to allow her at least to fulfill her contract. But it was obviously a losing battle. Pressured finally to comment on the Prince's dictum, Grace said resignedly, "If that's how he wants it, that's the way it will be."

MGM, for all its legal clout, was powerless to keep Grace Kelly making movies. If it insisted she report for her next scheduled film, *Designing Woman,* and she did not, its only recourse would be to sue her—and that would be impolitic from a public relations standpoint. Still, it was in MGM's best interest not to release her from her contract, for several reasons. It was possible that she would voluntarily return to Hollywood, in which case she would have to work for MGM.

Princess Grace at her loveliest, 1972. (BOZZACCHI, GAMMA-LIAISON)

Grace's first pinup, at six months, 1930. (THE BETTMANN ARCHIVE, INC.)

Pretty and self-possessed at eleven, 1940. (COURTESY OF THE ACADEMY OF MOTION PICTURE ARTS AND SCIENCES)

As a flower girl at a cousin's wedding, 1939. (LIFE)

Thirteen-year-old Grace serves as her sister Peggy's maid of honor, August 1944.

June 20, 1947: *(left to right)* Grace, Mr. and Mrs. Kelly, Kell, and Lizanne set off for England, where Kell will avenge his father's exclusion twenty-seven years earlier from the Diamond Sculls competition at Henley. (UPI/BETTMANN NEWSPHOTOS)

The men in young Grace Kelly's life. Harper Davis, Grace's high school sweetheart, at the time of his graduation in 1946. He died of multiple sclerosis in 1952. (COURTESY OF TEMPLE UNIVERSITY)

Fellow American Academy of Dramatic Arts student Mark Miller, with whom Grace shared an intimate involvement for several years. (COURTESY OF THE AMERICAN ACADEMY OF DRAMATIC ARTS)

Grace and her fellow summer stock actor Gene Lyons became "besotted with each other" during the summer of 1951. Miller, Richardson, and Lyons were each unaware of Grace's relationships with the others. (UPI/BETTMANN)

Don Richardson, an instructor at the Academy, became Grace's lover within hours of their meeting. Her parents' reaction to the affair was virulent. (COURTESY OF DON RICHARDSON)

A sultry 1954 pinup reveals the sex appeal behind Grace's girl-next-door image. (COURTESY OF THE ACADEMY OF MOTION PICTURE ARTS AND SCIENCES)

With Gary Cooper in *High Noon,* 1952. Cooper was the first of a series of much older, married leading men pursued—usually with success—by Grace.

Below: A publicity still from *Mogambo* (1953) features Clark Gable, Grace, and Ava Gardner in an appropriate safari pose. (© 1953 LOEW'S INC. REN. METRO-GOLDWYN-MAYER FILM CO.)

A rare public display of affection between Ray Milland and Grace on the set of Alfred Hitchcock's *Dial M for Murder,* 1953. Their clandestine affair nearly destroyed his thirty-two-year marriage. (KOBAL COLLECTION)

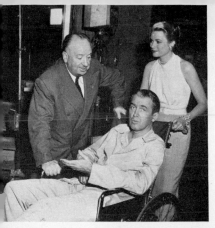

Hitchcock gives Grace and James Stewart some acting pointers on the set of *Rear Window*, 1954.

Alfred Hitchcock and Grace's first publicly acknowledged beau, Oleg Cassini, escort her to the Los Angeles premiere of *Rear Window*, August 16, 1954. (UPI/BETTMANN NEWSPHOTOS)

A deglamorized Grace as the long-suffering wife of an alcoholic actor in *The Country Girl*, 1954.

Marlon Brando, the Best Actor Oscar winner for *On the Waterfront*, congratulates Grace on her award as Best Actress for *The Country Girl*, March 30, 1955. (UPI/BETTMANN NEWSPHOTOS)

With William Holden in *The Bridges at Toko-Ri*, 1955. Their affair caused Grace a good deal of embarrassment and heartache—and led her to a psychiatrist's couch.

Grace's most sexually charged performance, opposite Cary Grant in Hitchcock's *To Catch a Thief*, 1955.

While at Cannes, Grace rekindles a 1952 romance with French matinee idol Jean-Pierre Aumont, and the lovers are captured by a hidden camera during an intimate luncheon.
(PICTORIAL PARADE)

Bing Crosby visits Grace on the set of *The Swan*, 1955. The two had a short-lived affair while Crosby's wife lay dying in 1952, and Crosby proposed marriage during the filming of *The Country Girl* in 1954.

John B. Kelly congratulates Prince Rainier as Grace and her mother look on after they announced the engagement at a tumultuous Philadelphia press conference, January 6, 1956. Rainier had courted her from across the Atlantic during filming of *The Swan*. (UPI/BETTMANN NEWSPHOTOS)

A few weeks later, Grace traveled to Hollywood to make her final motion picture, *High Society*, opposite Bing Crosby and Frank Sinatra. Here, she shares a tender on-screen moment with Sinatra. The two had dated in 1954.

Grace and Rainier are captured in an intimate moment during an engagement party at New York's Waldorf-Astoria hotel, January 10, 1956. (PICTORIAL PARADE)

Grace gazes out to sea as the *Constitution* carries her to her destiny. She later remembered feeling "as if I were sailing off into the unknown. I couldn't help wondering: 'What is going to happen to me?'" (COURTESY OF TEMPLE UNIVERSITY)

The scene in Monaco harbor as thousands of Monegasques, and Prince Rainier on his yacht, prepare to meet the *Constitution*. (MGM)

Grace and Rainier are married in Monaco's Cathedral of St. Nicholas on April 19, 1956. To Rainier's right is his mother, Princess Charlotte; to Grace's left are her parents.

The first official portrait of the Prince and Princess of Monaco, April 19, 1956.

Grace glows as she shows off the happy, chubby six-month-old Princess Caroline, born January 23, 1957. The photo is reminiscent of several of Grace's modeling assignments. (BOULET/GAMMA-LIAISON)

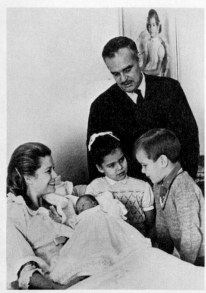

The Grimaldi family welcomes little Princess Stephanie, born February 1, 1965. (GAMMA-LIAISON)

Unescorted, Grace leaves the palace to attend an official function, 1972. (GAMMA)

Grief is etched on the faces of Prince Albert, Prince Rainier, and Princess Caroline as they follow Grace's coffin on foot during a procession through the streets of Monte Carlo. (MELLOUL/SYGMA)

Prince Albert jogs along a street near the campus of Amherst College in Massachusetts, April 1981. He later received a degree in political science. (SICCOLI/GAMMA-LIAISON)

Taking over the duties of First Lady of Monaco with dignity and glamour, Princess Caroline glows as she represents the royal family at the annual Rose Ball in Monte Carlo, March 1985. (APESTEGUY-GAMMA/LIAISON)

Two years after her mother's death, Stephanie also began to come into her own as a woman and a creative artist. (ADAM SCULL/GLOBE PHOTOS)

(To that end, MGM kept her contract in force until 1966 with a quasi-legal six-year "extension.") And, by keeping Grace under contract, the studio could extract concessions from her in return for releasing her from her next picture commitment.

Immediately MGM extracted. Grace would not be required to do *Designing Woman* if the studio could have exclusive film rights to her wedding. An agreement was reached for MGM distribution of the documentary, with a Monegasque crew, underwritten by MGM, filming the nuptials. After a 30 percent distribution cut, the studio would split the profits with the Monegasques (with Grace and Rainier's share going to the Monaco Red Cross).

The Wedding of the Century was released shortly after the nuptials and proved quite successful. But another MGM marketing ploy involving Grace backfired. The studio held back the release of *The Swan* until a week after the wedding to capitalize on the enormous publicity emanating from Monaco. "We thought *The Swan* was a good picture—a *really* good one," Dore Schary ruefully explained. "And we thought it was going to be an absolutely *tremendous* success. Here we're dealing with this fairy tale which turned out to be true. Then the marriage took place, with whole newsreels covering it. *Everybody* went to see the newsreels, then didn't bother going to see our film *The Swan*. They said, 'Yeah, we know about that but here's the *true* story.'" (The suggestion was also made that by the time *The Swan* was released, most people had had their fill of Grace Kelly.)

Four months after the disappointment of *The Swan*, however, *High Society* opened to box office success. Its reviews were mixed; one critic commented that Grace's performance suggested that "Her Serene Highness . . . seemed preoccupied, as though her mind might have been on other things." Others felt Grace was at her best. Audiences, however, found the film a sparkling comic and musical romp, and it proved a fitting denouement to Grace's short but spectacular film career.

* * *

Grace's uncertain future in films, and its vested interest in the wedding publicity, led MGM to heights of generosity as the nuptials approached. Her studio gave her a bonus of over $65,000 for 1956 and kept her on a weekly salary of $1,500 until several months after the wedding. It provided the services of its celebrated designer Helen Rose (whom Grace was supposed to have played in *Designing Woman)* to create her wedding dress, which cost $7,226. Grace enjoyed, free of charge, the services of a studio hairdresser during her first few months in Monaco, and one of MGM's top publicity men, Morgan Hudgins, assisted with the handling of the press during the wedding.

This last favor from MGM protected its own interests as much as Grace's. The press furor around Grace and Rainier since early January bordered on the phenomenal; wherever they appeared mob scenes usually broke out. The Prince was not used to such stampeding press interest, and he often reacted badly. The fact that Monaco had no press office did not make MGM any more sanguine about how the wedding would come off.

As things turned out, no amount of help from MGM was able to save the day in Monaco, and there were some early warning signs. Leaving Los Angeles in March, Rainier attempted to fly incognito under the alias C. Monte. Unsurprisingly, the ruse was discovered by reporters, who surrounded the Prince when he deplaned in New York's then Idlewild Airport. Asked once again whether Grace would continue her career, he replied, "No more movies for Miss Kelly!" He said he hoped his wedding would be a quiet one, and when a reporter asked him if he were weary of all the publicity, he replied, "A little bit. I expect that people will soon get sick of it. I know I am."

As Rainier returned to Monaco to resume his official duties and plan the wedding, Grace remained in Hollywood at MGM's request in order to present the 1955 Best Actor award. After handing the statuette to Ernest Borgnine for

Marty, Grace found herself, not Borgnine, the center of attention. Embarrassed and annoyed, she complained, "But *I* haven't won anything!" A reporter replied quickly, "Yes you have, you've won the Prince!"

A few days later Grace returned to New York to gather her trousseau and say goodbye to friends. She had less than three weeks before she would leave America aboard the SS *Constitution.* Wasting no time, she hired fashion consultant Eleanor Lambert to help her and purchased over twenty-five thousand dollars' worth of clothes from New York's most celebrated designers. There was a seven-thousand-dollar sable coat and a four-thousand-dollar mink, six cocktail dresses, four light dresses, two evening gowns, two ball gowns, a leopard skin coat, two light jackets, and twenty hats. Her luggage numbered four huge trunks and fifty-six other pieces. Her wedding dress was housed in a steel box that resembled a coffin, a ruse by MGM designed to fool reporters. In addition to her haute couture, Grace packed dozens of sweatshirts and pairs of dungarees; when Rupert Allan saw them in her suitcases he protested that she'd never wear them. "Oh yes I will," Grace replied. "All the time."

Grace didn't have too many people to say goodbye to in New York or Philadelphia; with her on the *Constitution* were seventy-two relatives and friends. Of those closest to her, only Lizanne and her sister-in-law Mary—both pregnant—did not make the trip. "They didn't want me there," Lizanne said years later. "They were afraid I'd have the baby in the church!" To everyone else, her goodbyes would be said as Princess Grace of Monaco, but until then the eight-day trip across the Atlantic would be one continuing party—at least for the guests.

For Grace, it began as an ordeal. "The trip was just bedlam," she said years later. "There was such confusion . . . mounting hysteria everywhere. Leaving New York was frantic. I hardly saw my mother the day we departed . . ."

The problems, not surprisingly, were caused by the other

"invited guests"—the press. Had Grace had her way, no journalists would have been on the ship—she asked the American Export Line not to sell any tickets to the press. But its reaction was so fierce that Grace relented; she allowed 110 journalists to accompany her on the voyage and agreed to several on-board press conferences. The first of these was a bad omen. Held while the ship was still docked, it degenerated into a near-riot as 250 reporters and photographers pushed, shoved, and jostled for position until Grace admitted she was "frightened." Morgan Hudgins, trying to keep things under control even as he was losing his footing, shouted, "Please, please! Behave, ladies and gentlemen!" Another publicity man snarled, "This is a press conference, not a riot. Unless you back up and give the lady some air, it will end immediately!"

Amid a cacophony of orders—"Wave for the camera, Grace . . . wave higher, so everyone can see!" "Take off your hat!" "Smile this way!"—most questions to Grace went unheard. At one point someone complained that "the movies," meaning the newsreel photographers, hadn't gotten Grace's wave on film. "That's your fault!" snapped Hudgins, and as an array of publicity people tried to quiet the commotion, Grace stood still and silent, looking out at the mass of faces in front of her, a trace of fear in her eyes, waiting for calm to be restored.

Finally, Jinx Falkenberg was able to ask her a question. "I wonder, Grace, if in this moment of excitement and some confusion, you have any thoughts about leaving this country and going on to this new life for you?"

"Well, Jinx," Grace replied evenly, "just getting married is a big step for any girl, and I have a lot of feelings about that. It's a very exciting thing and I'm very, very happy. Of course I'm a little sad to be leaving home, but I hope to be back very often."

After this melee (which *Editor and Publisher* described as "a disgrace to every profession represented at the conference") was over, Grace had a more agreeable task: broadcasting a greeting to the people of Monaco over Radio Monte

Carlo. To her soon-to-be subjects she said, "I would like to tell my future compatriots that the Prince, my fiancé, has taught me to love them. I feel I already know them well, thanks to what the Prince has told me, and my dearest wish today is to find a small place in their hearts . . ."

As the *Constitution* began to leave New York's Pier 84 on the morning of April 4, 1956, Grace stood at the railing, alone, gazing out into a mist. "The day we left," she said later, "our ship was surrounded in fog. And that's the way I felt— as if I were sailing off into the unknown . . . I couldn't help looking out into the fog and wondering, What is going to happen to me? . . . What sort of world was waiting for me on the other side of that fog?"

Chapter Thirteen

The eight-day voyage of the *Constitution* from New York to Monaco gave Grace a chance to party with her friends, pay her respects to relatives on both sides of her family and, occasionally, to reflect on what the future might hold for her. Sometimes, she was seen walking alone on deck; those who saw her instinctively left her alone. Frequently duty called in the form of prearranged interviews and photo sessions. Pictures of the crossing show us Grace playing shuffleboard, Grace running along the deck with the weimaraner puppy given to her by family friends in Philadelphia, Grace lounging on deck, her parents on either side of her, Grace sitting amid dozens of young nieces and nephews. She was surrounded by goodwill and best wishes, and this helped alleviate her nervousness and apprehension. She reacted with delight when the *Constitution*'s sister ship, the *Independence*, flashed the message "Good luck, Gracie!" as it sailed by.

While Grace enjoyed a degree of prenuptial insouciance, Prince Rainier grew irritable at the staggering amount of work needed to plan the wedding and its festivities. Sensing that the press could easily turn what he intended as a solemn occasion into a circus, he barred journalists from the ceremony. As his intended discovered after her own such dictum, members of the Fourth Estate do not react calmly to their exclusion from newsworthy events. Once again, a howl of protest led Rainier to change his mind—a decision he would come to regret.

Rainier's ill-temper in the weeks before the wedding was

explained as the result of a toothache, but observers noted little improvement in his disposition after the offending molar's extraction. Rainier took a brief respite from his princely duties on April 8, when—as his bride-to-be's ship steamed toward Monaco—he attended his bachelor party at an inn nestled in the nearby hillsides of southern France. The press made much of the fact that Father Tucker had not been invited, suggesting that Rainier was angry with the priest for speaking too freely about the details of his courtship. (Father Tucker, like Mrs. Kelly, had "written" a series of articles on the events leading up to the betrothal.) More likely, Father Tucker's exclusion resulted from a desire to avoid the dampening presence of a priest at what is traditionally a freewheeling occasion.

Four days after the party, at six-thirty in the morning of April 12, Rainier boarded his yacht, the 340-ton *Deo Juvante II* ("with God's help"), his wedding present to Grace, to await her arrival. By the time he sailed out of the Bay of Hercules to greet the *Constitution* and take Grace ashore, twenty thousand Monegasques, journalists, tourists, and other curiosity seekers had crowded the casino terraces, the harbor breakwater, and the streets along the shore, waiting in a light rain to see and cheer Monaco's soon-to-be princess.

As Grace stood at the head of her ship's gangway, the scene before her seemed like an elaborate location setup for an epic film. Monaco's harbor is one of the world's loveliest sights; calm azure water surrounded in a half moon by white buildings which dot the hills jutting up almost directly from the shore. Streaking toward her was the Prince's white yacht, surrounded by dozens of other boats carrying photographers and well-wishers. Overhead, helicopters and a seaplane buzzed.

As the *Deo Juvante II* neared, Grace exclaimed to her parents, "I see him!" The Prince was standing on the ship's bow, and as Grace waved to him, he returned her greeting with a salute. Grace laughed with delight. A tender bridged the way between ocean liner and yacht, and the sun, as if on cue, broke through the clouds as Grace descended the gangplank wearing a navy blue waisted coat over a matching dress, white gloves, and a large, saucer-shaped white hat. With her poodle, Oliver, in one arm, she greeted her prince by extending her free hand, which Rainier grasped warmly. Whether because of Rainier's princely reserve or the awkwardness of Oliver's presence, the couple neither embraced nor kissed, prompting headlines to point out, "Prince Gives Miss Kelly Kissless Hello in Monaco."

Rainier led Grace, followed by her parents, into the yacht's cabin, where they had a few minutes alone. Then the yacht cut away from the tender, circled the *Constitution* once, and headed back into Monaco's harbor. In farewell, the ocean liner that had carried Grace to what she called "my destiny" paid her a majestic farewell with four resounding blasts of its horn. Throughout the harbor, the smaller ships tooted their horns and blew their whistles in response. Onshore, a train whistle, a trolley Klaxon, the boom of a cannon, and the blasts of fireworks added to the cacophony of greetings for Grace.

As the yacht approached the shoreline, Grace stood at its bow, and for the first time she saw the thousands of people who had lined up as far as the eye could see to greet her. They cheered lustily when they saw her and waved wildly. As the whistles, horns, and cannon continued their salute, the seaplane overhead—owned by Aristotle Onassis—dropped thousands of red and white carnations on the yacht and into the sea around it. It was an intoxicating experience, and Grace drank in every drop.

When the yacht had docked, Prince Pierre and a host of Monegasque officials boarded for a champagne reception at which welcoming speeches abounded. After an hour the journalists waiting onshore began to clap rhythmically for the couple to emerge, and they did. Onshore, Grace was given a lei, which Mrs. Kelly had to enlarge to fit over her daughter's hat. (The hat, sightseers complained, prevented them from seeing Grace's face.) As the wife of a Monegasque official slipped the ring of flowers over Grace's head, she said to her, "You look happy, my dear." Grace replied softly, "I get happier and happier."

As they drove to the palace in the Prince's green Chrysler, cheering Monegasques lined every foot of the winding streets; as they entered the palace gates, Rainier's honor guard in their red-feathered helmets snapped to attention. And a cry of bugles saluted Grace as she entered her future home.

The rest of Grace's immediate family soon followed, awestruck by the pink opulence of Rainier's 220-room palace. (Rainier had repainted the entire structure and renovated several of the public and private rooms for his wedding festivities.) A luncheon for twenty-three people introduced the Kellys to the Grimaldis for the first time. Grace and her family met Rainier's mother, Princess Charlotte, his sister, Princess Antoinette, and his stepmother, Princess Ghislaine. If the luncheon was meant to further impress the Kellys, it did: there were two butlers stationed behind every chair in the dining room. "The servants had so much braid," Jack Kelly said, "you couldn't tell them from the generals."

After the meal Grace and her parents settled into the palace's apartments, while the bridesmaids and wedding guests were ensconced in Monte Carlo's posh Hotel de Paris. Grace took a short nap, then dressed for a private dinner with the Prince. Afterward, Rainier left to sleep at his villa in Cap-Ferrat while his exhausted bride-to-be fell into bed and tried to get some rest.

Over the course of the next five days, Grace would need all the rest she could get. Her wedding, which she had naïvely expected to be dignified and solemn, turned into a media circus the likes of which the world had never seen. "It was a nightmare, really, the whole thing," Grace said years later. "It was a difficult time to go through." On the "Today" show in 1985 Princess Caroline recalled, "My parents *hated* their wedding. They didn't even look at pictures of it for a year . . ."

Rita Gam, one of Grace's bridesmaids, recalls how difficult it was for Grace to handle the chaos: "Nobody ever went through that kind of an onslaught. It's a testament to her sense of balance that she handled it as well as she did. But she was thrown off base and surprised. She wanted to do it right. She wanted to please the press, and it cost her something in terms of an intrusion on her life. But she opted to play the game."

Doing so cost Grace something in terms of her physical stamina as well—she barely stood up under the strain. Film of the wedding ceremony reveals a woman tense and strained, dark circles under her eyes. "It was partly seriousness about getting married," Grace later explained to a journalist, "and partly the fact that there were over fifteen hundred journalists in Monaco—most of them behind the altar and hanging from the rafters." When she left for her honeymoon, she was ten pounds lighter than she'd been when she left New York two weeks earlier, and one journalist described her as "a wreck, her face gaunt with tension and fatigue, her body reed-thin."

Everything had begun with great promise. Prince Rainier proclaimed that he wanted "the richest ceremonials of the past" observed for his "beautiful wife," with no effort or expense spared. Throughout the principality, three miles of red carpet was laid, champagne cascaded, hundreds of yards of red and white material were formed into a flag by schoolgirls on the day of the wedding, and sumptuous galas were held, including a performance at the Opera House by Margot Fonteyn and the London Festival Ballet. The night before the civil ceremony hundreds of Monegasques serenaded the couple in the palace courtyard, dancing in traditional costumes of red and white as the Alsace Boys' Choir sang. When Grace retired to her rooms at midnight, a glorious fireworks display lit up the sky.

Had these celebrations been held in a vacuum, the joy Rainier intended them to convey would have been unmarred. But the wedding of the Prince and the movie star was of interest to far more than just Rainier's subjects, and therein lay the problem. Within two days not only fifteen hundred journalists and seven hundred wedding guests but untold numbers of sightseers invaded Monaco, creating utter chaos and prompting Morgan Hudgins to wire his MGM boss Howard Strickling, "Impossible to imagine confusion here."

Rupert Allan, who accompanied Hudgins, now says, "It was all Rainier's fault, really, because of his ignorance. He had no idea how to handle so many reporters and photographers." In fairness to the Prince, no one could have foreseen such an onslaught: interest in his wedding surpassed the coronation of Queen Elizabeth II several years earlier. UPI sent *twenty* correspondents, including Gloria Swanson on "special assignment." The International News Service designated nine, including Arlene Francis, Britain's ascerbic Lady Docker, and wedding party member Elizabeth Robertson. NBC sent nine reporters—three more than had covered D day for the network. CBS sent eleven. In all, thirty-one countries were represented, including Yugoslavia, and the wedding in the Cathedral of St. Nicholas was to be televised live to over thirty million people in nine countries, a television first.

Despite this overwhelming media presence, Rainier had no press office, held neither press conferences nor briefings, and offered no "photo opportunities" for the men and women whose editors were judging their performances on what they dispatched from Monaco. Frustrated, even panicky, photographers began to take drastic measures. At first they appealed unceremoniously to Grace's better instincts. Leaving a gala, she was confronted by scenes of Monegasque policemen roughly pushing photographers back. An angry newsman called out, "Miss Kelly, they're treating us like bums here!" Another exhorted, "Is this fair, Miss Kelly?" Whatever her feelings, Miss Kelly said nothing.

Bad tempers weren't improved by the increasingly heavy rain that had abated for only short periods since Grace's arrival. Before long, frustration turned to fisticuffs as newsmen fought Monegasque police, then each other. Within days, professional journalists had turned into hooligans. Photographers peered through guests' hotel windows or spied on Grace and Rainier as they took romantic walks; one stationed himself on the balcony outside Rainier's window at the Cap-Ferrat villa and sang dirty songs, hoping to raise the Prince's ire enough so that His Serene Highness would storm out in anger and have his picture taken. The ploy did not work.

After a luncheon given by his sister, Rainier left her villa by car with Grace at his side. He was greeted by a phalanx of photographers. When he attempted to inch his way through them, one threw himself on the ground directly in the car's path. Rainier finally made his way by, but he had had enough. He issued a stern statement: "A grave incident has happened today. There are certain limits of good behavior that should not be passed, and they have been passed. Some of you, in order to get a sensational picture today, did not hesitate to indulge in intolerable practices." As a result, Rainier went on, only three photographers would be permitted into the throne room to cover the civil ceremony, and none would be allowed into the garden party afterward.

A new howl of protest ensued, added to by John B. Kelly, who criticized his future son-in-law's "autocratic air" and said he would "have to have a talk with that young man." Surprising criticism of Rainier came as well from Father Tucker, who said his Lord Prince was behaving "like a spoiled boy." Rainier's subjects reacted with anger to Kelly's remarks and shock to Father Tucker's, but Rainier was chastised. When the man designated by the Prince to "handle" the press refused to come out of his hotel room, Rainier asked Morgan Hudgins's help (Hudgins was there as a wedding guest, in no official capacity). Hudgins suggested daily press briefings in French and English (the language barriers had frequently magnified problems and inflamed tempers) and strongly urged the Prince to allow himself and Grace to be photographed for at least several minutes each day. Rainier agreed, but he was wary. "I don't want this wedding to become a circus," he said rather belatedly. "I want to see pictures before they're handed out. For I know . . . certain photographers . . . will take fifty pictures of you, and then use only the one in which you're blowing your nose."

The photographers were somewhat mollified, but the reporters, less visible and less belligerent, were no less miffed at the lack of hard news. Many took snipes at the Prince and his tiny country, or reported on their colleagues' reporting, or blew silly rumors out of all proportion. Lady Docker, planning to entertain guests at the Cabaret restaurant at the casino, was refused admission because the Kellys were hosting a private party. She fired off a stinging protest to the palace, then wrote a piece in which she huffed that Grace wouldn't have worn her huge white hat on arriving had she known "the size of Rainier's yacht. It's only 135 feet long and 340 tons. My husband chartered that same ship before Rainier bought it and I'd call it a bit snug."

Lady Docker wasn't alone with unflattering things to say. Various dispatches described Monaco as "seedy and rundown," an "absurd postage-stamp kingdom," "the preshrunk principality." Rainier was rudely dubbed "Ray" and "Shorty." Fred Sparks of Scripps-Howard made a bet that Grace would not still be married to Rainier in five years—if she ever married him at all: "I hate to be offering Grace any advice but she is public property like the *Mona Lisa* and I urge her to stop, look and listen before she lets her head be turned by dreams of marbled halls. The marbled halls of Monaco . . . lack central heating and the plumbing would worry a camel and the furniture belongs in a museum and collects pyramids of dust . . ."

The Kellys didn't escape unscathed either. Reports circulated that the Prince's staff had been "scandalized" by Grace's sister Peggy and her children wearing shorts in the palace; Lady Docker quoted Randolph Churchill as sniffing, "I didn't come here to meet vulgar people like the Kellys." If many of the Kellys were out of their element, none was more so than John B. One story that always got a laugh when repeated among the press boys was that Jack had frantically called a Philadelphia reporter friend and asked if he could come over to his hotel and use the bathroom. Kelly, it seemed, was all alone in the palace, couldn't find a restroom, and couldn't ask any of the staff where it was because he didn't speak French. He took a palace limousine to his friend's hotel room, knocked frantically for admission, and was able to relieve himself.

Some reports dwelled not on the events unfolding in Monaco, but on the coverage of those events. Dorothy Kilgallen, fascinated by her own problems, wrote, "I have eleven pieces of luggage, but there's just no way of covering a royal wedding without the proper equipment—a sapphire mink stole, an ermine wrap, a little chinchilla wrap, a white cashmere coat, a gold brocade evening raincoat—journalism is growing more complicated every day." (Grace did not want to invite Kilgallen—or Hedda Hopper, Louella Parsons, or Sheilah Graham. Bill Hegner recalled trying to convince Grace to invite Kilgallen, because she was "the Number One Eastern Woman Columnist. Grace was dead set against inviting her: 'I hate her guts. I despise her as a person,' Grace told us. Finally, Grace granted her okay but only if she would be kept a deck apart from Kilgallen so that at no time would there be any opportunity for them to bump into one another." Hopper, Parsons, and Graham *were* excluded.)

Ironically, the usually poisonous Kilgallen provided some of the most lyrical, romantic descriptions of the ceremony, prompting Arthur Lewis to comment, "I can attribute this only to a common belief that all women cry at weddings even when they loathe the major participants."

More typically, Kilgallen also supplied the wryest description of her own profession's deportment during the wedding week: "The only really bright chaps here are the journalists for the sensational British papers. They solved the whole problem and haven't a care in the world. They just make up their stories—and believe me, they are a lot better than the stuff we conservative toffs are sending back home."

Stories not invented were grossly exaggerated. Reports circulated that Grace was "furious" with Rainier for not kissing her when she alighted onto his yacht; that (this from Kilgallen) Grace had "cured" Rainier's "mental block" about being shorter than she by "forcing" him to dance with her in public. Bob Considine weighed in with the news that the Kellys were undergoing an "agonizing reappraisal" of Rainier after finding him "lots nicer back in Philadelphia" and now "rather tense and distant."

To be sure, not all the "circus" trappings of "the wedding of the century" were created by disgruntled journalists. The carnival air was embellished nicely by thousands of tourists and the Monegasques themselves, some of whom hawked absurdly expensive "souvenirs," including a kerchief featuring a photograph of the royal couple, priced at five dollars. Some of the principality's less sentimental citizens, the forerunners of today's scalpers, sold their tickets for the various galas to the highest bidders.

As the commercialization of Monaco's wedding reached absurd proportions, Rainier, through a spokesman, protested. "His Highness is sorely afraid that somebody is going to advertise soup or soap or something in connection with his marriage." The Kelly family lawyer warned against any use of the Kelly or Grimaldi names, images or seals on any product whatsoever. But there was nothing to be done about the American television networks, which solicited sponsors to pay for their unprecedented coverage of the marriage. ABC, in a comical lapse of good judgment, sold airtime to the Peter Pan Brassiere Company. A happy Peter Pan executive cabled dealers to "be sure you have adequate stock on hand of Peter Pan bras and girdles! This is the most romantic event since Romeo and Juliet!"

Columnist John Crosby's comments of April 10 had proven prophetic: "Prince Rainier has complained that he doesn't want any commercialization of his wedding and everyone laughed heartily . . . I can't remember anything so rich in comic possibilities since the sailing of the Ford Peace Ship during World War I."

To some wedding guests that week, Monaco resembled a battle zone, because milling among the invitees and the rain-soaked masses were dozens of pickpockets and thieves. The latter managed several quite spectacular heists, including fifty thousand dollars' worth of jewels from Mrs. Matthew H. Mc-Closkey, wife of the treasurer of the Democratic party, and ten thousand dollars' worth from Grace's bridesmaid Maree Frisby Pamp. Kept from the press was the fact that Mrs. Kelly, too, had been victimized. Art Buchwald's reaction to all this was to announce that "Prince Rainier III is so furious over the jewel robberies that have taken place at Monaco during the last week that he has decided to ban all jewel thieves from the wedding. This drastic measure has raised a howl of protests from jewel robbers of every nationality who were sent there to cover the wedding." Buchwald then quoted an outraged thief: "I am shocked at the Prince's attitude. We have only stolen jewels from Philadelphia people and we haven't even bothered the Aga Khan."

Publicly, Grace reacted to the "Monaco melee" by retreating into the "plastic egg" Cary Grant had described. She took on an air of composure during public functions befitting a woman who would soon be addressed as "Your Serene Highness," but in fact she was maintaining a protective distance from situations that might have driven her to distraction. One observer noted that she seemed "lost in reverie" at one gala, and Dorothy Kilgallen wrote worriedly, "I fear Grace is slipping away from us."

Privately, the chaos took its toll on Grace. She was unable to sleep, as upset by Rainier's reactions to what was happening as by the events themselves. At the wedding rehearsal, the dark circles under her eyes were so bad she wore sunglasses indoors to hide them from photographers' prying lenses. The rehearsal, however, went off well; Rainier had agreed to allow several reporters to witness the run-through.

Afterward, he chatted with them and admitted, "I want to get out to sea as fast as I can. It will be the first time I will have been glad to leave my little country."

On the morning of April 18, Grace and Rainier, as she later put it, were "half-married" in a civil ceremony in the throne room of the palace. Wearing a beige-rose dress of lace over silk taffeta and a close-fitting Juliet cap, she sat stiffly erect in a high-backed gilt and damask chair a few feet from Rainier, facing the Monegasque throne (in which monarchs sit only during coronations). Both Grace and Rainier seemed ill at ease. She gazed straight ahead as if in a trance, he fidgeted, bit his finger, ran his finger under his collar, obviously uncomfortable under the huge television arc lights trained upon him from just a few feet away. "That was a man in a daze," Rainier said shortly afterward. "The work, worry, and tension were almost intolerable . . . By the time the ceremonies started, I was a nervous wreck."

The room, filled with family members and dignitaries from twenty-four countries, became unbearably warm and sticky since the rain outside still had not abated; the ceremony, in French, seemed to go on forever. After asking Rainier the unnecessary question, "Do I have His Serene Highness's permission to proceed?" Judge Marcel Portanier delivered an obsequious litany of "the impressive and intimidating presence in this historic place, the throne room, of the most eminent representatives of the great and numerous nations which have wished on this happy and moving occasion to demonstrate so brilliantly their vibrant sympathy for the Sovereign Prince of Monaco and his most gracious fiancée . . ."

After continuing in that vein at length, Judge Portanier then read the portions of the Napoleonic code applicable to marriage: mutual fidelity and assistance, protection of the wife by the husband, obedience to the husband by the wife. The wife is obligated to cohabit with her husband and follow him wherever he goes. The husband must supply his wife with her daily requirements, according to his means.

That done, Portanier recited the seemingly endless list of

Rainier's titles—142 in all. He then asked the couple if they each took the other in matrimony. Both answered *oui* in barely audible voices. The judge then declared that, unless there were any objections, Rainier Grimaldi and Grace Patricia Kelly were man and wife. An enormous register was brought in for each to sign. After receiving her guests, Grace relaxed for the first time that day with a glass of champagne. Shown a list of her own 140 titles, she laughed and exclaimed, "Oh no!"

At an enormous reception in the palace courtyard, three thousand Monegasques were treated to cake and champagne as the Prince and Grace mingled nervously among them. It was the first time many of the citizens of Monaco had had a chance to give Grace a close-up look. "Her complexion is perfect," said one, "astonishing . . ."

That night Stan Kenton performed *Homage to a Princess* at the Opera House while the London Festival Ballet danced. There followed a pas de deux by Margot Fonteyn and Michael Soames. Grace, resplendent in a white organza gown encrusted with pearls, rhinestones, and sequins and wearing a diamond tiara in her hair, held hands with her new husband, himself dressed entirely in white.

After midnight Grace and Rainier, although man and wife in the eyes of the law, once again retired to separate lodgings. Grace protested that such adherence to niceties was "Victorian," but Rainier understood his countrymen and their religion: he and Grace would not be truly married until united in the eyes of the church. And that would not be until the following day.

Thursday, April 19 dawned, to the relief of everyone, with brilliant sunshine bathing Monaco. It seemed that when Grace most needed it—the moment of her arrival, the day of her wedding—the sun obliged with an appearance from out of the dreariest skies. From this time forward, Monegasques would call long-awaited sunshine "Princess Grace weather."

At nine-thirty guests began to ascend the red-carpeted

steps of Monaco's ornate Cathedral of St. Nicholas, passing erect footmen and sentries with bayonets cocked. Spectators watched Aristotle Onassis, ex-King Farouk of Egypt, Gloria Swanson, Dorothy Kilgallen, Ava Gardner (flanked by Morgan Hudgins and Rupert Allan), the David Nivens, the Aga Khan, and representatives of dozens of nations and royal families enter through the Gothic façade of the limestone white building.

Inside the cathedral—cleaned so thoroughly one report referred to the removal of "ten-year deposits of dust"—was awash with flowers: the altar covered with white lilies, lilacs, and hydrangeas illuminated by candles, the chandeliers hung with gilded baskets filled with white snapdragons. The entire ceremony, rich with beauty, splendor, and the "ceremonials of the past," made an awesome spectacle for the thirty million people watching it on television.

By ten fifteen all six hundred guests were seated. Grace emerged from the palace on the arm of her father, and she was a breathtaking vision of loveliness. Her gown was a shimmering creation which seemed exactly what it was: a labor of love from Helen Rose, designed to befit its wearer perfectly as much as call attention to itself. On its own terms, the gown was a spectacle worthy of MGM, the most expensive dress Rose had ever made. Its 125-year-old rose point lace was purchased from a museum; added to it were twenty-five yards of silk taffeta and one hundred yards of silk net. Thousands of tiny pearls were sewn on the veil; even the three unseen petticoats were decorated with tiny blue bows.

More important to Rose than splendor, however, was a design *suitable* to Grace Kelly and to the occasion, and the dress is a masterwork in that respect. Highly traditional and elegant, the gown at the same time highlighted Grace's youthful slimness with its perfect fit along her arms, shoulders, neck, and tiny waist. There could be no doubt that Monaco's future princess was a very young, very beautiful woman.

Grace, escorted by her father, entered the cathedral at ten thirty. She was followed by four flower girls tending to her ten-foot train of beribboned tulle, two pages, Peggy (the maid of honor), and six bridesmaids—Judy Kanter, Rita Gam, Maree Pamp, Carolyn Reybold, Sally Parrish Richardson, and Bettina Gray—all dressed in yellow silk organza. As the bridal party took its position on either side of the altar, Grace, her face gravely serious, stood facing Monaco's bishop, Monsignor Gilles Barthe, Father Tucker, and the Kelly family's parish priest, Father Cartin. When Father Tucker informed Jack Kelly that he could be seated now that Grace was at the altar, he responded that he would remain by her side until the Prince arrived.

A fanfare of trumpets heralded His Serene Highness's presence. He was resplendent in a uniform of his own design, featuring golden epaulets and a plethora of medals celebrating elements of French and Italian military history. Across his chest from shoulder to waist hung the red-and-white sash of the Order of St. Charles. Rainier was attended by three best men: his cousin Comte Charles de Polignac, his friend and house-governor, Lieutenant-Colonel Jean-Marie Ardant, and Kell.

When Rainier reached the altar, Jack Kelly took his seat and both Prince and princess-to-be kneeled before Monsignor Barthe. Grace, although showing the strain of the previous weeks, seemed enveloped by a profound inner peacefulness. Never once did she smile, glance around, or react to the rustle as television technicians adjusted the microphones amid the flowers on the altar in front of her or the arc lights hanging from the rafters above her. Later, she spoke ruefully of "reporters hanging from the rafters," and Rainier added to a reporter, "During this wedding in front of an altar there were cameras and microphones everywhere. Such lack of dignity and solitude. Reflecting on this afterwards, we both agreed that we should really have got married somewhere in a little chapel in the mountains. That is the sort of impossible desire one has after these things."

To her credit, Grace never once allowed any of this to distract her. There was no lack of dignity, despite the circus trappings, because Grace herself brought to the proceedings a serenity befitting them.

The ceremony itself was, as *Time* put it, "a simple, age-old sacrament, in essence no different than that used by the humblest—" Monsignor Barthe addressed Grace and Rainier: "Both of you are aware of the duties of marriage. You are both children of God." To Grace he said, "It is easy to find about your qualities of the spirit and heart, and one finds in you the features used in the Holy Scriptures to describe the ideal wife." To the Prince: "You are not alone. Christ offers you his support. It will help you find saintly joy in the united family which you wish."

The bishop admonished Rainier to temper his authority with love and tenderness and Grace not to lose sight of the fact that physical beauty was fleeting and of no importance. Despite the microphones and loudspeakers, the hushed congregation could not hear the whispered replies to Barthe from Grace and Rainier. When the bishop asked, "Rainier-Louis-Henri-Maxence-Bertrand, will you take Grace Patricia, here present, for your lawful wife, according to the rite of our Holy Mother, the Church?" and addressed the same question to Grace, the assembled guests had to assume that both had replied, *"Oui, je veux."* Then the bishop said the words millions had been waiting to hear: "I declare you united in marriage in the name of the Father, the Son and the Holy Ghost."

Six-year-old page Sebastian von Furstenberg approached the altar, carrying two rings on a silver salver. In his nervousness, he dropped one; it was smoothly retrieved by Father Tucker. Rainier had trouble slipping Grace's ring onto her finger until she helped him with it. They did not kiss, although Grace glanced affectionately at her new husband during the one-hour nuptial mass that followed the ceremony. After the last benediction, the couple rose, genuflected, and turned toward the congregation. The Prince offered his bride his arm, and, still grave in their demeanor, they walked out of the cathedral past their beaming guests. Only then did Grace relax and smile at her husband, who returned her affectionate glance for the first time. As they entered a waiting Rolls-Royce, Grace said something to her prince that made him laugh. They rode in the open car through the streets of Monaco, holding hands, and arrived at the tiny peach-colored church near the harbor which is the shrine of the martyred Saint Dévote, patroness of Monaco. As the Prince watched, his plumed helmet cradled in the crook of his arm, his wife prayed to Dévote to bless her marriage, and she lay her bridal bouquet at the feet of a statue of the virgin saint who brought Christianity to Monaco.

Religious ceremony observed, it was time for celebration. A second wedding reception, this one just for the six hundred guests, was held in the palace courtyard. Champagne flowed to accompany the caviar, smoked salmon, shrimp, ham, salami, soup, cheese, jellied eggs, salmon with cucumber salad, cold lobster, and chicken served on enormous tables. After lunch, the couple cut the five-tier wedding cake, which was taller than either of them, with the Prince's sword.

Then, in an unorthodox move, the entire wedding party attended a soccer game at the National Stadium. Afterward, while other festivities continued, Grace and Rainier changed clothes for their honeymoon. After tearful farewells to her family and friends, Grace accompanied Rainier aboard the *Deo Juvante II.* They waved to the assembled crowd as the boat began its way out of the harbor and two parachute-bearing rockets shot into the air and dropped two huge banners, the flags of Monaco and the United States. Once out of sight of their subjects, the Prince and Princess of Monaco collapsed exhaustedly into deck chairs.

With the crew of nine trying to be as inconspicuous as possible, Grace and Rainier used the cruise as a time to recuperate and get to know each other. The first night Grace became seasick, and the boat dropped anchor just out of sight of Monaco harbor. The second day all the stress she had undergone got to Grace, and she became ill with the flu. After the first week, however, she was fine, and the couple proceeded with seven languid weeks of their honeymoon.

They cruised the Riviera, the Balearic Islands, and the coasts of France and Spain. They went ashore in Madrid, where they lunched with Generalissimo Franco, the leader of Spain. In Palma de Mallorca, Grace shopped. In Corsica, empty beaches beckoned them and they enjoyed each other, completely undisturbed for the first time since they had met. But when they went into town, Rainier recalled ruefully, "an English tourist walked up and calmly stepped between us while his wife took motion pictures. The lady then looked up and blandly requested us to remove our sunglasses so she could get better shots."

Back in Monaco the wedding guests, tourists, and journalists dispersed, most retaining memories only of the pageantry and beauty of what they had just experienced. "That was some wedding," Jack Kelly said in his inimitable way. "There has never been another like it." To him and the other guests, it appeared that Grace's tribulations were over. In fact, they were just beginning.

Chapter Fourteen

The "unknown" that Grace had contemplated aboard the *Constitution* was now at hand, and the fear, bewilderment, loneliness, and alienation she felt as she attempted to adapt to her new environment can scarcely be overstated —or easily comprehended by anyone who has not been through a similar situation. As Lizanne puts it, "Her first year over there was really bad. What she went through! She used to say she didn't know how she got through the first couple of years. She had *no idea* of what it meant to be the Princess of Monaco—and she was scared to death."

The adjustments every new bride faces are difficult enough under any circumstances. They were excruciatingly so for Grace, who could barely have been more isolated as she began life as a princess. As soon as she and Rainier returned from their honeymoon, he plunged back into the day-to-day responsibilities of running his country. Grace was left alone for hours at a time, with little to do and no one with whom to communicate. She and Rainier lived in his bachelor quarters off a courtyard on the ground floor of the palace, and they were, a friend said, "dank, dark and gloomy," a condition that did little to lift Grace's spirits.

Her family and friends were five thousand miles away, and the people around her all spoke a foreign language with which she was not nearly as familiar as she thought she was. Before long, Grace found herself lonely and depressed. "At first," she said, "I thought I wouldn't be able to cope."

Several years after her marriage, Grace told a reporter, "The biggest change in my life wasn't the palace. It was the adjustment to marriage itself. I lived alone in New York and in California, and the entire schedule of my life centered around my work. I had to get to the studio on time; I had to arrange my meals to fit my schedule. My career was the central focus of everything I did. Now, my life centers around my husband."

This was true to an extraordinary degree; and what saddened Grace the most during her first year as princess was the realization that the lives of everyone else in her world centered on her husband as well—and she was the least equipped to share most aspects of his life with him. She knew nothing about the political intricacies of the principality, chief among Rainier's concerns. She did not share his friends, nor even his acquaintances. What should have been inviolably her domain—their home—was only marginally under her direction.

Beyond these exceptional problems Grace faced, her husband was little more than a stranger to her. There had been no time for either to be exposed to, much less work out, the personality conflicts newlyweds often encounter. Moreover, the personalities of Grace and Rainier seemed custom-made to result in strife. Rainier, an absolute monarch, was used to having things his way. Occasionally he would capitulate to his wife's needs and desires, but more often he imperiously refused to. Grace's experiences with her parents had made her resentful of dictatorial, arbitrary judgments and decisions, and Rainier's were often unbearable for her. Bill Hegner recalled that she "cried a lot and called her friends cross-Atlantic and said Rainier was terrible, difficult to get along with. She was homesick and he's a strong-willed person."

Rainier is also, apparently, a man with a formidable temper, as Lizanne vividly recalls. "There was a great adjustment for Grace living with a new husband. Grace was a little spoiled, and Rainier—hah!—was *very* spoiled and getting his way all the time . . . Grace and Rainier had their differences—whew! They were both very strong-willed and definite. And Rainier had a Latin temperament, and he could blow up like crazy. Grace was amazing, she stayed calm. She could handle him pretty well. If I was there and Rainier got mad and blew up, I'd leave the room. He'd get mad and he'd sulk."

Even in their calmer moments, Grace and Rainier did not communicate well. She was used to openness with her loved ones, to sharing one's problems and listening to a friend's. Rainier's psychological walls, his guardedness, left him uncomfortable discussing his innermost feelings—even with someone as close to him as his wife should have been. Grace hoped to help her husband through his darker moods; instead she found herself rebuffed, and she in turn hesitated to confide her own fears and frustrations to him. The Prince later said he intuited Grace's loneliness and need for a close friend, but they never discussed it, and he regrets not having done more to help her.

The overwhelming loneliness and restlessness Grace felt during her first year in Monaco threatened to undo her. She hated not having anything to do on a regular basis; after six months as princess she made the extraordinary statement, "I have not lived in the palace long enough to establish a daily routine." Her principal pastimes, in fact, seemed to be answering her mail and waiting for her husband to come down from his office one floor above their apartment after a day's work. She ran up enormous phone bills calling home and wrote innumerable letters to friends. (She missed her friends more than her family; she was still resentful of the way they'd treated her over the years, and her hurt over her mother's "betrayal" with the newspaper series would take years to soften. On more than one occasion Grace muttered the cliché, "You choose your friends but your family you're born with.")

Phone calls and letters were scant comfort. Before long, she developed insomnia and a propensity for crying jags. (Her pregnancy, discovered six weeks after her marriage, added greatly to Grace's fragile emotional state.) She begged her friends and family to visit her, but they couldn't so soon after the wedding because of the expense and time involved. (Lizanne, in fact, did not visit Monaco for the first time until 1960.)

Grace longed to make friends in Monaco, but her position made it impossible for her to become familiar with anyone outside the palace. Worse still, she realized that within the palace—in what should have been her home—she was an outsider. As she later wrote to Don Richardson, "Many people here treated me as someone from Mars for a long time." Lizanne recalls, "Quite a few people were not too happy about Grace being over there. And they gave her a *very* hard time." With shock and dismay, she quickly realized that most of Rainier's servants, rather than embracing her as their new princess and the woman who would bear their prince an heir, resented and disdained her. She was an interloper, an actress, and—worst of all—an American. Her poor French was considered proof of her general inadequacy; her attempts to change any palace routine were usually ignored. Her discomfort with protocol was looked upon as boorish; her American tastes in food, decor, and fashion were, to those who were supposed to do her bidding, *insupportable*.

Paradoxically, while Grace felt lonely and alienated, she was rarely alone. The palace had a staff of hundreds, all there ostensibly to serve her. Grace couldn't leave the palace alone; and she couldn't walk more than a few steps outside her private quarters without someone inquiring, "May I help you, Your Highness?" Grace longed to say, "Yes, you can sit down and talk with me about what was in the news this morning and what's coming up in the fashion world!"—but of course she couldn't. Grace thought with irony of the poetic lament, "Water, water everywhere,/Nor any drop to drink."

In an effort to help his wife through this difficult period, Rainier appointed a young woman about her age, Madge Tivey-Faucon, a friend of Gisele Pascal's, as Grace's lady-in-waiting and charged her with teaching Grace French. "Tiv," who should have been the closest thing to a friend the palace had to offer Grace, harbored a pseudoaristocratic European distaste for the Princess's unreconstructed Americanism; after she left the palace six years later, she wrote a series of articles detailing some of Grace and Rainier's most intimate idiosyncrasies and what she saw as their peccadilloes, chief among them their tastes for things Yankee. Tiv was of little help to her mistress when it came to teaching her French. Whether it was the fault of the teacher or the pupil, Grace never was able to master her adopted language to the point of fluency. (A few days before the marriage, Rainier spoke glowingly of his bride to Father Tucker. When the Prince praised her command of French, Father Tucker muttered, "They say love is blind. Apparently, it is also deaf.") She was frequently unable to comprehend what was being said to her—few of the people around her bothered to slow their speech patterns for her benefit—or communicate what she desired; this caused a myriad of problems with her staff.

Grace's insecurity with her new language led her, during audiences and galas, to remain virtually silent—a stance that the Monegasques misinterpreted as icy reserve. This and the fact that Grace's public appearances during the first two years of her marriage were minimal caused her subjects to wonder just how much she cared about them. There was acute disappointment among many residents of the principality that "their" new princess was rarely on view.

So unfamiliar, and uncomfortable, was Grace with the requirements of protocol (necessary within the palace as well as without) that she dared not venture forth into the public's scrutiny more often than necessary. The new Princess was drilled in the do's and very definite don'ts that her position demanded: she must never appear in public except with her husband or a lady-in-waiting; she must always wear a hat at public functions, including those held inside the palace; her signature must be "Grace de Monaco," nothing else; should she refer to her husband in correspondence with the pronoun form, it must be capitalized (He, Him); she would be curtsied to by all women who met her and referred to as "Your Highness"; formally she would be known as Her Serene Highness.

Further, there were the rigid requirements of public ceremony. Grace tried to master everything, but often it made her
head ache.

If Grace had hoped that her in-laws might help her
through her period of adjustment in Monaco, she was sorely
disappointed. Rainier's mother and sister both kept their distance from Grace, which added to her loneliness and frustration. As late as 1972, after Grace had been a member of her
family for sixteen years, Princess Charlotte still had not accepted her. That year Grace wrote to Don Richardson about
a trip she'd taken to Charlotte's villa, a handsome Renaissance château in the North of France. She described the
building as "fascinating . . . but cold as a witch's tit."* Then
she added, "Of course, my mother-in-law's attitude toward
me does nothing to warm up the atmosphere."

Charlotte's dislike of Grace was rooted both in disapproval
of her status as an American, an actress, and a commoner,
and in a personal situation Grace could not have foreseen.
"Grace and Rainier were very friendly with Prince Pierre,
Rainier's father," Lizanne explains. "Charlotte and Pierre did
not have a very happy divorce. Grace and Pierre got along
very well, so Charlotte and Grace did not get along. It was as
simple as that. Grace had great problems with Rainier's
mother. Cold was not the word for Charlotte's attitude toward Grace . . . And Princess Antoinette wasn't any happier about the Prince marrying an American actress than
Charlotte had been."

Concerned about his wife's state of mind, Prince Rainier
suggested that she busy herself with a major project: renovat-
ing and redecorating the palace. Most of the building's 220
rooms were in states of decay and disrepair. Many areas had
not been used for over a century; tapestries peeled from the
walls, cobwebs completely obscured the frescoed ceilings. As

* In the handwritten letter, Grace crossed out the word "tit" and substituted
the more acceptable "teat." Apparently, she was ever conscious of her image,
even while writing to Richardson.

Rainier put it, "My predecessors let it get into such a state of neglect that it was almost falling to pieces." Lack of money precluded a restoration during Rainier's first seven years as sovereign. Considerably richer after his marriage, and with tourism already increasing and promising future solvency, the Prince felt able to undertake a major renovation of the eight-hundred-year-old palace. (It proved so expensive that paid tours were instituted to defray the cost, arousing a storm of controversy that was only partly diffused by the allotment of a portion of the proceeds to Monaco's Red Cross. "I can't afford to restore it and maintain it as it should be out of my own pocket," Rainier said.)

The restoration of the palace's public rooms proceeded slowly and without much input from Grace. The bulk of the work was repair of sagging roofs, peeling plaster, and warped window casings. In many of the rooms no redecorating was planned, just a general sprucing up: fabrics were replaced, wallpaper rehung, and the gild on furniture and picture frames cleaned or reapplied.

Where Grace was able and eager to make her own taste felt was in the suite of six private rooms in which she and Rainier lived. The Prince had refurnished the apartment in preparation for Grace's arrival, but not wholly to her liking, and he allowed her to completely redecorate. Characteristically she called upon someone from her past to help out—decorator George Stacey, with whom she'd designed her New York apartment. True to form as well, Rainier exploded when he heard Grace had brought in Stacey. "A decorator!" he bellowed at her. "Never in the history of my family have we had a decorator! One does that sort of thing oneself." Grace didn't argue, didn't throw a fit—but she was able to convince her husband to allow Stacey to do the job.

Grace had retained her New York apartment until months into her marriage,* but she decided toward the end of 1956

* According to Lizanne, Grace also left her personal financial holdings on the American side of the Atlantic. "My husband was a stockbroker," she says,

to give it up and use its contents in the palace, hoping this would make her feel more at home. All her furnishings, including drapes and carpets, were shipped to Monaco, and most were used in the apartment's salon, a favorite room of Grace's. There she was surrounded by her cream damask-covered sofa and armchair, and the blue-and-gilt seventeenth-century French conversation chair that had been one of her first purchases. "They are like old friends," Grace said of her possessions. "I would sooner have them than a lot of new things."

Grace's refurbishing met with Rainier's approval, with a few exceptions. In one instance her lack of familiarity with European custom enraged him. When Grace placed white chrysanthemums in the guest suite in anticipation of a foreign dignitary's stay, Rainier exploded, "For God's sake! In Europe those are the flowers of the tomb! Get them out of here!" But on the whole, Grace's personal touches made the palace atmosphere warmer than it had been for decades. "She's transformed it from a mausoleum into a home," Father Tucker said. "A few years ago it was the deadest place imaginable. The Prince hated it so much he even preferred to spend an evening with me in my little salon at the Church of Saint Charles. The Princess is a born homemaker."

Preparing for the renovation lifted Grace's spirits, but once the decisions had been made about furniture pieces and colors and fabrics, there was very little for her to do—the palace had someone on staff for just about every job. For Grace to supervise the work was impossible because of the language barrier, and so she once again found herself lonely and restless. She expressed some of these feelings in letters home, but she always put a brave face on so that only those friends who read between the lines were aware of Grace's unhappiness. Few did. "I'm ashamed," said Judy Kanter, "to say how insen-

"and he handled Grace's accounts for the first five years of the marriage. There was never community property between Grace and the Prince. All her holdings and money stayed in the United States. What Grace had was always hers."

sitive I was to Grace's loneliness in those early years. I projected my myth of a fairy-tale marriage onto her."

To Grace, at no time was it ever that. "I never saw anything 'fairy-talish' about it," she said years later. Even so, the first year of her marriage was so difficult and so strife-torn that a woman with less determination to succeed in the eyes of the world, less motivation to prove her mettle to her family, and less belief in the religious sanctity of marriage might well have called it quits. (There was, indeed, precedent for such an action. Rainier's great-grandmother, Princess Mary Victoria, was an eighteen-year-old Scottish aristocrat when she married Prince Albert. Within a year she had presented him with an heir, Louis, but Mary found the people of Monaco, its dry, hot weather, and her increasing loneliness intolerable and left the principality forever. The marriage was later annulled by the Vatican. Her successor, Princess Alice—who had brought that six-million-dollar dowry—also left the principality for good after ten years, following a bitter altercation with her stepson, Prince Louis.*)

Grace, however, had learned her mother's lessons well. To her, marriage was for life, problems were to be overcome, and appearances were to be kept up at all costs. Walking up the aisle she had thought, "Here I am. This is a one-way street now. There's no way out of this."

But her commitment to her marriage didn't alleviate her alienation or her homesickness. So great was the latter that Grace prevailed upon her husband to take her on a visit to the United States in September, less than five months after the wedding. "I am, in a sense, going home," she told a reporter. The couple remained in America two months, using as a "base" Grace's apartment in New York. The Prince attended to some business affairs; he and Grace were enter-

---

* If, as Charles Kelly said, there had never been a good Kelly marriage, one needs to look far back to find a good Grimaldi union as well. Rainier's parents, grandparents, and great-grandparents all suffered at least one failed marriage—a remarkable record in a Catholic country during an era in which marriages were most often kept intact at all costs.

tained by President Eisenhower (their visit, one observer noted, "threw the White House staff into an unprecedented tizzy"); and Grace visited with friends and happily shopped in New York's finest boutiques for maternity and baby clothes.

Grace's pregnancy brought her twenty-six additional pounds and that singular glow most expectant mothers exude —she looked healthy and prettier than ever. But her friends noticed a difference in her: that abstracted remoteness that only strangers had seen before. Most laughed it off as the requisite royal serenity; it was partly that but partly as well a result of the defensive wall Grace had erected to cope with her intimidating surroundings in Monaco. At a dinner party given in her honor by a friend, Nawab Mir Nawaz Jung, the Pakistani ambassador to the United Nations, the guests spoke with animation about the theater and the movies. Grace, an observer noted, "entered into the conversation—but with the detachment of someone who had never been within a thousand miles of a motion picture studio."

If Grace had entertained any hope at this point that she was anything but public property, that the chaos surrounding her engagement and wedding were an aberration, this was dispelled by her trip to Philadelphia. Wherever she went, alone or with the Prince, near-riots of press and onlookers erupted. Grace had come to accept a degree of this as a movie star, but she was taken aback by how far it had grown beyond anything she'd experienced before. The Prince abhorred it. Lizanne recalls, "He didn't like coming over here very much, because the press fell all over Grace. In the beginning, it was a madhouse—the poor things couldn't even go outside. People would stand in front of the house and gawk, and it was really very bad. Rainier didn't like it at all."

Equally distressing was the presence of the secret service men needed to protect the royal couple wherever they went in public; outside their private quarters, they could never be alone. In a restaurant an extra table would always be booked for the security men, and this may have been the reason for an unusually large lunch tab that disturbed Jack Kelly. His nephew Charles V. Kelly, Jr., recalled his very agitated uncle asking him if he'd eaten at the Barclay's restaurant. Charles replied that he had, but only infrequently because it was expensive. "Damned right it's expensive," Jack Kelly fumed. "I just got a bill today from them. Ninety-five bucks! Lunch for four people." In 1956 lunch in the best Philadelphia restaurant, with a fine wine, cost at most twelve dollars per person.

"My son-in-law must have ordered every damned expensive dish on the menu," Kelly went on. "And *he* had no money, so what they did was sign my name to the check." Jack Kelly paid the bill but muttered for months afterward, "What in God's name could four people have eaten for lunch that cost ninety-five dollars?" Charles recalled once feebly suggesting, "Well, maybe Rainier had his sandwich toasted."

As far as the press was concerned, Grace's pregnancy was "hard news," and no reporter failed to ask her about it at every opportunity. Philadelphia newsman Taylor Grant recalled interviewing Grace on the subject. "I asked her if she'd decided yet on a name for the child. She said no and as she did I saw her cast a slightly worried look at the Prince. Just enough to let me know I hadn't been letting him in on enough of this interview . . . So I turned to Rainier and asked him. He just couldn't wait to answer. He laughed and said, 'We've only decided what *not* to name it . . . I will never name the child Elvis.' "*

In November, Grace and Rainier returned to Monaco to await the birth of their baby and heir. If Grace had an official duty as Princess of Monaco at this point in her tenure, this was surely it. The preparations for the birth occupied her amply over the next three months, and the happy anticipation she felt at becoming a mother helped her repress her feelings of dissociation and loneliness.

---

* By 1956 the hype surrounding young rock 'n' roll singer Elvis Presley had reached outlandish proportions.

Chapter Fifteen

On August 2, over Radio Monte Carlo, Prince Rainier had announced to his subjects that his wife was expecting a baby. "It is a great joy for me to associate you all in our new happiness," Rainier said. "This must reinforce our hope in the future." The impending birth of Monaco's heir stirred joy in the Monegasques and renewed world interest in the tiny country. Once again a circus mentality took hold: in London insurance brokers set premiums for insurance against no heir being born, and in Monte Carlo casino gamblers were laying money on the baby's sex: the odds were five to seven the child would be a boy.

As the birth neared, the world's press again streamed into Monaco, hoping for scoops, inside stories, and the first pictures of the royal infant. Lack of news, as before, resulted in absurdity: much was made over the fact that Rainier had bought a pony, an act somehow interpreted as an indication that the Prince expected his child to be a boy. Rainier explained it meant nothing of the sort.

Her pregnancy proved uneasy for Grace. She felt nauseated for months: "They told me about morning sickness, but they didn't tell me you could be sick all day every day." Her childhood tendency to colds and infections returned; she seemed to suffer an interminable series of sore throats and viruses. She also became ravenously hungry at all hours of the day and night, and she gained over twenty-five pounds. Pregnant women are urged to eat well, but Grace went so far that her doctor told her she was eating too much.

Grace's preparations for her baby's arrival became, in the

absence of any other pressing obligation, all-consuming. She read books on natural childbirth and breast-feeding, and she worked closely with George Stacey to convert a room within the palace apartments into a nursery. "He's designed a really ingenious cabinet and shelving arrangement for the baby's linen!" she wrote home.

Toward the end of 1956, as her condition began to show more and more, Grace rarely ventured out of the palace. On one of her outings, as she made her way to her car to return to the palace, a crowd of subjects gathered around her. A woman pushed forward and suddenly put her open hand on Grace's belly, rubbed it, and wished her luck. Grace and many in the crowd laughed, but Madge Tivey-Faucon gasped in horror. It wasn't until Grace was in the car and the potential danger of the situation was impressed upon her that she became frightened. From then on, even Grace's simplest excursions from the palace were sheathed in security.

This encounter led Grace and Rainier to change their plan to have her give birth in a hospital. The Prince was already concerned about the growing hordes of press and photographers in Monaco. Now there was fear that the Monegasques themselves might get carried away in their excitement, and a jostling by either press or subjects could not be risked. Citing the Monegasque tradition that princely heirs be born in the palace, Rainier announced the change of plans. The newsmen were sorely disappointed—they had already asked the ambulance driver to slow down as he passed a preappointed spot so that cameras could catch Grace in labor.

Hastily a library in the apartments was converted into a delivery room and draped in green silk. (An Irish superstition says that surrounding a newborn baby with green will assure the child a pure, happy, and prosperous life.)

The child was due early in February, but in mid-January Grace's gynecologist, Dr. Émile Hervet, told her that the delivery would probably be sooner. Hervet and two colleagues remained in Monaco to await the birth, and Grace telephoned her mother to ask her to be at her side for the delivery. Mrs. Kelly arrived shortly before Grace went into labor.

Traditionally the citizens of Monaco learn of the birth of their prince's heir by a salute of cannons; 21 firings signified a girl, 101 a male heir. On January 20 a twenty-one-gun salute was heard, setting off jubilation in the land, but it was a false alarm: the firings were in honor of the visiting Sultan of Morocco.

Grace began her labor at 3 A.M. on January 23 and was taken to the delivery room. Rainier waited in an adjoining room, chain-smoking and pacing nervously as the hours wore on without word. After sunrise Prince Pierre, Princess Antoinette, and Mrs. Kelly joined him for the wait. At 9:27 A.M. Grace delivered without anesthetic a healthy, eight-pound, three-ounce girl. When she saw the child, Grace wept. Dr. Hervet described the baby's wails as "like a melody resounding through the palace." Rainier, moved by both the personal and political implications of this birth, gazed at his daughter for several minutes, then kissed his wife. He phoned the news to his mother.

Outside the palace, a young cyclist got the word and raced to the harbor. A cannon on the waterfront roared twenty-one blasts—and this time the Monegasques knew it was the real thing. As soon as the cannon stopped, fourteen church bells around the principality began pealing, and boats in the harbor sounded their horns—led by Aristotle Onassis's yacht, *Christina,* its siren audible six miles away.

As Grace cradled her daughter and sipped champagne, Rainier went to a nearby chapel to pray, then addressed his subjects. "My beloved wife, the Princess, has given birth to a baby princess who has been given the name of Caroline Louise Marguerite. Thank God and rejoice." In a traditional ceremony, Monegasque government officials were brought in to view the infant and be assured that she was indeed their prince's heir. Then television cameras were rolled in to broadcast the sleeping face of Monaco's littlest princess to her subjects.

A national holiday was declared. School was let out, Monte Carlo's sole prisoner was freed from jail, gambling ceased, free champagne was served throughout the principality, and red-and-white bunting was draped over every available surface. Monaco's sovereignty was once again assured.

Back in Philadelphia a reporter asked Grace's father for his reaction to the heralded arrival. His response was in character. "Oh shucks," he said. "I wanted a boy."

Although Jack Kelly's bluntness was typically insensitive, he expressed a sentiment many others felt but were too polite to reveal. Monaco had never had a princess at its helm of state, and unless Grace produced a male heir, the Monegasques would never feel completely comfortable with Rainier's successor. People the world over, in fact, apparently would have preferred a little prince: of the thousands of baby gifts sent to the palace before the birth, almost all were intended for a boy. There were stacks of clothes in the nursery sent by well-wishers, almost all boys' suits and pullovers. Only one dress could be found among the piles. Grace, indifferent to the sex of her child, said in a newspaper column shortly after Caroline's birth, "If we have a boy later on he will become the heir to the principality; but he will never be more important or dearer to us than the present heir, our firstborn, Caroline."

In the same column, Grace revealed that she was breast-feeding her baby. An American public heavily wooed by advertised modernity and convenience, and yet still prudish in matters of health and sexuality, was shocked by both the fact and the admission. Bottles, formulas, and disposable rubber nipples had taken the place of a mother's breast, particularly among the middle and upper classes, and Grace's decision seemed to fly in the face of progress. To her, this "advance" was abhorrent: nothing was more important to her than the spiritual and physical closeness of mother and child; manufactured "conveniences" distanced a vulnerable and dependent human being from its chief nurturer. Grace was surprised by the disapproval. Breast-feeding, she retorted, was "wholly normal and right—I never considered anything else." Later Grace would become involved in the La Leche League, to which breast-feeding is a carefully considered political issue. But in 1956 her decision was made purely on maternal instinct.

Six months after Caroline's birth, newspapers reported a kidnap threat against the royal baby. The palace had received unsigned letters detailing an abduction plot, the reports said, and although Grace and Rainier considered the threats only a "vicious prank," they were taken seriously enough that a group of Swiss plainclothesmen were sent to guard the child at the family villa in Gstaad, where they were vacationing.

The parents were horrified by the international coverage the threats received; they feared that it might put a madman in mind of just such an abduction. The palace issued an official denial of the story, and Prince Pierre told a reporter, "If Prince Rainier had received any anonymous letters threatening my granddaughter, I, as a grandfather, would be much less calm than I am this morning." The palace asserted that the security measures around Caroline were routine. (It was sadly true that threats against all members of the royal family had become a fact of life.)

Two months later Grace gave her first press interview since the birth of Caroline. Sounding every inch the proud mother, she said of her daughter, "I must agree with people who say she's gorgeous. She weighs nineteen pounds now, has big fat cheeks and very long legs. She has dark blue eyes like her father and she's even getting more hair—with the beginning of a blond curl which we are coaxing along. She's got her first tooth, a bottom one, and she was pretty fussy when it came too. Now she's chewing everything she can get into her mouth. She has chewed her bedclothes, all my beads, my husband's ties, and even the ears on our poodles."

Grace denied that she was pregnant again; she said that reports that Rainier had ordered profile pictures of her destroyed were false: "I myself killed those pictures. I don't like looking fat, especially when I've lost weight during vacation playing tennis and hiking. I weigh about 120 pounds now. That's above my old movie weight but my husband refuses to let me lose weight—he says I was too thin before." In fact, Grace was two months pregnant at this point, but for whatever reason she preferred to deny it. She did admit, "I'd like to be pregnant again, and sooner or later those rumors of my pregnancy are going to be true."

She had conceived again less than five months after Caroline's birth. "It's hard to remember *not* being pregnant in those days," she said later. Rainier's strong desire for a son may have had something to do with the immediacy of Grace's next conception, but in any event, on March 14, 1958, the Prince of Monaco had his heir apparent: Grace gave birth to an eight-pound, eleven-ounce boy whom the Grimaldis named Albert Alexandre Louis Pierre. Once again Grace delivered in the palace, and as Dr. Hervet stepped out of the delivery room he said simply to Rainier, "My Lord Prince, I congratulate you on your son and heir."

This time, the excitement was so great there was no waiting for the cannon salvos. One of the palace staff stuck her head out a window and yelled to the crowd gathered below, "It's a boy! It's a boy!" Aristotle Onassis, informed that a child had been born to the Prince, telephoned the principality from his London hotel suite in order to hear the number of cannon shots. After the twenty-second blast, he hung up. There were seventy-nine more. For this birth, Grace received two million orchids and, from the Prince, "a river of diamonds."

His voice faltering, Rainier once again took to the airwaves. "Monegasques and residents of the principality, you will understand my emotion and very great joy in announcing to you that the Princess, my beloved wife, has given birth to a little prince. Let us thank God for this new happiness, this proof of His special blessing."

One of the Grimaldis, however, wasn't all that happy about the new addition. Caroline later recalled that shortly after Albert's birth, "I was taken to see my mother. She was holding Albert in her arms. I had a little bouquet of flowers I was supposed to give her, and everyone kept saying, 'Go on, give your mother the flowers,' but I wouldn't. Finally, I just threw them at her."

Motherhood was to Grace her most important role, and she was determined to carry it out well. Hurt by her mother's delegation of many of her maternal duties to nurses, Grace vowed to herself that she would do better by her own children. After Caroline's birth, she told a reporter, "I'm not going to let public life or anything else push me out of my job as a mother. In America children of wealthy parents are so often given over completely to nurses from the start. Mine is not going to be." Grace was asked how her own childhood would influence her upbringing of her children, and her response was described as "cautious": "I think you have to give a child love and understanding—and, above all, treat him as an individual."

Still, Grace wanted to guard against any overreaction in her avoidance of what she saw as the deficiencies in her own upbringing: "Even if there were things that your parents didn't do for you, that doesn't mean you ought to do that particular thing for your child. He might not require it."

While Grace tried hard not to give her children "over completely to nurses," she did engage them. Margaret Stahl, a sweet-faced young maternity nurse from Switzerland, was the first, joined by Englishwoman Maureen King after Albert's birth. Grace hired nurses roughly her own age, so that she would not feel intimidated by an overbearing older woman with entrenched ideas of her own. Prince Pierre may have been instrumental in that decision; Rainier and Antoinette's nurse, he told Grace, was a formidable woman who tyrannized him: "I was never allowed into the nursery to see my children."

Caroline's and Albert's nurses were helpmeets to Grace, nothing more. The parents had very definite ideas about child rearing, particularly of the princely variety. Albert's upbringing posed special problems; he had to be groomed to one day take over Monaco's helm from his father. Don Richardson says, "The boy was totally isolated from Grace. She was able to visit him and eat with him and all that, but his upbringing was entirely in his father's hands, because he was training him to be the prince."

Grace's sister Peggy confirms that Albert was being "trained" by his father, and she adds, "Albert's godfather Prince Louis—Rainier's cousin—was just as instrumental in Albie's upbringing. He had to be groomed to take Rainier's place as the leader of the country." But, Peggy says, "Grace had a lot to say about Albie's upbringing, too. She was the one who wanted to send him to camp in the United States . . . Rainier went along with that. He was willing for his children to have the American influence that they did."

That influence was unavoidable. As the children grew older, their sensibilities were more or less equally American and Monegasque. The only caution was that they shouldn't confuse the two. They were taught French and English, for instance, but were allowed to speak only one language at a time—to avoid developing a hybrid of the two tongues.

"Hybrid" is perhaps as apt a term as any to describe the rearing of the littlest prince and princess. Just as in the marriage of their parents, conflicting necessities often arose. Both children needed to understand as much as possible the niceties of protocol and the responsibilities of their positions. At her official third birthday party, for example, Caroline acted as hostess to twenty-five children. While Albert's attentions were focused on the birthday cake, Caroline "received" the other children as they bowed and curtsied to her. Such an exalted position created problems for the little girl; as one observer asked, "On what basis do you play with somebody who has to bow to you?" To help balance things a bit, Grace began a class within the palace when Caroline was four that included other Monegasque children, to allow her daughter to interact with other girls her own age (presumably, they did not have to bow to her). The following year, Albert and two other boys joined the class.

Caroline and Albert's rarefied life, according to their cousin Grace LeVine (Lizanne's daughter, the child she was carrying at the time of Grace's wedding), was as natural to them as any other. "When you don't know anything else, you don't miss it. When I went over there at a very young age, being followed around by a nanny really bothered me, and I was glad I wasn't growing up there and had to always answer to somebody. You couldn't just run out to the backyard anytime you wanted to . . ."

Grace was always on guard against the children's developing a regal hauteur. When Albert said sharply to a butler, "You may take my plate away," Grace told him to do it himself. It took some doing, however, to make Caroline respectful; Madge Tivey-Faucon recalled that when the child would call her in the morning to fetch her for her private lessons, she would yell into the receiver, "I'm awake!" and hang up. Eventually, through reprimand and example and lack of special treatment, Grace and Rainier were able to avoid having their children turn into royal monsters. "I don't think they realized they were anything special for a long time," Maureen King recalled.

Grace's sometimes unorthodox child-rearing methods became the talk of Europe during the early 1960s. A typical story tells of how the Princess got Caroline to stop biting her little brother. Warnings didn't work, and Albert did nothing to defend himself. Finally, Grace took Caroline's arm and bit it, hard, to show her how it felt. Caroline stopped.

"I'm afraid I'm very severe at times," Grace said. "Outsiders might think I'm too hard on the children. But I give them just as much love as I do discipline, and it seems to work out very well."

There were times, however, when Grace seemed anything but disciplinary. Observers marveled at the freedom Albert and Caroline were given. In Europe children are most often "seen and not heard," and are relegated to separate parts of the house during meals and activities involving adults. Grace and Rainier frequently brought their children along on state visits, and it was not unusual for them to burst into official functions and interrupt their father. Several times Grace was permissive even by American standards. During an artist's exhibit, Madge Tivey-Faucon reported, Caroline had the artist "tearing her hair" by running up and down the aisles, sliding on the polished floor of the gallery. Grace did nothing but look at the pictures. And during a reception for ex-Queen Victoria Eugenia of Spain, at which precious ornaments were on display in the palace drawing room, Albert and Caroline tore around the room "like a hurricane," Tiv wrote, touching the artifacts "with irreverent baby fingers. . . . The Princess just went on looking at the collection. She did not bat an eyelid."

The children's displays of temperament often went unpunished; Grace interrupted evening plans whenever Caroline wailed as she and Rainier were leaving the palace—which, according to Tiv, was almost always. "The Princess can never resist her daughter's tears," she wrote. "She turns back at the first sob . . . the Princess bends over the child and consoles her gently until she stops crying. This may last a quarter of an hour. But the Princess never becomes impatient or angry. To avoid these frequent dramas, she often prefers to bring Caroline and Albert with her."

The children could scarcely have been less alike. Caroline, it seemed, had inherited her father's Latin disposition as well as his dark looks. She was mercurial, quick to laughter and to tears, strong-willed and definite, and jealous of any attention paid to Albert, especially by her father. Albert, clearly, took after his mother, from his fair hair and skin to his disposition —an "easy, sweet nature," as Grace put it in a letter to Don Richardson. Willing to let his sister bite him at will without complaint, he was quiet, self-involved, able to sit through mass at the age of two and a half without fidgeting. Both children were enormously bright, but while Caroline's intelligence took the form of scattered curiosity and mimicry, Albert's was more linear. Once, at the circus, Rainier had to continually coax his son to watch the performers rather than read the program; Albert was intensely interested in whether the acts were doing exactly what the program stated they would do.

There was no way to avoid spoiling the children with material lavishness; practically every palace visitor brought toys for Albert and Caroline, and they were frequently duplications of toys the children already had. On one occasion, French President and Mme. Charles de Gaulle arrived with a doll for Caroline and a red rocking horse for Albert. After a few minutes Grace whispered frantically to Madge Tivey-Faucon, "Fly down to the nursery, Tiv, and hide Albert's red horse!" The children expressed only mild interest when she did so, and when Mme. de Gaulle gave Albert the horse, he took it eagerly, never mentioning that he already had one just like it. "Madame de Gaulle was delighted," Tiv wrote, "and the Princess sighed with relief."

Caroline's collection of dolls was housed in its own specially built cabinet; one doll, a gift from America, came complete with a trousseau including a bikini, cocktail dress, and evening gown. Aristotle Onassis sent Albert a miniature car that ran on electricity and duplicated every aspect of a real automobile. Rainier, according to Grace, was frequently the worst offender: "Sometimes he goes too far as a disciplinarian, but more often he goes too far by spoiling them. He's likely to arrive loaded down with presents because he hasn't seen them for ten days. Once, when we were in Spain for the coronation of Juan Carlos, he spent a whole afternoon saying he had to bring something back for [the children]. I kept telling him, 'Forget it, they don't need anything.' There was nothing to be done. He went off on a hunt for Spanish records. He has always loved running around the shops . . ."

Never far from Grace's mind was the vulnerability of her children to harm. The publicized kidnapping of young Eric Peugeot sent Grace into a near-panic for Albert's safety. "I am afraid," she told Tiv. "There are so many maniacs capable of anything." And an outbreak of infantile paralysis led the Princess, according to Tiv, to have "the nursery quarantined: neither the children's nurses nor I were allowed to leave for a month."*

On another occasion, Grace received a letter from a doctor in America who wrote that he had seen a photograph in which she was holding Caroline's arm in a way that could result in dislocation. "I advise you to be very careful," the doctor concluded, "for it could be very painful for your child and frightening for you." Grace vowed to be more careful in the future, but only a few days later, at the family ranch at Roc Agel, Grace heard screams coming from the garden. "It was Caroline," Tiv wrote. "The young nursemaid had done this very thing when she was taking Caroline for a walk, and the child's arm hung like a puppet's. I thought the Princess was going to faint. Then suddenly she pulled herself together and flew at the nurse. This is one of the rare times I saw the Princess lose her self-control."

Roc Agel, although just a few miles from the palace, afforded the royal family an entirely different lifestyle than that of "the Rock." The Prince purchased the building and sixty acres in 1957, and by 1959 Grace had renovated the structure into a charming farmhouse with a tiled roof, heavy beams, and stone walls. There, the Grimaldis lived a far more self-sufficient lifestyle. The children pitched in with the chores, Grace tended to the vegetable and flower gardens, Rainier cared for the animals and rode the horses. More than anything, Roc Agel was Rainier's concession to Grace's homesickness; there, she could be more herself than anywhere else except Philadelphia: the kitchen she'd designed was entirely American (including the plumbing), and symbolically, one of the bathrooms was covered with stills from Grace's movies. Usually the family would barbecue hamburgers and hot dogs;

---

* Tiv doesn't say whether the three were confined to the nursery or the palace. One hopes it was the latter.

if the weather was bad, Grace would prepare experimental Chinese and Italian dishes, with varying success.

It was important for Grace and Rainier to maintain a sense of balance by getting away from the strictures, pomp, and protocol of the palace; it was even more vital, they felt, for the children to do so. Caroline and Albert not only needed to learn self-sufficiency, their parents believed, they also had to remain level-headed about their stature: they were royalty, yes, but they were not put on earth to be waited upon. Lizanne LeVine recalls that the children learned this lesson very well: "They could come to anyone's house here in America and make their beds, clean up their rooms, pitch in with dinner and the dishes. They were taught to do that, not that they should expect someone to wait on them all the time."

To raise children in a bilingual, bicultural environment, to give them a balanced outlook while never letting them forget the responsibilities of their positions, to make them understand the subtle and not-so-subtle differences among Monegasque, French, and American customs and sensibilities, could not have been an easy task for Grace and Rainier. But these would prove among the couple's easier challenges. More difficult would be molding individual, self-confident personalities among children whose parents were not only the vortex of their world but of their country's as well. Many children feel inadequate to live up to their parents' accomplishments; how daunting this must then have been for Caroline and Albert.

As her children grew up, Princess Grace was most often heralded in women's magazines as "Monaco's Perfect Mother." She was no more so than any other woman has ever been. She was a good mother, loving, concerned that she do what was right for her children. But she made mistakes, and she repeated a few of the ones *her* mother had made with her (the irony of which was not lost on her). Years later, as Caroline grew into womanhood, a great deal of friction developed between mother and daughter and caused them both great pain. To Grace, the realization that it was the kind of up-bringing she had worked so hard to give Caroline that caused much of her troubles with her daughter was the most painful thing of all.

Chapter Sixteen

The birth of her children, more than anything else, cemented Grace's commitment to Prince Rainier and to Monaco. If the difficulties she faced in her first two years of marriage sometimes led to thoughts of escape, they crossed her mind no longer. She was determined to be the best possible wife for her husband, the best possible mother for her children, and the best possible princess for Monaco. William F. Buckley's analysis of her commitment to the life she had so hastily chosen is apt: "If she had decided to become a nun rather than a princess, there would not have been a distinctive difference in her approach to her vocation."

Rainier's marriage to Grace Kelly, as his advisers predicted, helped turn Monaco's economy around. By the end of the 1950s, annual tourism—from which most of Monaco's income was then derived—had nearly doubled its 1954 total. The number of visitors staying in the country just for a day rose to nearly a million, while large numbers of the more well-heeled, who might stay for weeks and spend thousands in the hotels, restaurants, and casinos, once again made Monaco the most glamorous and exclusive resort in Europe. The high cost of vacationing there—at least two hundred dollars a day for a couple, exclusive of gambling considerations—helped Monaco avoid the scourge of more "common" tourists who had descended upon Cannes, Nice, and Saint-Tropez. As it had been in the previous century, Monaco became the playground of the superwealthy as its annual income rose into the tens of millions. During this period, the yearly stipend granted the royal family nearly tripled to $321,000 by 1961.

Had she done little else, Grace would have fulfilled her obligation to Monaco by producing a royal heir and re-establishing the country as a tourist magnet. But her responsibilities were ongoing, and she tried to fulfill them to the best of her abilities. Many of them she dreaded—a scheduled appearance at an official function often caused her physical distress—but others she welcomed, and still others she created through an intense interest in improving some aspect or other of Monaco life.

One of her first "crusades" involved Monaco's hospital. When it was renamed in honor of her in 1958, Grace took a zealous interest in improving the institution. Appalled by the cold, antiseptic rooms, she badgered the hospital staff to warm up the wards with paint and decorations, but she met with resistance. The administrators cited expenses and argued against what they saw as Grace's naïve belief that adding amenities in the hospital would help patients recover, but Grace was undeterred. She at first brought in flowers and hung paintings on the walls; later she began fund-raising efforts. Wearing down the bureaucrats with her persistence, the Princess got her way: she even chose the colors and new decor.

Grace saw a similar need at Monaco's home for the aged, but among those people what was needed was more than a cheerier decor: it was human companionship that was lacking. Often without families (or left ignored by what family they had), the residents saw no one except their attendants for months at a time. Grace created an Assistance Center made up of volunteers who visited the home at regular intervals (she herself often among them), materially improving the quality of life of people whose days had been blurs of monotony and loneliness. "She brought us heart," one resident said, and her concern for them began to melt whatever misgivings her subjects may have had about her.

Grace's most important duty early in her reign was as president of the Monaco Red Cross, a position she took over from Rainier. The organization, involved in the international relief network, served Monaco essentially as an adjunct to the state welfare system in providing help to those in need. Eventually Grace expanded its impact with day care centers for working mothers, an orphaned children's center, courses in home nursing for expectant mothers, and first aid training.

Grace attended all meetings of the Red Cross administrative council, settled disputes, and eventually made most of the decisions without need of consultation. Perhaps her greatest contribution was with fund-raising. The state's yearly stipend was not nearly enough for the organization to fulfill Grace's expansive vision for it; she established the annual Red Cross charity ball as the social event of the year in Monaco and one of the most glamorous events of its kind in the world. Over the ensuing years, the lavish costume ball would be attended by some of the world's most important people, from royalty to Grace's Hollywood friends: the Richard Burtons, Frank Sinatra, Sophia Loren, Gina Lollobrigida, and all in spectacular costumes. The most fantastic, of course, was always worn by Grace, who one year had to be transported to the gala in a van, because her headpiece, spreading out several feet with golden spikes, wouldn't fit inside an automobile: "I looked like Radio Monte Carlo," Grace laughed. The Red Cross gala was always her favorite public event—an opportunity to see many of her old friends, dress extravagantly, and raise a great deal of money for a cause to which she had made a strong commitment.

But always there is Grace's dichotomy. The concerned, committed Princess could just as easily forget her responsibilities, sometimes childishly. Madge Tivey-Faucon recalled going to fetch Grace for a Red Cross meeting. She smelled something burning and warily opened the door to the library. Inside Grace was playing with a seal that Rainier had given her, bearing the family's coat of arms. She was heating variously colored waxes, experimenting to see which ones looked the best. "When she saw me," Tiv wrote, "she gave a little jump like a girl caught doing something naughty. There was melted sealing wax all over the place. The round table and the carpet were strewn with matches and crumpled envelopes. She continued to play like this until she suddenly perceived that the time had slipped away and she had missed her scheduled Red Cross meeting."

On occasion Grace used her royal prerogative as a shortcut. Preparing to meet General Charles de Gaulle on a trip to Paris with Rainier, Grace decided she should be as familiar with de Gaulle's life and career as possible. She asked Tiv to get her the general's memoirs at the library, then had another aide read the book and prepare a résumé of it for her.

When lacking diversion, either serious or playful, Grace succumbed to boredom, making no attempt to fill her periods of free time. After her children had started school, Grace spent a large part of her day in bed. "At first, when she went to bed in the middle of the day, I thought she was ill," Madge Tivey-Faucon wrote. "I had to get used to it. And so did the Prince. The telephone can ring, the visitors can wait, the Princess sleeps, and orders are given not to wake her."

Grace's lethargy left her less able to function well on certain occasions, and less able to handle her responsibilities when they converged, as they frequently did. She wrote to Don Richardson that her duties often left her feeling exhausted and "like the one-armed paper-hanger."

Grace tried to alleviate her boredom and homesickness in any way she could. She was, a friend said, "childlike" about parties and excited about seeing her friends; she was indefatigable at the gatherings, resisted attempts to get her home, and often remained, drinking champagne, until early in the morning. This was true as well when she entertained at home, where she would play games or reminisce with old friends until daybreak.

Nothing pleased Grace more, in fact, than to have visits from her show business friends; seeing them renewed her link to her past, brought her news of her beloved profession, allowed her to laugh and let her hair down as she could with no one else outside her family. To be certain that she missed no one who happened to be traveling through France, she subscribed to Maggi Nolan's "Celebrity Bulletin," a daily listing of prominent visitors to Paris. She constantly extended invitations through phone calls and letters to old friends in the United States to come and visit her, and if she ran into someone unexpectedly anywhere near Monaco, she would not allow a refusal.

Mark Miller recalls attending a social event in Paris with his wife and in-laws early in the 1960s. "I hadn't seen Grace in a few years; she had invited me to the wedding but I couldn't go, and then I got married and started raising children, and we got out of touch. Grace walked into this gala with her father-in-law, and flashbulbs were popping and people were gawking. She started to pass where we were standing, and she saw me standing there. She put her hand up to shield her eyes so she could be sure it was me, then she exclaimed, 'Herbie! What are you doing here?', threw her arms around me, and kissed me. Everyone was astounded. Her father-in-law didn't know who I was, and my in-laws had no idea that we were friends, and here she was calling me Herbie. It was very funny. Everyone was thinking, Who is this guy? Reporters started asking me, 'Who are you?'

"Grace just ignored them and kept asking me what I was doing there. I asked her the same thing. She said, 'I live here.' I said, 'I thought you lived down the coast.' She said, 'Knock it off, you know damn well where I live.' She told me she was pissed that I didn't come to the wedding, and that I must come down with my relatives and visit her in Monaco, and I should call her. She wrote down her phone number. All this is going on with about fifty cameramen and reporters surging around us, and she's writing her phone number on a piece of paper against the wall."

Miller and his wife drove to Roc Agel a few days later, where Grace and Rainier entertained them. Miller brought Albert a pair of pistols and a holster, because Grace had told Albert that Miller, a Texan, was a "cowboy." "Apparently he absolutely loved them and wore them for years afterward," Miller says, "until he finally grew out of them."

"In honor" of Miller's Southern background, Grace made pitchers of mint juleps. "We got absolutely bombed and laughed about the jillions of funny things that had happened to us. And we kept in touch after that. You don't usually have that kind of lasting friendship with people you go to school with, especially if you've been romantically involved—usually you break up and that's that, you never see them again. She tried to keep her friends."

When the Millers began to leave, Grace and Rainier expressed concern. "They tried to get us to stay the night because she said the road was absolutely treacherous and she told me, 'You can't go down that road, we've had too many mint juleps.' She was right, of course, but we had to leave. Well, I literally inched my way down those roads."

In her letters Grace constantly urged her family and close friends to visit her. As often as possible, they did. Stories of these visits abound and indicate diverse reactions to Monaco and the palace. Lizanne, who visited for the first time in August 1960, "adored" it: "It's so elegant, my God, to have someone serve me in bed and all that, do my clothes—you take off something and it's whipped to the laundry, washed and ironed, a button sewn on if you need it. It's very nice. But Grace also made it homey; in the apartment they would make their own breakfast every morning. When we went over there, there were a few big events, but mostly we'd play games and it was great fun. And of course, when we went up to Roc Agel, there was nobody around, so you could do whatever you wanted to and we had great times there."

Grace's father, however, was never comfortable in the palace. His nephew Charles V. Kelly, Jr., recalled, "If there was anything [Jack Kelly] loathed, it was pretentiousness. He hated Monaco, where you'd have servants all over you. He'd say to them, 'Go away! I'll call you when I need you.' Whereas my uncle George adored the palace and the life that went with it. But Uncle Jack couldn't bear the protocol in Monaco."

Grace's father was also extremely uncomfortable with the fact that his newest son-in-law—a breed for which he never concealed his contempt—was more powerful and important a man than he was. Grace's final attempt to attain stature in her father's eyes took the form of marriage to a man born to a position in life that Jack Kelly, with all the hard work and money in the world, could never achieve. In Monaco, his son-in-law was the man around whom everything revolved—an untenable situation for a man used to being the center of his own world. True to form, Kelly had mocked the palace atmosphere during the wedding week when he arrived at a friend's hotel room to play gin rummy: "I got out on a twelve-hour pass but I want to be back on time so I won't get jugged for going AWOL." Later, during the game, he said, "I expect more respect from you commoners."

Not everyone in the Kelly family was impressed, either positively or negatively, by Grace's palace life. Grace LeVine remembers taking in stride her first visit, when she was seven. "We had a great time over there, but my biggest memory is of the typhoid shots we had to get in order to go. We stayed for three weeks. It was really very normal. It wasn't anything grand, I wasn't awed by it or anything. She just lived in a bigger house than we did, that's all. I guess when you grow up around that kind of thing, you just take it in stride."

Of all Grace's friends and relatives, Kell was always the most impertinent about Grace's exalted new position. In the middle of the stuffiest social event, Kell would slap his sister heartily on the back and introduce her as "my little sister, Gracie." Depending on her mood, Grace would love it or be mortified. (Kell wasn't the only one of Grace's intimates to do this, and it irritated Tiv: "Such familiarity," she wrote, "destroys at one blow the careful staging built up by protocol around the Prince and Princess.") Kell took delight in playing practical jokes on Grace and Rainier. Philadelphia Congressman Jack Edelstein, a close friend of Kell's for years, recalled paying a visit to the palace with Kell. They decided that Kell would tell his sister that he was bringing along Japan's premier world-class diver. "So I went out and bought a ridiculous swimsuit," Edelstein recalled. "I had a pair of extra-large kind of Japanese teeth made by my dentist . . . And I was wearing a big pair of dark glasses which covered my face.

"Jack told Grace and Rainier that we were fortunate to have this Japanese with us because he was willing to give a diving exhibition in the palace pool. Well, Kell brought out Grace and Rainier and there I was standing up on the diving board looking completely ludicrous . . . I looked over at Rainier and Grace watching me. In a Japanese accent I informed them quite seriously that I was a 'Jupe,' that my mother was a Japanese and my father a Jew. I could see that Grace was trying hard to preserve her dignity. Well, after some double-talk about what a famous diver I was, I stepped back to the start of the board, took a run to the edge, and did a tremendous belly flop. Then they caught on and howled; Rainier was hysterical."

One of Grace's relatives strongly protested a royal family practice during a visit of his. When Charles Kelly sat down to dinner in the palace dining room, he noticed that two dogs were also in the room. Rainier passed two silver bowls of dog food to Grace, who set them on the floor for the animals. Charles was appalled. "I told Grace either the dogs go or I go. I had no intention of eating *my* meal with a pair of slobbering beasts. The dogs went; I stayed."

Around Easter in 1961, according to Tiv, a visit by Cary Grant and his wife, Betsy Drake, created friction between the Prince and Princess. So excited was Grace over the Grants' arrival that she met them at the Nice airport—"an honor usually reserved for her mother," Tiv wrote. A photographer captured Grace kissing Grant in greeting, and the photo appeared in local newspapers the next day. The Prince was displeased. "He was always jealous, in spite of himself, of his wife's friends from the days before their marriage," said Tiv. "He was doubtless also afraid that this friendly embrace might remind the gossips of the passionate kisses between Cary Grant and Grace Kelly in front of the camera." (When the Prince had screened *To Catch a Thief* in the palace theater, Tiv recalled, he had taken the unusual step of barring staff members who lived in the palace.)

"The Prince did not hide his bad humor during the Grants' stay at the palace," Tiv went on. "He spoke to no one. He sulked . . . The Princess was cool—her usual attitude to her husband's moods."

Grant felt that Tiv's memory of the events was strongly skewed. "The Prince has never been anything but charming to me," he said. "We are very good friends. I do not have any recollection of a coolness on the part of the Prince toward me during that stay in Monaco."

Grace's strong desire to have her friends visit her was rooted in far more than nostalgia—she was dreadfully lonely. She still had not, after several years in her new home, acquired a single close friend. A gregarious person who loved interacting with people she liked, Grace attempted to improve the chances of developing friendships with some of the Monegasques by inviting them to the palace for cozy family dinners. The results were disastrous. The guests, it turned out, felt extremely uncomfortable being so intimate with their princess, and the dinners were just long patches of embarrassed silence punctuated by awkward civilities. Disappointed, Grace abandoned the experiment.

Indeed, for the duration of her life in Monaco, Grace's best and closest friend was her husband. Rainier later admitted that it took time for a genuine love to develop between them, but it did grow with the birth of their children and their strong need for each other. Madge Tivey-Faucon recalled the affection between them: "There is nothing more touching than to see the Prince put his arm around the Princess's waist as they come out of the *grande salle à manger* after luncheon or dinner. The gesture is infinitely graceful and never fails to move those present. Often, in the evening, when the Prince leaves his office in the palace, he takes his wife by the arm and leads her to the white Jaguar. They escape like lovers, to dine in some little restaurant not far away."

Still, the fundamental differences in their personalities kept Grace and Rainier from achieving an ideal marital closeness. Often, according to Tiv, Grace would speak to Rainier and be ignored—"The Princess must certainly suffer when she asks him a question and it remains unanswered." What affinity they did share Grace attributes to their religion. "The Catholicism in our marriage was a very strong link between us," she said in 1974, "and it helped . . . because there weren't too many other mutual bonds."

Grace and Rainier shared few interests. While she watched opera, ballet, and theater presentations in Monaco with rapt attention, the Prince could be counted on to fall asleep shortly into the performance. "People pretend not to notice," Tiv wrote, "but everyone is in on the secret. All the musicians from the Monaco National Orchestra are aware that he can rarely last out the first bars, despite nudges from the Princess." On one memorable occasion, Rainier fell asleep at a banquet while the Queen of Spain was telling him a story. Usually at such times Grace poked or kicked her husband awake. This time, the embarrassed Princess was at the other side of the table and could do nothing.

Conversely, Grace shared few of her husband's enthusiasms; she had no interest in skin diving, archaeology, motorcar racing, or zoology. When the Prince burst excitedly into the library to announce that one of his chimpanzees was pregnant, Grace didn't interrupt her conversation with Tiv. The Prince grew impatient: "You don't seem to know how important this is! . . . It's very rare for a chimpanzee to breed in captivity!"

"All *rightie,*" Grace snapped. "I'll *knit* her something!"

It took Grace years to feel comfortable among the people in Monaco. At first she avoided public appearances, so much so that magazine articles soon appeared calling her "The Invisible Princess" and captioning illustrations of Grace among the

Monegasques "Rare Photo." When she did appear in public, it was with great discomfort. "She keeps away from people, flees from her popularity," Tiv wrote, adding that Grace attended a gala opera performance "as though she were going to an execution." If she were applauded by her subjects, "she might give a faint smile. People would shake their heads and say, 'She just does not know how to do it. It would be so easy to love such a beautiful Princess!' "

There were several reasons for Grace's reserve. The kidnap threats against her children, and the near-paranoia of her staff about interaction between crowds and Princess, had left her wary. Her lack of self-confidence in her role as princess was often crippling. Her difficulty with the language, her unfamiliarity with protocol, her fear of embarrassing her husband, even her near-sightedness, kept her inside her "plastic bubble" during public appearances. The result was that the woman her friends knew as warm and full of life was not only alienating her subjects, but distancing herself in social situations that might lead to new friendships and alleviate her loneliness. Once again, the diverse elements of Grace's personality were at war.

To the world outside Monaco, however, it appeared that Grace Kelly had fitted herself easily and elegantly into the cloak of royalty. Her beauty dazzled the most cynical statesman, and her reserve, although born of terror, was viewed by many as appropriately regal hauteur. By the early 1960s, Princess Grace had become one of the world's most admired, celebrated, and imitated women—a fact that mystified some observers. Maurice Zolotow, profiling Grace in 1961, began his article, "One of the curious questions of modern public opinion is why the world's imagination continues to be intrigued by a certain tall, slender, thirty-two-year-old blonde, who is married, has two children . . . and has for six years contributed absolutely nothing of any world-shaking social, artistic, political, or economic importance that would justify the amount of attention she gets . . . She is one of the seven most publicized women of the past decade in the international press, her six sisters being Princess Margaret, Marilyn Monroe, Brigitte Bardot, Elizabeth Taylor, Jacqueline Kennedy and Queen Elizabeth II of England. More is being published about Princess Grace today in the European and American newspapers and magazines than there was in 1954 when she was at the height of her power and fame as one of Hollywood's most formidable motion-picture stars . . ."

Her movie star-become-princess mystique served her well, of course, but so did her singularity as the wife of a head of state. Few political consorts were as beautiful, as elegant, as fashionable, as charming in personal encounters as Her Serene Highness, the Princess of Monaco. The same glamorous qualities that separated Jacqueline Kennedy from other wives of heads of state distinguished Grace, and it was she who charmed Charles de Gaulle years before Mrs. Kennedy's triumph at Versailles. Just as Jackie won the hearts of the French people in 1961, so did Grace during a state visit in October 1959. That Grace would enchant the French President had been predicted by *Le Monde:* "The presence of Princess Grace at [the Prince's] side will undoubtedly give more splendor to this latest expression of Franco-Monegasque friendship."

Grace was more nervous about this engagement than she had been about any other; political matters between France and Monaco were at a sensitive stage (and would reach the crisis point three years later), and Rainier was anxious for all to go well. Grace diligently studied the résumé of de Gaulle's memoirs she'd had drawn up (but she still couldn't bring herself to read the entire corpus) and found herself unable to eat or sleep for several days before the visit.

All went perfectly at the official reception at the Élysée Palace. Grace enchanted the general with her beauty, her knowledge of his military exploits, and her insistence on speaking to him only in French (he found her lapses of grammar and pronunciation charming). *Paris Presse* reported, "Grace of Monaco reigned over fifteen ministers and three hundred subjects at the Élysée." During the next three days,

Grace won the hearts of most Frenchmen with her visits to hospitals, factories, and orphanages. As Jacqueline Kennedy did several years later, Grace stole the spotlight from her husband, but Rainier could not have been anything but delighted. "The best ambassador I have is Grace," he said, without overstatement.

Occasionally public adoration of Grace got out of hand. Rainier dreaded trips to America, where the press rarely left him and his wife alone for more than a few minutes at a time, but compared to the chaos generated by the Grimaldis' visits to some other countries, the United States was a haven of privacy and respectful decorum. When Grace and Rainier visited Italy in 1957, the couple had to be surrounded by policemen to protect them from paparazzi; when they made a pilgrimage to Grace's ancestral Irish homestead in 1961, over one hundred people were injured in a tumultuous welcoming melee.

The visit to Ireland proved a highly emotional experience for Grace. Perhaps because she had been separated from her American roots and was living within an alien culture, she developed in the early 1960s an intense new interest in her Irish heritage. Ireland, although not a part of the Continent, was a member of the European community; and for Grace, reestablishing her Irishness brought her closer, in a small way, to her new compatriots. The avidity of her interest led her to purchase a library of *five hundred* books on Irish history and culture.

Early in 1961, Grace decided to visit her ancestral home in County Mayo. Rainier arranged for a state visit with Irish President and Mrs. de Valéra, and Ireland prepared an enormous welcome. The Irish were feeling a great deal of national pride—John F. Kennedy had just been inaugurated as America's first Irish-Catholic president—and the visit of the granddaughter of Irish emigrants who had become a princess brought out tens of thousands of cheering people of all ages as Grace stepped off the plane at the Dublin airport. En route to the hotel, the car in which Grace and Rainier were riding was rocked by a crowd that filled the street from side-walk to sidewalk; outside the hotel, the crowd refused to dis-perse until Grace appeared on her balcony to wave to them.

The most emotional point of the trip came as Grace paid a visit to the thatched hut in which her grandfather John Henry Kelly had lived before coming to America. On the way Grace heard small schoolchildren standing along the route chant "Princess Grace! Princess Grace!" as they waved little red Monegasque flags; as she climbed the steep hills to the whitewashed cottage, she wept softly as a crowd of observers broke into "Kelly, the boy from Killann."

Her emotion almost overcame her as she sat in one of the cottage's two rooms, talking with Ellen Mulchrone, the el-derly widow who then owned the Kelly homestead, eating scones and drinking Irish tea. Grace listened avidly to stories about the Kellys of County Mayo, and her superstitious na-ture was intrigued by Mrs. Mulchrone's story of a fortune-teller's prediction, given to her years before: "A beautiful woman will visit you from Europe, and her all dripping in diamonds. . . ."

Grace and Rainier toured the countryside, went fishing with one of Grace's cousins, a local fisherman, and stayed at the local inn, a modest establishment. The entire pilgrimage was a spiritual odyssey that brought back into sharp focus for Grace the sense of her own cultural heritage that had been blurred in the American melting pot and nearly obliterated within the national chauvinism of Monaco and France.

As moving an experience as the trip was for Grace, recountings of the trip by her relatives back in Philadelphia were not immune to the patented Kelly family irreverence. Grace's niece, Mary Daly, sister of Charles V. Kelly, Jr., told the story this way: "When Grace was there at the house for the first time it was during an awful heavy rainstorm. The place consisted of two rooms plus an outhouse. Grace had to go. So she said to the old lady, 'May I use your bathroom?' The lady said, 'Well, it's really too rainy out there. Come with me, dear.'

"She took Grace into the bedroom and gave her a potty, which Grace used, covered it over, and said to the woman, 'What shall I do with this?' So the woman told her, 'Don't worry, dear, I'll dispose of it.'

"And do you know what my brother Charles said? 'Dispose of it, hell! I'll bet the old woman bottled that pee and sold it.' "

Chapter Seventeen

The difficulties Grace faced in the first years of her marriage were compounded by a series of political and financial crises that threatened her husband's—and Monaco's—sovereignty between 1956 and 1965. Grace, while never a direct part of the decision-making process, advised her husband, cajoled him, acted as a sounding board, and worked to help him keep his temper under control. Faced with struggles over the very existence of his country as he knew it, Rainier frequently vented his anger and frustration on his wife. She, characteristically, remained calm, allowing him to let off steam. But the pressures built up in her too, and household staff members often saw her wandering the palace corridors in the middle of the night, unable to sleep.

Rainier's political problems began not long after his ascension to the throne. Just twenty-six and inexperienced, he was unable to win over Monaco's tradition-bound National Council to his vision for the modernization of Monaco. Particularly controversial was his plan for an ambitious railroad tunnel through Monaco, and a landfill project to add dozens of acres to the country and allow for the erection of corporate offices, high-rise apartment buildings, and tourist attractions. Rainier knew that Monaco's future lay in economic expansion; traditionalists feared that "modernization" would destroy Monaco's charm and character. And, although Rainier was looking ahead toward economic solvency, his opponents saw the enormous expense of his plans, looked at the country's depressed economic condition, and wondered where the money would come from.

Faced with bureaucratic foot-dragging at almost every turn, Rainier, by birth and training an absolutist but bound by Monaco's constitution, burned with frustration. What slow progress he was making in his plans was interrupted in 1955 by the first serious crisis of his reign. Monaco's Precious Metals Society, the country's biggest bank, declared bankruptcy after overinvesting in a consortium designed to exploit Monte Carlo's radio and television station. The bank's failure under any conditions would have been a blow to Monaco and to the Prince, but the fact that members of Rainier's household occupied positions in the Society proved severely damaging to his personal prestige. Angered by the potential loss of their own investments and eager to capitalize on the Prince's embarrassment, members of the National Council called for the resignation of three of his closest aides. Rainier at first angrily resisted but was soon forced to accede to the demand.

The unsavory situation played into the hands of Rainier's domestic foes, who used it as an example not of corruption but of incompetence. How, they asked loudly, could this young prince be trusted with an enormous modernization project if he couldn't even manage to keep a Monegasque bank solvent? It was a question that would continue to dog Rainier.

The future of the Precious Metals Society was assured after a group of French companies took control of it, and several anonymous loans appeared on its books—loans from various sources, all controlled by Greek shipping magnate Aristotle Onassis. Onassis's help was accepted but not particularly welcomed by Rainier, who knew that the Greek's motives for helping to keep Monaco solvent were anything but unselfish. As the Prince would later bitterly say, "Onassis wants to turn Monte Carlo into Monte Greco."

The forty-six-year-old Greek billionaire was not as well known in America as he would be a decade later when he married President John F. Kennedy's widow, Jacqueline, but in much of the rest of the world he was renowned for his enormous wealth, personal flamboyance, beautiful twenty-six-year-old wife, Christina, and his yacht of the same name, which he had converted from a destroyer into a virtual floating palace at a price of two-and-a-half million dollars. Onassis had been enchanted with Monaco since the age of sixteen, when, as a refugee from his native Smyrna, he had stood on the deck of a ship heading for Buenos Aires and been captivated by the romantic harbor lights of Monte Carlo.

Three decades later, then several times a millionaire, Onassis viewed Monte Carlo not only as a beautiful memory but as a financial opportunity. At first he attempted to buy the decrepit Winter Sporting Club building as a tax-free headquarters for his shipping fleet, but the SBM informed him that the building was neither for sale nor for rent: Rainier and the other members of the SBM did not countenance the presence of so powerful a figure at their doorstep.

Used to getting his own way, Onassis simply bought the SBM. He acquired, directly and through dozens of satellite companies he owned in Central and South America, a majority of the company's shares and thus a controlling interest in the corporation. When the takeover was completed in 1954, Onassis announced this latest acquisition.

Faced with this fait accompli, Rainier tried to look on the bright side: one of the world's wealthiest men now had a vested interest in the economic fortunes of Monaco (indeed, one year later came his rescue of the Precious Metals Society), and he knew that Onassis's circle of high rollers would now be more attracted to Monte Carlo than ever before. Further, Onassis personally assured the Prince that he shared his vision of a modernized and economically vivified Monaco. Rainier liked Onassis, a man of great charm and personal magnetism, and came to welcome his promised cooperation in Rainier's vision for Monaco's future.

The rapprochement between these two powerful and autocratic men had soured so badly by 1954, however, that Onassis stormed out of a palace meeting after Rainier told him, "Mr. Onassis, your money has brought you everything except an education. You were badly brought up." In late 1955 they spoke to each other only through exchanges with interviewers. Asked by a reporter about Onassis's contributions to Monaco since his acquisition of the SBM, Rainier could barely control his anger. "That man! I won't have anything to do with him . . . he came here two years ago with a lot of big talk about wanting to help me modernize Monaco. We listened to him. We went out and hired engineers to survey his projects. And what happened? Nothing except that we wasted money on the preparations."

Onassis, for his part, responded as to a wayward child. Asked by the same reporter who had interviewed Rainier, "What has he got against you?" Onassis responded, "Did that kid have the nerve to say something nasty about me? What was it? I thought when we got him that boat, he wouldn't talk so much."*

Petty rhetoric aside, Rainier deeply resented Onassis's apparent view of Monte Carlo as a plaything, and its prince as a puppet. Onassis's advice was usually sound; it was he, in fact, who had pressed Rainier to seek a prominent wife, perhaps an American actress, in order to enhance Monaco's attraction as a tourist magnet. But, as he often did, Onassis overstepped his bounds with a crude and ill-advised attempt to put his advice into action. Unbeknownst to the Prince, Onassis and publisher Gardner Cowles put out feelers to Marilyn Monroe about the prospect of marrying the Prince of Monaco. That Monroe was not Catholic, had been married twice before, and had exactly the wrong public image for the Princess of Monaco appears not to have occurred to Onassis.

Marilyn was apparently intrigued. Asked if she thought the Prince would want to marry her, she replied, "Give me two days alone with him and of course he'll want to marry me." But she was clearly unsuitable as a prince's consort, and this behind-the-scenes maneuvering on his behalf, Rainier has said, served only to "disgust" him.

* Onassis, it seems, had "arranged" for Rainier to get a "bargain" price on the *Deo Juvante*.

Rainier's advisers had hoped that his marriage to Grace, along with its many other advantages, would help calm his domestic opposition and smooth his relationship with Onassis. It did achieve the latter. Onassis was reportedly "overjoyed" at the announcement of the impending nuptials; he donated a million francs to the Monegasque Red Cross in celebration, and as a wedding present gave Grace a lavish tiara and bracelet of diamonds and rubies. Onassis found himself completely charmed by Monaco's new Princess, as did opera diva Maria Callas, with whom Onassis had begun a longtime relationship following his divorce from Christina. Grace and Callas developed a close, mutually admiring relationship.

With Grace as a calming element between Onassis and her husband, the two couples began to mesh socially, dined together often, took cruises on the *Christina*. Over the next several years, a sometimes uneasy but generally pleasant détente developed between Rainier and "Ari." It wasn't to last, and before the final estrangement, Monaco's prince would face the two worst crises of his reign.

Prince Rainier's marriage to Grace Kelly did not, as he had hoped, calm his political troubles in Monaco. Grumbling among his opposition resumed with the wedding itself; the circuslike nature of the event, so distasteful to Rainier, was cited as another example of his managerial ineptitude. Grace's aloofness and growing reputation as the "Invisible Princess" did little to charm her husband's more skeptical compatriots into endorsing his modernization programs.

The situation reached its nadir in 1958. Work on the railroad tunnel had proceeded, despite opposition from the National Council that grew stronger with each delay and cost escalation. Monegasques who wanted constitutional reform used the discontent generated by Rainier's management problems to demand a new Constitution, one that would give the National Council more power. All that body could presently do to challenge a princely proposal, except to bog it down in red tape, was veto the entire state budget, an extreme and belligerent action the council had never before taken.

Unable to stop the tunnel project, the National Council used Rainier's call for additional funds for the Oceanographic Institute as an excuse to force matters to a head: claiming that expenditures were too high, the council renewed its call for constitutional reforms and refused to approve the 1959 budget.

Long beleaguered and now deeply angry, Rainier refused either to back down or to negotiate. With similar actions by his predecessors Albert I and Louis II as precedents, he suspended the Constitution, abolished the National Council, and outlawed any political assemblies or demonstrations. As he announced his action to his stunned subjects, Rainier blamed the council's "obstructionism" and attacks on "the plenitude of my princely powers." He promised that the measures were temporary and that he would, in his own good time, grant the principality a new Constitution.

Rainier's opponents bitterly attacked the move as a "coup d'état" and labeled him a dictator. They had a point: his actions were unconstitutional. To resolve the budget impasse, Rainier's legal options were limited to dissolving the existing National Council and calling an election to create a new one. This would have been an effective move, but it was not enough. Rainier, buffeted by critics for ten years, felt the time had come to assert his unassailable sovereignty as Prince of Monaco—or be forever a vulnerable and embattled leader.

The action resolved the impasse to the Prince's advantage, but it created deep-seated resentments against the royal couple that affected their day-to-day lives—particularly Grace's. She had made acquaintanceships among several of the women with whom she worked on various charities and guilds, and she hoped that close friendships might develop. But many of these women were the wives of her husband's political enemies, and Rainier's abolition of the National Council made civility, much less friendship, difficult to maintain. Even Grace's sister-in-law, Antoinette, had married one of the leaders of her brother's opposition, widening the rift between her and Grace.

The political climate in Monaco remained static until 1962, when Rainier and his opposition came together to fight the worst external threat to their country in over one hundred years. Ironically, it was precipitated, as was Rainier's domestic opposition, by his modernization and expansion policies. In an attempt to bolster Monaco's economy, Rainier had set out to lure new businesses into the country—and the lack of personal, corporate, land, or inheritance taxes in the principality was a strong lure indeed. In less than two years, over one hundred companies—most of them French, German, American, and British—relocated to Monaco, occupying the gleaming new skyscrapers built as part of Rainier's master plan, and bringing hundreds of new jobs to the principality.

Charles de Gaulle, fond of Rainier and Grace, watched the situation with alarm. The relocation of dozens of French corporations to Monaco meant that France was losing millions of francs in taxes, and the treaty of 1918 specifically forbade Monaco to act in opposition to French economic interests.

France took no action until Rainier's concern over increased French investment in Radio Monte Carlo led him to suspend trading of the company's stock on the Paris stock exchange. State-owned French companies were interested in gaining control of the radio and television entity, particularly since its broadcasts extended into North Africa and reached hundreds of thousands of French citizens living there since the days of French colonial rule. Rainier was determined to keep control of his country's media, and he issued the order to prevent any further sale of stock.

The Prince's action outraged de Gaulle. Not only was Monaco now competing economically with France, but Rainier had directly interfered in a matter of financial and political importance to the French government. Through Monaco's French Minister of State, Émile Pelletier, the de Gaulle government insisted that Rainier rescind the ban. He refused and dismissed Pelletier. The minister, angered by Rainier's rash action, reported to de Gaulle that the Prince was "anti-French." France, it seemed to de Gaulle, had no recourse but to come down hard on Prince Rainier.

Three months later it did so. Rainier was notified that within six months Monaco must "align its fiscal policies with those of France"—essentially, charge its residents and corporations taxes that would then be paid over to France. If it did not do so, the dictum warned, there would be "juridical consequences." These were not enumerated, but rumors circulated that they could include cessation of gas, water, and electricity supplies from France to Monaco.

The threat to Monaco, and to its prince, was enormous. If Rainier acceded to the French demands, Monaco's sovereignty and its uniqueness would be severely compromised. The chief reason for its economic boom, lack of taxation, would cease to exist—and along with it Rainier's glistening vision of a new Monaco. If he stood firm against the French, his subjects could suffer severe hardships, and, as several newspapers speculated, he might be forced to give up his throne.

Faced with the stark reality of his country's vulnerability, Rainier backed down. He rescinded the ban on trade of Radio Monte Carlo stock and wrote to de Gaulle to express his loyalty to France and to point out that French taxation of Monegasques had the potential to destroy the fabric of Monegasque life—and perhaps the country itself.

De Gaulle's government ignored Rainier's letters and allowed the ultimatum to stand. Faced with an external threat far greater than any he'd confronted from his own countrymen, Rainier attempted to gather forces within Monaco. He made overtures to his opposition by reestablishing the National Council, promising a new Constitution, and calling an election in October. As he had hoped, his opponents were eager to work with him to resolve the problem with France, and he appointed several of them to negotiate the situation.

Talks began, but by the time the six-month "grace period"

had expired, no resolution had been achieved. In a show of force, French customs officials took post along the France-Monaco borders, hassling tourists. The crunch had come. Monaco was rife with fears that French warships would fire on the harbor, or that de Gaulle might decide to rid himself of recalcitrant Monaco by nuclear obliteration.

The struggle of a tiny principality against a world power riveted international attention, much the more so because Grace Kelly was its princess. Grace, in fact, may have been instrumental in the ultimate compromise that was achieved. World opinion, never a minor consideration in international affairs, played a strong role in France's treatment of Monaco during the confrontation. The people of America and Britain, particularly, sided with Monaco in this David and Goliath struggle—principally out of affection for Grace and her family. De Gaulle knew he could not make good on his threat without creating a world hue and cry far greater than would ever have arisen before the Prince's marriage, when few outside Europe had heard of Monaco. He agreed to a compromise.

The agreement called for the taxation only of French citizens or corporations relocated to Monaco within the previous five years. All others would remain exempt, and Monaco would retain its independence. Thus France regained its recently lost revenue, but ironically—given de Gaulle's concern over increasing non-French influence in Monaco—the agreement also had the effect of severely slowing, and in some cases, reversing, the flow of French companies and people into Monaco. Still, the rapprochement saved face for all concerned, restored some of France's income, and ensured Monaco's sovereignty. As such it was a monumental achievement.

With the completion of a new Constitution (which, with Grace's urging, granted suffrage to women for the first time), Monaco's domestic problems were resolved. The document reaffirmed the Grimaldi family's rights and powers as hereditary monarchs, but it acceded a great deal of constitutional and judicial power to the National Council and Monaco's courts. While much of world opinion saw the document as antiquely autocratic, it was in fact revolutionary, bringing Monaco, as one observer noted, "from the seventeenth into the nineteenth century."

Through all of these struggles, Grace attempted to preserve her sense of humor. As her husband stood his ground and asserted his "princely powers," Grace gave him a framed cartoon clipped from *The New Yorker*. It depicted a king and queen lying in bed as she says, "Don't pull your divine rights on me, Buster. . . ." It always made Rainier laugh to look at it.

With two major threats to his reign and vision vanquished, only one potential problem remained for Rainier: Aristotle Onassis. Grace and Rainier had remained friendly, if not intimate, with Onassis and Maria Callas; in July 1961 the foursome took a cruise aboard the *Christina,* sailing to Majorca, where they joined famed hostess Elsa Maxwell and designer Vera Maxwell, a new friend of Grace's, in taking over the Hotel Son Vida's orchestra during a boisterous party. Elsa played the piano, Rainier manned the drums, Callas shook maracas, and Onassis sang love songs in French and Italian. Grace laughed and applauded, her clapping hands keeping time to the music.

Onassis's devil-may-care lifestyle and open affair with Callas shocked many puritans, most of whom assumed that Grace was among their number. The revelries of Onassis and his associates as described by the press were roundly condemned, and there were reports that Grace "strongly disapproved" of Onassis's lifestyle and relationship with Callas, and she associated with him only because she had to. Some stories somehow found a link between Grace's disapproval of Onassis and the Vatican.

Such assumptions, of course, were nonsense, part of the public perception of Grace as just short of saintly. Writer Maurice Zolotow, profiling Grace in 1962, made short work of the rumors from his knowledge of her background. With utmost discretion, Zolotow commented, "For ten years before her marriage, Grace Kelly lived and moved and worked in the theatrical circles of New York and Hollywood. She went out with men who were highly sophisticated. How ridiculous to imagine that she could be shocked by the Onassis-Callas affair."

Although the two men enjoyed good times together, Onassis's position as owner of the SBM became increasingly problematic for Rainier. As Grace put it in an interview, "I don't think that Mr. Onassis's investment in the Société des Bains de Mer of Monte Carlo is of very great importance to his over-all empire. He has so many more and bigger investments than Monte Carlo. I feel that his ownership of the majority of shares, and therefore a controlling interest, in the casino of Monte Carlo has been more for his own amusement than a serious business affair."

Clearly, Grace was parroting her husband's opinion; Rainier had not missed Onassis's comment that his two favorite "playthings" were his yacht and the SBM. But even as a play toy, Monaco was losing appeal for Onassis. By the early 1960s he rarely visited Monte Carlo, reluctant to revive memories of a beloved wife who left him. Rainier perceived Onassis's financial decisions involving the SBM as purely selfish, unfettered by concern for Monaco's future—or its tradition-bound past. Worse, Onassis seemed subject to whims and bizarre changes of heart—as when he suggested to Rainier that gambling be abolished in Monte Carlo because it was immoral. Stunned by Onassis's apparent lack of awareness of Monegasque realities and by the blinding contradiction inherent in Onassis's words, Rainier could only remind the world's most controversial tycoon that ethics were not usually counted among his strong suits.

By 1966 Rainier realized that he would have to regain control of the SBM if he were to complete his plans for Monaco's future and become, finally, its undisputed ruler. To gain support in what could prove to be a messy public battle, Rainier enlisted the advice and support of the National Council and conferred with President de Gaulle before hatching a plan: Onassis's control of the SBM would be diluted by issuing six hundred thousand additional shares in the corporation, shares that would be bought up by Monaco, thus returning the controlling interest to the Monegasques. Onassis fought the move in the Monaco Supreme Court, but unsurprisingly he lost his case. A younger and more enthusiastically combative Onassis might have gone to the mat with Rainier over the issue but, wealthy beyond measure and courting Jacqueline Kennedy (whom he married two years later), he not only capitulated to Rainier's plan but sold all his shares in the SBM (at a profit of nearly 1,000 percent).

Finally, after fourteen years of struggle, criticism, and crisis, Prince Rainier was indisputably in control of Monaco. He had held firm, negotiated, manipulated, and fought his way out of a series of crises that might easily have daunted a lesser man. He was well on his way to the realization of his dreams, the fulfillment of his creative and spiritual needs. His wife, however, was not as fortunate. During the myriad problems that monopolized her husband's interest and took away much of the support he might have given her, Grace faced two of the greatest spiritual and creative upheavals of her own life. From them, she did not emerge nearly as well.

Chapter Eighteen

The debilitative effects on Grace of her husband's political troubles during this period were deepened by her own physical and spiritual trials. She suffered two miscarriages, both of which may well have been caused by the strain she was under. She wanted several more children, but it wasn't until 1965, seven years after Albert's birth, that she would be able to carry a child to term.

Early in April 1959, newspapers reported that Grace had been taken to Clinic Cecil, a Swiss luxury hotel converted into a hospital, and was suffering from a "rare intestinal disease." Rumors flew that she had cancer, that she had miscarried, and that she was undergoing gynecological surgery. The reports were fueled by the fact that Grace had left Monaco to be hospitalized, and that the Kelly family's personal physician, Dr. James Lehman, had flown to her side. On April 4, it was announced that Grace had undergone an appendectomy performed by Dr. Lehman, and the operation was a success. Lehman stressed during a press conference that the operation was for the removal of Grace's appendix "and nothing else."

Prince Rainier and Mrs. Kelly, who had flown over on short notice to be at her daughter's side, both greeted Grace when she was returned to her room after the operation. She remained in the clinic for a week, then spent another week resting at the Hotel Beaurivage in Lausanne.

Just over a year later, Grace was again in a hospital—this time to visit her father. Jack Kelly had begun to feel ill early in 1960, and on May 30 he underwent exploratory surgery on his stomach. Grace spoke with her mother by telephone from Monaco; Mrs. Kelly told Grace that her father was doing well and that there was nothing to worry about. But her mother had sounded so tired, and her optimism rang a little false. Grace called Dr. Lehman, who had performed the surgery, and asked him about her father's condition. Lehman reassured Grace that all was well, but when she asked him if her father would still be able to attend a planned family reunion in Ireland, where a cousin was to be married a few weeks later, Lehman said no; the reunion, in fact, had been canceled.

Rather than setting her mind at ease, the conversations upset Grace. Her mother and Dr. Lehman were just trying not to worry her, she was sure; if the reunion had to be canceled, her father's condition must be grave. Within a few hours, she boarded a plane to Philadelphia, accompanied by her personal secretary, Phyllis Blum, who had become a close friend and confidante.

When Grace arrived at the hospital, she wasn't allowed to see her father immediately; a nurse explained that a doctor was with him. The concern etched on her face deepened as she sat waiting in the hospital corridor; the nurse reassured her that it would be just a few minutes longer. When the nurse returned to tell Grace it would be okay for her to go into her father's room, she noticed that Grace paused before entering, took a deep breath, straightened her body, and brought a smile to her face. She was here to cheer her father, and she could not let him see how concerned she was.

The visit *was* a cheerful one; Grace remained chipper as she and her father discussed inconsequentialities. Neither acknowledged what both by then knew: Jack Kelly was dying of cancer. After ten or fifteen minutes, sensing that he was tiring, Grace bid her father goodbye.

Kelly, unaware that Grace knew how ill he was, did not discuss his condition with her; but with others, he was wittily resigned to death. Kate Shea, who had worked for him for years, recalls a conversation she had with him in his hospital room. "Kate," he'd said to her, "Margaret came in with Dr. Lehman and told me I have about four weeks. What do you think of that?"

"Mr. Kelly, that's in the hands of God."

"Yes," Kelly responded. "But I'll tell you what, Kate, if I go up or down, I'll put in a good word for you."

Grace remained in Philadelphia for two weeks, unrelentingly cheerful, always attempting to buck up her family. During this period Jack was allowed to leave the hospital for what was to be his last public appearance: he testified as a character witness for Dr. Lehman and his wife, who were accused of defrauding the United States government of nearly three hundred thousand dollars in unpaid income taxes. The prosecuting attorney, Walter Alessandroni, recalled the impact of Kelly's appearance. "My God! What guts it took for him to come to court that morning. He looked absolutely awful, bent over like an old man. And when you think about how rugged and handsome he was. He *must* have known he was dying, but that wasn't going to stop him from testifying for an old friend. He managed to put on the old Jack Kelly smile and even waved his hand at me when the nurse led him out."

Grace flew back to Monaco on June 13, homesick for her family and aware that she had done all she' could for her father. On the plane all the cheerfulness and stoicism she had displayed for her family dissolved into tears and melancholia. In the two years that Phyllis Blum had worked for the Princess, she had never seen her cry. Now Grace had no strength in reserve. "She told me she wanted so much to be loved by her father," Phyllis recalled. "There was nothing she wouldn't do for him. But she could never get what she needed in return."

Her father's impending death left Grace crushed with sorrow, frustration—and anger. Now there would never be an opportunity to talk with him, to perhaps understand why he had treated her the way he had. No chance for them to reach, as many fathers and their children do, a reconciliation born of increased understanding, one of the other. She would never know if her father had loved her and not been able to show it; if he had indeed been as proud of her as she had tried to make him with just about every adult action she had undertaken.

Her tears of confusion—had she, after all, somehow let her father down?—would alternate with anger. There was nothing she could do to please him. He had made fun of Prince Rainier, and to *newsmen.* When a reporter commented on the Prince's short stature, Kelly had joked, "Yeah, he's only titty-high to Grace." In his desire not to appear a social climber, Kelly protected his own ego at the expense of ridiculing his daughter's fiancé. Once Grace was married, Jack Kelly let his disdain for the palace be known, and he made only two trips to Monaco in the years between the wedding and his death.

Immediately Grace was overwhelmed by guilt over her feelings of resentment against her father. To the sympathetically silent Phyllis, she began a catalogue of his attributes, praising his strength of character and his strongly held values. As these thoughts filled her again with overwhelming sadness, she dissolved anew into tears. Phyllis was stunned by the startling ambivalence of Grace's feelings toward her father, and by the deep sadness those feelings created in her, a woman of thirty-one.

Just a week after Grace returned to Monaco, she flew back to Philadelphia to attend her father's funeral. He had died of cancer on June 20, four months short of his seventy-first birthday. Within days of his death, copies of Jack Kelly's will were selling briskly at seven dollars a copy. It made fascinating reading, not only for its revelations of Kelly's financial affairs, but also because it was written largely by Kelly himself and offered revealing glimpses of his personality.

Kelly bequeathed all of his personal property—clothing, trophies, champion rings, and jewelry—to Kell. The remainder of his property—the furniture and the houses in Philadelphia and Ocean City—went to his wife, who also received one third of his wealth, valued at nearly two million dollars. The rest was to be divided equally among his four children.

Kelly watchers were surprised by the "small" amount of money in Jack Kelly's estate. They were unaware of the fact that over the preceding ten years, Kelly had given between five and seven million dollars to his children and each had received a substantial sum upon turning twenty-one. Shortly after Grace's marriage, Dorothy Kilgallen reported that Kelly had turned over stock holdings valued at close to one million dollars to each of Grace's siblings. This may have been Jack Kelly's gesture to avoid resentment on the part of Kell, Peggy, and Lizanne over his dowry payment to Prince Rainier. In any event, the bulk of Jack Kelly's wealth had been turned over to his children well before his death.

Kelly expressly excluded from his will, written in 1953, any man who might marry one of his daughters. Future sons-in-law were further not to be allowed to buy stock in John B. Kelly, Inc.: "Since I have chosen my employees . . . I would rather see them as stockholders than many of the Romeos that I see presenting their charms to the tunes of mandolins under the windows at 3901 Henry Avenue. There is also the possibility that some Burlesque girl with a sweater might sell Kell a bill of goods . . . I don't want to give the impression that I am against sons-in-law—if they are the right type, they will provide for themselves and their families and what I am able to give my daughters will help pay the dress shop bills which, if they continue as they have started out, under the able tutelage of their mother, will be quite considerable."

Then Jack Kelly, who had caused his wife such distress with his philanderings and his daughter Grace such sorrow by withholding his approbation, remarked that "My wife and children have not given me any heartaches." And the father who had forcibly shaped his son's very existence and constantly interfered in Grace's happiness wrote, "I am not going to try to regulate your lives, as nothing is quite as boring as too many 'don'ts.' "

His children must have smiled in spite of themselves. Clearly, the man to whom appearances were everything was writing his will for public consumption, presenting himself in a light often precisely the opposite of the truth. In closing, he pontificated: "In this document I can only give you things, but if I had the choice to give you worldly goods or character, I would give you character. The reason I say that is, with character you will get worldly goods because character is loyalty, honesty, ability, sportsmanship, and, I hope, a sense of humor."

Grace returned to Monaco in a deep depression. Rainier understood and left her alone. "She was oversensitive to [the Kellys]," he later said. "They mattered terribly much to her— more, it certainly seemed, than she mattered to them . . . Though there were strong family ties with the Kellys, there wasn't a lot of heart."

Grace's despondency lasted for months. Often, at the least opportune moment, she would break down, unable to control her emotions. Madge Tivey-Faucon recalled one such occasion: "I can still see her, seated beside her husband on the little balcony that overlooks the Cour d'Honneur. There was a concert that night and they were playing Chopin. Suddenly she was overcome with some emotion. She had to get up and go into the *salle des gardes* . . . and everyone thought, for a moment, that she was seeing herself once more on her wedding day, coming down the great marble stairs on her father's arm."

Grace's fragile emotional state after her return from her father's sickbed left her less able to cope adequately with a situation new to her marriage: rumors about her husband and another woman. A perhaps well-meaning but more likely mischievous "friend" informed her that while she was in Philadelphia, Prince Rainier had celebrated his thirty-seventh birthday by dancing until dawn with Grace's new lady-in-waiting, the petitely feminine Zénaide Quiñones de León. Confronted by his wife, the Prince explained that his party had also included Madge Tivey-Faucon and several other guests, and that he had danced with all the women. Madge corroborated the Prince's version of the evening.

When she returned to Monaco from her father's funeral,

Grace discovered that the rumors had not died down, and that several differing stories about what happened were making the rounds of Monaco society. Jealous and uncertain, Grace found no other option but to dismiss her lady-in-waiting, and Zénaide was fired. It would not be the only time Grace would be confronted with doubts about her husband's fidelity.

By early 1962 Grace had come to terms with the death of her father, but another void in her life was causing her restlessness, anxiety, and resentment: she acutely missed the fulfillment of acting. For the first few years of marriage and motherhood, her creative needs had been sublimated to her new responsibilities. Now, with palace life having fallen into a routine, and both Caroline and Albert in school, she found herself aching to express herself through some kind of creative outlet.

Since the day she announced her engagement, Grace had been continually asked if she would ever make another movie. At first, after her marriage, the answer was always no—she had given up her career in order "to make a real home for my husband and my children." By 1959 she admitted to a reporter, "I miss acting."

The subject had come up, jocularly, in 1959. The first official offer she received to return to films came from producer Spyros Skouras, who wired Aristotle Onassis that he was producing the biblical epic *The Greatest Story Ever Told* and wanted Grace to play the Virgin Mary and Maria Callas to play Mary Magdalene. He would pay each woman a million dollars. Onassis read the wire to Rainier, Grace, and Maria aboard his yacht. Grace dissolved in laughter. "The Virgin Mary? No way!" she exclaimed. "Mary Magdalene, yes . . ." The offer was turned down.

One year later Grace was again asked to play the Virgin Mary, this time by MGM for *its* biblical epic, *King of Kings*. The thinking obviously was that Grace would have little excuse to turn down such a sanctified role because surely her Catholic subjects couldn't object. Grace agreed, and she asked Rainier if she could accept the offer. But the Prince, extremely sensitive to his people's views, felt they would consider such a portrayal by their princess a sacrilege. Moreover, they would view such a move, he was sure, as a sign that Grace was "going back to Hollywood" and, in appearance if not in fact, deserting her country. He refused to allow it. Grace, left with no choice but to turn the offer down, was furious.

His wife's reaction to his dictum shocked Rainier. At first he had viewed her desire to return to films as a passing nostalgic whim. He reminded her that she had hated Hollywood. "Yes," she replied. "But I didn't hate *acting.*" After she turned down *King of Kings* her mood darkened; she remained uncommunicative for days, sometimes weeks at a time. Rainier, not an insensitive man, realized that there was a fundamental void in his wife's life. He told his biographer in 1966 that there were "times, you know, when the Princess [was] a little melancholic—which I quite understand—about having performed a form of art very successfully, only to be cut away from it completely." The Prince acknowledged that of all Grace's difficulties in adjusting to her marriage, "the hardest thing for her was to give up her career." What she missed the most, she told him, was the creation of something that was entirely her own. "You are creating things here," the Prince replied. "Yes," Grace said, "but not alone."

The matter arose again and again, frequently exploding into bitter quarrels. Grace would cajole, plead, burst into tears, but Rainier held his ground. Privately, however, he had begun to realize that Grace's discontent was something he would have to deal with sooner or later.

Early in 1962, Alfred Hitchcock sent screenwriter/novelist Evan Hunter a copy of Winston Graham's novel *Marnie* and asked if he would be interested in adapting the book into a screenplay. Hunter found the heroine fascinating. "Marnie is a puzzlement," he said, "an enigma. A fearful, fascinating enigma. There are so many aspects of her character to balance and juggle. She must be clever and witty and warm. But she is also afraid and mysteriously remote."

The description could have been of Grace Kelly—a fact not lost on Hitchcock or Hunter. After reading the novel, Hunter told Hitch, "There is only one actress who could possibly handle the part."

Hitchcock, ever sly, responded, "You mean we'll have to wait until *Cleopatra* is finished?"

"I don't mean Elizabeth Taylor," Hunter replied.

"Would you be referring to a certain lady who prefers to make her residence outside these shores?" Hitchcock asked.

"Yes," said Hunter.

"Then we agree," Hitchcock replied. "Let us wait and see."

"Not once did either Hitch or I mention Kelly's name," Hunter said. "But we knew. After that we used a code word for her. HSH—for Her Serene Highness."

Hitchcock was worried about Grace's reaction to the script, because in addition to Hunter's litany of Marnie's characteristics, she was, he said, "terrified of physical contact with men. If a man touches her she becomes violent." Marnie was also a petty criminal: "Her pursuit of crime," Hunter explained, "is a substitute for sex."

A compelling character for any actress—but for HSH? If Rainier didn't think she should play the Virgin Mary, would he let her play a frigid thief who, during the film, is raped? When she received Hitchcock's offer, Grace was overjoyed. But she expected strong resistance from her husband.

Rainier's surprising reaction was prompted both by concern for his wife's mental health and by his affection and respect for Alfred Hitchcock. He told Grace he would allow her to play the role if the filming could take place during the family's customary vacation period and not interfere with any of her official duties. He explained the decision to a friend: "I think that anyone who has spent so much time on their craft as the Princess has, and she's so good at it, it's a waste. And she gets pleasure in doing it. She should do it . . . it would be right for her to do it. Why should a talent like that go?"

Grace was overjoyed, Hitchcock and Hunter were happily surprised, and the announcement was made on March 18, 1962: Her Serene Highness Princess Grace of Monaco would make a film for Mr. Alfred Hitchcock beginning in August and return to Monaco by November. The last piece of information was furnished to counter any Monegasque fears that the Princess was deserting her country.

Still, the uproar was immediate and tumultuous. Grace's subjects were appalled. In the middle of the showdown with France, when he most needed support, their Prince's consort was going back to Hollywood. That she would return home in November did nothing to ease concern; she could, conceivably, make picture after picture from now on. Monegasques interviewed on the street expressed dismay: "She would be slighting our country," said one. Another exclaimed, "What about her kissing the leading man? That would really be the end!" A saleslady commented, "I could no longer respect her if she goes to Hollywood." Another resident asked an American reporter, "Would you like it if President Kennedy and Sal Mineo shared top billing?"

Most of Hollywood was thrilled with the news, with a major exception: MGM's executives. They fired off a letter to Grace expressing pleasure at her return to films but adding that "your intended employment by anyone other than MGM is . . . disturbing." In a letter to Hitchcock, they were more specific. Grace represented "an important but unused asset of this company." The studio's position was that Grace's contract was in suspension until such time as she returned to films, and thus had more than four years to run. Hitchcock's lawyers responded that the contract's original seven years had expired and that it was their opinion that the contract could not be suspended and had thus run out. Depending on the strength of MGM's righteous indignation, a potential legal battle loomed large.

But it was, first and last, the objections of her subjects that caused Grace to back out of the project. As she told a reporter, "I have been very influenced by the reaction which the announcement provoked in Monaco." For Grace, the timing was particularly unfortunate. Had Monaco not been embroiled in what could be a life-and-death struggle with France, she might have been able to ride out the storm and make her movie, but at this juncture it was simply impossible. Grace was bereft. It was clear to her now there was no possibility that she could ever return to acting, ever fulfill this profound need within her. Forced to accept a very unpleasant reality, she needed to convince herself all over again, as she had before she married, of the correctness of sacrifice and unselfishness. This time, however, she was not disillusioned with her career but achingly nostalgic for it. In 1956 she had told herself that life in Monaco would be more rewarding than life in show business. Now she knew better—but there was nothing she could do about it. As she put it in *Playboy* in 1966, "One has to choose in life."

It was a resignation born of a sense of duty. When she was asked if she was happy, she replied, "I don't expect to be. I don't look for happiness. So perhaps I am very content in life, in a way." Asked how she would define happiness, she replied, "I suppose being at peace with yourself. Not anxiously seeking for something, not being frantic about not having something."

"Are you at peace with yourself?"

"Well, I understand myself. But I argue with myself all the time, so I guess I'm not really at peace . . ."

"Since you haven't found peace of mind, what do you think will help you achieve it?"

"Well, I have many unfulfilled ambitions . . ."

Faced with the immutability of her situation, Grace, as she had so often before, put the best face on for things. She threw herself into her work as Monaco's Princess; she developed small enthusiasms for crafts like embroidery and painting; she tried to put her discontent out of her mind.

Grace's suppression of her creative frustrations after the *Marnie* debacle harked back to her interaction with her family before her marriage. Then her flauntings of convention were always followed by contrition when she was confronted by her disapproving parents; her paramours always eventually went by the wayside if her parents opposed them. In marriage, an attempt at "rebellion" like accepting the *Marnie* role, once rebuffed, would be followed by a renewed commitment to self-sacrifice rooted in her religious training, a "reaffirmation" of her "vows." At times like these, she would say, "I don't think anyone has a successful marriage . . . without sacrifice."

Two and a half years after the disappointment of *Marnie,* Grace had a happy diversion: her third child, a daughter named Stephanie Marie Elisabeth, was born on February 1, 1965. After two miscarriages, the baby's healthy birth was a joyous occasion for Grace and Rainier. Like Caroline's, Stephanie's delivery was a little earlier than expected; no sooner had Grace met her mother at the airport and sat down to lunch with her than she went into labor. Grace was rushed back to the palace, where she delivered Stephanie in the same room in which Caroline and Albert were born. The two children listened for the cannon shots to learn whether their new sibling was a boy or a girl. When the blasts ended at twenty-one, Albert exclaimed proudly, *"I* got a hundred and one!"

Stephanie's birth helped divert Grace's attention from her frustrations about her creativity and gave her an additional rationale for her self-denial. "Acting is something that takes a great deal of time and concentration," she said in 1969. "When you're married and have children, that alone makes acting complicated because when you're acting you have to think of yourself first, and when you're a mother you just can't do that."

As she had at the time of Caroline's and Albert's births, Grace threw herself into motherhood with devotion. She again breast-fed her baby and rarely let nursemaid Maureen King take full charge of the child; when she was freed from her duties, Grace spent every available moment with her baby. With Caroline and Albert now both in school, Stephanie received, for much of the day, Grace's undivided maternal attention.

Stephanie, the youngest child, separated from Albert by seven years and a family blessing after Grace's miscarriages, was shamelessly doted upon and spoiled. As her personality developed, it became clear that she was the most independent and strong-willed of the children, besting even Caroline in that regard. She could be willful and stubborn, refusing at even an early age to show tears or capitulate to punishment— "I could have beaten her like a gong," Grace said, "without making her give way."

"I was always the headstrong child in the family," Stephanie has said. "My mother and father called me a rebel at two years old." But she wasn't an evil child, and her charm could melt the hardest heart. If the personalities of Grace's three children could have been combined into one, that child would have come close to duplicating their mother. Albert's gentle shyness, his reserve and timidity, his sensitivity and resignment to duty all recalled the child Grace. Caroline's and Stephanie's rebelliousness, their lack of attention to the rules, their intellectual curiosity, and their ambition for diversions duplicated their mother's inner self, revealed during her years in New York and Hollywood. Without discounting their father's influence on their personalities, Grace's children are a remarkable duplication of her own striking duality.

The second half of the 1960s was the happiest period in Grace's married life. After the deep disappointment of *Marnie,* she put her creative longings out of her mind, suppressed her frustrations, and refused to allow herself to be victimized by dashed hopes. Many of the trials she faced in her first decade as princess were behind her; she had weathered her apprenticeship successfully. She had grown comfortable with royal protocol, familiar with what was expected of her and how to achieve it. She understood the customs and idiosyncrasies of Monaco and—as she called it—"the Latin mentality," and she knew how to avoid the pitfalls that often stemmed from them.

Further, she had proved herself to the people of Monaco through her actions and her example, and they had grown to love and admire her. She said in a letter to Don Richardson that it had taken her a while to understand the Mediterranean temperament: "Many of the people here treated me as someone from Mars for a long time." But by 1972 she felt confident about her place in Monegasque culture and wrote Richardson: "They have accepted me now."

Her relationship with Rainier had improved over the years as well. The couple had made difficult adjustments; they were now more comfortable with each other, tolerant of each other's peccadilloes and idiosyncrasies. No longer was either wounded by the other's lack of interest in some enthusiasm or other; they had come to accept that they were separate people, that they could go their own ways and follow discrete interests and still love each other. This had not been a realization easily reached. So strong a discord was created by their differing temperaments, Grace admitted in 1974, that only their mutual religious beliefs pulled them through. "The Catholicism in our marriage was a very strong link between us, and it helped . . . because there weren't too many other mutual bonds . . . Marriage is not an end in itself. It takes a lot to make it work. Two people are changing and growing all the time."

After so many obstacles, internal and external, that might easily have destroyed many another marriage, Grace's was finally "working." The public and private crises Grace and Rainier had weathered had drawn them closer together, given them a strong bond. And with his country firmly within his control, his sovereignty unchallenged, Rainier had mellowed, softened, grown closer to his wife and children. The family saw more of him, and when they did his attention to them was undivided, unfettered by matters of state.

* * *

There *were* sadnesses during these years. Rainier's father, whom Grace adored and remained close to, died in 1965. In 1967, during a visit to Montreal's Exposition, Grace fell ill and was rushed to the hospital. There it was discovered that a baby she was carrying had been dead within her for several days. Grace was despondent; she wanted more children, especially a companion for Stephanie, who was so far removed in age from her brother and sister. And, at nearly thirty-eight, Grace feared that she would not be able to have any more children. As it turned out, she never did have another pregnancy.

🍄 4 🍄

Monaco's Lonely Lady

The closing of the movie is just five minutes of Grace being herself . . . In a way, it's almost spooky. It's the last time she ever appeared on celluloid, and there are moments that are very revealing of her personality—standing alone in the palace, looking down at a boat going by, or picking a flower, all alone, very sad. She talked about the meaning of life and how life would be meaningless if there wasn't pain. It was very strange. She was a lonely person.

Robert Dornhelm,
director of *Rearranged*

Chapter Nineteen

On November 12, 1969, Grace turned forty—and the occasion affected her badly. Despite the fact that she looked more beautiful than ever—her face had thinned to reveal a lovely bone structure—she viewed forty, as many women of her generation did, as the beginning of the end. As such, it stirred anew her feelings of loss at not pursuing her creative dreams. Now she felt it was too late to return to films even if she somehow became free to do so. This left her with a profound sense of regret—and an exaggerated dread of turning forty.

Since the day she became Princess of Monaco, Grace had perfected an inpenetrable veneer of propriety. In public she was always the elegant princess, the epitome of reserve and composure. During interviews she invariably maintained a regal demeanor, said only what the public would expect of her, revealed little of herself, and smiled glacially rather than answer a question she found distasteful. Various interviewers described her as "rehearsed" and "stiff"; her smile "plastic" and "frozen"; her answers "boring."

The approach of forty, more than anything before or since, changed all that. With stunningly uncharacteristic frankness, Grace talked about her aversion to this birthday in an interview with William B. Arthur for *Look* magazine: "I'm an absolute basket case. I can't stand it. It comes as a great jolt. It really does. It hits one right between the eyes . . . All I can think of is Shakespeare's 'When forty winters shall besiege thy brow/And dig deep trenches in thy beauty's field,/Thy youth's proud livery, so gazed on now,/Will be a tattered weed, of small worth held . . .'

"For a woman, [forty] is torture, the end. I think turning forty is miserable . . ."

Grace's reaction to turning forty foreshadowed the discontent that would grow within her as the 1970s unfolded. By then, her stifled frustrations once again began to assert themselves in the tug of war within her, and this time self-denial would lose. Stephanie had begun kindergarten, and Grace's life had settled once again into a rut from which she sometimes longed to scream for escape. Although enormously busy with her duties as Princess, Grace rarely felt fulfilled by them. As their tenth wedding anniversary approached in 1966, Prince Rainier had asked Grace what she would like as a present. She replied, "A year off." She didn't get it—then or ever. She wrote to Don Richardson in 1972 that her life was so busy and hectic she felt "like the one-armed paper-hanger." In a 1979 letter, she wrote of returning to Monaco from a trip to the United States to face "a lot of social nonsense and thousands of hot, sweaty tourists." She longed, she wrote, to escape to Roc Agel in the secluded hills above Monaco for "a few weeks of peace and recuperation."

Still, rather than cut back on her activities and obligations, Grace constantly added to them—because a work load that drove her to exhaustion was preferable to having too much free time. With not enough to do, or plan, or look forward to, Grace became bored, restless, nostalgic for her friends; she would dwell on the frustrations of her creative drive and descend into depression. It was vital to her mental health that she keep every moment full, even at the risk of physical exhaustion.

Her days during this period were long ones. Usually—"if I can drag myself out of bed"—she arose at 7:00 to prepare breakfast for the family and help get the children off to school. She then would dress and go to her office, one floor below Prince Rainier's, to review the daily details of running the palace. This might take up to an hour; it involved a majordomo, three butlers, five maids, six footmen, her personal maid and the Prince's valet, the housekeeper, Princess Stephanie's nurse, two chefs, twenty laundresses, several chauffeurs, gardeners, electricians, painters, and upholsterers. Day laborers dealt with unexpected problems. "It's a small world all its own," Grace said. "There's always a crisis, or a problem. Of course it gets tiresome . . . I sometimes feel hemmed in, very hemmed in."

(In 1971 Grace made a surprising admission: she could not say how many people were employed in the palace. Defensively, she added, "You see, whole households with children live inside the walls—it's a whole world unto itself." On another occasion, she was asked how many rooms the palace has. "I really couldn't say," she replied. Then she added, "I can never tell what counts as a room.")

Grace's daily chores also involved answering the hundreds of letters she received each week, many addressed to "Grace Kelly" and expressing admiration for a performance seen on the "Late Show." Some were requests for help from her subjects, whom she occasionally agreed to see and assisted whenever practicable.

If an event were planned for an evening that was likely to keep her out late, Grace would try to nap, but it was far more difficult for her to find the time to sleep during the day than it had been at the beginning of her marriage. Now there were usually meetings of the Red Cross or the Princess Grace Foundation or the Garden Club to fill up her afternoons.

Although Grace's devotion to the work of the Red Cross was sincere, and her delight at its annual costume ball total, the Princess Grace Foundation and the Garden Club, her own creations, were much closer to her heart. She began the foundation in 1964 to encourage local artisans, whose work was sold in a boutique Grace supervised. She opened a second shop in 1970, and by the mid-1970s all her earnings from her various outside activities were given over to the foundation, whose commitments were now much more far-reaching. The organization began to assist artists the world over and expanded to include cultural pursuits—principally the international ballet school founded by Marika Besabrasova, which was renamed the Academie de Danse Classique Princesse Grace. Grace hoped that the academy would help restore Monte Carlo as a leading ballet center; her interest in dance, which had not flagged since her studies as a teenager, continued to be expressed through projects and involvements during the 1970s.

Grace conceived the Garden Club, her other major personal interest in Monaco, in 1968 out of her passion for flowers and her desire to become a little closer to her subjects. With the club's treasurer, Jardin Exotique director Marcel Kroenlein, Grace hiked for hours several times a week in the hillsides of Monaco, learning the Latin names of the myriad plant life and collecting wildflowers. The club's members included ordinary Monegasques, not just the wives of members of government, and that gave Grace an opportunity to get to know some of her subjects without the awkwardness that had surfaced during her dinner party experiment. "The atmosphere of the Garden Club was very friendly," one of the members said. "She made links, joined us together. Now we each give parties for the club; it contributes to the spreading of human contact in Monaco." The club was far more than a social exercise, though, contributing heavily to charity and decorating hospitals and old people's homes on holidays. On the surface apparently the kind of organization created for dilettantes, Grace's Garden Club became—principally because of her passion and ambition for it—an internationally important center for flower-arranging competitions and highly lucrative charity fund-raising.

Grace's belief in breast-feeding led to her appointment as honorary president of the Monaco branch of the international La Leche League, an organization extolling the physical and psychological benefits to children of breast-feeding. As the organization's most famous supporter, Grace was invited in 1971 to speak before a convocation of members at Chicago's La Salle Hotel. "It was the sweetest thing," she said. "Babies crawling all over the lobby, up and down the stairs. Mothers carrying babies in pouches on their backs, and all so concerned and eager to do the best thing for their children." Grace's comments to the group are revealing of her beliefs about motherhood and the family. She later commented, "I think the family structure is in real trouble. It's crumbling. If children are going to grow up stable and strong, and make a reasonable world, it has to begin with a loving, responsible mother and father, a close family, physically and emotionally. Where else is a child to learn respect for authority, consideration for other people, a regard for decency? It all begins with a close family who love one another."

To the assembled members of the La Leche League, Grace said, "I will not be the first to compare life to a never-ending relay race, a handing on by us of the torch of life out of the past to be carried into the future by our children . . . The act of breast-feeding, the giving of food and security from within our own persons, is an integral and vital moment in the passing on of that torch." Grace acknowledged that formulas and bottles had gained popularity because of the hectic lifestyles of the day, but she averred that the avoidance of breast-feeding was an unacceptable avoidance of maternal responsibility. "Breast-feeding calls for discipline on the part of the mother. Sometimes, at the beginning, it can be both painful and discouraging. There is help of many kinds for these, but the greatest of all in overcoming them is the determination of self-control sparked by concern and responsibility for the child."

To Grace, a mother's willingness to sacrifice for her children was perhaps the most important element in raising children properly; it helped to create within the family a "well-being that comes from the natural act of unselfishness . . . The breast-feeding mother is living for the happiness of another besides herself."

It was the credo by which Grace had lived all her married life. She had made sacrifices again and again for her husband and her children. She had done what was expected of her, denied her own needs for the benefit of her family. The reason is perhaps best revealed in her statement, "Nothing is more important to me than a harmonious family life." In 1972 things were going well. The children, now fifteen, fourteen, and seven, were good-looking, athletic, bright, and for the most part well-behaved. While their independent spirits sometimes caused trouble, it was nothing their strict parents worried too much about. Grace was bursting with pride over all three of them, especially so since they were a positive reflection of her competence as a mother. In an October 1972 letter to Don Richardson, she called her children "my jewels . . . so wonderful, sweet and adorable." Her daughters, she wrote, have very strong personalities and are both "terribly bright." Caroline, nearly sixteen, was, Grace wrote, "much more sensible than I was at that age—or any age for that matter." She described their relationship as "lovely."

Prince Albert was depicted by his mother as a quiet but strong young man, and a dreamer, possessing "an easy, sweet nature—which the girls take advantage of, naturally."

Stephanie, Grace wrote, "is a seven-year-old teenager—very bossy and much too clever." A long line of nannies and governesses were exhausted by the child—to the extent that Grace, as she wrote this letter, had no one to care for Stephanie in the evenings. Still, Grace added, "She is very affectionate and has irresistible charm, which saves her from being impossible."

In September 1971, Grace enrolled fourteen-year-old Caroline in St. Mary's Convent at Ascot, England—exactly the kind of place where an upstanding, upper-class Catholic mother would send her daughter. When Grace visited the school for the first time, she seems to have remembered well her years in Catholic school. Headmistress Sister Bridget remembers thinking her "quite prim and proper." Grace wore her spectacles, which she always avoided doing in public, pulled her hair back severely, wore a sensible gray suit, and maintained an air of great seriousness throughout her conversations with the nun. The desired effect was achieved; Sister

Bridget recalled that the impression Grace made upon her was of "shining good" and of "total sincerity and integrity."

Caroline, an intelligent and intellectually curious girl, did well at St. Mary's; she earned praise from the nuns and was graduated in 1973 with the equivalent of a high school diploma at sixteen. Grace couldn't contain her pride; she spoke glowingly of Caroline's scholastic achievements, implying during several interviews that credit for her daughter's fine character rested with her and Rainier. Asked by one journalist if they were ideal parents, Grace replied, "Not at all. But we do our best, and so far, so good . . . By their fruits, you shall know them."

It was exactly this perception that caused Grace the great anguish she felt when Caroline's behavior began to change. "Caroline went a little crazy," Lizanne says, "and Grace had a fit. She *really* had a fit, but there wasn't much she could do. There's only so much you can do but sit on them or lock them in a closet."

Caroline's rebellion against the strictures under which she was raised was not unusual, nor was it particularly outrageous —but it was conducted in public, and that mortified Grace. If her daughter's scholastic achievements reflected well on Grace's talents as a mother, what could photographs of Caroline smoking, drinking, nightclubbing, and sunbathing nude with a boyfriend say about her upbringing, and about her parents? To Grace, who had said, "There is nothing more creative and wonderful than forming the personality of children and training them to meet life . . . the whole harmony of spiritual well-being of the family depends on the wife and mother," Caroline's behavior was a body blow and a source of numbing embarrassment.

Grace first noticed the change in her daughter's personality when Caroline returned from St. Mary's. No longer was there the special mother/daughter closeness that had caused her to boast in a letter to Don Richardson that "we have a lovely relationship"; no longer did the girl confide her innermost feelings and problems to her mother. Grace tried to be philosophical about this, but it hurt her. "There's a certain point up to which a mother and daughter can share all confidences," she said in 1974. "But there are confidences a daughter will share only with friends her own age. A girl of seventeen can't have a woman of forty as her pal."

Worse for Grace was the fact that Caroline was no longer a little girl who did everything she was told with a polite "Yes, Mommie." Sixteen, away from her parents for two years, Caroline's "little character" had developed into full-fledged rebellion against parental strictures. Grace tried to lay down the law, but in most cases she found herself completely frustrated. Asked in 1974, "How do you manage children whose home is a palace, who have titles, and who want to live just like other kids their age," she replied frankly, "I don't manage them, at least not completely. Do you know anybody who does? I try . . . We win some and lose some."

Grace frequently became completely exasperated with Caroline—"I've often been tempted to strangle her"—but at the same time, she found herself admiring her daughter's gumption; she saw something of herself in Caroline. "There has to be this breakaway," she said. "I did it. I rebelled against my family and went to New York to find out who I was . . ."

Caroline's "breakaway," as it turned out, was to Paris. She had expressed a desire to attend the École Libre des Sciences Politiques and study government, as her father had done, and both Grace and Rainier were pleased enough with that. They knew that she would first have to earn a French high school diploma, and that entrance into École Libre would be several years off. But Caroline insisted on studying at a lycée in Paris, where, she argued convincingly, she would get the best possible preparation.

For a time Grace had entertained the thought of sending Caroline to school in America in order to round out completely an education that had begun in Monaco and continued in England. After much thought, she changed her mind. America, she said, "was just too far. And with all the dope in the schools and the things going on, I wasn't too anxious to send her to America . . ."

The implication that Grace didn't trust her daughter to resist temptation was amplified when Grace decided that Caroline could attend school in Paris only if she accompanied her. Although Grace would sometimes say that Caroline was "more together than I was at that age," she later admitted to a reporter that she considered her daughter "in other ways . . . more vulnerable." Because of this, Grace decided, she and Caroline would live together in the family's apartment on the elegant Avenue Foch, one of the streets spoking out from the Arc de Triomphe.

Caroline did not want her mother to live with her in Paris, and she said so, loudly. Didn't her parents trust her? Why couldn't she live with family friends, as they had also discussed? She could handle things, she assured her parents, and she would, after all, still be "chaperoned." Rather against her better judgment, Grace agreed. Caroline left for Paris, accompanied by a friend, to live with close friends of the Grimaldis.

Almost immediately the French paparazzi descended upon her. In Monaco it was possible to control photographers (any who angered the Prince could be detained by the police) but in Paris it was not. They literally camped out in front of Caroline's residence, incessantly snapping her every departure and return, hounding everyone who lived there day and night. Driven to distraction, Caroline broke into tears and cried, "Why do I have to be a princess? I hate it!"

Word of this was all Grace needed to justify a return to the plan she had favored all along: she and Stephanie would move to Paris and live with Caroline on Avenue Foch. Worry about Caroline and a desire to spare the family friends the burden of dealing with the paparazzi were only two of the reasons Grace wanted to go to Paris, however. Another major reason was that, by 1974, she was eager to spend some time away from Monaco. Two years later, when she joined the board of 20th Century-Fox and began attending its meetings in Los Angeles, Don Richardson asked her why. She replied, "It gets me away from Monaco at least four times a year."

Living in Paris allowed Grace to "get away from Monaco" for six months at a time, and this was tremendously important to her. It was becoming more and more difficult for her to sublimate her interests and her creative drives for the political necessities of the principality. Her feelings of frustration, boredom, and loneliness, so long suppressed within her, now were undeniable. Her children, away at school much of the time and drifting away from her as they grew older, no longer provided a substitute for her artistic drives. Neither did her activities as Princess—which, as she had complained to Rainier, had never brought her the kind of satisfaction that her own individual enthusiasms did, and which had in many ways become routine and uninteresting.

Life in Paris, Grace felt, would restore in her much of the joie de vivre that was ebbing away from her in Monaco. She would see more of her old friends, make vibrant and fascinating new ones, and become a part of the shimmering Paris cultural scene. With great enthusiasm, and with the protests of both her daughters ringing in her ears, Grace moved with Stephanie into the Avenue Foch apartment.

The move was counterproductive on all counts. The onslaught of the paparazzi did not decrease but grew worse (the photographers now had *three* princesses to pursue). Grace found herself still caught up in Monaco's affairs, which now had to be dealt with long distance, leaving her less time than she had hoped for her own pursuits. And her efforts to protect Caroline from cosmopolitan temptations failed completely. By mid-1975, the eighteen year old had developed into a striking beauty with a voluptuous figure, and as one of the world's most famous teenagers (a *Time* cover had helped considerably in that regard), she was also one of Paris's most socially sought-after young women. It did not take much time for her to discover the pleasures of Paris's nightlife and the attractions of its men. Before long, the newspapers of Europe began publishing almost daily photos of Caroline partying at various Paris discos with attractive young jet-setters at her side: Henri Giscard d'Estaing, son of the French President, British playboy Nigel Pollitzer, French pop star Philippe Lavil.

The press had a field day. Headlines called Caroline "The Playgirl Princess" and "Caroline the Heartbreaker." The implication was that she did nothing but party, which was of course not the case. Caroline tried to defend herself. "I only go out to a party once a month—maybe not that often—but the press will sometimes use my head on somebody else's picture. I've sued for that."

The truth lay somewhere in between Caroline's protests and the press's exaggerations. Many journalists of course amplified everything out of all proportion, but it could not be denied that Caroline, when she did go out, behaved in a way strongly suggestive of rebellion against her strict upbringing and of defiance of her mother. She was photographed nuzzling her escorts, smoking, and drinking too much in clubs; one photographer caught her wearing a dress with a neckline that plunged to her waist and revealed, according to *Time,* "a bit more of Caroline than caution." Grace was mortified. Her daughter, to her way of thinking, was shaming the family, sullying the reputation for perfect motherhood Grace had worked so hard to build. A furious row between the two ensued, in which Caroline openly defied her mother. "It was very difficult for Grace to shame Caroline into toeing the line," Don Richardson says, "because by then Caroline had heard things about her mother's past. So whenever Grace would fight with Caroline, Caroline would shout back at her that she hadn't *exactly* been a model young woman either, so who was she to preach? It was very difficult for Grace."

Grace told friends that Caroline was being "impossible," and she was so frustrated that she let down her guard and confided her travails to a British journalist—and, in an extraordinary moment, criticized her daughter publicly. "We have our differences about clothes and boyfriends," she said in reference to Caroline's indiscreet outfit. "There was nothing wrong with the dress. It was the way that she wore it—or rather the way she didn't watch how she was wearing it. It may have been dark in the nightclub, but she should have kept an eye on what the photographers were doing. That ugly and very upsetting picture went around the world. We were distressed and so was she. She learned her lesson the hard way . . ."

Caroline's public chastisement embarrassed her and brought home to her the difficulty she faced in attempting to carve out a persona distinct from her family—and from her mother. If being a princess was a daunting responsibility, being Princess Grace's daughter was doubly so. Her mother, Caroline admitted, "was a point of reference in all things, from the smallest detail to the most important thing." As such, she was a most difficult standard to live up to. "My mother is beautiful but she is rather reserved. She is a marvelous housewife, full of self-control, always impeccable down to the smallest detail. I sometimes find it difficult to do the things Mother expects of me."

Practicing self-control and living a lifestyle of which her mother could be totally proud proved impossible for a vibrant young woman who found herself presented with opportunities for unaccustomed excitement at every turn. The pleasures of nightlife attracted her more strongly than they might have had her upbringing been less protective—and Caroline, despite Grace's growing protestations and the increasing friction between mother and daughter, was unwilling to forgo them.

Grace's anguish over Caroline's behavior extended far beyond the usual motherly concern. She was still painfully aware of the heartache her own rebellion had caused her as a young woman, and the thought of Caroline learning that lesson as painfully as she had was agonizing. Even worse was her realization that all her efforts to teach Caroline moral discipline and social propriety had in many ways had exactly the opposite effect, that she had contributed to her daughter's behavior with her rigid and unceasing demands for circumspection in all things. It had been so as well between her and her own mother, to be sure, and Grace found herself angry and depressed at the thought that she was, unconsciously, emulating many of Mrs. Kelly's worst traits: "I remember as a girl saying, 'I'll never say that to my children.' But now I find myself echoing the same phrases."

Matters grew steadily worse. Always an enthusiastic student, Caroline lost interest in her studies, and for the first time in her academic career she failed to do well on her semester finals. When Grace spoke to her about the matter, Caroline announced that she did not intend to return to school after completion of the school year. At her wits' end, Grace took Caroline back to Monaco, and a series of highly charged confrontations between daughter and parents ensued, during which her father convinced Caroline that the best course for her would be to enroll in Princeton University. Grace and Rainier had discussed the matter, and they agreed that Caroline must be removed from the temptations of Paris. Despite her concern about drugs in America, Grace felt Princeton was far enough away from a cosmopolitan area that Caroline's attentions wouldn't be diverted from her studies.

Caroline was very unhappy about being torn from the pleasures of Paris, but she was being told, not asked—and the thought of living over four thousand miles away from her mother did have its appeal to her at this point. She agreed, was accepted at Princeton, and informed the school that she would enroll in the fall of 1976.

Grace breathed a deep sigh of relief. She would still worry about Caroline, to be sure, but she wouldn't be confronted with daily anxieties—what she didn't know wouldn't hurt her. And Caroline would be close enough to the Kellys to call upon them if she needed to. It seemed like the best possible solution to the "Caroline problem"; apparently, this particular family crisis was over.

In fact, it was just beginning—because, several months before Caroline was set to leave for the United States, she fell in love.

Chapter Twenty

If Caroline had emulated her mother's rebellious youth with her Parisian exploits, she did so all the more in her choice of a lover. Philippe Junot was seventeen years older than Caroline, an attractive and sophisticated jet-setter, witty and brimful of Continental charm. Comparisons to Oleg Cassini and Jean-Pierre Aumont follow naturally, but unlike those men, Junot had no clear-cut profession; most often he was described as a man who "works in investments." The only incontestable label that could be placed upon him was "playboy." He boasted of aristocratic heritage, but that was unproven; he claimed to have been graduated from the New York Institute of Finance, but at the time he attended the school it was not issuing diplomas.

Grace viewed her daughter's relationship with Junot with great wariness. He was an enigma at best, and as such represented a dangerously unknowable element in Caroline's life. Was he a fortune hunter? A publicity seeker? Was he using Caroline for some other ends, whatever they might be? Grace fretted, but she also told herself that Junot's considerable advantage in age and experience might help Caroline settle down.

She was wrong. Junot was a dedicated hedonist, a jet-setter whose examples to Caroline included pulling his pants down in the middle of a disco and pouring a bottle of whiskey over his head. While her parents squirmed, a delighted Caroline was falling in love. "Philippe has given me the first freedom I've ever known in my life," she said. Again, her mother was confronted with the unpalatable fact that Caroline's behavior was a reaction to her upbringing, and the pain of it stung more deeply with each reminder.

The "freedom" Philippe gave Caroline resulted in the single most embarrassing episode in this period of trial for Grace. In an echo of the Jean-Pierre Aumont lunch photos episode, a hidden photographer captured Philippe and Caroline aboard a yacht. Rather than revealing a few romantic gestures, however, the photographs as published showed a nude Caroline sitting and reclining on deck, and Philippe kissing Caroline's bare breasts. This time Prince Rainier fully shared Grace's fury and, according to reports, shortly thereafter called Caroline and Philippe into his study and "gave them hell." Both were apologetic and respectful to Rainier (as Caroline had not always been with Grace), but afterward Caroline began to spend less time in Monaco and in the Avenue Foch house and more time in Philippe's Paris apartment —which, according to Caroline, "helped me to have some independence and provided me with an escape . . ."

The ultimate independence and the ultimate escape, Caroline knew, could be attained only through marriage. Early in 1977 Philippe asked her to marry him, and Caroline, just turned twenty, happily agreed. When Junot asked Prince Rainier for his daughter's hand shortly thereafter, the Grimaldis felt stricken. Here was the worst possible situation parents could face: a daughter dizzily in love and joyously contemplating marriage—but to a prospective husband who was clearly unsuitable and likely to bring her heartache. The best that could be said for Junot, in Grace and Rainier's eyes, was that he was frivolous and irresponsible. The worst, they didn't even want to think about.

Grace and Rainier could not bring themselves to approve of the marriage but, they feared, neither could they forbid it. Grace recalled the pain her parents' opposition to her suitors had caused her, and she didn't want to inflict that on Caroline. Worse, to refuse Caroline permission to marry might push her irrevocably away from the family. Parents must beware, Grace had said, of "slamming the door [on their children] . . . you have to leave that door open because when it's closed, it's finished."

As her own parents had with her and Oleg Cassini, Grace urged Caroline and Philippe to put off any thoughts of marriage for a year, using as an excuse Caroline's youth and plans to attend school. To the parents' great relief, they agreed. Caroline, who had refused to attend Princeton after meeting Philippe, instead would attend the Sorbonne and work toward the French equivalent of a bachelor's degree in psychology, and afterward they would reconsider marriage. For the immediate future, the crisis had passed.

While the Kellys' gamble had worked—Grace and Oleg's relationship had waned on its own—the Grimaldis' did not. Nine months after they had agreed to postpone marriage plans, Caroline and Philippe again approached her parents for permission to wed. This time, they would not be swayed.

By now Grace's opposition to the marriage had hardened into a firm resolve to forbid it. She was convinced that Caroline was setting herself up to have her heart broken—if the marriage took place, Grace told friends, it wouldn't last more than two years. It was Philippe's reputation as a ladies' man that worried Grace the most. "Grace did not *at all* want Caroline to marry Philippe," Lizanne recalls. "It was a case of history repeating itself, if you think back to Grace and my parents. But Grace wasn't opposed to Philippe for the same reasons my parents opposed Grace's beaux; after all, he wasn't already married, and he was Catholic. But Philippe had quite a reputation as the playboy of the world. Grace and Rainier's biggest worry was that Caroline would not be Philippe's only woman, even after the marriage."

Grace urged her husband to formally forbid Caroline to marry Junot. He considered it, but such a step, he argued, might cause an irrevocable rift in the family—Caroline could well decide to marry outside Monaco and outside the church. When Rainier threatened Caroline with just such a ban, she coolly informed him that she would not defy it—she would simply live with Junot out of wedlock. Faced with her daughter's determination to remain with Philippe, married or not, and unwilling to risk the scandal that one of its princesses "living in sin" would cause in Catholic Monaco, Grace, with great reluctance and trepidation, agreed to allow Caroline and Philippe to have a church wedding in Monaco.

Worried and doubtful, Grace tried to talk herself into sanguinity on the subject; perhaps marriage would help settle Philippe down, perhaps Caroline's strength of character would help her weather the crises Grace was sure would arise. But she could not convince herself that Caroline was doing the right thing. She repeated her "two years" prediction on the eve of the wedding and told Rainier resignedly, "Well, perhaps it's for the better. This way she'll have a successful second marriage."

Her doubts about the future of the marriage didn't prevent Grace from striving mightily to give her daughter a marvelous wedding. A sumptuous ball was held the night before the civil ceremony, attended by a great many members of present and former European royalty. The British press made much of the fact that no members of their royal family attended, and neither did anyone from the Dutch, Belgian, Danish, Swedish, or Norwegian royal families. An odd snub, feebly explained by press secretary Nadia LaCoste as the result of "previous engagements." She told the press, "Obviously, they have busy lives and many commitments and it appears they were unable to fit Caroline's wedding into their respective schedules. Anyway, this is not a state wedding. We are reserving that for Prince Rainier's son Albert. This is basically a private affair and Her Serene Highness Princess Grace and Prince Rainier only want their close friends."

Eight hundred "close friends" attended the ball, and four hundred attended the wedding, including the aforementioned lesser royalty and Grace's Hollywood friends—Frank and Barbara Sinatra, Gregory Peck, Cary Grant, David Niven, and Ava Gardner among them.

Grace and Rainier were determined to prevent the circus

atmosphere that had marred their wedding from recurring: the Prince issued an order barring the manufacture and sale of wedding souvenirs, and he banned all but official photographers from the ceremony. To assure privacy, the Prince also banned all helicopters from the air above Monaco for four days. (One photographer, who thought he had circumvented the ban by flying over the palace in a hang glider, had his film confiscated when he landed.)

During the wedding rehearsal, Grace directed the principals as Prince Rainier shot videotape. Later, the family—with David Niven adding his expert advice—critiqued the proceedings with an eye toward perfection the following day.

On June 28, after a small prewedding lunch hosted by David Niven at which Frank Sinatra sang "My Way" to them, Caroline and Philippe were married, as her parents had been, in a civil ceremony in the palace throne room. The following day, the same bishop who had married her parents joined Caroline and her husband in holy matrimony in the courtyard of the palace.

The wedding was a lovely one; the bride's parents fought back tears, and Caroline gave in to hers. As the new Mr. and Mrs. Philippe Junot left on their honeymoon, her parents wished them every happiness—and Grace had never meant anything more. To friends who knew of her skepticism, she said, "I hope I'm wrong."

Grace and Rainier succeeded in their efforts to keep Caroline's wedding sedate and dignified. In a letter to Don Richardson, Grace wrote that the wedding went off well, with "a simple country atmosphere." It had been a great deal of work for her "because I was determined not to go through anything like ours in '56, when the press made a circus of it all." She added with wicked delight that "they were sore that they couldn't do the same this time."

Despite all the success of the festivities, and Caroline's apparent happiness, there was one immediate, negative impact from the marriage. As Grace wrote to Richardson, "Rainier went into a decline." She explained that the Prince "did not like the idea of his baby girl marrying anybody," and that he "took it all personally." For Grace's part, she allowed as to how it would take some adjustment "to accept a stranger into the family circle." Still, she concluded her letter on an optimistic note, telling Richardson that there were no problems.

Up until nearly the last minute, Grace continued to believe that. Caroline was determined to make her marriage work, as much to prove her parents wrong about Philippe as for her own happiness. But Grace's principal fear about Junot—that he would revert to his playboy ways—was borne out within just a few months of the wedding. Word of indiscretions began filtering back to Caroline, and confirmation came when a photographer caught Philippe dancing with an ex-girlfriend at Studio 54 in New York when Caroline thought he was in Montreal on a business trip. Hurt and angry, Caroline decided to fight fire with fire and went out with a former paramour of her own.

The marriage continued to disintegrate from there. Grace LeVine, Caroline's cousin, spent a year in Monaco and became a close friend and confidante of Caroline's. "She loved him, she really did," Grace recalls, "and she was a wreck when the marriage broke up. She knew what she was getting into when she married him, but she was so much in love she convinced herself everything would be okay. Philippe was a *very* charming man, and he did change his ways before the marriage. But after that it was all downhill. There wasn't any *one* thing that broke the marriage up, there were a lot of them —I don't know all their names. Caroline agonized over what was going on. We'd stay up all night talking about it, we went through every pro and con you can possibly imagine—'Well, he's this, he's that, he's done this, he's done that.' "

Her mother, although aware that there had been bumpy stretches in the Junot marriage, was unaware of the seriousness of the problems Caroline was facing. On September 3, 1979, she wrote to Don Richardson, "Caroline and Philippe seem happy and she looks better than ever—so married life must agree."

Grace didn't realize the depths of Caroline's marital problems because Caroline didn't want her to. As Lizanne explains, "Caroline didn't want her mother and father to know that they had been right about Philippe. She was putting a good face on things. Grace didn't know anything about what was going on and Caroline didn't want to tell her."

For a long time, Grace LeVine adds, Caroline refused to admit even to herself that her marriage was doomed. "She ignored problems for a long time and told herself, 'Okay, I'm going to make the best of this.' But finally it was just too much."

In May of 1980, there was no longer any way for Caroline to conceal her anguish. After a loud public battle with Philippe at the Monte Carlo Grand Prix, she finally admitted to her mother that her marriage was in trouble—and that she doubted it could be saved. Grace was shocked, both by the situation and by the fact that Caroline had let things go so far without seeking her comfort and advice. Clearly, Caroline needed to confide in someone, needed to pour her heart out. But she wouldn't turn to her mother as she had when she was a little girl. Wanting to help her daughter in any way she could, but unable to reach her, Grace looked to the other side of the Atlantic and called Grace LeVine. "Can you come over and stay for a couple of weeks with Caroline?" Grace asked her niece. "Because she's miserable." Her cousin came over but, she says, "by then Caroline had just decided, 'Forget it, it's over.'"

Grace hurt deeply for her daughter's unhappiness, doubly so because of the guilt she felt at being partly to blame for Caroline's need to rush into marriage, and she reacted with a deep depression. Rainier's reaction took the form of fury at Junot; "I really believe the Prince would have throttled him at the end [if Junot had showed up]," Rupert Allan said.

Despite the Catholic stricture against divorce, ending the marriage was obviously the only way out for Caroline, and her parents gave her to understand that they would rather risk scandal and censure from Monaco's more pious citizens than prolong Caroline's sorrow. Without discussing the matter with Philippe, Caroline, through Nadia LaCoste, issued a statement in August announcing that she and Junot had separated, and in October the divorce was final. Philippe was bitter; he blamed the failure of his marriage on Grace and Rainier. "There were problems with [Caroline's] parents," he told a reporter. "I like them, they're great, but if they ever saw Caroline unhappy, everything got exaggerated. What I really wanted was some time for Caroline and me to be alone and work out our problems. But then her parents interfered, and the press—and the whole thing became impossible."

With Caroline's divorce, a deep heartache was behind Grace. But there were others in the second half of the 1970s, big and small, new and lingering, which gnawed at her and left her with a sense of hopelessness. Her letters to him during this period, Don Richardson says, "all reflect tremendous loneliness. They were very sad letters. She was very unhappy toward the end." Grace's situation in Monaco, like Philippe Junot's marriage, had become "impossible."

Chapter Twenty-one

Her experiences during the second half of the 1970s brought to Caroline an abrupt and painful maturation, but she emerged from them a wiser and happier woman. Her mother did not fare as well. Grace suffered deeply through her daughter's problems; that Caroline neither sought nor welcomed her help with them came as a bitter blow. For years Grace had taken pride in being "mother confessor" to many of her nieces and nephews, someone to whom they could turn in times of trouble. In 1979 she wrote to Don Richardson that she had spent a month "playing psychiatrist" to a niece who was going through a difficult period. It was, she admitted, "not an easy job."

Lizanne fills in the details: "That was my brother's daughter, Lizzie. She had anorexia. It was a difficult time. Kell and his wife Mary were divorcing, and they couldn't help—Lizzie didn't want their help. She wanted to get away, so Grace suggested she go over to Monaco. She thought that would be a good solution. Grace thought she could solve any problem. We used to say, 'Grace, you cannot wave your magic wand every time . . .'"

Some of the problems with which Grace had been beleaguered over the prior few years had been on the other side of the Atlantic. She suffered along with her sister Peggy through her two failed marriages and the teenage elopement of her daughter. But Grace's strongest empathy and sorrow was reserved for her brother, Kell, whose life began to unravel in the late 1960s and fell apart in the mid-1970s. Like Grace, he had not emerged well from the Kelly family structure.

In 1968 Kell rebelled against his upbringing by leaving his wife and six children for life as a playboy. "I'm tired of doing everything everybody else wants me to do," he later said. "The old man pushed the hell out of me." His niece Marion Smith added, "What he's doing now he should have done with the high school crowd. Suddenly his father's gone; he's got money; he's a good-looking man. It's delayed adolescence." Kell had begun seeing other women several years before he walked out on his family, and he had assumed that his wife, Mary, knew all along. But it came as a shock to her when the husband of a married woman Kell was seeing told her about the liaison. When she confronted him, Kell was surprised that she hadn't been aware. "What he told me during this period of time!" she said. "Things that I never had any idea or even imagined. You see there was so *much*. How *many* other people there had been and the fact that he was absolutely amazed. He'd assumed that I'd known all of this and just had been discreet and not said anything."

Mary filed for divorce in 1968, but after pressure from Mrs. Kelly, she dropped the action. Kell left his family and he and Mary remained separated for eleven years. During this time Kell lived his life as a carefree bachelor—a life that would, principally because of his mother, come back to haunt him.

By 1975 Kell had become a Philadelphia city councilman while still running the family's brickworks, and he decided to seek the Philadelphia Democratic Policy Committee's endorsement to run for mayor. Local pols considered him a strong candidate and he was expected to receive the Democratic backing and very likely win the election—something his father had been unable to do forty years earlier. Kell asked Grace if she would come to Philadelphia and help his campaign, and she agreed. His assistant Kathy McKenna recalls the occasion: "I think that Grace and Kell had a great fondness for each other, and that was exemplified when he was seeking the nomination for mayor. Grace came to Philadelphia and made an appearance at the City Council. I just can't tell you what happened in that room. The chamber was packed—both floors. There was all manner of press. She accompanied him to each councilman's desk, one by one. And I have to tell you, they fell over themselves. Most of those men had only read about her—and there she was, larger than life, talking with them. It made a *tremendous* impression. Grace could have done without all this, but she did it for her brother, because she knew how important this was to him."

But John B. Kelly, Jr., as mayor of Philadelphia was not to be. On the eve of the announcement that Kell had indeed received the Democratic backing he sought, his mother telephoned the president of the Philadelphia City Council and the chairman of the Democratic Policy Committee to *discourage* them from endorsing Kell for mayor. Kathy McKenna recalled, "It went something along the lines of, 'If you endorse my son as the Democratic party's candidate for mayor of this city I will go on television and I will tell the city that it should not have my son for mayor and I will tell the city why . . . And I will financially support his opponent.'"

Needless to say, Mrs. Kelly's gambit worked. "Obviously," Kathy McKenna said, "the party decided it wasn't going to run a family feud. This was a political campaign and they didn't need any subdivisions. [Mrs. Kelly] destroyed her son, she destroyed this forty-eight-year-old man; she treated him like an erring little boy. He defied her once and she was going to fix him and *she did* . . . Kell was totally devastated. When the news came he disappeared; no one knew where he was. Eventually he called me from his apartment. He'd gone home to get himself together because he was thoroughly embarrassed—humiliated that his mother would do this to him. His voice sounded like ashes, there's no other simile."

Mrs. Kelly's rationale, as so often before, centered on family pride and the importance of keeping up appearances rather than on what her children needed to fulfill themselves. Several months before he decided to seek the nomination, Kell had been seen out on the town with Rachel Harlow, the glamorous owner of a Philadelphia night spot. What raised eyebrows about this liaison was that Harlow was a transsexual who had spent most of her life as Richard Finocchio. Kell didn't think it was all that big a deal. "I went with her just a few times . . . Of course she is a gorgeous person. Good-looking! And so we went and the people were fascinated; she was the center of attraction the whole night. I thought, What the heck . . . The extent of it was *grossly* blown out of proportion. I guess people wanted to talk about it. They wanted to tell and retell it. And Rachel didn't help, you know. Because anytime she was interrogated by anybody from the press she'd tell them, 'I have nothing to say.' Well, when you say *that,* you *imply.*"

The implication was enough for Mrs. Kelly. She was already worried that Kell's rival for the nomination, Frank Rizzo, would sully the Kelly name by harping on Kell's separation from his wife and his reputation as a playboy; what would he do with information about Harlow? When Mrs. Kelly heard a report that the Republicans were planning to produce a poster with Rachel's picture and the legend, "Will Harlow Be Philadelphia's First Lady?" she got on the telephone.

The episode debilitated Kell, and Grace watched with sorrow and alarm as her once-proud brother declined. In 1977 he pleaded guilty to a drunk-driving charge. He divorced his wife of twenty-five years in 1979 and remarried in 1981. He died in 1984 at the age of fifty-seven.

The bitterness Kell and, by extension, Grace felt toward their mother over her destruction of his political future evaporated a few months afterward when she suffered a crippling stroke that left her without reasoning power. As of 1987, she remained in that condition and was not aware that Grace and Kell are deceased.

That Grace couldn't "wave her magic wand" to prevent the suffering she and her family were going through depressed her. Each frustration of her creative instincts, each quarrel with her daughters or husband, each piece of bad news from Philadelphia, ate into her, wore away the psychological armor she had worn for years. She thought ironic the public's perception of her life as a fairy tale. Time spent in Monaco merely left her lonelier, made it easier to dwell on her problems and lack of fulfillment. More and more, she wished for escape from her situation—both emotional and physical. Her comment to Don Richardson that serving on the 20th Century-Fox board allowed her to "get away from here at least four times a year" was echoed when her friend Fleur Cowles asked her to contribute several lines to a book on flowers that Cowles was preparing. With sad irony, Grace turned around what many had seen as her "fairy-tale" marriage: "I would try," Grace wrote, "to find a freshwater pond on the island for my water lilies with the hope that their large leaves will attract frogs. Who knows? One might turn into a handsome prince who would be decent enough to whisk me off this lonely island and take me back to civilization . . . After all, I am really a city girl at heart."

An extraordinary opportunity for Grace to return to "civilization" arose in 1976 when director Herbert Ross offered her *either* lead in a film he was preparing, *The Turning Point.* The story revolved around two old friends, one an aging ballet star, the other a woman who gave up a promising dance career for marriage and motherhood. The subject, obviously, appealed mightily to Grace, as did the brilliantly constructed script and the strong central characters. What better film in which to return to movies—a serious motion picture about the dance, directed by one of Hollywood's most respected talents? She was enormously flattered by the offer, and especially so by the choice of roles she was offered, and Grace *ached* to say yes. Discussions with her husband, however, made it clear that now, as before, a return to films was out of the question.

Once again Grace was crushed with disappointment. After more than twenty years of self-denial, she was less and less willing to let it continue. Perhaps the burgeoning women's movement had helped stir the dormant resentments Grace had held ever since she had been forced to turn down a role for the first time; it is as likely that she had simply come to the end of her patience with self-sacrifice. Inevitably, this new state of mind drove a deep wedge between husband and wife, one that widened as the years progressed. But it did not change Grace's course.

If she couldn't alleviate her angst and flex her creative muscles through a return to films, Grace decided, she would do so in whatever "acceptable" way she could. In the latter half of the 1970s, she became involved in so many new, personally fulfilling enterprises that she wrote to Don Richardson, "It is a wonder that my head is still above water (at least I think it is)." Along with the duties of her position, her new enthusiasms frequently left her "exhausted." But she had to become involved in projects of her own, activities that brought her creative fulfillment and took her mind off her problems and responsibilities. Or, she feared, she would go mad.

The first of these grew out of an earlier escape mechanism —Grace's habit of walking and collecting flowers for hours among the footpaths of Monaco's hills. She loved the peacefulness of the area, and she took great joy in the variety and color of the wildflowers for which the Mediterranean coast is famous. It saddened her, though, when the flowers died, and she began pressing some of them in the pages of books to preserve them. When Mrs. Henry King, a friend from Philadelphia, introduced her to the art of pressed flower designs, Grace had a new obsession. She spent hours arranging and rearranging dried flowers into pleasing patterns. Once she had created a design she liked, she would return to it several days later, make whatever adjustments her fresh eye deemed necessary, then paste the flowers into a permanent collage.

Grace found the work not only artistically fulfilling but calming as well. "As the designs begin to take shape," she later wrote, "you get the same feeling of tranquillity as doing needlework." She compared herself to other women who had few diversions from family responsibilities: "No wonder Victorian ladies spent hours making pressed flower albums and pictures." Once Grace became absorbed in a design, her concentration—and her happiness—was total; observers told her that in the midst of her work she would talk softly to herself "like a cat purrs."

That Grace took pride in these delicate works of art as *her own* achievements can be seen by her signature; she signed each "GPK"—her initials before she became Grace of Monaco. But simply to produce the collages was not enough—that afforded her emotional escape, but not physical. And so she decided to publicly display her work. In 1977 the collages were exhibited at a gallery in Paris, where Grace attended the opening and posed for a series of photographs; in 1978 she designed a line of bed linens featuring her floral designs for the Spring Mills Company and appeared at a sales conference in New York to promote them; in 1980 a collection of her collages, *My Book of Flowers,* was published by Doubleday, and Grace embarked on a tour of America to publicize it.

Grace was "nervous and anxious" about the exhibit and sale of her work, she wrote to Don Richardson. She felt, she said, that she was "really sticking my neck out" by showing her collages at an important Paris gallery.

After the show, Grace wrote that it had been a success and all her pieces were sold. Still, she revealed that all during the exhibit "I was terrified that someone would suddenly appear and arrest me for taking money under false pretenses. But I got away with it!"

Although flattered by the offer from Spring Mills to turn her collages into a line of bed linens, Grace's principal reason for proceeding with the venture was the fact that, by donating her profits to the Princess Grace Foundation, she could infuse that organization with a good deal of money. But by agreeing to so commercial an exploitation of her work, much more so than by exhibiting, Grace *was* sticking her neck out— and *The Village Voice* cheerfully wielded an ax on her in its report of her appearance at the Spring Mills sales conference. In an article entitled, "Say Goodnight, Gracie," Mara Wolynski wrote, "Flower pressing is, perhaps, the most depressing art form known to man . . . But that is what Princess Grace does as she sits in her studio high above the streets of the best tax shelter in the world. And, so everyone could see what she does, a slide show was presented which the Princess narrated. In it, we saw Grace Kelly wandering through the mountains with a basket in her hand like a demented Heidi, Grace Kelly squatting over a half-dead flower soon to be plucked for one of her collages, Grace Kelly curling her lips around a pencil as she adds another fern to her framable morgue—'I guess I'm just a scavenger at heart,' she says . . . Then it was time to go to the third floor where samples of the sheets were reposing in the viewing room. They were dead-looking indeed . . ."

Despite snide dissents like this one, most observers found Grace's collages lovely, and the varied forms in which they were presented to the public was each a gratifying success. Maurice Rheims of the French Academy wrote of Grace's creations, "Floral art is the fruit of an ancient tradition based on the sole desire to faithfully reproduce the original. Because there is such perfection in nature that no artist can depict forget-me-nots, primulas and eglantines that are more exquisite than the original or surpass colors and forms."

Grace found a good deal of contentment in her flower creations, and a sense of professional accomplishment in their financial success. But none of this fulfilled her in the way that performing could. In 1977 she was presented with an opportunity to appear again on film, not as an actress but as a narrator. She leaped at the chance—and in the bargain made a stimulating new friendship.

Robert Dornhelm, an attractive, thirty-year-old Hungarian director later based in Austria, had made a documentary film for American producer Earle Mack, *The Children of Theatre Street,* about Russia's Vaganova Institute, the world-renowned ballet school that had produced some of the dance's greatest talents. Dornhelm and Mack both wanted a celebrated person to narrate their film. "We considered Dame Margot

Fonteyn and Paul Newman and Joanne Woodward," Dornhelm recalls. "But Monaco had just announced that their ballet school had been renamed after Princess Grace because of her dedication to it, and the ballet in Monaco had ties to the Russian ballet, and it seemed right for Princess Grace to do the narration." Grace expressed interest but said that she wanted to view the film before committing herself.

Dornhelm carried a 16-mm print of the film under his arm to Paris, where he borrowed a projector from a friend and showed his film to Grace and a Russian great-aunt of Prince Rainier. "Thanks to this wonderful lady, the atmosphere watching the film was incredible," Dornhelm says. "She recognized streets in Leningrad and had lots of old memories come back. At the end of the screening, we were drinking vodka and celebrating and making plans, and it was totally clear that Grace wanted to do the narration."

Prince Rainier agreed that this was a suitable project in which to put Grace back in front of a camera, and Dornhelm went to Monaco to film her onstage at the Monte Carlo Opera House, and later on a boat in the harbor. There is a strong contrast between the tight, reserved Grace in the Opera House and the carefree, windblown Grace on the boat. "She was nervous at first about her reading," Dornhelm says, "but by the time we filmed in the harbor, she was much more at ease. It worked well to show the two sides of Grace. She definitely had a dual personality. She was, for instance, *Princess Grace,* of whom we were all in awe, and yet she was terrified of our producer. Whenever I'd express some unhappiness with him she'd say to me, 'But he's the *producer.* You *have* to be nice to the producer.'

"She wrote most of the narration herself. She wanted to be creative. We used to joke—but it wasn't a joke really—that she had gotten the perfect part as Princess. She was very serious about her work. She was nervous before takes, but she was also extremely disciplined. She was a very passionate actress and she loved her work. She regretted giving it up, she absolutely did."

The film was a major critical success and a moderate financial one, and it won an Academy Award nomination as Best Documentary of 1977. To the dismay of all involved in the project, the Soviet Union banned the film when Earle Mack refused to delete references to the Vaganova's three famous defectors to the West—Mikhail Baryshnikov, Rudolf Nureyev, and Natalia Makarova. "I feel very sad that the Russian people are not able to see it," Grace said. "However, I think it would be a pity to omit the reference, because you certainly can't deny the dancers' existence."

When a reporter asked her if she thought she might be criticized for glorifying an aspect of the Soviet Union, she bristled. "I think we're dealing with art and beauty, and that really has nothing to do with politics, does it?"

By far the most pleasant by-product for Grace of *The Children of Theatre Street* was the special friendship she developed with Robert Dornhelm.* They could not have been less alike, but Dornhelm feels that this helped rather than hindered their relationship. "I think one of the reasons we got along so well was that I was so opposite anything she had known before. I had just left Vienna and my family, I was an adventurer, I didn't care a whit about royalty, and I think in a way she liked that, being exposed to a fresh attitude."

Grace, aware that Dornhelm was at first intimidated by her and her surroundings, made great efforts to put him at ease. As their friendship grew—and as Dornhelm became aware that Grace was fascinated by his intellect and his opinions— he grew emboldened enough to instigate what he calls "ideological disputes" with her. "After a while she allowed me to comment, and criticize her. I knew my place, but still I reminded her at times about her own attitudes. She was a funny mixture of social concern, which came from her American background, and far-right politics, which also came from America, mixed with the French. She was fond of quoting her

---

* Dornhelm won critical praise in 1986 with his first feature film, *Echo Park*, starring Tom Hulce and Susan Dey.

uncle George to the effect that when you're young, you have to be a Communist, but after you're thirty, if you're still a Communist, you've remained a fool. I've always been interested in social matters, the individual, and I told Grace that when she dealt with individuals, she was very socially concerned, but when it came to countries, that wasn't so true. I reminded her that countries are made up of individuals."

Grace was unaccustomed to such intellectual sparring, and she found it—and Dornhelm—very stimulating. The two became closer than Grace had been to anyone outside her family since her marriage. They spent a great deal of time together, visiting museums, walking through the streets of Paris deep in conversation, traveling across Europe and the United States, first to promote *The Children of Theatre Street* and later to raise money for a variety of ballet schools. So comfortable were they with each other, in fact, that rumors arose suggesting that their friendship had evolved into a romance. Dornhelm's friends described him as "enamored" of Grace, and she wrote to Don Richardson to describe Dornhelm as "a dear boy who reminds me a bit of you. He could almost be our son . . ." Richardson, in fact, heard the rumors that Grace and Dornhelm were having an affair and turned down an invitation to meet him because "I didn't want to sit with him on either side of Grace like bookends—you know, before and after."

Dornhelm denies that his relationship with Grace was romantic. "I take it as a compliment that people assume that, but we just had a very special friendship—and that was surprising, because who was I? But she needed to talk to somebody who wasn't royalty or a member of the upper ten thousand who have all the money and power. She always told me that she dreamed about the days when no one would care about her and she could be a bag lady wandering through the Metro in Paris carrying her bags. We had good times together. People noticed that we laughed a good deal and danced a lot. Our relationship was under a very good star."

Grace's affection and regard for Dornhelm led her to an

uncharacteristic action when he was snubbed at a gala reception for the opening of *The Children of Theatre Street.* "The film premiered at the Paris Opera," Dornhelm explains, "and it was a major event—only *The Magic Flute* had been screened there before. It was a lavish gala with the entire French ministry, the French President and his wife, dozens of big stars, Grace and her family, my mother and I, and the artistic director of the film, Oleg Briansky. I put together the evening's festivities. Afterward the French minister of culture threw a private banquet for Grace and her family, the Russian ambassador, and lots of other people, and neither I nor Oleg Briansky was invited. I told Grace and she said she would look into it, she was sure that 'there must be a mistake. Surely the director of the film and the producer of this evening should be invited to the banquet.' She was told that there was simply no room for us. She said, 'Fine,'—and she and her entire family boycotted the banquet. Instead, we all went to a brasserie after the screening and waited thirty minutes for a table. That's a good example of her rebellious side. It required courage to snub all those people, and it was a very nice thing to do for us."

Grace worked again with Dornhelm in May of 1979, in a scripted movie she produced centered on her annual flower-arranging competition in Monaco. She had long wanted to put the event, one of her favorites, on film, but wasn't sure how it could be done. She didn't want to do a straight documentary, she wrote to Don Richardson. She discussed the subject with Dornhelm and a friend, French novelist Jacqueline de Monsigny, and the three came up with an idea involving an astrophysicist who comes to Monte Carlo to give a lecture, and through a series of misunderstandings ends up in the bouquet competition. "It is not bad considering the low budget," Grace wrote, "and all was shot in one week . . . It is kind of fun."

The film, entitled *Rearranged,* starred Grace as herself and actor Edward Meeks, Monsigny's husband, as the astrophysicist. It proved to be the last time Grace would appear on film.

"The closing of the movie," Dornhelm says, "is just five minutes of Grace being herself. I don't know why I shot this footage; I suppose I just wanted to capture as much of her radiance as possible while I could. In a way, it's almost spooky. It's the last time she ever appeared on celluloid, and there are moments that are very revealing of her personality, standing alone in the palace, looking down at a boat going by, or picking a flower, all alone, very sad. She talked about the meaning of life and how life would be meaningless if there wasn't pain. It was very strange. She was a lonely person."

Grace's special friendship with Dornhelm and the creative and intellectual stimulation he brought to her led her to discuss many different projects with him. For one film that Dornhelm was not able to finance, she would have served as the casting director—"She had good instincts about who would be right for each part," Dornhelm says. Another project, also stillborn, was a documentary about child prodigies; despite Grace's support Dornhelm was unable to raise enough money to make it.

In 1982 Grace confided to Dornhelm that she thought the time was nearing when she would be allowed to return to feature films. Excited by the prospect, he sent her a copy of a 1952 book by Gore Vidal, *A Search for the King,* suggesting that he direct and she star in a film version of the book. She loved the idea. "It was a medieval troubador story and very disrespectful toward royalty," Dornhelm says, "but that didn't bother Grace. She wrote to me that she thought it had 'all the elements I can handle.' But she wrote, 'You'll have to do some serious rewrites because the love story isn't quite believable—I don't know if that's because Gore Vidal wrote it or what, but you should work on that.' "

Dornhelm recalls Grace's excitement over the project with sadness: "We might have been able to put something together for Grace's return to films—but I received her letter a few days after her death."

Grace struck up a friendship early in 1982 with a young man remarkably similar to Dornhelm. Boyishly handsome

Swedish actor Per Mattsson, then thirty-three, was in Holly-wood for a role in the Richard Chamberlain TV movie *Wallenberg*. He was invited to a dinner party at New York's Russian Tea Room for the producers and financial backers of the film. To his surprise, Princess Grace was one of his fellow dinner guests.

"She was warm, relaxed and happy," Per said. "We were the only actors at the dinner and we both felt a little out of place. Neither she nor I really knew any of the other guests."

Grace and Mattsson spent the evening in conversation, talking about film and acting, and about their respective children. "Grace was worrying a great deal about her daughters at that time," Mattsson said. "She felt that they were living wild lives, wandering around the world. She said they wasted far too much money and lacked something to really strive for."

Mattsson found Grace so charming and personable that he couldn't help but ask her why she usually projected such a cool and distant image. "It's a role I'm forced to play," Grace replied. "It comes with the title of Princess."

Although Mattsson is a movie star in Sweden, he couldn't quite believe that he was having an intimate conversation with the legendary Grace Kelly. "I had even more reason to pinch myself when it was time for coffee," he said, "because Grace and I stole away from the others and went up to her suite at the Helmsley Palace. She sent her bodyguards away and we sat and played the piano and sang duets until five in the morning."

Mattsson found Grace "plump but still very beautiful." The next day, he was again surprised when she telephoned him and invited him to lunch. He was picked up by a limousine and met Grace in a restaurant, where they sat in a section cordoned off by rope. "We had twelve tables to ourselves. She was more frigid and formal than the day before. Still very nice, but so terribly formal. Back in her official role, as it were."

Grace and Mattsson kept in touch during the remainder of

1982, and she repeatedly invited him to visit her at her Paris apartment. Busy working, Mattsson was never able to accept. In September she again extended an invitation to Paris and this time Mattsson made arrangements to go. As he sat down to write her a note to fix a time for their meeting, he heard the news that she had been in an automobile accident.

While Mattsson attempted to find the address of Princess Grace Hospital, he learned that Grace had died. "I was deeply shocked as I tore up my letter to her. I don't like talking about this period. Several people close to me died around this time.

"I miss Grace very much. She was a wonderful woman."

Chapter Twenty-two

The creative exercise that fulfilled Grace the most during this period, that took her away from Monaco the most frequently, and that caused the greatest rift between her and her husband, was her poetry readings. As with *The Children of Theatre Street,* the opportunity presented itself to Grace in the form of an invitation—and she once again jumped at it. Writer-director John Carroll had been asked to fashion a program for the Edinburgh Arts Festival to commemorate America's bicentennial celebration. He wanted a well-known American to read the work of American poets, and he was at a loss to find one.

At lunch with British journalist Gwen Robyns, Carroll described his quandary. Robyns was at work with Grace on an authorized biography, and she suggested her to Carroll. "She loves poetry," Robyns explained, "she reads a lot and is very interested in literature and all the arts. Let me write to her and tell her what you are doing."

When she received Robyns's letter, Grace made a lunch date with Carroll in Paris. No sooner had he finished his well-thought-out presentation designed to convince Grace to join him than she responded that she would be absolutely delighted. It seemed a perfect solution to her dilemma—as a friend put it, "A way of returning to the stage without returning to the stage."

The recital, held in September 1976 in a small two-hundred-seat eighteenth-century chamber redolent of Scottish history, was a gratifying success for Grace. Reading the American poet Elinor Wylie's *Wild Peaches* with noted English Shakespearean actor Richard Pasco and the American Richard Kiley, Grace held her own, even with having to affect a slight Southern drawl. Carroll, although excited by the glamour and box office draw Grace brought to the program, had wondered whether she could rise to the peculiar challenges of poetry recital. "Having worked in the theater," Carroll said, "I know that quite well-known people are not always good at reading from a script or a book. They may be good at learning their lines, but there is a difference." Grace did not disappoint him. "Princess Grace has the timing, the feeling to perfection. She's got a soft, very good speaking voice with a marvelous range. And she has a great sense of humor."

For the first time since she appeared onstage at Elitch Gardens, Grace performed before a live audience. Although she wasn't acting a script, to her mind she wasn't merely *reading* either: her attempts to understand and interpret her pieces weren't too far distinct from her preparations for a role. "Grace worked hard," Carroll said, "but not like most actors, who would read and re-read and re-read it aloud, playing with phrasing, intonation, modulation and so on. Grace tried principally to get an intellectual grip on the poem itself."

Her fear that she was "sticking my neck out" by exhibiting her flower collages was nothing compared to her apprehension as she prepared for the Edinburgh Festival. Thus the favorable critical reaction—the BBC called her recital one of the poetry highlights of the year—was tremendously gratifying to her. She wrote to a friend of how much this meant to her: "I'd have just crawled into a hole and died if they hadn't liked me."

Carroll was so pleased with the success of the festival that he immediately asked Grace to repeat her triumph at Stratford-on-Avon in England the following year. Carroll devised a tribute to Shakespeare to be held at the Holy Trinity Church. "When Princess Grace arrived at the church," Carroll recalled, "I was waiting for her outside. In a very charming gesture, she had brought a lovely rose which she thought we could put on Shakespeare's tomb."

The Stratford appearance, at which Grace read selections from *Twelfth Night* and several sonnets, was equally successful, and word got back to the United States. The American International Poetry Forum invited Grace to repeat her Edinburgh program in Pittsburgh in 1978, and she accepted with pleasure; it would give her a chance to spend some time in America and be near her family. But rather than repeat herself in just one city, Grace and Carroll decided that they would create an entirely new program and "tour" with it. Grace ultimately took a "poetry and prose entertainment" entitled "Birds, Beasts, and Flowers" to six American cities, offering readings from various writers germane to those subjects. Grace's earnings from these programs were donated to the World Wildlife Fund.

In America, where poetry readings are less popular than in England, audiences derived more pleasure in seeing "our own Grace Kelly" than in hearing her performances. *New York Times* poetry critic Mel Gussow put it succinctly when he wrote, "The black-tie Washington audience paid $20 a ticket not to hear poetry or to listen to Mr. Pasco, but to see Princess Grace. She clearly upstaged her own performance . . . In no sense was the recital demanding—either on the actors or the audience (which did not stop the man sitting behind me from being loudly restless)." (Another "restless" audience member was Grace's brother, Kell, who chattered with his date from his front-row seat all through Grace's recital in Philadelphia.) Gussow did offer Grace some praise, however: "The evening . . . is carefully composed to show the Princess off to her best advantage. With her silky voice, her poise and her precise diction, she is eminently suited to read delicate and light verse."

Some observers found great humor in one of Grace's selections. Bruce Vilanch, whose irreverent comic sensibilities have made him a top comedy writer, particularly for Bette Midler, was involved with ABC's TV show "Omnibus," which in 1981 wanted to tape and air one of Grace's recitals. "I called her in Monaco and asked her what she wanted to do.

She said, 'I'd like to read that wonderful old American piece "The Owl and the Pussycat." ' So I said, 'That's very nice, who are you going to play, the hooker or the boyfriend?'* She said, 'Oh, they warned me about you.'

"It turned out that the only place on her tour that year where we could put together a crew and film her performance was in Nashville, at the Grand Ol' Opry, and her charity at that recital was La Leche. So off we went to Nashville along with two thousand breast-feeding mothers to hear Princess Grace recite 'The Owl and the Pussycat' with this marvelous old English character actor John Westbrook. Up she got, and she started reading the poem, and this old actor is looking tenderly into her eyes and saying, 'Oh pussy, my pussy, my beautiful pussy. What a beautiful pussy you are.' All I could think of was, Here's America watching Princess Grace being called a beautiful pussy, and we were on the *floor* in the control room as we're taping it. We thought it was a *riot.* I thought the ABC censor would *freak out,* but I looked over at the control booth and he was sitting there *enthralled* with the poem, completely oblivious to the fact that there's any kind of double entendre going on here at all." Grace's recital aired exactly as she had delivered it, but, Vilanch says, "as predicted nobody watched it, because it was aired opposite '60 Minutes.' "

Between 1976 and 1981, Grace read poetry all over Europe and the United States, including a recital before the Queen Mother at St. James's Palace. In November 1979 Grace wrote proudly to Don Richardson, "I have (just happen to have) an extra copy of my review from Dublin which has lifted my spirits to new heights and enabled me to face fifty on Monday." Richardson, a man who has devoted his life to creative expression and the teaching of acting, found Grace's letter depressing. "She's so goddamn proud of this

---

* Vilanch was referring to the Broadway play and 1970 Barbra Streisand movie that borrowed the poem's title but was otherwise quite unlike the children's verse.

review, after she's won an Academy Award and been a princess. She felt a need, after all that, to remind me that she is an important person, that she existed, or else why write and tell me that she had recited some poetry in a little joint in Ireland? When I read that I felt like crying. I thought, To be that unfulfilled, after all she had achieved, is the saddest thing in the world."

Robert Dornhelm agrees. "Her poetry readings were a step in the right direction, but I don't think a very fortunate one, because while she was performing, it didn't have the same impact for her that it would have had if she were doing it on film."

Grace's numerous outside activities had the desired result of getting her away from Monaco, but the problems, isolation, and frustrations she faced there were always still present whenever she returned. In fact, her decision to lead a life of her own away from the principality worsened the pressures she faced at home because it caused a serious rift between husband and wife. Prince Rainier did not want Grace to become involved in activities that took her away from Monaco for months at a time, but she proceeded with them anyway. Every time she prepared to leave home on another project, a quarrel ensued—but unlike before, Grace did not capitulate to her husband's demands.

Rainier responded by largely ignoring whatever Grace was doing; no pretense of great togetherness was made by Grace or Rainier after the mid-1970s. For two years he refused to attend any of her poetry readings; only when he realized that their success was a diplomatic bonus for Monaco did he appear at one of her programs. When she was honored for her acting career at a star-studded gala in Philadelphia in early 1982, he stayed home.

There were other, more serious schisms between Grace and Rainier in the years before her death. Reports appeared that when Grace was at home in Monaco, the couple no longer shared a bedroom in the palace. Family friend Bill

Hegner told author Arthur Lewis in 1977, "They didn't communicate that well physically even if they've had three children. She fulfilled her commitment and they've stuck it out because it's mutually beneficial. Now she can live in Paris and meet her friends again. She travels a lot . . ."

Rumors that Prince Rainier was having extramarital affairs abounded in Monaco and reached print several months before Grace's death. She, apparently, was aware of her husband's transgressions. Don Richardson recalls, "She used to write to me and complain about the girls Rainier had in Paris. She was very unhappy about it."

Grace, for her part, appears never to have had an extramarital affair. There has never been a whisper of a paramour for Grace, except Robert Dornhelm, and he says, "I doubt very much that Princess Grace had an affair with anybody. How could she? Everywhere she went reporters and photographers dogged her. They drove her crazy. I'd like to think that she did have affairs, because they would have been good for her. But I really don't know how she would have done it."

Her trips away from Monaco were a way for Grace to avoid the increasingly frequent arguments with Rainier. Their fights over her life away from the palace and his "girls in Paris" led to nothing but each pursuing more fervently what had angered the other. It was a vicious cycle that resulted in tremendous pain for both of them. Two months before Grace's death, the *National Enquirer* ran a story entitled "Princess Grace: Our Marriage Is Over." Citing palace insiders, the magazine painted a grim picture of a battling couple who "dislike each other intensely." On a trip to Bangkok, the article went on to say, they staged loud public battles in their hotel lobby and Rainier refused to escort Grace to a charity function after their presence had been advertised. While she attended the affair, Rainier ate in the hotel restaurant. Grace reportedly was "furious."

Adding as well to Grace's vexations toward the end of her life was a most unwelcome repetition of her tribulations with Caroline in the now-rebellious Stephanie. She had had little trouble with Albert, although he was not, according to his cousin Grace LeVine, the model son he has been painted. "Oh, Albert went through a rebellion of his own," she says. "But nobody pays any attention when it's a boy doing it. If a daughter gets a little wild, the press really plays it up. But boys get away with murder." Still, whatever rebellion Albert went through, it was mild and short-lived. Rarely linked with women, rarely seen partying, Albert completed his studies at Amherst College in Massachusetts, then joined the French Navy. In Albert, Grace had a son who came wonderfully close to her ideal.

This was not the case with Stephanie. Over the years Grace had spoiled her third child shamelessly. "You get a little tired with the third one and you give in to keep the peace," she said. Grace hinted at her daughter's difficulty in her letters to Don Richardson, but always with affection. In a 1979 letter she described the fourteen year old as "something else again. A very special child—difficult but sensational. She has been here before . . ." In 1974, Grace had said, "I should have been beating her like a gong long ago."

A mercurial, creative, affectionate, clinging child, Stephanie had leaned upon her mother in every area, and as she had been with Caroline, Grace was friend, mentor, and confidante to Stephanie for years. Again, however, that changed. At sixteen, suddenly desirous of independence, Stephanie had become willful and headstrong, and not only spurned her mother's counsel but violently rejected much of her upbringing. She hated being a princess, she would scream during family quarrels, and she would not act like one. Even at thirteen, she had refused to wear anything but pants to her sister's wedding ball and was forbidden to attend unless she wore a dress. She stayed away. Many fights between mother and daughter were over clothes; the two were once seen in a Paris boutique arguing over what to buy.

In school Stephanie resisted authority as well. She broke rules against smoking and leaving campus, and she was ordered to repeat a year at the strictly Catholic Institute St.

Dominique in Paris when her academic results were poor. Instead, Grace removed her from the school and enrolled her in a more liberal Catholic school, Charles de Foucauld. There, under dire threat from her mother, Stephanie buckled down and was graduated in the spring of 1982.

But she also infuriated her mother with indiscreet liaisons with Urbano Barberini, the twenty-one-year-old son of wealthy Italian socialites, and Paul Belmondo, seventeen-year-old son of French actor Jean-Paul Belmondo. Stephanie, then barely sixteen, was seen necking and photographed cuddling with Urbano on a beach, prompting Grace to ban further visits to the seaside spot. A few months later she met Belmondo, with whom she was more discreet. But the two were inseparable at parties, frequently spending all their time alone together in a corner.

Worried, and feeling a disturbing sense of déjà vu, Grace insisted that Stephanie return to Monaco and limit her dates with Belmondo. Now it was Stephanie's turn to be furious. The two argued violently and often, each fight tearing at Grace's heart and increasing her hurt and anger. During the summer of 1982, the fights only increased, as Stephanie tried again and again to assert her independence. Grace worried terribly. Stephanie was only seventeen. She had never had *this* much trouble with Caroline at that age. . . .

All of this had driven Grace to distraction, and she had, since the middle 1970s, relied increasingly on anesthetizing alcohol to take her mind off things. Grace had always enjoyed a strong cocktail, and stories abound from her friends about drinking with Grace and, in Mark Miller's words, getting "absolutely bombed." Her friend Anthony Burgess told of Grace fixing him drinks "that knocked your head off." Ava Gardner said, "Give her a couple of dry martinis, and Her Serene Highness Princess Grace becomes just another one of the girls who likes to dish the dirt." Rock Hudson told intimates that he and Grace had gotten "ripped to the tits" at a Rupert Allan party in the late 1960s. In 1971 Grace attended a fancy banquet thrown by the Shah of Iran in Persepolis, at which she imbibed freely until she was feeling a little silly. When the man sitting next to her lit up a cigar, Grace let loose with an unrestrained sneeze that popped all the buttons off the back of her shimmering gown. As her lady-in-waiting looked on in horror, Grace began to laugh until she was hopelessly hysterical.

But although Grace could get drunk with the best of them, her friends didn't start to worry about her drinking until the mid-1970s, when it seemed to them that she was drinking too much and for the wrong reasons. Clearly she was "letting herself go." What shocked her longtime friends the most was how much weight Grace was gaining, how puffy she looked around the eyes. As Robert Dornhelm expressed it, "People tend to gain weight when they're unhappy." One of the ways Grace had kept her weight down was to forswear alcohol for several months a year. "From August 15th until my birthday [November 12]," she said in 1976, "I go off the booze. I have a good send-off on August 14, then no more drink until my birthday. That way I lose weight and can wear all my clothes again."

By the mid-1970s she no longer bothered to stop drinking to control her weight. "What's the point?" she asked her friend Fleur Cowles. The result was that Grace put on a great deal of weight the last year of her life, weight that was especially disconcerting on a woman who had been so svelte all her life. Gore Vidal recalls, "A friend of mine traveled with her for a time and they shared a bedroom at one point. My friend went into the bathroom and saw Grace's bra—it was, as this woman put it, the kind her grandmother had worn— made of *canvas!* Miles of it. And she'd wash these things out herself and hang these huge canvases. These water wings would be in the bathroom. It was rather startling in this day and age. But she got fat, so she had to strap herself in."

Grace's drinking worried her friends all the more because when she was drunk, she would become careless about her actions and appearance and, even worse, mindless of her personal safety. For Grace to behave irresponsibly, even at a carefree party, was so out of character for her that her friends became deeply concerned. Don Richardson recalls one such instance at a party at Rupert Allan's home in 1979 to which Grace invited him and his wife. "She had started drinking quite a bit at that point. At the Rupert Allan party, she was hitting the bottle pretty good. She was letting herself go. The seams of her dress were open, her hair wasn't combed, her makeup was smudged. She put away a hell of a lot of drinks, and when it was time to leave, she insisted on driving home alone in this beat-up little convertible she'd arrived in. I was very worried about her driving, but she wouldn't listen to me, wouldn't let anyone else drive her home."

Chapter Twenty-three

On the brilliantly sunny Monday morning of September 13, 1982, Grace prepared to leave Roc Agel, where she, Albert, Rainier, and Stephanie had been staying, for an appointment with her couturier in Monaco. She needed to have several dresses altered before leaving that evening for Paris with Stephanie. She loaded her brown Rover 3500 with luggage and laid out the dresses needing alteration along the back seat to prevent them from wrinkling. Grace, who did not enjoy driving, usually was driven by her chauffeur, Christian Silvestri. But when he started to enter the car, Grace—aware that there wasn't room for three people in the Rover—told him, "That won't be necessary." When Silvestri reminded Grace of her fear of the tortuously winding road between Roc Agel and Monaco, she told him jokingly, "You can run behind us."

At around nine-thirty, the Rover, with Grace at the wheel and Stephanie beside her in the passenger seat, left the Grimaldi property and ventured out onto County Highway 53. The twisting road has over fifty sharp turns, many of them hairpin, and Grace negotiated them at a snail's pace. During the last five miles, truck driver Yves Raimondo was directly behind the Rover. He watched it make one turn, then another, without incident. But, about two hundred yards before the final and sharpest curve, Raimondo saw the car in front of him zigzag so badly that it almost sideswiped the mountain rocks on the opposite side of the road. Assuming "a lack of attention," Raimondo sounded his horn and, as he expected, the Rover righted itself as it continued down the roadway.

Then, to his growing horror, he realized that the car was not slowing down in anticipation of the dangerous turn ahead. "The corner came up," he later said. "I did not see it slow down . . . the brake lights didn't come on . . . she did not even try to turn and I had the impression that she was going faster and faster . . . [the car] disappeared over the edge."

All of the curves on the Moyenne Corniche have crash barriers, but this one, unlike the others, extends only halfway, because at that point a narrow dirt road runs off the main roadway at right angles. Grace's car barreled straight ahead, brushed against the edge of the barrier, passed over the entrance to the roadway, and careened off the hillside. It flew a few feet in the air, then crashed through thick underbrush and somersaulted several times before landing on its roof at the edge of a vegetable garden. The police photographs taken immediately after the accident reveal that the car's right side had been crushed flat in the fall down the hillside; the left-hand, driver's side of the car wasn't as badly damaged, and the door had popped open. Steam poured out of the car's radiator. It was 10:05 A.M.

Stephanie, injured but conscious and able to move, crawled out of the left-hand side of the car just as several residents of the area arrived. Her first words were, "Help my mother . . . My mother is in there—get her out!" Grace, who had not fastened her seat belt, was lying on her back amid the car's jumbled seats, her feet toward the front windshield and her head resting against the back window. There was little blood, but she was only half-conscious and did not respond to shouts.

Stephanie wandered to the steps of the nearby farmhouse, sobbing to the occupants that they must call her father. They didn't recognize her and asked who her father was. "He's the Prince. I'm his daughter, Stephanie, and *maman* is in the car." Calls were made to the *gendarmerie* and to the palace, and within five minutes two ambulances arrived. The attendants saw that there was no way to extract Grace from the car except to smash the rear window and pull her out through it;

they did so. She was obviously very badly injured. Her open eyes were glazed over, a gash ran across her forehead and her right leg lay at an odd angle. She did not respond when spoken to.

Grace and Stephanie, each in a separate ambulance, were rushed to Princess Grace Hospital. Rainier and Albert arrived shortly afterward but were not allowed to see them. Stephanie, the doctors discovered, was suffering from shock, a concussion, and a vertebra fracture that had come perilously close to paralyzing her. Grace's reactions to light and other stimuli were tested and were negligible, indicating severe brain damage. She was placed on a life-support system, and Dr. Charles Chatelin, head of surgery at the hospital, began four hours of surgery to treat her external wounds—a broken collarbone, broken femur, fractured ribs, severe gash in the forehead, and numerous cuts and bruises. Internally, Grace had sustained damage to her thorax and had a collapsed lung. Chatelin opened both her thorax (to remove blood and to bring air to her lung) and her stomach (to treat internal bleeding).

Her condition continued to deteriorate, however, and her electroencephalogram indicated she was falling into a coma. Dr. Chatelin and Dr. Duplay, head of neurosurgery at Nice Hospital, who had joined his colleague at Grace's side, realized that a CAT scan of her brain would be necessary. Princess Grace Hospital did not have the machine to do this; the only one in the area was owned by Dr. Michel Mourou in Monaco. Nearly thirteen hours after the accident, Grace was taken to Dr. Mourou's office on a stretcher. The elevator to his suite wasn't big enough to accommodate the stretcher, so Grace had to be carried up two flights of stairs. The scan was administered and revealed an area of massive bleeding deep in her brain that had caused extensive damage, and a smaller area of bleeding in the temporal lobe that, the doctors hypothesized, had occurred just before the accident. Grace, they concluded, had suffered a stroke, which most likely precipitated the accident, and had sustained such severe brain damage that she was unlikely to live. If she did, she would never again have use of her faculties. Grace was returned to the hospital named for her and was put back on life-support systems as her husband and children stood vigil and prayed for a miracle.

No one but those closest to the family knew the seriousness of the situation. Within hours of the accident, members of the world media descended on Monaco, eager for any detail. Nadia LaCoste, whose seasoned handling of the press had kept many another situation under control, was on vacation, and in her absence the job fell to an inexperienced member of the Grimaldi household. This, it turned out, made a bad situation worse. Pressed for some official word on Grace's and Stephanie's conditions and the reason for this seemingly unfathomable accident, the palace aide was unable to get the information he needed, either from Grace's doctors or from Prince Rainier. Wanting to protect his Prince, and his own job, the aide recalled Rainier's complaint about press sensationalism: "You have a bump with your car. Five minutes later it has become a bad accident. Next it is really dramatic: the car is wrecked and you are injured. It ends with you being thrown out into the road and killed."

Unwilling to give the press anything "really dramatic," the aide released an unofficial "official statement" that was inaccurate and misleading. Grace, it said, had suffered only some broken bones but "strict observation is necessary to diagnose any secondary complications," and Stephanie had suffered just some bruising. As to the matter of what caused the accident, the Monaco communiqué was a total fabrication. Perhaps assuming the only logical reason for such an accident must be mechanical failure, Rainier's aide wrote in his release that Princess Grace had "ascertained a brake failure."

The communiqué, in the light of subsequent events, gave rise to suspicions among newspeople that there had been a cover-up of the facts surrounding the accident. Within the next few days, rumors became rampant: Stephanie, under the legal driving age, had actually been driving the car (this rumor was given credence by reports from the first people who arrived at the crash site that Stephanie had crawled out of the driver's side of the car); Grace had been driving but she and Stephanie had had a violent argument that led her to lose control; Grace had left the palace in a rage after a fight with Prince Rainier and was in no condition to drive; the Rover had been tampered with by the Nice Mafia because Grace had fought to keep them out of Monte Carlo; the car had been whisked away by the palace before the authorities could examine it in order to conceal evidence; Prince Rainier had refused to allow the police to inspect the vehicle.

There is no way—short of a full explanation from Stephanie, which has not been forthcoming—to know what actually took place within the Rover on that tragic Monday. The official version is that Grace suffered a stroke and lost control of the car. What Prince Rainier has said Stephanie told him, however—"Mommy panicked. She didn't know what to do. She lost control"—would seem to work against such an explanation. Had Grace suffered a stroke, she would likely have blacked out and been unable, as Raimondo testified, to right the car after hearing a horn blast. Stephanie could have done so, but if she had, why didn't she also either press down on the brakes or attempt to maneuver the curve ahead?

There is so little plausible explanation for the fact that the Rover's brakes were never used and the car's trajectory was straight off the cliff that even the argument scenario doesn't convince; no matter how violently she and Stephanie may have been fighting, Grace surely would have realized that the curve was ahead and been cautious, especially after the near-miss of the zigzagging. The mystery, which may never be solved, is so compelling that more and more fantastic explanations keep popping up. In fact, a Paris stringer for one of the American tabloids, Patrick Wilkins, says, "The consensus among everyone I've talked to here in Paris is that Grace was so beside herself with all her problems, and so furious with Stephanie, that she just didn't care what happened to them anymore. A lot of people are convinced that Grace's death was a suicide."

That is the one theory that can never be proven, and we may never know the truth of any of them. But other rumors *can* be laid to rest. Captain Roger Bencze, who conducted the official investigation into Grace's accident as a member of the Mentone police force (the town in which the accident occurred) and is now a member of France's national *gendarmerie*, has spoken out for the first time for this book. With the confidential investigation file's depositions and photographs in front of him, Captain Bencze stated firmly that he believes the official version of the accident to be essentially correct, although he adds that "it was wrong for the palace to downplay the injuries."

Bencze stressed that "there was never any attempt to interfere with my investigation. I examined the car at four-thirty on September 13, in the company of the district attorney of Nice and the chief of police of Monaco. My inspection had been approved by the palace and no one tried to influence it. I found that the car had absolutely no mechanical problems. There was no evidence that there had been a fire, as was later suggested, and it was clear that the only possible way for Stephanie to exit was through the driver's side of the car. The fact that she crawled out of that side would in no way indicate that she was driving—it was the only way she could have gotten out." Examination of the photographs confirmed Bencze's statements.

Bencze believes that the evidence available could support the explanation that Grace suffered a stroke. "She might have lost awareness momentarily, as if she was falling asleep, and the sound of Raimondo's horn could have roused her. Then, as the effects of the stroke grew worse, she could have blacked out just before going over the cliff.

"There is no way of knowing for sure, of course, but in my official capacity—and just as a human being—I'm satisfied that there isn't all that much mystery involved in Princess Grace's death."

The original communiqué from Monaco—that Grace had been injured but was doing well—appears to have been not so much subterfuge as uninformed wishful thinking, because it wasn't only the press who were given this optimistic news, but Grace's intimates as well, including Nadia LaCoste—who was told that the situation wasn't bad enough to warrant her immediate return—and the Kellys. Later, reports appeared that Grace's family in Philadelphia was "furious" with Prince Rainier for "keeping from us" the extent of Grace's injuries. Lizanne denies this. "When the palace called me right after the accident," she says, "they didn't *know* how serious it was. They thought she just had a broken leg, that it was very superficial. They didn't know how serious the head injury was. When I spoke to Rainier the day she died, he told me it was very serious. But I don't think even then that he knew just *how* serious it was. He never kept anything from us."

Grace lingered, falling slowly into an ever deeper coma, throughout the night and morning of September 13–14. Her family—including Caroline, who returned from a trip to England at noon on Tuesday—kept a vigil at her bedside, anxiously conferring with the doctors, embracing one another, trying to hold on to a vestige of hope. At 6 A.M. the oscilloscope monitoring Grace's brain activity indicated that she was, in all but the most technical sense, dead. Her children kissed her, then left their father to be alone with his wife. At noon Prince Rainier gave the doctors permission to cease artificial life support. At 10:35 that evening, Grace died.

The news sent out a shock wave of incredulity: How could she be dead? Hadn't she merely suffered a broken leg in the accident? When the fact that one of the world's most beautiful, beloved, and seemingly charmed women had indeed been killed in an auto wreck sank in, both her friends and people who had never met her felt a profound sadness. To millions Grace had been, in Don Richardson's words, "a perfect canvas for everyone to paint a dream on." Her apparently unswerving commitment to her religious values and old-fashioned moral principles made her a shining example to those who felt such values far too quickly ebbing away. She was a symbol of self-sacrifice, of commitment to marriage and family, of dedication to one's professed principles.

Perhaps her knowledge that she was such a symbol had created much of her dread of that image crumbling during the family crises she faced, but it also caused a reaction to her death that far exceeded what might have been accorded a former movie star who married the prince of a tiny Mediterranean country. Grace's death elicited an outpouring of grief and affection throughout the world unparalleled since the assassination of John F. Kennedy in 1963.

Grace lay in state for several days in an open coffin. On Friday, September 17, the coffin was borne from the palace's chapel to the cathedral where she and Prince Rainier had been married twenty-six years earlier. World dignitaries, including Nancy Reagan and Princess Diana, sat in sorrow along with Grace's Hollywood friends, her former bridesmaids, and her family. Prince Rainier, Princess Caroline, and Prince Albert sat beside her coffin, a tableau of grief. Even in so sorrowful an atmosphere, observers were struck by the awful depth of Prince Rainier's desolation. He looked stricken, a man shattered by his loss. Cary Grant remembered his own reaction to Rainier's appearance: "I will never forget the way the Prince looked that day. Oh my God. Can there be any doubt that the man loved her with all his heart?"

Grace was laid to rest in the Grimaldi family vault in the cathedral on September 21, 1982. The inscription on a white marble slab says simply, "Grace Patricia, wife of Prince Rainier III, died the year of our Lord, 1982."

In one of those odd coincidences that seem to occur so often, Grace was asked by Pierre Salinger two months before her death, "How are you going to want to be remembered?"

Her answer, which was in several parts, included a desire "to be remembered as trying to do my job well, as being understanding and kind . . . I'd like to be remembered as a decent human being and a caring one who tried to help others."

That may well prove to be exactly the way in which Grace is remembered. For in those particulars of her life at least, there is no divergence between image and reality.

Epilogue

Once the shock eased, there was the numbing emptiness. For twenty-six years Grace and Rainier had *been* Monaco, and now one of them was gone. For the Prince there was no escape from pricking reminders of what had been. "She was terribly present all over the place," he said a few months after her death. "We've got constant reminders." In the weeks following the accident, family and friends worried about Rainier's ability to cope. "I think he's having a very hard time," said Lizanne. "He let Grace do a lot of things that he'll have to take over himself. I don't know how he's going to handle it."

To get away from Monaco seemed like the best solution. Rainier spent days on his ship, "being at sea as much as I can," and weeks at his mother's château in the North of France. Charlotte had left the Renaissance castle to him upon her death, and he and Grace had completely restored it after a fire. "There's a lot of hunting," Rainier said, "and I enjoy hunting, a lot of wild boar, and a lot of duck shooting. It's a different life and a different scenery, so it's a good change. The children enjoy it too."

In the grief-stricken period that followed Grace's death, it was the two oldest children who were strong for the father. "Rainier was so bereft," Rupert Allan said, "that Prince Albert stepped in and fielded most of the calls that were coming in from Grace's friends all over the world. He was grieving just as deeply—maybe even more so—but he managed to step in anyway. He showed a great deal of character."

During the funeral preparations, Caroline—as she would

later do in a more universal way—took over some of the duties her mother would usually have performed in such a situation. More than once, family members caught themselves starting to say, "We'll have to ask Grace," when confronted with a decision; more often than not, it was Caroline whom they turned to for advice. In the ensuing months Caroline looked after her father, who fell into a depression that affected his appetite, to make sure he ordered his meals from the palace kitchen. She also supervised the housekeeping staff. "Her father was very dependent on Caroline," says Grace LeVine. "Uncle Rainier was so devastated after Aunt Grace died that someone had to take over—and it was Caroline."

If Caroline and Albert had to be strong for Rainier, he needed to be strong for Stephanie. The physical pain of her injuries was nothing compared to the horror of her memories of the accident and her guilt at the battles she had waged against her mother in the months before her death. The intimations that she might have been in some way responsible for the accident weighed heavily on Stephanie. As Kell told the press, "I think maybe in some way she might be blaming herself for not having done something to save the situation." As to whether the facts of the accident might ever be unquestionably clear, a palace insider told *People* magazine, "The truth will eventually come out because there is a survivor—moreover one with a low barrier of resistance. I can't imagine that she will be able to keep it in forever with the questions following her around. At some point, she'll have to break."

Rainier visited his daughter several times each day in her hospital room and attempted to lift some of the burden she so suddenly had to shoulder. But there was little anyone could do. A few months after the accident, Rainier was asked, "How is Princess Stephanie?" He replied, "I think well, physically. The brace is off. The doctor says the healing is complete." Emotionally, though, he said, "I think she has a little bit of a second shot at realizing what's happened and how it's changed her life and how she has to make some decisions alone, which is difficult. She has to stop and think. It's very hard to advise her."

Their mother's death changed the lives of all three of her children, most vividly Caroline and Stephanie—and in ways, ironically, of which Grace would have approved. Each became more responsible, more focused, more as their mother would like to have seen them. Caroline, in fact, has in many respects taken her mother's place in Monaco as the country's "First Lady"; she is now president of the Garden Club, the Princess Grace Foundation, and the organizing committee for Monaco's annual Springtime Festival of International Arts. What has surprised seasoned Caroline watchers is the verve and commitment she has demonstrated in her new duties. Her work to realize her mother's dream of a Monaco ballet company bordered on the obsessive as she succeeded in convincing Parliament to release the money, hired a choreographer and artistic director, organized the company, and oversaw the restoration of Monaco's Opera House. A friend said, "Caroline has changed dramatically. Before, she was confused and unorganized. She had a lot of energy, but it was all spent in the wrong direction. Now she is calm, focused, in control."

A new marriage and motherhood have done as much to mature and settle Caroline as her mother's death had. As her marriage to Philippe Junot was ending, Caroline wrote in a notebook she kept, "I do not think I am the ideal woman for a man—with my tormented past, my uncertain present and perhaps my melancholy future." She went through several short-lived romantic flings after her divorce, notably with tennis star Guillermo Vilas and Ingrid Bergman's son, Roberto Rossellini. Then, late in 1983, she met Stefano Casiraghi, the twenty-three-year-old son of an Italian industrialist. Like Junot, he had no specific occupation; he worked with his father and struck out on his own with entrepreneurial enterprises. But that, according to a friend of Caroline's, is where the similarity to Junot ends: "It's easy to see why Caroline was attracted to Stefano. He is the opposite of Junot. He is thoughtful, hardworking, refined, conservative, smart . . . He is young in age but very mature. He has a lot of qualities her mother had. He is disciplined, devoted, reserved, warm. In him she has found her mother."

Prince Rainier was apparently unmoved by these similarities and did little to hide his disdain for Stefano. "The Prince makes it obvious that he feels Stefano is not good enough to be married to his daughter," one observer told *People*. But when Caroline and Stefano came to him in mid-December of 1983 to ask for his blessings for their marriage, Rainier could hardly say no: Caroline was three months pregnant. On December 20 the impending marriage was announced, and nine days later Caroline and Stefano were married in a civil ceremony at the palace.

On June 8, 1984, Caroline gave birth to a six-pound, ten-ounce boy the couple named Andrea Albert, after a friend of Stefano and Caroline's brother. Although much was made in the press of the infant's "noticeably premature" arrival, the birth of Prince Rainier's first grandchild was a joyous family occasion, a watershed in the Grimaldis' recovery from Grace's death. For Caroline, motherhood signaled the fruition of her newfound maturity. "I think Caroline and Stefano are very happy," Lizanne says, "and they're mad for that little baby. He's adorable—the cutest thing ever." For Prince Rainier, the birth symbolized the fact that, as he had said with forced optimism to friends after Grace's death, "life goes on." With the Casiraghis living in a villa just a few minutes' walk from the palace (a gift from Rainier to Caroline when she married Junot), the Prince has ample opportunity to dote over Andrea (and his siblings, Charlotte, born in August 1986 and Pierre, born September 1987). "Andrea looks just like Uncle Rainier," Grace LeVine says. Adds Lizanne, "A prouder grandfather you have never seen."

Although Caroline has stepped impressively into her mother's shoes, it is not something she has completely relished. "She *had* to do it," Grace LeVine says. "She had no choice.

But she has her own family now, and she can't wait for Albert to get married and take over."

The question of when—and whether—Prince Albert will take over for his father has intrigued Monegasques for years. Albert turned thirty in March 1988 and has for most of his life been preparing to succeed his father as ruler of Monaco. Unlike Rainier, however, Albert may not accede to the throne only upon the death of his predecessor, because Prince Rainier has said he plans to abdicate in Albert's favor "the day he feels ready"—in the near future, he hopes. "I've always said that I don't want to drag on. He's young, he's got plenty of stamina and will, and he knows the place well . . . I don't believe in making him wait until I die off." The transition, Rainier feels, will be much easier for Albert with his father still around to smooth the way. Rainier also, according to Lizanne, is eager to retire. "He is looking forward to it. He can't wait. There's a part of the palace that he says he's going to live in and leave the rest of the place to Albert. He's found his little niche. I think this will all happen after Albert's thirtieth birthday."

It is a responsibility Albert would rather not assume. Asked by an interviewer if he would be "happier not having to," Albert replied simply, "Much." But the noblesse oblige of his ascension was a fact of life for him from the beginning. "It wasn't a major topic of conversation," he said, "because . . . I was aware of what I was expected to do in the future." Until his mother died, however, he didn't much think about it and paid little attention to the inner workings of Monegasque politics. Grace's death—and the jarring reminder of mortality that came with it—led Albert to finally become intimately involved in his father's world. "He has started," Rainier said in 1983, "to go to government meetings, just to see how they work, what is discussed, what projects come up. He has done this only since his mother died, so he needs a little more acquaintance with the administration. Then I'd like to have him next to me to see how things get to me and how they have to be solved."

One of the reasons for Albert's lack of enthusiasm about succeeding his father is that, for now, he's having too good a time as the world's most eligible bachelor. During a 1984 visit to Los Angeles, his friend Todd Allan said, "He had an incredible party schedule. He's just having fun." Grace LeVine adds, "He has a lot of dates, but he's very discreet. He doesn't get nearly the kind of publicity Stephanie and Caroline get." Albert's calm personality has a great deal to do with that. A friend told *Interview*'s Christopher Buckley, "At an opening, we were swarmed by the cameras. He just stood very still, let them take their pictures, then turned on his heel and said, 'Thank you very much,' and walked away. You're not going to print photos of someone who just stands there and says, 'Thank you,' are you? But one of Caroline or Stephanie fighting or sticking their necks out is different."

As he has with Caroline and Stephanie, Prince Rainier disapproves of the people with whom Albert socializes. Lizanne recalls asking the Prince whether Albert was romantically involved with anyone. He replied, "I hope he's not serious about anybody in that group he's going around with."

Albert has dated Brooke Shields, Catherine Oxenberg, Lady Helen Winsor, Italian actress Patrizia Pellegrino (who called him "the most wonderful of lovers"), a West German porn actress who claimed Albert "could be" the father of her unborn child, and even Hart-breaker Donna Rice (in 1981), but apparently he has never had a serious romance. "I don't think he's ever been really involved with any one person," Lizanne says. "He's had girlfriends, but I don't think there's anyone who's gotten him in a serious mood." For his part, Albert offers only a general statement of intent: "I just know that I want a loving family, like the one my father and mother created for my sisters and me. My wife will have to understand the responsibilities involved in overseeing Monaco. It takes a lot of time and hard work. And I will follow in my father's footsteps in one regard: I will marry the woman I love."

Recently, friends say, Albert has begun a relationship with

Mary Wayte, a twenty-two-year-old Gold Medalist in the 200-meter freestyle at the 1984 Summer Olympics in Los Angeles. They have, at least, a serious interest in sports in common: Albert has been in training for the 1988 Winter Olympics bobsled competition. But no one expects any engagement announcement. As a close family friend put it, "Everyone's beginning to get a bit worried."

Prince Rainier, as publicly guarded as he is, has addressed the possibility that Albert may not marry. Asked on "The CBS Morning News" what would happen in such an event, Rainier replied, "He doesn't have to produce an heir. If he doesn't, Caroline or one of her children could take over." That isn't something that would please most Monegasques, who have a strong preference for princes, but neither is it, apparently, unthinkable.

Another reason for Albert's royal reticence is his insecurity about living up to Rainier's reputation. "Albert realizes," says Grace LeVine, "that his father has done an unbelievable job with Monaco and it's a hard shoe to fit into. He wants to be really ready when it happens." Albert apparently plans to continue his father's controversial policy of continued development of Monaco. "My father has been successful in developing Monaco from a quiet, low-key state with virtually no industry to a principality that is developing tourism, real estate, foreign business and foreign industry . . . If we can maintain this level in the areas in which we are strongest and find ways to expand it, we'll be in good shape."

Recently, Prince Rainier has given indications that he will stay on much longer than he originally intended, most probably because of Albert's reticence to take over. If he does, the lack of a Princess will become more and more serious a problem for his country. Already, tourism is down considerably in the five years since Grace's death, and many observers feel a new Princess for Monaco would reverse the trend.

The most frequently mentioned candidate to replace Grace as Monaco's first lady is Ira von Furstenberg, the forty-six-year-old sister of Sebastian von Furstenberg, the ring-bearer at Grace and Rainier's wedding. Former sister-in-law of Diane von Furstenberg and ex-wife of Spanish prince Alfonso von Hohenlohe, Ira is described by those close to her as a woman who would "rather be Marilyn Monroe than the Queen of England." Lusty and beautiful, she made twenty-six Italian movies in the sixties and seventies—"all bad, unfortunately," according to a friend.

Will Rainier and Ira marry? It appeared more likely before first she, then her son, spoke too freely about the possibility to the press. Caroline, who reportedly dislikes Ira and sees her as a threat to her own position in Monaco, used Ira's indiscretion against her in conversations with her father. One insider commented, "I don't think Rainier has the guts to confront Caroline at this point in his life. He likes Ira, but he doesn't want these problems."

As for Ira, she admits that "at the moment the whole thing is rather jeopardized. But you can never tell what happens in life . . ."

Almost since his birth, Albert has been said to be the most like his mother, in temperament as well as appearance, of the Grimaldi children. Certainly his inner calm, his reserve, his quiet dignity all call to mind aspects of the Grace Kelly personality. But it is, ironically, Stephanie—who looks like her father—who has become strongly reminiscent of the creatively ardent, emotionally searching young woman Grace was at the same age. She has had, after her breakup with Paul Belmondo, romantic flings with Alain Delon's handsome, muscular son Anthony, Swedish racecar driver Stefan Johansson, and other beautiful young men of the jet set, including Ted Kennedy, Jr. In 1986 she had a highly publicized affair with handsome young actor Rob Lowe, which lasted one month—just long enough to permanently end his engagement to actress Melissa Gilbert. Described, as her sister was, as a "playgirl," Stephanie is defended by her brother: "Why shouldn't a girl her age have a lot of boyfriends? It would be worse if she knew only one boy before she got married."

Like her mother and sister did before her, Stephanie has fallen in love with an older, sophisticated jet-setter and—again like them—she has faced harsh criticism for it. Stephanie met thirty-four-year-old, French-born Mario Oliver (né Jutard) in 1986 at his popular L.A. nightclub, Vertigo. They've been inseparable ever since, living together with a friend of his in a Coldwater Canyon hideaway.

Stephanie seems content to remain in Los Angeles. As the handsome blond Oliver expressed it to the *Los Angeles Times Magazine*'s Nikki Finke, "Here, they recognize me on the street and say, 'Who's that?' about Stephanie. But in Paris, they look at Stephanie and then at me. That's why she likes it better here."

"I live a normal life, a quiet life," added Stephanie. "I don't live the life of a star . . . Our favorite thing to do together is just laying back in the sun and seeing our friends and being real settled, like normal people . . ."

Unfortunately, Stephanie's hopes for a "settled, normal" life with Oliver have been upset by a storm of controversy over his past, his motivations in becoming involved with her and his acceptance by the royal family. Oliver cannot seem to put to rest the story of his arrest in 1982 on charges that he and a friend raped a nineteen-year-old college student at a party in exclusive Bel-Air. After a year, Oliver, as part of a plea-bargain, pleaded no contest to a lesser charge of sexual battery.

Oliver defended himself to Nikki Finke: "The thing is, I didn't rape her. I didn't rape any girl. I don't need to . . . Sorry, but I've even had some girls trying to rape me . . . I knew this girl. . . . She came to this party and I had sex with her. Something normal. Plus, she was really, really trying to pick up on me. . . . Eight days later, they came to the restaurant where I was working and said, 'Mario, you're accused of a crime.'"

Stephanie, well aware of Oliver's background and the persistent rumors that he is using her to advance himself and his nightclub businesses, appears unfazed by either. "Mario has his defects. He has some dark spots like everybody. Nobody's perfect."

Unsurprisingly, reports have surfaced of Prince Rainier's violent opposition to his daughter's relationship with the twice-married Oliver. Indeed, Mario would appear to be tailor-made for Grimaldi family ostracism, and he has not, in nearly two years, visited Monaco. "He has not met my father," Stephanie explained, "because the opportunity has not presented itself." She discounts reports of her father's opposition to the relationship: "If he weren't happy with me living here, he would have me back home on the next flight."

Stephanie's romance with Mario Oliver, it can safely be assumed, would not have met with Grace's approval. But her professional activities since Grace's death would have pleased her, because, in many ways, she is emulating her mother in that arena as well. While Caroline and Albert are admirably doing the jobs expected of them as members of the royal family, Stephanie promises, like her mother before her, to establish an artistic reputation of her own in endeavors distinct from the "family business."

Not that she hasn't, in the years since her mother's death, floundered and flailed about in an attempt to find her niche. Always a creative child, her passion as an adolescent had been fashion design. "I've always been interested in clothes from as early as I can remember," she said. "I used to love playing paper dolls with my mother—she would cut them out and I would dress the dolls." Intent on attending a fashion design school at the time of Grace's death, afterward she wasn't sure, as her father put it, "if she really wants to do that. She's just taking cooking courses now, nothing terribly serious."

Within six months she had made up her mind to enroll at the Fashion Design School in Paris. A year later, however, eager for some practical experience, she dropped out: "You lose time studying fashion in school," she explained. Her status helped her become an apprentice to Marc Bohan at Christian Dior in Paris, where she went to work every morning, designed fabric and jewelry, and made the connections that led to her next enthusiasm: modeling.

By the time she turned twenty in February 1985, Stephanie had become one of the world's most strikingly beautiful women. Her large soulful blue eyes, sensuous full lips, strong nose, opulent eyebrows, and air of petulant androgyny was the perfect fashion look of the 1980s, and when a Parisian modeling agency approached her, she excitedly accepted their offer to represent her. Within weeks she was appearing on the covers of magazines like *Company* and *Elle,* and creating a good deal of excitement. She was the perfect model: one who was already a world-famous celebrity. To clients her services were reportedly worth ten thousand dollars a day. Very quickly New York took note, and Stephanie got offers from every top American modeling agency to represent her in the United States. She turned them down, because her father was unhappy about this new and temptation-laden field she was toying with. "I don't think it is a fulfilling or important career," he said later.

A few weeks later, however, Stephanie was being represented by the Wilhelmina agency in New York. "It was a rebellious act against the family's wishes," said Frances Grill, owner of another agency, Click. Wilhelmina scheduled a whirlwind two-and-a-half-week New York visit for Stephanie in April 1985, during which she was to be presented at a Visage Club party and make herself available for photo sessions. As *Vanity Fair* put it, "Everyone in town tried to reach her. Hilton [Karen Hilton, Stephanie's agent at Wilhelmina] stiff-armed all but the *crème* in the best Studio 54 doorman fashion. 'I don't know how many people I said no to,' she says."

By the time Stephanie's itinerary was set, she was scheduled to be photographed for *Vogue, Life,* and *Mademoiselle.* ABC News, "Entertainment Tonight," and the "Today" show were set to film the photo sessions. *Rolling Stone* and one of the newsweeklies were preparing cover stories. The Visage party was the hottest ticket in New York.

Stephanie never showed up—and no one is certain why. Wilhelmina explained that she had been hospitalized for "women's problems." The *National Enquirer* said it was drug abuse. Another version was that Rainier had refused to let her go when the hoopla seemed to get out of hand. Frances Grill felt it was Stephanie who made the decision not to show. "To take a girl who's only twenty, who's never really worked, whose family is against it in the first place, to be booked for big parties, big PR—it's got to have scared her to death." Stephanie's only explanation: "I got sick of modeling and was afraid of being overexposed."

Whatever the reason, Stephanie went back to her drawing board at Christian Dior, and there befriended another young apprentice, Alix de la Comble, who was specializing in wedding gowns. "We sat at our boards in the same room for three months before we spoke," de la Comble said. "Then one day we both started trying on designer shoes, and we started laughing like a couple of children. From then on we were friends."

The two women shared a restlessness with the nine-to-five routine and an entrepreneurial spirit. Seeing a need for innovative swimwear, they worked in their spare time to develop avant-garde, provocative designs. Rather than offer their creations to their employer, Stephanie and Alix went into business for themselves and created a company—Pool Position—with their own resources. "We took a gamble, and we won," Stephanie said later. "My father didn't finance us."

In less than a year Pool Position had sold twenty-eight thousand suits priced at $80 to $150, helped along by Stephanie's international promotion tour early in 1986. By any standards, her enterprise was a success, and observers expected her to settle into a career as a celebrity fashion designer. She did, in fact, buy out her partner Alix, and is now sole owner of the swimwear company, which continues to thrive.

Apparently, however, Stephanie is intent on trying everything—and succeeding at it, too. On March 1, 1986, her first record, "Irresistible," was released in Europe, and within two months had sold eight hundred thousand copies and topped charts all over the Continent. There was talk that Stephanie planned a world concert tour to promote the record and that she was serious about building a show business career. "Who would think I could sing with this voice?" Stephanie said soon after the record's release, mocking her husky alto. "We worked on the record for four months, because it had to be extremely professional—I didn't want anyone to say I was getting by on my name."

Although that's just what many people did say, Stephanie's career gamble paid off. Her first album, *Besoin,* sold five million copies in Europe, making her one of the top-selling recording artists in the world. Although an earlier plan to break Stephanie out in the all-important American market sputtered, a second attempt is being orchestrated by the same management firm that handles Prince and Sheila E. Putting herself completely in their hands, Stephanie is said to be working on a totally "new look" involving her makeup, hairstyle and clothes.

Even further, Stephanie has been studying acting with renowned teacher and former actress Nina Foch. She hasn't yet decided whether to try her hand at the profession her mother triumphed in; she has told friends she wants to be certain she has real acting talent before setting herself up for comparisons to her mother.

Is Stephanie a privileged dilettante, dabbling in whatever seems fun and allowed to indulge her whims because of her status, or a tremendously creative force who has not yet found the best outlet for her artistic energies? She may well be both. Whether or not she makes the right decisions for herself remains to be seen, but her future promises not to be dull.

"By their fruits you will know them." This statement of Grace's, made in pride as her children entered adolescence, came back to embarrass her as first Caroline and then Stephanie publicly defied the strict and careful upbringing Grace had provided them. At this writing, however, five years after her death, Grace would be proud of her children. Both Caroline and Albert have, for the most part, risen to the challenge of their positions in life, as their mother did for so many years. And Stephanie, although conducting her personal life in a way that would have displeased her mother, has shown an artistic audacity that the rebellious young actress Grace Kelly would have loved.

In the Salinger interview two months before her death, Grace mentioned another way she would like to be remembered: "I suppose mostly in terms of my children and their children." It may have taken her death to set Grace's children on the proper course, but they seem intent now not on rebelling against the upbringing she gave them but rather on using it to create for themselves lives of which she would be proud. "She was terribly present all over the place," Rainier said. Clearly, she still is.

Notes

Key to Abbreviations:

LAT: Los Angeles *Times*
NYDN: New York *Daily News*
NYT: New York *Times*
DR: Don Richardson
PI: Personal Interview

Initial references to a Personal Interview include the date the interview was conducted. Abbreviated references are cited fully in the selective bibliography.

xiii   She has a blind confidence: Tivey-Faucon.

PART ONE

1   We were always: "The Story of Princess Grace: Once Upon a Time Is Now." Television documentary. NBC-TV, May 22, 1977.
What's Grace sniveling about: Levin.

Chapter One

3   No one except the library staff: PI with Geraldine Duclow, head of the Theatre Collection, Philadelphia Free Library, February 10, 1986.
4   "She's not upset": Lewis, p. 158.
7   A good example: Newman, p. 13.
"There never has been": Lewis, p. 11.
8   "Rowing is": Newman, p. 22.

9 "Did you ever know": Parsons.
10 "Coming back from": Martin(a).
   "Neither of them": Ibid.

Chapter Two

13 "our Prussian general mother": Bradford, p. 20.
   had several extramarital affairs: Lewis, p. 146.
   "messed up his only son's life": Ibid., p. 14.
   "Kell wanted to play": PI, October 20, 1985.
14 "I don't get that girl": Bradford, p. 25.
   "Don't worry": Lewis, p. 184.
15 "We'd all have": PI, January 7, 1986.
   "I always thought": Taves.
   "Grace was always": PI.
   "My older sister": Pepper.
   "She told such": Levin.
16 "Flossie was wonderful": Ibid.
   "I was always telling": Ibid.
   "I wonder": Taves.
   "I gave Grace": Levin.
17 "Grace never": PI, January 8, 1986. *(All Lizanne LeVine
      quotes in this chapter are from this interview unless oth-
      erwise indicated.)*
   "What's the use": Levin.
   "Grace was a very good": PI.
20 "The woman who played": Martin(a).
   "She understood": Bradford, p. 30.
21 "The teens are rather awful": Fisher.
   "She was nothing but": Kelly.
   "There was nothing awkward": PI, November 13, 1985.
   "Grace was a wild teenager": Marx.
22 "Men began proposing": Kelly.
   "When we picked Grace up": PI, May 6, 1987.
   "Grace had a pleasing": Newman, p. 36.
   "I think she was popular": Ibid.
23 "Because she was so young": Kelly.
   "I suppose we never knew": Ibid.
24 "It became terribly": Ibid.
   "At last": Bradford, p. 40.
   "At the time": Scullin.

25 "That was the year": Ibid.
"My husband knew": Kelly.
"She had never": Ibid.
"Let her go": Bradford, p. 41.
"Deep down": Levin.
26 "Mr. Diestel said": PI, November 20, 1986.
"She got away": Englund, p. 24.
27 "It all happened so quickly": quoted by DR, PI, November 8, 1985.
28 "Now I'm really going": Kelly.

Chapter Three

30 "We were turned on": PI, March 29, 1986.
"She was terribly sedate": *Time.*
31 Grace suddenly jumped: Gaither, p. 20.
"I went to a party": PI, November 13, 1985.
32 "I had this Texas drawl": PI.
"I was doing some modeling": Ibid.
33 "What we call": *Time.*
"I was terrible": Ibid.
34 "A candidate for": PI.
"I had several classes": PI, November 9, 1985.
"People would see her": PI, November 15, 1985.
35 "Grace, I found": Ibid.
"I never thought": Ibid.
"I was amazed": Richardson.
36 "She said yes": PI, November 4, 1985. *(All Don Richardson quotes in this chapter are from interviews conducted between November 3, 1985, and January 22, 1986, unless otherwise indicated.)*
"Jeez, you've brought some dull broads": Richardson.
37 "Grace and Don Richardson": PI.
38 "There's a man, isn't there": Kelly.
39 "I gave them the word": Robyns(a), p. 42.
41 "That next morning": PI.
"When the call came": Richardson.
At the end of the summer: Ibid.
42 "Grace said she was in love": PI.
"It was a promise": Richardson.
44 Mark Miller reports: PI.

Chapter Four

45 "Whenever they asked me": Levin.
46 "Everybody said I was too tall": McCarthy.
"I took her to Capp's office": PI.
Capp was arrested: NYT, February 12, 1972.
47 "Even at this early time": Englund, p. 30.
"I've got a part": Kelly.
"She got the part": Schulberg.
48 "When Raymond Massey arrived": Kelly.
"Though I knew": *Time*.
49 "We did a lot of silly things": Schulberg.
"How did we ever": Ibid.
50 "We were to wave": Ibid.
"She wasn't just another": Bradford, p. 58.
"She has no stove": Ibid.
"She's got no sex": letter from Steve Morris to the author,
October 25, 1985.
"Edie just flipped": PI.
51 "We've got a new girl": *Time*.
"I thought she looked pretty": Parton.
52 "She's perfect": *Time*.
53 "She said to me": PI.
54 "She explained": Kelly.
A man with "an inner": Englund, p. 46.
"Besotted with each other": Bradford, p. 64.
"I felt that he was not": Kelly.
55 "I didn't find out": PI.

PART TWO

Chapter Five

60 "Jay Kanter brought Grace": PI, November 15, 1985.
"She was a new face": Bradford, p. 61.
"It wasn't so much": Englund, p. 38.
"You ought to learn": Martin(a).
61 "I paid him": PI.
"Coop muttered": Ibid.
"She was just too special": Englund, p. 41.

62 "I prefer older men": Aline Mosby interview with Grace,
        July 10, 1954.
    "Grace fell in love": PI.
    "Grace was infatuated": Ibid.
    "Coop felt warmly": PI.
    "Coop was the kind of guy": PI, January 8, 1986.
63 "She was very serious": Arce, p. 241.
    "He's the one who taught me": Scullin.
    Accused Zinnemann of being: Englund, p. 41.
    "I'll never be able to thank": Scullin.
64 "Everything is so clear": *Time*.
    "She was very, very wooden": Bradford, p. 62.
    "An experienced": Englund, p. 43.
    "It cost five hundred thousand dollars": PI.
    "It was a wonderful": Scullin.
65 "I discovered": Levin.
    "All she did": Schary, p. 260.
66 "Darryl miscast her": Ibid.
    "He made the test": Ibid.
    "We certainly didn't object": PI, November 2, 1985.
    "She told me": Ibid.
67 "I was puzzled": Ibid.
68 "Guess what": Kelly.
    "Oh, Mother": Ibid.
69 "Grace was mad for Clark": PI.
    "She should never have been": Parsons.
    "What is there about this": Garceau, p. 237.
    "Grace was just a one-night stand": Bradford, p. 69.
    "Grace almost always": PI, December 1, 1985.
70 "It's the most beautiful": Bradford, p. 70.
    "She saw a lion": Ibid.
    "pass the bottle around": quoted by Lucille Ryman Carroll,
        PI, November 2, 1985.
    "That's the greatest compliment": Bradford, p. 65.
71 "If I cried": Carpozi, p. 139.
    "I was very fond of Clark": Santora.
    "It was almost as if": Carpozi, p. 139.
72 "Our waiter": Sinden, p. 170.
73 "The location was full": PI.

Ava told him: Higham, p. 136.
74 "Kelly, what the hell?": Bradford, p. 74.

Chapter Six

76 "An actress like Grace": Martin(a).
77 "In a horrible way": Ibid.
78 "Hitch made her": PI, November 9, 1985.
    "Working with Hitchcock": Bradford, p. 79.
    "Every good dramatic coach": Scullin.
    "I have such affection": Bradford, p. 79.
79 "Aren't you shocked": Spoto, p. 345.
    "I'd just get up": Ibid., p. 343.
80 "Hitchcock was fascinated": PI.
    "[He] would have used": Englund, p. 61.
    "It was very serious": PI.
    "I was aware of it": PI.
81 "I flew back": PI.
    "I don't know if they": PI, November 7, 1985.
    "Mal told Ray": PI, November 15, 1985.
82 "My father was concerned": Marx.
    "I don't like that": *Time.*
    "in our family": PI.
    "She and Scoop": Martin(a).
    "My mother and father": PI.
    "Grace came to realize": Ibid.
83 "In those days": PI.
    "I felt like": Martin(a).
    "I have nothing": PI, January 28, 1986.
84 "Word got around": PI.
    Joe Regan, a former: Arthur Lewis Papers, Temple University Library, Philadelphia, Pa.
    "She was a very 'touchy' ": PI.
85 "Grace was used": Englund, p. 127.
    "She's very cagey": Martin(a).
86 "Sometimes I think": Ibid.
    "For some personal reasons": Bradford, p. 81.
    "Grace *cold*": Parton.
87 "This was her fifth": PI, December 13, 1985. *(All quotes from James Stewart in this chapter are from this interview unless otherwise indicated.)*

"I was entranced": Englund, p. 62.
88 "There was a reason": Spoto, p. 348.
    "The bosom isn't right": Ibid.
    "She's easy to play to": Martin(a).
89 Grace "wasn't the slightest": PI, November 15, 1985.
    "Grace was kind of a tomboy": Ibid.

Chapter Seven

91 "The part of the wife": Martin(a).
92 "dressed as if": Ibid.
    "the girls at the Actors' Workshop": Ibid.
    he told fellow actor: Thomas, p. 104.
93 "brief but satisfactory": Ibid., p. 97.
    "so far she has only played": Martin(a).
94 "George and I": Martin(a).
    "We have big plans": Englund, p. 75.
    "*Somehow* we let Grace know": Martin(a).
    "I just *had* to be in": Scullin.
95 "Metro won't let us have you": Martin(a).
    "I'm always being given": Levin.
96 "I saw this *gorgeous* girl": PI. *(All Arthur Jacobsen quotes in this chapter are from this previously cited personal interview unless otherwise indicated.)*
97 "Sue said": PI.
98 "thought the part": PI, November 7, 1985. *(All Chico Day quotes in this chapter are from this interview unless otherwise indicated.)*
99 "Hey ol' buddy": PI with Robert Slatzer.
    "I don't mind telling you": Thomas, p. 98.
    "Bing was mad for her": Bradford, p. 88.
    "Grace called me up": PI.
    "I remember when Grace": quoted by Dorothy Kilgallen, January 13, 1956.
100 "Yours with love": London *Daily Express,* March 5, 1978.
    "I have been jealous": London *Sun,* March 20, 1978.
    "If I were": Martin(a).
    "She fell head over heels": PI.
101 "Bill was absolutely": PI.
    "I couldn't do that": Thomas, p. 99.
    "Bill liked Grace": PI.

"Bill Holden told me": PI.
"If I were to lose Ardis": Thomas, p. 135.
103 "I see you're": Bradford, p. 89.
"It doesn't take any stretch": PI.
104 "I know she got": Ibid.
"As an unmarried woman": de Vilallonga.
"With some actresses": Martin(a).
105 "She worked her head off": Ibid.

Chapter Eight

106 "All the men": *Time*.
"was a wretched experience": Levin.
107 "She would look at me": Bradford, p. 94.
"Our last scene": Granger, p. 306.
"I remember one time": Parton.
108 "a beautiful but dumb": Scullin.
"I don't want to dress up": *Time*.
"Dore Schary should have been": PI.
110 "The publicity people": Parton.
"If you made a gaffe": PI, October 16, 1985.
111 "Until I know people": Martin(a).
"I don't think it's anybody's business": McCarthy.
"I've been accused": Santora.
"It's nine-thirty": Martin(a).
112 "I don't think Grace": quoted by Erskine Caldwell, "Kelly Is a Lady," syndicated newspaper series, October 29–November 2, 1954.
113 "Popularity goes in eras": Parton.
"The boys came back": PI.
"She has great beauty": Parton.
114 "She was my ideal": PI, December 2, 1985.
115 "Dad gave each of us": PI.
117 "I was just happy": Levin.
"Peggy's the family extrovert": Martin(a).
118 "Grace, that will be enough": quoted in Levin.

Chapter Nine

119 "She was all that I wanted": Bradford, p. 91.
120 "the greatest": Englund, p. 117.

"When she broke up": Marx.

121   "Considering that the world": Gam.
     "We were very isolated": Robyns(b).
     "asked me what my intentions were": Marx.
     "I don't think": Robyns(b).
     "secretly engaged": Marx.
     "We had an understanding": Robyns(b).

122   "I had left the business": PI. *(All Cary Grant quotes in this chapter are from this previously cited personal interview unless otherwise indicated.)*

123   "No matter": Bradford, p. 94.
     "Three quarters": Parton.

124   "She will probably": Ibid.
     "Grace never complained": Ibid.

125   "She isn't one of those girls": Ibid.
     "I deliberately photographed": Truffaut, p. 168.
     "I think the most interesting women": Ibid, p. 167.

128   "Whose gardens are those": Englund, p. 82.

129   "was to show off": Spoto, p. 352.

130   "I don't approve": *Time.*
     "Should I shake his hand": PI with Kathy McKenna.

131   "I just received": Lewis, p. 162.
     "Now wait a minute": Ibid.
     "Oleg, you're": Kelly.
     "Once I am involved": Englund, p. 120.

132   "The weekend I spent": Marx.
     "I ate razor blades": Robyns(b).
     "Don, you're slipping in": Levin.

133   "Her family regarded her": Englund, p. 121.
     "I know for sure": Ibid, p. 128.
     "If one has": Ibid.
     "She kept seeing me": Marx.
     "she had changed": Ibid.
     "The most amazing thing": PI.

134   "Yes I *would* mind": Englund, p. 122.
     "It was very difficult": Robyns(b).

135   "There had been": PI.
     "You wouldn't believe": PI.

136   "She came to see it": PI.

"many acquaintances": Martin(a).
Prince Rainier asked Niven: Morley, p. 232.

Chapter Ten

138   "Do you think": Galante(a).
      "The words were": Ibid.
      the Prince had abruptly: Englund, p. 138.
139   "Was it possible?": Galante(b).
      "It would not do": Galante(a).
      "Tell me about": Galante(b).
140   "Their red and blue": Galante(a).
141   "It's unbelievable": Bradford, p. 111.
143   "We felt like": Englund, p. 129.
      "Grace's complexion": Galante(b).
144   "I was immediately": PI, May 7, 1986. *(All Jean-Pierre
           Aumont quotes in this chapter are from this interview
           unless otherwise indicated.)*
145   "The secret of": Reynolds.
147   "We live in a terrible world": Ibid.
148   "I don't think she feels": Bradford, p. 114.
      "Gracie, shall I": Kelly.
149   "I used beautiful fabrics": Rose, p. 103.
      "It's like a palace": Bradford, p. 116.
150   "The other day": Parton.
151   "Sometimes I saw her": Ibid.
      "I've met her": Galante(b).
      "I made up my mind": *Match.*
152   "I want to thank you": Englund, p. 131.
      "I almost knew": Levin.
154   "I am not shopping": Schoenbrun.

PART THREE

157   Of course I consider: Scullin.

Chapter Eleven

159   "At one point": Levin.
      "Christmas morning": Ibid.
      "We knew almost nothing": PI.
160   "Grace and Rainier seemed": Ibid.

"She hesitated": Kelly.
161 "Rainier was helping": PI.
"Everything was perfect": Levin.
162 "I don't think Grace was in love": PI.
"I think they bought": Lewis, p. 267.
"As the Prince of Monaco": Levin.
163 "I am living in a dream": Santora.
164 "Father, if you ever hear": Martin(b).
Gisele later married: Bradford, p. 113.
"Her family": Martin(b).
165 Prince Rainier was under the impression: PI with DR.
"They had her in stirrups": PI.
"You have to remember": Ibid.
"Grace told me": Ibid.
166 "I don't want any": Bradford, p. 124.
167 "The Kellys were": PI.
"For Grace to have": Englund, p. 142.
170 "Grace told Dore Schary": PI.
"She would never": PI, January 9, 1986.
171 "She looked at him": Hart-Davis, p. 34.
"Why on earth": PI.
"Grace had terrors": PI.
172 "If I'd met the Prince": Levin.
"She talked to me": Robyns(b).
"The fact is": Birmingham.
"I raised hell": PI.
173 "As far as": PI.

Chapter Twelve

174 "It's *Monaco*, Mother": Birmingham.
"Really, Grace": Kahn.
175 What is now Monaco: grateful acknowledgment is made to
    Steven Englund, whose excellent history of Monaco
    in *Grace of Monaco* provided the basis for this one.
182 "If Prince Rainier": Santora.
183 "struck Grace a terrible blow": Englund, p. 236.
184 "I've worked so hard": Bradford, p. 131.
"as big as": Englund, p. 146n.
"I vehemently opposed": PI, June 27, 1986.
185 "At the end of the song": Ibid.

"I could tell Grace was": Englund, p. 148.

187 "We thought *The Swan*": Lewis, p. 261.

189 "They didn't want me": Birmingham.

"The trip was just bedlam": Kahn.

191 "The day we left": Schulberg.

Chapter Thirteen

195 "It was a nightmare": Kahn.

196 "Nobody ever went through": PI, January 7, 1986.

197 "It was all Rainier's fault": PI, December 4, 1985.

198 "have to have a talk": Newman, p. 103.

"like a spoiled boy": Englund, p. 161.

200 Jack had frantically called: Lewis papers, *op. cit.*

"the Number One Eastern Woman Columnist": Lewis, p. 271.

"I can attribute this": Lewis, p. 275.

201 "His Highness is sorely afraid": Newman, p. 96.

203 "I want to get out to sea": Ibid., p. 106.

209 "An English tourist": David.

"That was some wedding": Newman, p. 112.

Chapter Fourteen

210 "Her first year": PI.

"At first I thought": Roderick Mann, "Fairy-tale Life with a Tragic End." LAT, September 19, 1982.

"The biggest change": Arthur(a).

211 "cried a lot": Lewis, p. 268.

"There was a great adjustment": PI.

212 "I have not lived": Arthur(a).

213 "Many people here": letter to DR, October 16, 1972.

"Quite a few people": PI.

214 "They say love is blind": Gaither, p. 166.

The new Princess was drilled: Englund, p. 206.

215 "fascinating . . . but cold": letter to DR, October 16, 1972.

"Grace and Rainier were very friendly": PI.

216 "My predecessors": Ellis.

"I can't afford": Ibid.

"A decorator": Tivey-Faucon.

217 "They are like old friends": Ellis.
     "For God's sake": Tivey-Faucon.
     "She's transformed it": Ellis.
     "I'm ashamed": Englund, p. 234.
218 "I never saw anything": *Playboy*.
     "Here I am": *Match*.
219 "entered into the conversation": Gaither, p. 174.
     "He didn't like": PI.
220 "Damned right it's expensive": Lewis, p. 194.
     "I asked her if": Ibid, p. 190.

Chapter Fifteen

222 "He's designed": Gaither, p. 174.
224 "If we have a boy": Grace Kelly, "Princess Grace Tells
     Details of Baby's Life," newspaper column syndicated
     by the Associated Press, March 1, 1957.
225 "wholly normal and right": Englund, p. 214.
     "I must agree": Curtis.
     "I myself killed": Ibid.
226 "I'd like to be pregnant": Ibid.
     One of the Grimaldis: Judy Fayaid, "A Job Fit for a Prin-
     cess, *Life,* April 1986.
227 "I'm not going to let": Ellis.
     "I think you have to": Levin.
     "Even if there were": Ibid.
     "I was never allowed": Bradford, p. 163.
228 "The boy was totally isolated": PI.
     "Albert's godfather": PI.
229 "When you don't know": PI, March 29, 1986.
     When Albert said: Bradford, p. 164.
     "I don't think they realized": Ibid.
     Grace took Caroline's arm: Englund, p. 284.
     "I'm afraid I'm very severe": Fisher.
231 "Sometimes he goes too far": "Grace Kelly—An American
     Princess," *Look,* Special Edition, 1982.
233 "They could come": PI.

Chapter Sixteen

235 "If she had decided": Englund, p. 364.

239 "I hadn't seen Grace": PI.
240 "It's so elegant": PI.
     "If there was anything": Lewis, p. 194.
241 "I got out": quoted by Earl Wilson in his New York *Post*
          column of April 17, 1956.
     "We had a great time": PI.
242 "So I went out": Lewis, p. 239.
     "I told Grace": Ibid., p. 20.
243 "The Prince has never": PI.
244 "The Catholicism": Bennetts.
245 "One of the curious": Zolotow.
248 "A beautiful woman": Newman, p. 133.
     "When Grace was there": Lewis, p. 114.

Chapter Seventeen

251 "Onassis wants to turn": Korrey.
252 "Mr. Onassis, your money": Ibid.
253 "That man": Ibid.
     Onassis, it seems: Ibid.
     "Give me two days": Robyns(a), p. 127.
     served only to "disgust": Englund, p. 139.
256 Even Grace's sister-in-law: Ibid., p. 231.
259 Grace gave him: Ibid., p. 244.
     Grace and Rainier had remained: Zolotow.
260 "I don't think that Mr. Onassis's": *Playboy*.
     Onassis seemed subject to whims: Englund, p. 264.

Chapter Eighteen

263 When Grace arrived: Britten.
264 "Kate," he'd said: Lewis, p. 197.
     "My God": Ibid., p. 196.
     "She told me": Englund, p. 235.
265 "Yeah, he's only titty-high": Lewis Papers, *op. cit.*.
266 Dorothy Kilgallen reported: Kilgallen column in New York
          Journal-American, April 16, 1956.
267 "She was oversensitive": Englund, p. 236.
     A perhaps well-meaning: Tivey-Faucon.
268 "The Virgin Mary": Bradford, p. 178.
269 "the Princess [was] a little melancholic": Englund, p. 238.

270 "Marnie is a puzzlement": Peter Evans, "Rebirth of a Frozen Goddess." London *Daily Express,* March 27,
  1962. *(All subsequent Evan Hunter quotes are also from
  this article.)*
  "I think that anyone": Bradford, p. 178.
272 "I have been very influenced": Englund, p. 243.
273 "Acting is something": Arthur(b).
274 "I was always": Calistro.
275 "Many of the people here": letter to DR, October 16,
  1972.

PART FOUR

277 The closing of the movie: PI, April 26, 1986.

Chapter Nineteen

279 "I'm an absolute basket case": Arthur(b).
280 "A year off": *Match.*
  "like the one-armed paper-hanger": letter to DR, October
  16, 1972.
  "a lot of social nonsense": Ibid., June 18, 1979.
281 "It's a small world": McManus.
  "You see, whole households": Bennetts.
282 "The atmosphere of the Garden Club": Bradford, p. 191.
  "It was the sweetest thing": McManus.
283 "I think the family structure": Ibid.
284 "Nothing is more important": de Vilallonga.
  "my jewels": letter to DR, October 16, 1972.
  "quite prim and proper": Bradford, p. 198.
285 "Not at all": Pepper.
  "Caroline went a little crazy": PI.
  "There is nothing more": quoted in the London *Times,*
  May 9, 1972.
286 "I don't manage them": Pepper.
  "I've often been tempted": *People.*
  "There has to be this breakaway": Pepper.
  "was just too far": Bennetts.
287 "more together than I was": Englund, p. 324.
  "in other ways": Pepper.
  "Why do I have to be a princess": Englund, p. 323.

288 "It gets me away from Monaco": PI with DR.
289 "I only go out": *People*.
  "It was very difficult for Grace": PI.
290 "We have our differences": to Jean Rook, London *Daily Express*, April 14, 1976.
  "was a point of reference": Englund, p. 325.
  "My mother is beautiful": "Princess Grace: The Problems of Being a Mother." *Good Housekeeping*, August 1976.
291 "I remember as a girl": Pepper.

Chapter Twenty

293 "Philippe has given me": Englund, p. 327.
294 "helped me to have some independence": Ibid.
  "slamming the door": Englund, p. 328.
295 if the marriage took place: *News of the World* (London), August 17, 1980.
  "Grace did not *at all*": PI.
296 "Well, perhaps it's for the better": Englund, p. 329.
  "Obviously, they have busy lives": London *Daily Mirror*, June 26, 1978.
297 "I hope I'm wrong": *News of the World*.
  "a simple country atmosphere": letter to DR, August 31, 1978.
298 "She loved him": PI.
299 "Caroline didn't want": PI.
  "She ignored problems": PI.
  "by then Caroline": Ibid.
  "I really believe": Englund, p. 333.
300 "There were problems": to Nick Fullagar, London *Daily Mirror*, December 2, 1980.
  "all reflect tremendous loneliness": PI.

Chapter Twenty-one

301 "playing psychiatrist": letter to DR, September, 1979.
  "That was my brother's daughter": PI.
302 "I'm tired of doing everything": Lewis, p. 211.
  "What he's doing now": Ibid., p. 208.
  "What he told me": Ibid., p. 257.
  "I think that Grace and Kell": PI.

303 "It went something along the lines of": Lewis, p. 178.

304 "I went with her just a few times": Ibid., p. 233.

305 "I would try": Marx.

306 "It is a wonder": letter to DR, June 18, 1979.
"As the designs": Grace.

307 "nervous and anxious": letter to DR, May 17, 1977.
"I was terrified": Ibid., August 31, 1978.

308 "Flower pressing is": Mara Wolynski. "Say Goodnight, Gracie." *The Village Voice,* November 27, 1978.
"We considered": PI. *(All Robert Dornhelm quotes in this chapter are from this previously cited personal interview.)*

310 "I feel very sad": Klemesrud.
"I think we're dealing": Ibid.

311 "enamored" of Grace: Englund, p. 346.
"a dear boy": letter to DR, August 31, 1978.
"I didn't want to sit": PI.

312 "It is not bad": letter to DR, September 3, 1979.

314 "She was warm": Winterhall.
"Grace was worrying": Ibid.
"I had even more reason": Ibid.

315 "I was deeply shocked": Ibid.

Chapter Twenty-two

316 "She loves poetry": Hall.
"A way of returning": Al Haas, "A $40 Evening of Poetry with a Princess." Philadelphia *Inquirer,* March 3, 1978.

317 "Having worked in the theater": Hall.
"Grace worked hard": Ibid.

318 Another "restless" audience member: Englund, p. 352.
"I called her in Monaco": PI, December 12, 1985.

319 "I have (just happen to have)": letter to DR, November 9, 1979.
"She's so goddamn proud": PI.

320 "Her poetry readings": PI.

321 "They didn't communicate that well": Lewis, p. 268.
"She used to write": PI.
"I doubt very much": PI.

"dislike each other": Noel Botham, "Princess Grace: Our Marriage Is Over." *National Enquirer,* July 6, 1982.

322 "Oh, Albert went through": PI.
"You get a little tired": Pepper.
"A very special child": letter to DR, September 3, 1979.
"I should have been": Pepper.

323 drinks "that knocked your head off": Englund, p. 359.
"ripped to the tits": Davidson, p. 102.
a fancy banquet: Englund, p. 337.

324 "People tend to gain weight": PI.
"From August 15th": quoted in the London *Daily Express,* September 1, 1974.
"What's the point?": Bradford, p. 216.
"A friend of mine traveled": PI.

325 "She had started drinking": PI.

Chapter Twenty-three

326 "That won't be necessary": Bradford, p. 220.
327 "The corner came up": police deposition, September 13, 1982.
"He's the Prince": Bradford, p. 221.
330 "Mommy panicked": Stolley.
"The consensus among": PI, May 13, 1986.
331 "it was wrong for the palace": PI, May 14, 1986.
"never any attempt to interfere": Ibid.
"She might have lost awareness": Ibid.
332 "When the palace called me": PI.
333 "I will never forget": PI.
"How are you going": interview aired on "20/20," ABC-TV, September 23, 1982.

EPILOGUE

335 "She was terribly present": Stolley.
"I think he's having": Carlson.
"There's a lot of hunting": Stolley.
"Rainier was so bereft": Carlson.
336 "Her father was very": PI.
"I think maybe in some way": Carlson.
"The truth will eventually": Ibid.

"I think well": Stolley.

337 "Caroline has changed": De Dubrovay.
"I do not think": Ibid.
"It's easy to see": Ibid.

338 "The Prince makes it obvious": Diliberto.
"I think Caroline and Stefano": PI.
"Andrea looks just like": PI.
"A prouder grandfather": PI.
"She *had* to do it": PI.

339 "I've always said": Stolley.
Rainier ". . . is looking forward": PI.
"Much": Buckley.
"It wasn't a major topic": Ibid.
"He has started": Stolley.

340 "He had an incredible": Bacon.
"He has a lot of dates": PI.
"At an opening": Buckley.
"I hope he's not serious": PI with Lizanne LeVine.
"the most wonderful": Green.
"I don't think he's ever been": PI.
"I just know that I want": Bacon.

341 "Everyone's beginning to get": Colacello.
"He doesn't have to": "The CBS Morning News" interview, July 25, 1986.
"Albert realizes": PI.
"My father has been successful": Bacon.

342 "rather be Marilyn Monroe": Calacello.
"I don't think Rainier": Ibid.
"at the moment the whole thing": Ibid.
"Why shouldn't a girl": Bacon.

343 "I live a normal life": Finke.

344 "If he weren't happy": Ibid.
"I've always been interested": Calistro.
"if she really wants": Stolley.
"You lose time": Calistro.

345 "I don't think": "The CBS Morning News."
"It was a rebellious act": Duka.
"Everyone in town": Ibid.

346 "To take a girl": Ibid.

"I got sick of modeling": Calistro.
"We sat at our boards": Ibid.
"We took a gamble": Ibid
347   "Who would think": Ibid.

Selective Bibliography

Cited in addition to books are newspaper and magazine articles quoted more than once within the text. Other sources are listed only in the Notes. Each entry is preceded by the abbreviation used to identify it within the Notes.

Arce. Arce, Hector. *Gary Cooper: An Intimate Biography.* New York: William Morrow & Co., 1979.

Arthur(a). Arthur, William B. "Grace Kelly's Life As a Princess." *Look,* February 5, 1957.

Arthur(b).———. "Princess Grace Turns Forty." *Look,* December 16, 1969.

Bacon. Bacon, Doris Klein. "The Yuppie Prince." *Ladies' Home Journal,* April 1985.

Bennetts. Bennetts, Leslie. "Climbing the Tower to See the Princess." Philadelphia *Sunday Bulletin,* March 31, 1974.

Birmingham. Birmingham, Stephen. "The Fairy-tale 25 Years Later." *McCall's,* March 1981.

Bradford. Bradford, Sarah. *Princess Grace.* New York: Stein and Day, 1984.

Britten. Britten, Ruth. " 'Please God, Don't Let My Father See Me Cry.' " *Photoplay,* September 1960.

Buckley. Buckley, Christopher. "H.S.H. Prince Albert of Monaco." *Interview,* January 1986.

Calistro. Calistro, Paddy. "Stephanie." Los Angeles *Times,* April 11, 1986.

Carlson. Carlson, Peter. "Living with the Memories." *People,* November 15, 1982.

Carpozi. Carpozi, George. *Clark Gable.* New York: Pyramid Books, 1961.

Colacello. Colacello, Bob. "The Princess Who Could Save Monaco." *Vanity Fair,* October 1987.

Curtis. Curtis, Olga. "Princess Grace Hoping for Boy Heir to Throne." New York *Journal-American,* September 11, 1957.

David. David, Lester. "Even a Prince Needs Privacy." *This Week,* January 13, 1957.

De Dubrovay. De Dubrovay, Diane. "Monaco's Reigning Beauty." *McCall's,* September 1986.

de Vilallonga. de Vilallonga, Jose Luis. "Interview with Princess Grace." London *Star,* October 30, 1979.

Diliberto. Diliberto, Gioia. "A New Beginning for Monaco's Princess." *People,* June 24, 1985.

Duka. Duka, John. "Desperately Seeking Stephanie." *Vanity Fair,* July 1985.

Ellis. Ellis, Jennifer. "Around the Clock with Grace and Rainier." *American Weekly,* June 30, 1957.

Englund. Englund, Steven. *Grace of Monaco.* New York: Doubleday & Co., 1984.

Finke. Finke, Nikki. "L.A.'s Royal Romance." *Los Angeles Times Magazine,* July 26, 1987.

Fisher. Fisher, Graham, and Heather Fisher. "The Prince and I." *Ladies' Home Journal,* October 1961.

Gaither. Gaither, Gant. *Princess of Monaco.* New York: Henry Holt & Co., 1957.

Galante(a). Galante, Pierre. "The Day Grace Kelly Met Prince Rainier." *Good Housekeeping,* May 1983.

Galante(b).————. "The Inside Story of How It All Began." *Look,* April 11, 1961.

Garceau. Garceau, Jean with Inez Coche. *Dear Mr. Gable: The Biography of Clark Gable.* Boston: Little, Brown & Co., 1961.

Gam. Gam, Rita. "That Special Grace." *McCall's,* January 1983.

Grace. Princess Grace with Gwen Robyns. *My Book of Flowers.* New York: Doubleday & Co., 1980.

Granger. Granger, Stewart. *Sparks Fly Upward.* New York: G. P. Putnam's Sons, 1981.

Green. Green, Michelle. "Taking Grace's Place." *People,* September 28, 1987.

Hall. Hall, Anthea. "Gracing the Occasion." London *Daily Telegraph,* June 11, 1978.

Hart-Davis. Hart-Davis, Phyllida. *Grace: The Story of a Princess.* New York: St. Martin's Press, 1982.

Higham. Higham, Charles. *Ava: A Life Story.* New York: Delacorte Press, 1974.

Hudson. Hudson, Rock and Sara Davidson. *Rock Hudson: His Story.* New York: William Morrow & Co., 1986.

Kahn. Kahn, R. T. "Amazing Grace." *Ladies' Home Journal,* September 1982.

Kelly. Kelly, Mrs. John B., as told to Richard Gehman. "My Daughter Grace Kelly." Los Angeles *Examiner,* January 15–24, 1956.

Klemesrud. Klemesrud, Judy. "Princess Grace Makes a Movie—But It's No Comeback." New York *Times,* December 18, 1977.

Korrey. Korrey, Edward M. "The Monte Carlo Story." *Look,* May 1, 1956.

Levin. Levin, Robert. "Why Grace Kelly Became a Princess." *Redbook,* February 1957.

Lewis. Lewis, Arthur H. *Those Philadelphia Kellys.* New York: William Morrow & Co., 1977.

Martin(a). Martin, Pete. "The Luckiest Girl in Hollywood." *Saturday Evening Post,* October 30, 1954.

Martin(b). Martin, John. "Grace Kelly's Secret Child-Bearing Test." *Inside Story,* October 1956.

Marx. Marx, Linda. "Grace Kelly of Philadelphia." *People,* September 5 and 12, 1983.

Match. Paris Match. "Twenty Years of Happiness." March 13, 1976.

McCarthy. McCarthy, Joe. "The Genteel Miss Kelly." *Cosmopolitan,* April 1955.

McManus. McManus, Margaret. "Why Princess Grace Won't Look Back." Philadelphia *Evening Bulletin,* July 23, 1971.

Morley. Morley, Sheridan. *The Other Side of the Moon: The Life of David Niven.* New York: Harper & Row, 1985.

Newman. Newman, Robert. *Princess Grace Kelly.* Derby, Conn.: Monarch Books, 1962.

Parsons. Parsons, Louella. "Grace Kelly." Los Angeles *Examiner,* May 23–25, 1954.

Parton. Parton, Margaret. "What Makes Grace Kelly Different?" *Ladies' Home Journal,* March 1956.

People. Ward, Penny, and Kevin Dowling. "By Grimaldi Out of

Kelly, Caroline Is Royalty's Most Spirited Thoroughbred." *People,* August 30, 1976.

Pepper. Pepper, Curtis Bill. "Princess Grace's Problems As a Mother." *McCall's,* December 1974.

Playboy. Playboy, "Interview: Princess Grace." January 1966.

Reynolds. Reynolds, Lisa. "Ooh La La." *Motion Picture,* September 1955.

Richardson. Richardson, Don. "Kelly": An unpublished manuscript.

Robyns(a). Robyns, Gwen. *Princess Grace.* New York: David McKay & Co., 1982.

Robyns(b).———. "Grace: Her First Love." *Ladies' Home Journal,* September 1983.

Rose. Rose, Helen. *"Just Make Them Beautiful."* Santa Monica, Calif.: Dennis-Landman Publishers, 1976.

Santora. Santora, Phil. "A Prince for the Girl Who Has Everything." New York *Daily News,* January 8–13, 1956.

Schary. Schary, Dore. *Heyday.* Boston: Little, Brown & Co., 1979.

Schulberg. Schulberg, Budd. "The Other Princess Grace." *Ladies' Home Journal,* May 1977.

Scullin. Scullin, George. "The Girl Who Dares To." *Motion Picture,* March 1955.

Sinden. Sinden, Donald. *A Touch of the Memoirs.* London: Hodder & Stoughton, 1982.

Spoto. Spoto, Donald. *The Dark Side of Genius: The Life of Alfred Hitchcock.* New York: Little, Brown & Co., 1983.

Stolley. Stolley, Richard B. "The Legacy of Princess Grace." *Life,* March 1983.

Taves. Taves, Isabelle. "The Seven Graces." *McCall's,* January 1955.

Thomas. Thomas, Bob. *Golden Boy: The Untold Story of William Holden.* New York: St. Martin's Press, 1983.

Time. Time. "The Girl in White Gloves." January 31, 1955.

Tivey-Faucon. Tivey-Faucon, Madge. "Inside the Palace with Princess Grace." *Cosmopolitan,* March 1964.

Truffaut. Truffaut, François. *Hitchcock/Truffaut.* New York: Simon & Schuster, 1967.

Winterhall. Winterhall, Zenita and Johan Helmertz. "Per Mattsson Tells of His Meeting with Princess Grace." *Den nya Husmodern* (Sweden), June 29, 1987.

Zolotow. Zolotow, Maurice. "Grace of Monaco." *Cosmopolitan,* December 1961.

Index